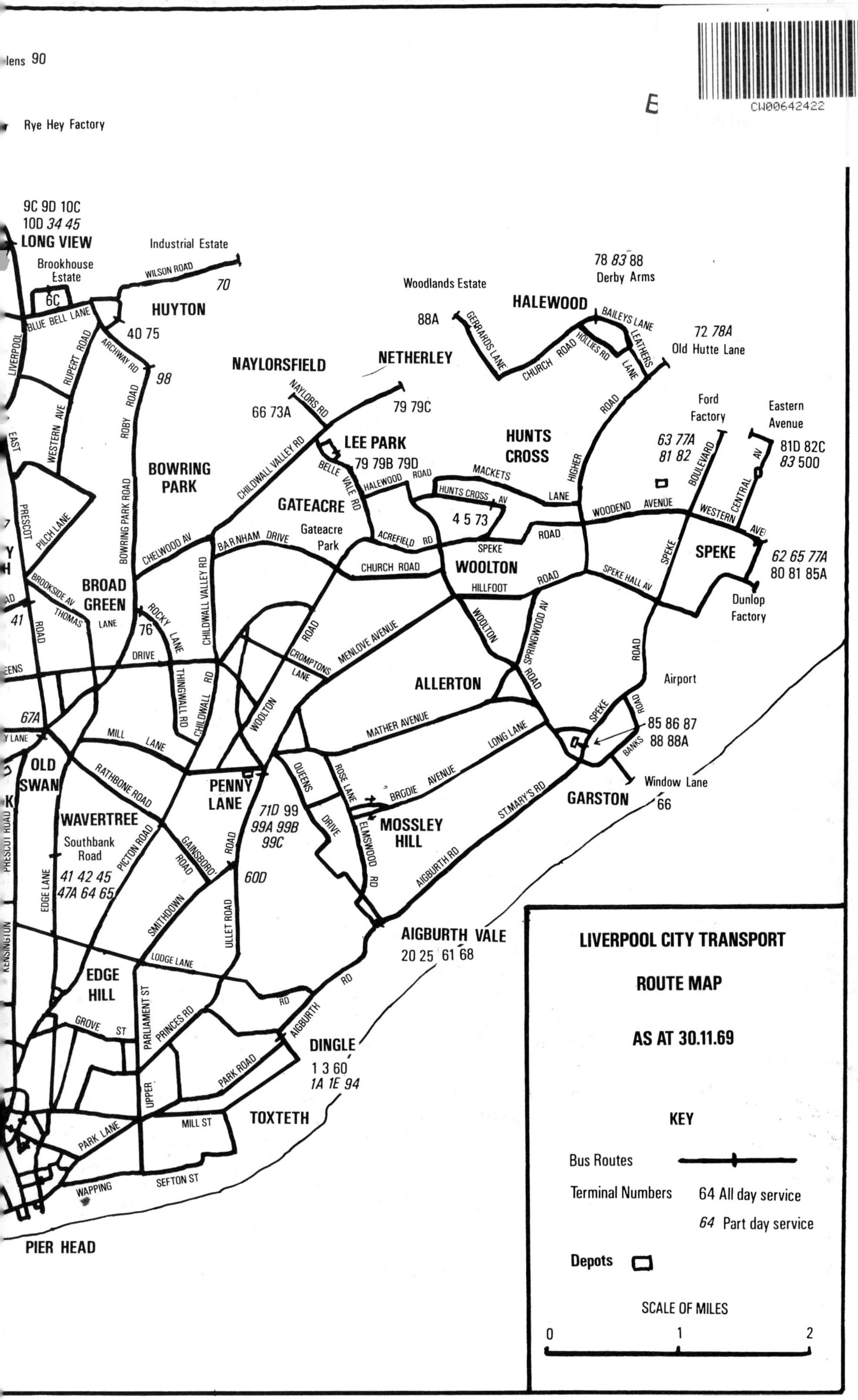

16.95

CW00642422

lens 90

Rye Hey Factory

9C 9D 10C
10D 34 45
LONG VIEW

Industrial Estate

Brookhouse
Estate

WILSON ROAD

70

6C

HUYTON

BLUE BELL LANE

LIVERPOOL

40 75

78 83 88
Derby Arms

Woodlands Estate

HALEWOOD

88A

BAILEYS LANE

72 78A
Old Hutte Lane

GERRARDS LANE

HOLLIES RD

LEATHERS

CHURCH ROAD

LANE

NETHERLEY

NAYLORSFIELD

WESTERN AVE

RUPERT ROAD

ARCHWAY RD

ROBY ROAD

98

EAST

79 79C

NAYLORS RD

66 73A

LEE PARK

79 79B 79D

BELLE VALE RD

HALEWOOD

ROAD

MACKETS

LANE

HUNTS CROSS AV

HUNTS
CROSS

HIGHER ROAD

Ford
Factory

63 77A
81 82

BOULEVARD

Eastern
Avenue

81D 82C
83 500

CENTRAL AV

BOWRING
PARK

BOWRING PARK ROAD

CHILDWALL VALLEY RD

GATEACRE

Gateacre
Park

ACREFIELD RD

CHURCH ROAD

4 5 73

ROAD

WOOLTON

HILLFOOT

SPEKE

ROAD

WOODEND

AVENUE

WESTERN AVE

SPEKE

62 65 77A
80 81 85A

Dunlop
Factory

CHELWOOD AV

BARNHAM DRIVE

PILCH LANE

PRESCOT

BROAD
GREEN

BROOKSIDE AV

THOMAS LANE

41

ROCKY LANE

76

DRIVE

CHILDWALL VALLEY RD

CHILDWALL RD

ROAD

CROMPTONS LANE

MENLOVE AVENUE

WOOLTON ROAD

SPRINGWOOD AV

ALLERTON

MATHER AVENUE

LONG LANE

SPEKE HALL AV

Airport

SPEKE ROAD

ROAD

BANKS ROAD

85 86 87
88 88A

67A

EENS

QUEENS

MILL LANE

LANE

RATHBONE ROAD

WOOLTON ROAD

ROSE LANE

BRODIE AVENUE

ST. MARY'S RD

GARSTON

Window Lane
66

OLD
SWAN

PENNY
LANE

71D 99
99A 99B
99C

QUEENS DRIVE

ELMSWOOD RD

MOSSLEY
HILL

AIGBURTH RD

WAVERTREE

Southbank
Road

41 42 45
47A 64 65

PICTON ROAD

GAINSBORO ROAD

SMITHDOWN ROAD

60D

ULLET ROAD

RD

AIGBURTH VALE
20 25 61 68

EDGE LANE

PRESCOT ROAD

KENSINGTON

EDGE
HILL

GROVE ST

PARLIAMENT ST

PRINCES RD

LODGE LANE

RD

AIGBURTH RD

DINGLE
1 3 60
1A 1E 94

UPPER PARK LANE

PARK ROAD

MILL ST

SEFTON ST

TOXTETH

WAPPING

PIER HEAD

LIVERPOOL CITY TRANSPORT

ROUTE MAP

AS AT 30.11.69

KEY

Bus Routes

Terminal Numbers

64 All day service

64 Part day service

Depots

SCALE OF MILES

0   1   2

Liverpool Transport

Volume 5 — 1957-86

Liverpool Transport

Volume 5—1957-1986

by

J. B. Horne, C.Eng., MIGasE.
and
T. B. Maund, FCIT.

designed by
John A. Senior

with additional photography by
Reg Wilson
and
Ken Swallow

Transport Publishing Co Ltd : Glossop : Derbyshire : England

Typeset and produced for the Publishers by
Mopok Graphics, 128 Pikes Lane, Glossop, Derbyshire
Printed and bound in Great Britain

CONTENTS

Subscribers to this volume

D. P. Acock
A. J. Affleck
S. R. Allchin
J. J. Amey
D. Anders
R. Atkinson
G. D. Austin
W. I. ap Simon
Dr J. R. Bacon
D. M. Bailey
M. Bailey
W. C. Bailey
J. F. Baker
Dr P. Banister
A. E. Barrow
A. Bartlett
Rev P. M. Battersby
E. L. Beamer
R. A. Beaumont
C. Beech
R. Bell
R. L. Bell
A. C. Bellamy
M. A. Bernero
A. J. Bertram
J. M. Bettle
D. Bevan
A. Blanchard
L. Bland
K. P. Blinston
R. A. Bott
F. Bowering
D. S. Braisted
J. P. Bramley
A. D. Broughall
N. Brown
J. A. Bryant
C. Buckley
K. W. Buckley
D. G. J. Burch
D. A. Butler
P. T. Byrne
A. Cassidy
R. D. Caton
D. J. Catton
B. T. Channon
N. Chapple
J. G. Chattwood
H. B. Christiansen
S. Christie
J. M. S. Clark
J. A. Clarke
G. N. Clarkson
H. Cobham
J. P. Coffey
D. R. Cole
M. G. Collignon

B. Cook
A. M. Cooke
J. C. Cooke
B. O. Cooper
Dr E. Courte
C. R. Cowlin
M. C. Crabtree
D. R. Crease
K. F. Crompton
P. J. Crossley
D. J. Cunningham
W. S. Cunningham
J. L. Daley
N. A. Davidge
C. P. Davies
J. K. Davies
T. H. Davies
R. J. Devaney
D. K. Dewar
J. Diandas
A. M. Dixon
G. M. Dodd
M. G. Doggett
K. Donnelly
J. Dreifus
R. P. Drew
P. W. Duckett
C. S. Dunbar
G. Earl
D. L. Edwards
R. F. Edwards
C. V. Ehrke
M. Elliott
G. Ellis
Rev J. F. Ellis
K. D. Evans
M. D. Evans
D. R. Farnworth
F. J. Farrell
D. Farrer
C. E. Fawcett
N. G. Fellows
R. Fleetwood
D. R. Forsyth
E. E. Foxwell
E. A. J. J. Furnell
E. A. Gahan
D. W. Garland
M. Gaywood
L. A. Gibson
Col G. K. Gillberry
R. M. Gillespie
R. F. Glaze
R. J. Gleave
D. E. Gledhill
W. Goddard
G. D. Gordon

N. Griffiths
P. Griffiths
L. Grinstead
C. H. Haddrill
P. J. Hall
D. Hancock
T. R. Hardiman
G. P. Harris
R. Harrison
B. Hayes
R. A. Hayhow
E. N. C. Haywood
J. W. Hemley
R. G. Hemsall
M. D. Henderson
N. F. Henley
I. A. Herdman
M. Heyneck
H. Heyworth
S. Higgins
D. E. Hilton
R. N. Holden
D. Holmes
N. A. Holt
M. B. Hopkinson
J. D. Howie
A. Howley
C. F. Hunt
P. J. Huxford
C. Hyelman
C. F. Isgar
D. E. Jackson
W. E. James
D. A. P. Janes
P. N. Jarvis
F. E. M. Jenkins
A. M. Jervis
A. Jobson
D. E. Johnson
E. R. Johnson
A. E. Jones
D. A. Jones
P. A. Jones
H. E. Jordan
D. R. Keenan
J. C. Kenney
R. J. Kenworthy
D. M. Kirby
A. W. Kirkpatrick
J. D. Knowles
P. Kuivala
P. A. Legon
C. J. Lent
C. Lewis
D. B. Littlewood
E. A. Lloyd
Dr E. K. Lloyd

J. M. Lloyd
W. M. Lloyd
D. M. Loxley
H. Luff
I. Lynas
G. Lyon
N. Macmahon
R. G. Manders
C. D. Mann
J. W. Manvers
D. S. Marriott
Dr P. H. Marriott
J. A. Marsden
R. Martin
C. A. Mayou
J. McCafferty
I. McIntosh
B. D. McKee
K. McKelvie
I. G. McMStewart
J. M. Melbourne
C. M. Mercer
D. J. Meredith
A. P. Mernock
D. C. Mitchell
D. J. Mitchell
P. R. Mitchell
F. A. Moffatt
M. H. Mogford
T. Molyneux
K. Moody
H. C. Moore
D. Moran
J. D. Moran
J. Moreau
T. B. Morrison
E. W. Morton
H. Moss
J. L. Muir
C. J. Murphy
J. M. Murphy
A. G. Murray
L. J. Myerscough
G. C. Nelson
J. G. E. Nye
J. Oley
P. Oppmann
R. D. Owen
H. O'Neill
G. H. Page
N. W. Palfreyman
S. Palmer
T. Parkinson
R. E. Parry
G. G. Paton Williams
J. R. Payne
G. K. Peacock

W. G. Pealing
R. J. Pennell
M. C. Perkins
J. R. Pinfold
R. Pleuler
E. R. Pollard
J. H. Price
B. K. Pritchard
J. I. Pulford
J. M. Purdy
R. Pybus
A. A. Pye
D. Quine
G. Radley
C. G. Read
Dr G. P. Reed
E. Richards
J. H. Richards
D. Ricketts
F. J. Riehl
A. E. Rimmer
C. C. Roberts
D. Roberts
D. F. Roberts
D. W. Roberts
G. P. C. Robinson
P. B. Robinson
S. G. Robinson
I. Ross
F. T. Rowan
P. G. Rudd
B. J. Rusk
H. J. P. Rutherford
Capt B. A. Sampson
G. G. Saunders
L. Sayer
H. R. Schmoll
D. J. S. Scotney
E. G. Scott
T. H. Shears
K. H. Shepherd
J. Simmons
J. R. Simpkin
J. S. Sisson
S. A. Skeavington
R. J. Skiming
C. A. Skinner
A. J. Slater
J. L. Slater
J. Small
G. E. Smith
H. D. Smith
P. T. Smith
D. Smithson
A. Smyth
D. H. D. Spray
J. D. Spurr

R. H. Stevens
M. D. Street
N. R. Strong
N. Sturtz
J. W. Suckling
K. Sullivan
B. Sunners
K. W. Swallow
T. C. Swiney
J. Symons
W. B. Tabler
R. B. Tait
L. J. Taylor
T. Taylor
D. T. Thomas
Dr W. G. Thomas
D. N. Thompson
R. F. V. Thomson
P. Thorley
J. C. Thornber
A. F. Tieuli
A. Tilston
D. A. Tipton
C. J. W. Townson
N. J. Treacher
E. Tschop
C. J. Usher
E. R. Vaughan
A. P. H. Velthoen
D. Vivyan
J. M. Wagstaff
Rev R. H. Wagstaff
I. P. Walker
M. J. Waring
A. C. Warton
A. J. Watkins
Dr H. Watson
R. Watson
N. F. Weatherley
W. J. Webster
T. Wedgwood
B. Weeden
G. Welburn
C. B. Wheble
D. E. Wilkinson
H. Williams
J. P. Williams
P. Williams
A. A. Williamson
A. C. Williamson
R. Williamson
J. F. Windsor
J. R. Wingfield
J. D. Winteridge
J. M. Woodman
L. P. Worboys
M. C. Wright

The extension to Kirby created a rural tramway which contrasted greatly with the city centre.

The brief twilight between trams and buses on Edge Lane is exemplified by this picture of a Leyland PD2 working to the tram timetable on the late afternoon of 14th September 1957.

INTRODUCTION
and Review of the Series

Since Volume One of Liverpool Transport was published in 1975, the authors have acquired a considerable quantity of additional material and, by popular request, a selection of photographs from the tramway era has been included in this volume in the form of a Prologue. Rail transport in the streets of Liverpool covered almost a century because it was in March 1859 that an omnibus fitted with retractable flanged wheels was placed experimentally on the rails of the Dock Board's railways by its inventor, W. J. Curtis.

Horse-drawn omnibuses had been at work in the town for almost 30 years having originated as feeders to the first interurban main line railway between Liverpool and Manchester, opened in September 1830. After initial problems, both mechanical and bureaucratic, had been overcome, the 'railway omnibuses' became firmly established, running along the Line of Docks until the opening of the Overhead Railway in 1893.

An experimental tramway between Sheil Road and Old Swan, then outside the city boundary, was laid down in 1861 but removed the following year by the Turnpike Trust. Not until eight years later did the horse-drawn tramcar finally come to the city's streets with the opening of a route between the City Centre and Dingle on 1st November 1869.

Looking east from the northern end of Pier Head terminus in 1900, towards George's Dock Gates, St. Nicholas Church and the Overhead Railway. Indicators were in short supply so Liverpool-type Preston car No. 172, like the direct-stair Preston car at the left, carries a paper sticker on each dash plate.

Liverpool, from the Landing Stage   Valentine's Series

Following the opening of the route to Dingle in November 1869, a line to Walton followed but the Liverpool Tramways Co lacked the resources to expand the network fully and in 1876 a merger with omnibus interests created the Liverpool United Tramways and Omnibus Company. In 1879 the Corporation purchased the tracks and leased them back to the company. Many additional lines were constructed including a network in the Oxford Street and Catharine Street areas which was never used because of the danger of runaways on the steep hills. Reports of their use during the electrification period have not been confirmed.

The Corporation allowed the tracks to fall into disrepair and it was the prospect of having to pay heavy damages to the company which first led to talks about municipalisation of the tramways. The Corporation took over on 1st September 1897 and immediately obtained Parliamentary powers for a much extended electrically operated system; in the meantime, the trams and buses taken over from the company were effectively utilised to improve the existing network and develop new routes. The first electric car ran in public service on 16th November 1898, once again between Dingle and South Castle Street.

The electrification of the whole system, including many extensions, was achieved within four years during which time over 400 new cars were placed in service including, initially, quaint single deckers of American design and diminutive German cars with trailers. However, orthodoxy prevailed and by the end of the Edwardian era, a distinctive type of Liverpool car with closed top deck but open end balconies was well established. The tramways, with low fares and frequent services, revolutionised life in the city and its environs, stimulating suburban development, widening the horizons of leisure pursuits and contributing to the mobility of labour.

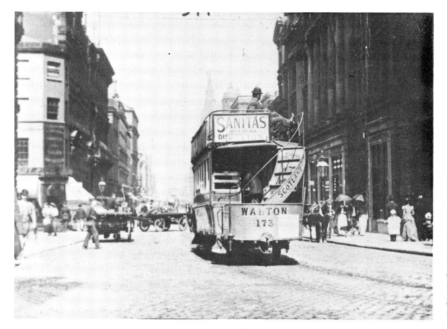

Horse car 173 probably dated from the early 1880s and was reportedly single-ended at least for part of its life. Note the knifeboard (back-to-back) upper-deck seat. It is seen in Dale Street near the Town Hall traversing the single line 'Inner Circle' which all city cars used as a terminal loop. There were different colours for each principal route and this one was brown.

London Road in the 1890s with a seven-window knifeboard car probably one of several built by Starbuck of Birkenhead in 1882; it is bound for Breckfield Road North (Robson Street) and has a third ('trace') horse attached to help it ascend the steep gradients. The other car on the left is of a newer type with garden seats on the upper deck.

(Above) Horse car 316 was one of the last to be built in the 1890s being not dissimilar in design to some early electric cars. It was one of seven used on a service between Breckfield Road and Strand Road with a 3d transfer facility to Seaforth as shown on the supplementary board. This route was extended and continued for many years as electric tram 18 and, eventually, bus 33. These cars had reversible garden seats on the upper deck and the lower saloon was illuminated by oil lights which also served as external lights.

Late Victorian Liverpool—a misty view of Upper Parliament Street at Kingsley Road in 1899 with knifeboard horse bus on the Smithdown Road route. The tramway track and overhead supported by an elegant centre pole with twin gas lamps, is not yet in use and traces of the never-used horse car track into Kingsley Road, leading to Beaumont Street depot, are just visible, bottom left.

Liverpool all but eliminated open top cars by 1905. Car 305 is shown in original condition before receiving its top cover in October 1904. Note the waterproof aprons to protect the upper deck passengers, hanging on the rail, in accordance with municipal bye-laws. The hexagonal glass indicators are for the Outer Circular but the car is without route boards, the brackets for which can be seen above the decency screen. When new in 1900 the car had Peckham wire tray lifeguards and four-sided end indicators. Taken inside Lambeth Road Works, this view clearly shows the useful wooden board above the trolley wire. It caught dewired trolleys.

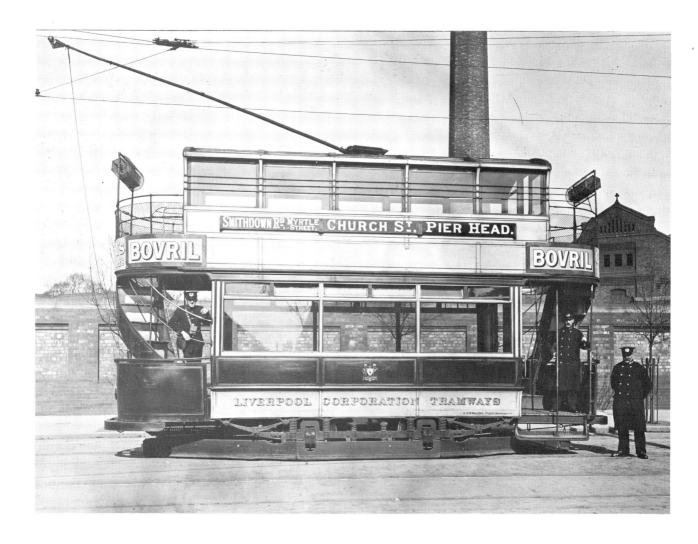

(Facing page)

Several essentially Liverpool features are shown in this picture of a Bellamy car taken outside the Refuse Destructer and Generating Station adjoining Smithdown Road car shed in March 1907. The car is un-identified but it was probably in the high 400s. Note the external rails preventing passengers from leaning out too far when the Magrini-patent upper deck windows were all wound down simultaneously by the conductor; they were continued round the offside of the balconies where there was a seat for three. The attachment of the plough lifeguard to the truck is clearly visible. The reversible route boards were in three sections, but were rarely changed in service.

Long before 1908, when this official photograph was taken, Liverpol's fleet was highly standardised. Near-identical Bellamy-roofed four-wheelers ran almost all services, although the addition of top covers to the earlier batch of direct-stair Preston cars gave them another lease of life. This view is from Church Street across the busy Paradise Street/Whitechapel junction into Lord Street; a horse-drawn 'Liverpol Flat' blocks the junction so east-west drivers let their cars drift slowly forward, awaiting the policeman's signal to cross. Note that all the cars have sliding roof panels but none are open; they are probably stuck fast. The tramwaymen are sporting their white 'P&O' cap covers. The photographer seems to have had the use of a tower wagon for this, one of a series of photographs taken around 27th June 1908. They were intended to record traffic congestion, a recurring theme.

Decorated tramcars formed part of most tramway undertaking's fleets and Liverpool was no exception.

To celebrate the Coronation of King George V and Queen Mary in 1911, there was an inter-depot decorated car competition. All the entries shown here were Bellamy cars and show the detail of the type of car in its prime to excellent effect. Liverpool used the plough type lifeguard despite Board of Trade opposition. The Smithdown Road entry, car 544, was destined to be the last of its class, being withdrawn in July 1949. It was a wide-bodied car with transverse seats on the lower deck.

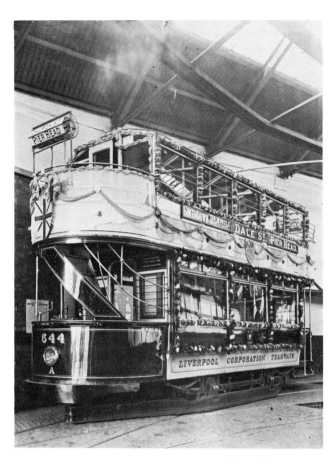

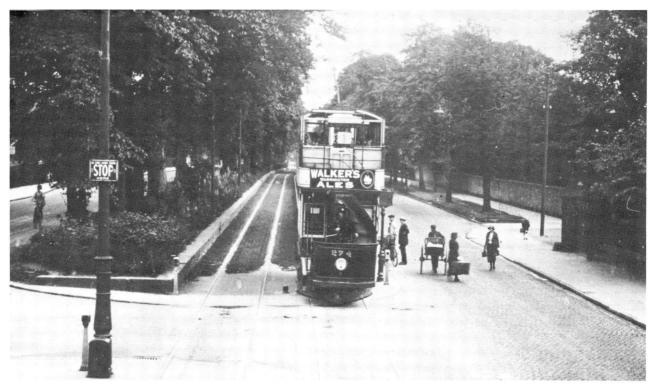

Aigburth Road was a classic example of the famous Liverpool 'grass tracks', the rails having been transferred from the street in stages during 1921-24. Bellamy car 274 was built by Dick, Kerr in 1900 as open top and covered in 1904. Note the revolving hexagonal glass indicator, set so that two names were visible from ground level and the reversible route number sign which would have '33' on the other side. This car was withdrawn in 1934.

Car 70, seen on the new Bowring Park extension in 1914, was of the 'Straight Staircase' (or 'Little Emma') type with short top cover and virtually no protection for the driver. It was one of 81 such cars built by Dick Kerr in 1899-1900 and top covered in 1907-8. Seven, including No. 70, were withdrawn in 1920-21 to be completely rebuilt as Priestly balcony cars. Six others were converted back to open top condition in December 1925 when it was hoped to take over the Great Crosby tramway but negotiations fell through and they were scrapped without further use.

The opening of the Broad Green and Bowring Park extension in 1914-15 brought with it the first of Liverpool's famous 'grass tracks', built on reservations, mainly on a centre median strip. It was the forerunner of 27 miles of such high speed track though the 1914-18 War delayed the further development of this improvement. The War brought enforced neglect and many other serious problems.

The Corporation's first motor buses were acquired with the business of the Woolton Motor Omnibus Co Ltd on 1st November 1910. In 1919, buses were used on a network of services designed to relieve pressure on the tramways and thereafter outer suburban feeder routes were started. Competition from private operators serving areas outside the sphere of the tramways, such as Crosby, Ormskirk and Widnes, gathered momentum and by 1925 private buses, albeit heavily restricted, had breached the city walls. The Corporation unwisely built up a varied fleet of unreliable buses, competing with its own trams, and by the end of the decade of the twenties, the undertaking was in serious financial trouble.

Despite a steady programme of tramway extension and rolling stock renewal, at first in the old tramway works in Lambeth Road and, from 1928, in the new Edge Lane works, there was little technical advancement and such improvements as vestibules and upholstered seating came reluctantly and late.

An Agreement with the major company bus operators, sponsored by the railways, laid a solid foundation for the future co-operation of municipal and private enterprise. New management embarked on equipping the tramways with modern cars, worthy of the miles of reserved tracks which were further extended into new suburbs. New modern buses replaced the obsolescent vehicles of the twenties.

Water Street in 1925 with Bellamy and Priestly standard cars. Car 514, new in 1908, is equipped with a stencil route number, mounted lower than the more common reversible glass type. It is turning into George's Dock Gates to reach the North Loop on route 22A from Aintree. Car 647 was quite new at the time as was the Walton Hall Avenue (44) service on which it was running. Note the variety of vintage traffic, the cab with the hood down and the ornate public house lantern.

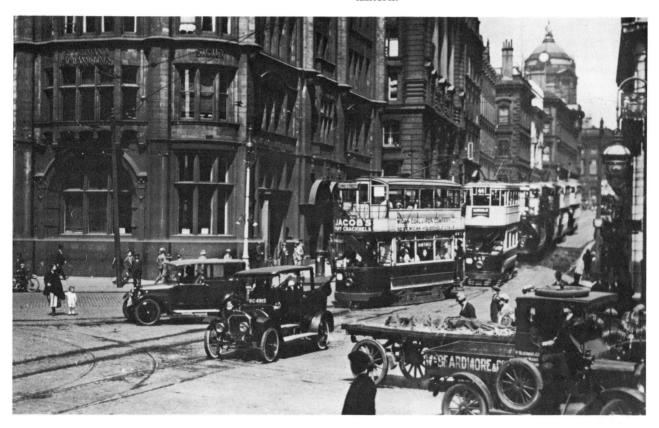

ALL CARS GOING WEST
STOP
ON REQUEST

South Castle Street terminus about 1947 with 1933 bogie car 778 on the clockwise Outer Circular with rebuilt Standard 469 about to turn on to its terminal siding in Preesons Row. The open fronted standard in the background is on a depot run to Dingle. The bogie car shows a red route number denoting a Castle Street service, a convention which had just been officially abandoned. Its domed roof was inspired by London County Council car No.1

A wartime view of Lime Street Quadrant. 1931 bogie car 767, with white blackout fender and masked headlamps, heads north to Walton despite its incorrect destination display. The siding on the left was the terminus of Seaforth and Litherland routes 24 and 28. The normally cream parts of the car bodies have been painted wartime grey.

Modernised Priestly standard car 305, new in 1931 as No.214, was rebuilt in 1938 with a new 8 ft EMB truck. It is seen at Seaforth in 1947 behind a grimy Baby Grand on route 18 to Breck Road. The bystander is studying the announcement of a meeting to be addressed by Willie Gallacher, the only Communist to be elected to the British Parliament.

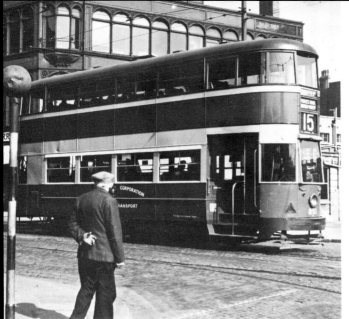

Marks bogie car 851, fitted with new destination blinds, was looking smart in the post-war livery when seen in Castle Street in 1948. Route 15 to Croxteth Road was the shortest all day tram route and, after conversion to bus operation, eventually lost its identity in longer routes.

Standard car 719, already rather full, loads more passngers outside the Employment Exchange in Leece Street. When it entered service in 1926, it had been fitted with a 10ft. wheelbase radial truck but this had been replaced by a 8ft. 6in. standard truck; a wartime vestibule was fitted. Despite the wartime livery, the car still presents a smart appearance.

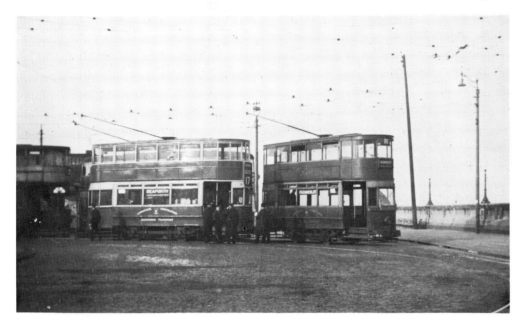

Priestly standard cars on the North Loop at Pier Head in immediate post-war days. The leading car on route 22 to Fazakerley has a utility vestibule fitted in response to strong trade union pressure. The centre car has been fitted with large indicators but retains its original truck while the dilapidated car just visible to the left is still unvestibuled and in the maroon and cream livery.

Unhappily, the outbreak of war in 1939 prevented the completion of the programme and, despite spectacular wartime extensions to serve war factories, a decision was made in 1945 to replace the tramways by buses. Aerial bombardment all but brought the tramways to a halt in 1941 but the indomitable spirit of the corporation's staff, augmented by men from neighbouring towns, restored services in an incredibly short time. The 'planning mania'

of the late war years resulted in a reversal of the pre-war pro-tramway policy and when peace returned, Liverpool was committed to the replacement of all its tramways by buses. Wartime arrears and post-war problems reduced the tramways to a state of near-dereliction and it was only during the last five years or so between 1952-57 that a gradually reducing network was able to present a more acceptable face to the public.

St. Nicholas Place, between the Liver Building and the Floating Roadway, probably in the first few months of the war. Note the white paint on the poles and the steel water main at the left, a branch of which crosses the footpath. These mains enabled an emergency fire-fighting supply to be pumped from the Mersey when the ordinary mains were damaged by bombing. People tripped over them in the blackout and they were sometimes extended across the tram tracks, interrupting the service. Car 742 was Liverpool's first to have a permanent windscreen and was known as the 'Crystal Palace' when new in 1927; see Volume Two, page 171. After some years at Green Lane 742 moved to Walton and then to Litherland depot.

Reconditioned car 318 pauses in Church Street to be passed by a vehicle which also relied on home-produced fuel. Note the boarded-up shop windows in this circa-1942 view.

Liverpool's worst-ever tramcar accident was the collision and subsequent fire involving car 913 and a coach belonging to Gore's of Southport on a workmen's contract at Kirkby on Saturday 14th April 1945. The fire is believed to have been due mainly to fuel from the petrol-driven bus; three passengers lost their lives and twelve were injured.

The last trams in Liverpool ran in public service on 14th September 1957.

A number of the social changes which were to erode the traditional concepts and structures of public transport had their origins in wartime and post-war events and had considerable influence on the relative economics of the various modes. Low cost, frequent tramway operation thrived on routes of medium length with high population density. The dilution of residential density in the inner suburbs had already begun with slum clearance in the thirties and the devastation caused by the air raids accelerated it. Unfortunately the planners, almost invariably blind to the need for public transport and stubbornly determined to ignore its basic economics, pressed ahead with schemes to disperse whole communities to distant 'new towns'. The city became an apple without a core and public transport was called upon to carry people long distances at subsidised fares in circumstances which reduced fleet utilisation.

A Baby Grand passes beneath the Overhead Railway Structure in the last tramway days of 1957. The railway had already succumbed to the bus on 30th December 1956.

Number 272 disgraced itself on the last day of tramway operation. Two other Baby Grands were needed to push it up Brookside Avenue as the brakes could not be released.

The bogie streamliners sold to Glasgow for further service were transported in this special trailer. Meanwhile wholesale destruction of other cars took place at Edge Lane, as seen below. Only three streamlined trams survived; the sole bogie car, 869, is currently undergoing restoration at the National Tramway Museum, Crich, Derbyshire, whilst of the two surviving Baby Grands, 245 was stored in Liverpool for many years and is currently being considered for renovation to operational condition whilst 293, the official last car, is preserved in the USA.

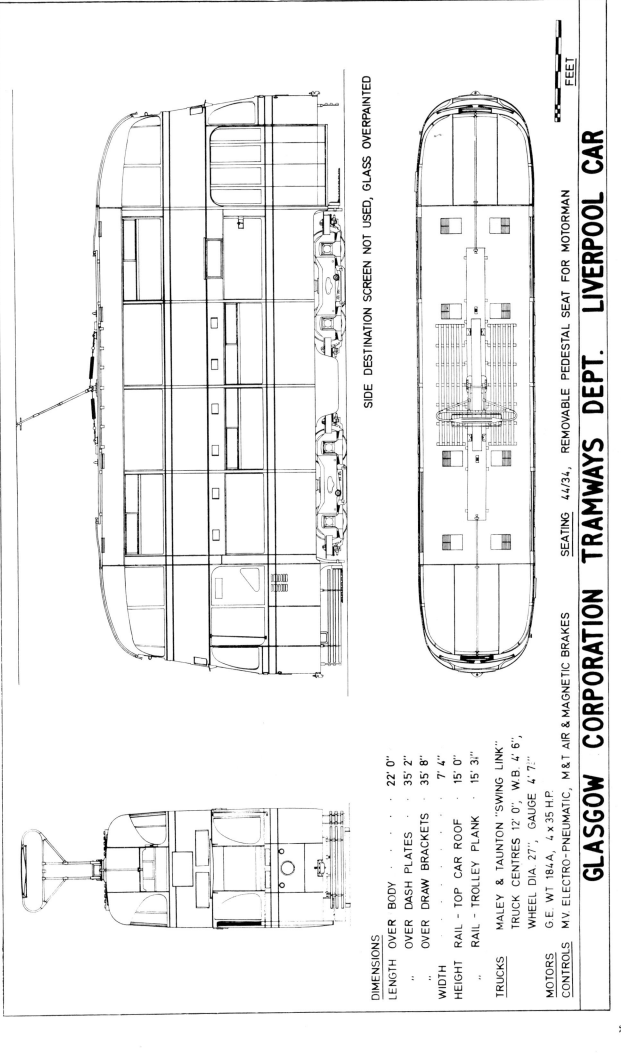

SIDE DESTINATION SCREEN NOT USED, GLASS OVERPAINTED

FEET

DIMENSIONS

LENGTH OVER BODY . . . . 22' 0"
"   OVER DASH PLATES . . 35' 2"
"   OVER DRAW BRACKETS . 35' 8"
WIDTH . . . . 7' 4"
HEIGHT RAIL - TOP CAR ROOF . 15' 0"
"   RAIL - TROLLEY PLANK . 15' 3⅜"

TRUCKS   MALEY & TAUNTON "SWING LINK"
         TRUCK CENTRES 12' 0", W.B. 4' 6",
         WHEEL DIA. 27", GAUGE 4' 7½".

MOTORS   G.E. WT 184A, 4 x 35 H.P.
CONTROLS M.V. ELECTRO-PNEUMATIC, M & T AIR & MAGNETIC BRAKES   SEATING 44/34, REMOVABLE PEDESTAL SEAT FOR MOTORMAN

GLASGOW CORPORATION TRAMWAYS DEPT. LIVERPOOL CAR

The grandiose schemes for nationalisation of all forms of transport for which legislation was passed by the post-war government unsettled the operators, all of whom were opposed to them even when municipal ownership was vested in councils of the same political hue. But the prevailing political policies had many more lasting effects on the fortunes of the providers of public transport. Labour was encouraged to become more militant leading to higher wages and costs; the five day week and shorter working hours accentuated the peak and reduced vehicle utilisation further. Social policies kept fares unnaturally low in relation to other commodities without any formal substitute for the lost revenue. Public transport became less profitable and the resultant economies made it less attractive, not only to the passengers but to the employees. Whereas a regular job on the tramways had been much sought after in pre-war days, there were now better paid jobs in industry with regular hours and every weekend free. The price regulation exercised by the Traffic Commissioners kept transport wages down and despite the nucleus of loyal, long serving employees, the standard of worker — and service — deteriorated.

By 1957, the change in leisure travel patterns caused by the popularity of television was well-established and much evening and weekend off-peak revenue had been lost. Fleet utilisation declined further, making the peak hour workers' services more expensive to operate as there were fewer miles over which to spread the fixed costs. An increasing threat was the proliferation of private transport, less severe in Liverpool than in some other areas, as car ownership tended to remain below the national average in many areas of Merseyside.

Apart from causing traffic congestion which impeded public transport, car ownership eroded the off-peak periods even further. Whereas only one member of a family might use the car to go to work, leaving the other members on public transport, the whole family tended to use the car for leisure pursuits. Elaborate traffic management schemes, whilst improving traffic flow, often took the bus away from its customers and caused further loss of bus patronage.

The previous four volumes described events in times of growth and expansion but this volume deals with thirty traumatic years during which it can be said without exaggeration that a revolution took place in public transport in Liverpool as, indeed, it did throughout the land.

It was a time which saw great social change, labour militancy and frightening cost inflation. Traditionally minded management fought a rearguard action, trying to balance the books in situations which constantly changed for the worse.

The parlous financial state of public transport generally led to the passing of the Transport Act 1968. Private enterprise was effectively eliminated from passenger transport on Merseyside and, with the wider spread of financial responsibility, the vociferous local authorities were at last obliged to match their mouthings with money.

From 1969, passenger transport in Birkenhead and Wallasey, across the river in Cheshire, came under the same management as that in Liverpool and the transport undertaking was further enlarged to embrace St. Helens and Southport in 1974. Although this is a book about transport in Liverpool it has been difficult to avoid mentioning happenings in some of the other towns which made up the enlarged undertaking. Batches of buses were frequently distributed around the outlying depots and transferred between districts and divisions. Indeed, in the seventies, this practice enlivened the transport scene in Liverpool immeasurably. However, the changes which the formation of the PTE ushered in were not sufficiently sudden and radical to justify breaking the story at 1969. Continuity of management at Liverpool ensured that many progressive ideas developed by Liverpool Corporation were put into practice under the new regime and also transferred across the river.

On Merseyside's buses the pace of change was accentuated by the policy of developing the local rail network at the expense of road services. Political upheavals in local government did nothing to ease the burden of public transport and finally, a government committed to privatisation policies, alarmed by the constantly increasing cost of subsidies, enacted a new set of rules which certainly revolutionised bus operating. The sequel is controversial and whilst the broad course of events in the post-deregulation era has been summarised in the final chapter, no attempt has been made to describe or analyse this period in depth. These events are too recent and their detailed examination must be left for a later occasion.

(Facing page)
Journey's End — almost! Baby Grand 293 being unloaded at Boston on arrival in the United States. The body was separated from the truck for shipment.

47 THE LAST MUNICIPAL YEARS

As the last trams made their way into Edge Lane Works on 14th September 1957, the Liverpool Transport undertaking reached the climax of 12 years of planning and nine of active changeover from trams to buses. Much has been written on the economic aspects of the conversion but little on the economic influences which affected the road passenger transport industry as a whole. These stemmed from the rigid application of the principle of price control established by the Road Traffic Act 1930 and acceptance that the need for a fares increase must be proved, very publicly, whilst running the gauntlet of the uninformed opposition of all sorts of pressure groups from non-operating local authorities to trade unions and church organisations.

Most bus fares in 1951 were the same or lower than 20 years earlier, a result of the positive aspects of wartime operations which enabled all loss-making mileage to be shed and what remained to be maximised and operated very profitably. The post-war boom continued the trend of burgeoning revenue until the demand peaked around 1950.

If bus fares had been allowed to rise moderately during and after the war in line with other commodities — or at half the rate of railway fares — the bus operators would have been saved many of the problems of the late fifties and sixties. It would have been prudent to have accumulated adequate reserves to cover arrears of maintenance and fleet replacement but, where reserves existed, they were used to subsidise fares and local authority rates for political reasons instead of for the purpose intended. The fifties saw the imposition of penal taxes on fuel which kept the industry under constant financial pressure until a government grant was introduced in 1964.

Liverpool's last trams were given a rousing send-off as the procession left the Pier Head just after 5 o'clock on the 14th September 1957. The heavy rain of the afternoon finally stopped and the sun broke through, much to the relief of the many photographers in the large crowd. As the procession set off to Bowring Park, led by Car 293, seen below, every ship on the river sounded its hooter or siren to give a never to be forgotten send-off. Car 293, in its unique reversed livery, would shortly resume its maritime connection when it left for the American tramway museum at Kennebunkport.

Four separate queues, two each side of the stop sign, were accommodated at one loading point in Lord Street, giving an indication of the traffic potential of that time. AEC Regent III A3 had a Crossley body and was part of an order for 100 buses delivered between June 1953 and March 1955. The full width bonnets were designed by Liverpool Corporation and fitted by Crossley. The Crosville Bristol immediately behind is on a short working to Speke and will follow virtually the same route as A3 to Garston.

One result of this was that transport wages did not keep pace with those in industry and, with the widespread adoption of the five day working week, the bus industry, with its unsocial hours, became even less attractive. In the post-war era labour became more mobile and, whilst job opportunities on Merseyside lagged behind those in more prosperous areas, daily travel to and from places 12-20 miles distant was acceptable if the take home pay made it worthwhile. When the motor industry came to Liverpool, hundreds of men forsook the business of running buses for five-day jobs with better pay and conditions and more leisure. Manning problems on the buses then became very serious. Staff shortages encouraged labour militancy and much management time, which might have been spent on maintaining and improving the quality of the service, was dissipated in solving constant labour disputes.

Staff shortages contributed in no small measure to loss of patronage because the service became unreliable and slovenly attitudes and incivility abounded. If it had not been for that strange local quality, be it real or imagined, sometimes summed up as the Scouse Factor, which frightened many industries away from Merseyside, the problems might have been even worse.

The popularity of television and a determination to own personal transport were established factors and the most perfect bus service would not have stemmed their advance.

Service Reductions

The impact of social change on traffic carried was under constant study. In the General Manager's report dealing with revised services to follow the tramway conversion, the Committee's attention was drawn to the underlying trends. The number of private cars registered had increased by 145% between 1945 and 1955 and traffic losses tended to be greater in the off-peak periods. In Liverpool, mileage operated had increased every year and many new facilities had created their own demand so the number of passengers carried had not decreased. But the density of traffic had declined from 11 to 8.6 passengers per mile operated between 1939 and 1956, a fall of 22%. This reflected the fall in residential density in the inner areas and the lengthening of the average passenger journey. In a nutshell, the department was having to work harder to keep its passengers.

The Suez crisis in late 1956 and early 1957, which led to petrol rationing and reductions in bus services, showed to what extent services could be reduced without significantly affecting passenger carryings. Comparisons are clouded by the Overhead Railway replacement services but 1956-57 showed a 12% increase in revenue over the previous year for a 9% increase in mileage.

In March 1958 the General Manager drew the attention of the Committee to the national trend of reduced traffic after 7.00pm, largely because of television, and the following month he submitted draft proposals for frequency reductions. It was proposed to withdraw services 7C, 21, 77 and 506 in the evenings and reduce frequencies on selected services from 10 to 12 or 15 minutes, 15 to 20 minutes and so on. Twenty-seven services were to remain unaltered. A sub-committee was appointed to discuss the problem of falling revenue with the trade unions; national and local trends were analysed. Service changes following tramway conversions and the provision of new services to developing housing estates made it difficult to assess trends with accuracy but, after a series of censuses, the following percentage reductions, based on 1952 traffic, were quoted:-

	National %	Liverpool %
1953	2.3	0.5
1954	3.5	1.6
1955	3.7	2.6
1956	5.3	5.4
1957	6.7	5.5

Revenue after 7.00pm on the routes surveyed was 3d per mile (8%) lower than the average revenue for the day and observations on Monday 27th October 1958, a fine mild evening, when 1619 trips were checked, revealed average loads of 16 passengers inwards and 23 outwards between 8.00pm and 11.30pm. A similar census taken earlier in the year, nearer the city centre, showed an average load of 14 inward and 27 outward.

There was an urgent need to economise as, although the Department's accounts showed a credit balance of £61,630 at 31st March 1958, a recent wage award was expected to cost £150,000 per year. Deficits of £15,400 were predicted by 31st March 1959 and £171,000 by March 1960 if no economies were made. Reductions of about 7% in total mileage were suggested, mostly in the evenings but with some off-peak cuts during the day.

By November 1958 cuts on Sundays were also being proposed and the General Manager recommended withdrawing 20 peak buses (2%) as this would have reduced expenditure by £30,000 per year. It was accepted, however, that there would be some inconvenience to passengers and possibly further loss of traffic. The cuts would save 2.5 million miles annually.

There was opposition from many quarters — trade unions who feared job losses, individual councillors and other pressure groups and it was a very watered-down version of the proposals which was eventually implemented on 16th November 1959, 20 months after action had first been proposed. This was a typical example of the Committee's and Council's attitude to the serious problems which public transport faced during the next two decades.

Mileage peaked in 1958-59 at 41.9 million, an increase of 24.7% in nine years. It subsequently declined to 32.4 million in 1967-68 and to 24.7 million in 1968-69, the latter steep fall being the direct result of a lengthy strike.

In every environment problems give rise to solutions and the bus operators, hamstrung by more than their share of statutory restraints, were no exception. The fifties had seen the emergence of the underfloor engined single decker with 25% more seating than its predecessors and then the lightweight vehicle with a relatively small engine, designed to reduce fuel costs. By constant lobbying, the government had been persuaded to increase the permitted dimensions of buses in stages and, in general, the high capacity vehicle which needed a more powerful engine was seen as a better proposition than a lightweight vehicle using less fuel and likely to have a relatively short life. Whilst the companies, and particularly Ribble, quickly took advantage of the relaxations, Liverpool Corporation, with a standardised orthodox fleet which was already too numerous for its requirements, cautiously acquired three experimental vehicles in 1959, meticulously testing each one before coming down in favour of the Leyland Atlantean for the next generation of the city's buses. Whilst Liverpool's version of the model avoided some of the problems experienced by earlier users, the large capacity double-decker was five years late coming to the city's municipal routes.

Liverpool's first Atlantean, E2, was a distinctive vehicle in a fleet of front-engined double-deckers. The large opening windows at the front of the upper deck were a prominent but perhaps unattractive feature.

After 1960, the rate of passenger loss accelerated to 14% over the next five years. By 1969, passengers carried were below 200 million per annum compared to 360 million in 1960. Mileage reductions were not commensurate but the use of large capacity buses reduced mileage appreciably, though at the cost of wider service intervals. Atlanteans were placed in service, route by route, over a period of just over four years commencing with routes 86/87 on 4th February 1963 and finishing with routes 2/30 on 24th April 1967. In every case, frequencies and peak hour augmentation were reduced.

From 1st April 1962, the four traffic divisions were reorganised into two. The North Division covered Litherland, Walton, Green Lane, Stanley, Carnegie Road and Edge Lane depots while the South assumed responsibility for the city centre, Speke, Garston, Dingle and Prince Alfred Road. In December 1965, the Department's name was changed from Liverpool Corporation Passenger Transport to Liverpool City Transport.

Outer Suburban Development

In the fifties and sixties, an outer ring of new suburbs, many designed for low income groups, began to develop along the eastern perimeter of Liverpool and Bootle. Some of them were logical extensions of the immediate post-war housing schemes but others, such as Netherley and Knowsley were completely new. This was despite the acres of derelict land near the centre which remained from the blitz and which now grew rapidly as slum houses were demolished or bricked up. Off-peak requirements could usually be met by the extension of existing services but all had a high peak hour demand and complex school requirements, exacerbating the continuing tendency for the peak to shorten and reducing bus utilisation. This placed a further strain on transport services as the distances involved were such as to limit most vehicles to one trip in the peak hours. Furthermore, the city council's tapering fare policy, designed to make living in these far flung suburbs affordable, ensured that these trips were unremunerative. As the south-eastern estates at Halewood, Netherley and Naylorsfield were built in what had been Crosville's very rural territory, complications arose with the company fare scale.

The transport operators tried in vain to convince the planners of the need for a good spine road for bus services with turning facilities at the terminus. In the case of Halewood they got the message across but the later stages of the development were abandoned and sections of the bus road, which had been built across the fields, lay derelict and unused.

Eventually, the wisdom of redeveloping the inner areas was recognised but in both inner and outer suburbs hundreds of families were housed in tower blocks which nobody wanted, leading to vandalism and other social ills from which neither the buses nor the drivers were protected. In some cases, the premature demolition of modern structures has followed. Events have proved that other traumatic population movements to Skelmersdale, Runcorn and Winsford were largely unnecessary as the population of Merseyside as a whole declined.

The County Borough of Bootle, having extended its boundary to include Netherton, developed the area both residentially and industrially while the traditional industries along the line of docks gradually died away. In due course, Sefton Estate was built to the north. Communication between the northern suburbs was inhibited by the presence of numerous weak bridges, some of them moveable, across the Leeds and Liverpool Canal. The loss to the canal of commercial traffic facilitated the rebuilding of several of these and the strengthening of bridges in Fleetwoods Lane, Wango Lane and Waddicar Lane gave the bus network much greater flexibility.

Two classic features of the Liverpool of the 'sixties — the Atlantean bus and the tower block redevelopment. Neither was to be without its problems, but whereas the Atlantean was capable of being improved the high rise accommodation was recognised as a disaster, being demolished prematurely in many instances.

Netherton

Magdalene Square was designated the hub of residential Netherton and Bootle Corporation installed bus lay-bys and passenger shelters, a contribution to the cost being made by Liverpool City Council. Following the completion of new roads, route 28 from the city and 53A from the Black Bull were extended the short distance from St. Oswald's Lane to the Square on 30th September 1957. The extension of route 56, which approached from the other direction, had to await the reconstruction of Fleetwoods bridge and this was completed in August 1958. Buses on 57A reached Magdalene Square only in 1961, having been first extended along Bridle Road to Hereford Drive in 1958.

The industrial estate at Heysham Road and Leckwith Road, on the south side of Dunnings Bridge Road, was within walking distance of most of the Netherton housing. Individual factory requirements were served by special unadvertised buses not just on the routes which passed nearby such as 53, 54 and 59 but on others which diverged from their normal routes. Thus one could see the odd 61 which made its way to the Black Bull to regain its normal course. Ribble used the numbers W54 and W59 on some of these works buses and, in 1964, provided direct facilities from Maghull after settlement of a dispute with Liverpool Corporation as described in Chapter 49. A common-sense relaxation of the joint working arrangements had allowed the Corporation to start workers' route 95B in July 1961, giving Netherton residents better access to Gillmoss.

The direct route from the city via Stanley Road and Linacre Road (55), which terminated with route 56 in Fleetwoods Lane at St. Nicholas Avenue, was not extended to Magdalene Square, but was diverted along Almond's Turn to the corner of Buckley Hill Lane as the first houses on Sefton Estate were occupied in September 1966. At peak hours, part of the service continued to turn at St. Nicholas Avenue as 55A and this became an all day service in April 1967. Route 55 was eventually extended along the unimaginatively named Northern Perimeter

Road to a specially constructed lay-by in September 1971 but almost 12 years were to elapse before road improvements enabled buses to reach this area direct from Dunnings Bridge Road through what remained of Netherton village.

Peak hour services to Magdalene Square were further augmented by the extension of the Overhead Railway replacement route 1E from Litherland via Ford and Fleetwoods Lane on 16th June 1969, the day when road improvements at last enabled the Line of Docks buses to follow the dock road throughout. The extension of 1E was agreed with Ribble as a quid quo pro as described in Chapter 49.

Kirkby

Kirkby's greatest period of development was during the early fifties and the pattern of services had been established following the abandonment of the 19 and 44 trams in November 1956. The Northwood estate was completed and routes 44D and 544 and industrial service 35 were extended from their temporary Minstead Avenue terminus to Roughwood Drive in April 1959. An additional service to Northwood was provided from March 1960 by route 92B which also served Westvale, the last sector of the Kirkby residential area south of the railway to be completed. There were several main road realignments as arterial roads were built which would eventually link up with the M57 motorway and some erstwhile through routes such as Ingoe Lane and Ribblers Lane were stopped up or relegated to a minor status. Later, Hornhouse Lane and its roundabout on the East Lancs Road, briefly the tram terminus in 1943, almost disappeared beneath a realignment of Coopers Lane. Valley Road (an extension of Longmoor Lane), County Road and Moorgate Road were designed to cater for through traffic.

There were many minor changes to services as the final layout of the town took shape. A small temporary bus station was built adjacent to the Civic Centre in Cherryfield

A lonely terminus was the Northern Perimeter Road turning point on the outskirts of Netherton where a special layby was built for buses. Atlantean 1968 with Alexander body waits time on route 30A to Pier Head via Netherfield Road during the period when route 30 ran through to Crosby.

Kirkby Industrial Estate, Main Gate, frequently termed 'Kirkby Admin', was an important terminus. This March 1966 view shows St. Helens Corporation 1961 Leyland PD2A L10 with 64-seat East Lancs body on the St. Helens-Kirkby service, overtaking unpainted Liverpool PD2 L309 on route 93. The latter was one of 30 buses delivered in 1957 with Crossley frames but stored until 1961 when it was completed by Metro-Cammell. Note the hopper windows. Route 93 buses made a circuit of the Industrial Estate before returning to the Pier Head via Fazakerley.

New buses replacing old trams always created a good impression and the fleet of Crossley-bodied Leylands used for the conversion of the 19 and 44 routes were no exception.

Drive though few services used it as a terminus. All-day facilities to the Industrial Estate were excessive and the section of East Lancs Road east of Moorgate Road generated virtually no traffic between the peaks. The tram replacement route 19 which, oddly, had followed the main road to Hornhouse Lane was curtailed off peak at Lower Lane as 19C in July 1963, the Moorgate Road variant, 19A, being extended past the Industrial Estate to Hornhouse Lane. In effect, the 19 group now followed the course which logically the trams should have taken twenty years earlier.

A second Northwood limited stop service (592) took the place of some journeys on 92B from February 1964 when 92A was also rerouted to pass the Civic Centre and extended to Pagemoss on Saturday and Sunday afternoons. There were thus three limited stop services between Kirkby and the city centre.

Residential development now spread north of the railway line and the Tower Hill estate was built along Shevington's Lane, a district hitherto served only by the Tuesday and Saturday Ribble route 305. A shuttle 15B between Tower Hill and the Civic Centre commenced running on 25th January 1965 when new schedules should have been introduced for all services in the Breck Road corridor to coincide with conversion to Atlantean operation, but had to be postponed for five days as leaflets were not ready. It was then consolidated in a new 15D service through to the Pier Head.

The Department had done its best to serve the new town and the positioning of the large new garage at Gillmoss was part of the overall plan. But the costs were high and it was to prove difficult to reconcile the political desire for low fares with the loss of traffic and other changes of subsequent decades.

Naylorsfield and Netherley

These estates were extensions of the immediate post-war housing development at Gateacre and Belle Vale; the prefabs were cleared away and new housing extended north and east. The area was served by route 73A from the city via Ullet Road and Woolton Road, 79C and 79D from the city via Wavertree and Childwall Valley Road, the intersuburban 66 from Garston and the interurban 89, Speke-St.Helens. There was also the hourly Crosville H23 to Widnes, Runcorn and Chester.

The Lee Park estate adjoining Belle Vale Road came first, the 66 making a loop through it from February 1958 when experimental one-man operation started. The 79s followed in May with a terminus at the corner of Lee Vale Road.

From November 1961, the Corporation provided a service for the Gateacre Park private housing development, a variant of the 79s (numbered 79B) running half-hourly between South Castle Street and Well

Lane via Barnham Drive, being extended to Thurne Way in 1963. The area consolidated until early 1969 when housing in Naylorsfield, west of Naylors Road, began to be occupied and route 66 was extended about 400 yards from the Bridge Inn. From May 1969, 73A was extended to Brinton Close and at the same time 79B was projected during the off-peak from Thurne Way along Gateacre Park Drive and Gateacre Brow into Lee Park. The later diversion along Grange Lane followed road improvements in 1973.

Meanwhile the Woodlands Estate at Netherley was in need of a service which was temporarily provided by extending the Garston-Halewood (88) service along Church Road and Gerrard's Lane as 88A. Construction of the Netherley estate proper involved realignment of the B5178 road both to discourage through traffic and to form two sides of a perimeter road. The first city connection was the diversion of 73A at peak hours from Naylorsfield round three sides of the perimeter road from January 1972. At the same time 66 started using the Naylorsfield perimeter road and then continued along Caldway Drive to Woodlands. Buses numbered 79 were extended along Childwall Valley Road to Caldway Drive in September 1969 and the Lee Park time tables on 79B, C and D were revised simultaneously. Future trends were foreshadowed by the withdrawal of the 79D Dale Street/Tithebarn Street service on weekday evenings and all day Saturdays and Sundays in favour of a hybrid 79B route via London Road, Lime Street and Church Street. In May 1970, the 79 was extended to Woodlands Estate and the 88 cut back to its normal terminus at Halewood (Derby Arms). A Rapidride

These views of L521 taken on its first day in service — 4th February 1963 — and L721, taken on 19th March 1966 when three months old, show the minor differences between the first and second batches of Atlanteans. The rear end of the later vehicles was smoothed out into one gentle curve and ventilating windows added to the front upper deck. Both wore the original livery with the cream window surrounds extending round the front end and were equipped with the two-line lower case route indicator.

service (479) was commenced three months later and industrial services 65A to Edge Lane in 1971. The opening of the Belle Vale District Centre in 1973 stimulated traffic to some extent and various minor diversions were made to improve passenger access.

Hunts Cross and Halewood

The first Corporation service to reach Halewood village

was the 88 from Garston which was extended from Hunts Cross in May 1959 via Baileys Lane. A new all-day route 78 between Hunts Cross (Mackets Lane) and Pier Head via Kings Drive, Woolton Road and Wavertree, started in October 1962, the peak hour route 78 (the former 72B) being renumbered 78A. The latter was diverted from the Speke Road route to Mackets Lane a year later.

In 1964, the 78 was extended along Higher Road to Leathers Lane with a 20-minute all-day service and, in August 1965, these buses and the peak hour 83 to and from Speke, were extended to the Derby Arms, Halewood via Leathers Lane, which became the spine road of the development. A week later, Crosville H19/20 were similarly routed but 88 remained on Baileys Lane until May 1966. The extension of 78 to Halewood was first proposed in January 1964. Although within the Corporation's operating area, it was opposed by Crosville before the Traffic Commissioners on the grounds that the frequency was excessive and passengers would be abstracted from their service which had been provided over many years when the area was sparsely populated. A terminal loop via Wood Road, Hollies Road, Church Road, Baileys Lane and Leathers Lane was adopted in November 1966 to eliminate buses turning at the Derby Arms. Halewood was now very well served with seven buses an hour to the city centre, four Corporation and three Crosville. As previously mentioned, the 88 was temporarily extended to Netherley in 1969-70 and it was to be another eight years before the facility was restored and the 88 linked with the 66 as a circular.

Knowsley and Cantril Farm

A small housing estate was built at Knowsley village and a direct half-hourly service from the Pier Head started in February 1961, the Lyme Cross (9) service being reduced from a quarter to a half hour service to supply the necessary buses. There was a combined quarter-hourly service to the top of Stockbridge Lane. In July 1965, the Knowsley service was extended from Sugar Lane end to the top of Frederick Lunt Avenue.

The name 'Cantril Farm' had been used to describe a terminus in Princess Drive since 1949 when route 12 was extended on conversion from trams but, from 1967, housing spread into the area of Huyton-with-Roby Council and the now familiar perimeter road, so wasteful of bus miles, developed. A variant of the 12 group, (12C) commenced in June 1967 with a bus every half hour between a point on Haswell Drive and Pier Head via Melwood Drive and West Derby Road. It was extended along Haswell Drive to the underpass at Birtle Croft a year later and to the Waterpark Drive shops in October 1968, the daytime frequency eventually giving a bus every 10 minutes. The layout of the estate was such that every bus had to almost completely circumnavigate it. In due course industrial routes to and from Kirkby, Gillmoss, Seaforth and Edge Lane were added. Years in the future, in 1984, the part of the estate outside the city of Liverpool was renamed Stockbridge Village, in an effort to improve a somewhat tarnished reputation. Eventually, as blinds were replaced, this was adopted by the PTE.

The MALTS Study

In the post-war years, many opportunities to improve the environment and layout of the city streets were lost. Lord Street was rebuilt virtually on the foundations of the structures demolished in the 1941 air raids, where a little imagination could have produced a wide boulevard, extending into Church Street and revealing the elegance of the Bluecoat School. The appointment of Graeme Shankland, the eminent town planner, in the early sixties came too late but it produced the Shankland Plan which introduced the concept of separating traffic from pedestrians and gave birth to the rejuvenation of long neglected places in the city centre such as Queen Square and Williamson Square, while retaining the narrow by-ways such as Hackins Hey with their quaint shops and pubs. One of the plan's features was a series of elevated walkways which were subsequently abandoned, resulting in the new underground railway station at Moorfields decanting its passengers at first floor level.

In 1962 the Liverpool Junior Chamber of Commerce undertook a survey of transport on Merseyside and its report recommended the formation of a Merseyside Transport Authority with a monopoly of road passenger transport. The area covered would have been bounded by a line drawn through Neston to Ellesmere Port and then from Runcorn through Widnes, St. Helens and Ormskirk to Formby. It was seen as essential that the body should be entirely divorced from local politics and the local authorities should have no part in its management and no share in its profits.

Meanwhile the various local councils had established a Steering Committee on Merseyside Traffic and Transport following visits in October and December 1961 by the then Minister of Transport, Mr. Ernest Marples, MP for Wallasey. Membership consisted of representatives of all the local authorities and transport operators, planning authorities and the Dock Board, under the chairmanship of a Ministry of Transport official.

Sub-committees were established to consider cross-river traffic, highways and transport services, and a Merseyside Conurbation Traffic Survey was commenced in 1962. A number of censuses were taken and an enormous amount of information regarding travel habits was assembled and published. A plan for additional highways and river crossings was drawn up to meet 1982 traffic forecasts. All parties were agreed that great benefit would follow the extension of the Mersey Railway on a circular route under the city centre with additional stations connecting with the main line stations which, with the construction of a burrowing junction at Hamilton Square, Birkenhead, would double the capacity of the line. The railway management had advocated a scheme of this kind in the fifties.

The Transport Sub-Committee was also unanimous in its wish to create a cross-river authority with control over the road tunnels and ferries but there was no such unanimity on the question of an overall transport authority for the area. It was, of course, understandable that the Crosville and Ribble companies did not favour any arrangement which would deprive each of them of an important part of their operating areas and thereby completely upset their financial stability. 'Private enterprise' bus undertakings, even before some of them had become state-owned, had for over thirty years been run on the principle of cross-subsidisation. The companies had maintained many unremunerative services in North Wales, Cumberland and Westmorland with the help of the revenue from heavily trafficked services in urban areas such as Merseyside.

The outcome of these preliminary surveys was a major investigation which became known as the Merseyside Area Land Use and Transportation Study (MALTS), the contract for which was awarded to the Traffic Research Corporation (later renamed Peat, Marwick, Kates & Co.), a Canadian consultancy firm. The Study was directed towards the needs of Merseyside as a whole in 1991. Meanwhile the City Planning department had produced a number of schemes which, if adopted, would have had a radical effect on local transport. Some of these were strongly criticised by professional transport men who, as usual, had not been consulted. The schemes for pedestrianisation, implemented during the next two decades, were generally unsympathetic to the requirements of bus passengers and pleas for buses-only lanes and turning facilities to give better access fell on deaf ears.

Traffic Management

The rapid growth of road traffic in the sixties and seventies created great problems of congestion in all towns and cities, with an adverse effect on public transport. Irregular operation caused by traffic delays affected a wide area, including suburbs remote from the source of the trouble, and this unreliability tended to drive more passengers to private transport thus aggravating the problem. Measures intended to reduce this congestion sometimes had repercussions on public transport as a slight diversion caused by a one-way traffic scheme, could involve an operator in thousands of additional, unproductive miles when it had to be traversed by several close interval services. A further irritant was the moving of stopping places from old established points convenient to the needs of the public, to sites chosen solely from the point of view of traffic flow. A great deal of short distance traffic was lost because of this. It was even suggested that future designs for buses should mimic trains by having entrances on both sides so that stopping places could be sited on the 'wrong' sides of one-way streets where this was more convenient and there is no doubt that such a device would be superior in many instances to existing arrangements. Traffic congestion was already causing serious peak hour delays by the autumn of 1947 when outward journeys during the evening peak hour were speeded up on routes 73, 80 and 82 by allowing fully loaded buses from the Pier Head or Castle Street to divert via Strand Street or South Castle Street, Canning Place, Duke Street, Upper Duke Street and Canning Street, thus avoiding the most congested part of the city centre.

In broad terms, the traffic management schemes put into effect in Liverpool during the sixties were disastrous for public transport. It is true that buses moved more freely but there was little regard for the convenience of bus passengers. As is so often the case, the planners were concerned more with numbers of vehicles rather than numbers of people. The very first city centre traffic scheme of any importance, introduced on 11th December 1950, created a gyratory system round St. George's Hall, (though Lime Street remained two-way also William Brown Street until it no longer had trams), and disrupted the bus terminus in St. Johns Lane which had existed since 1929. Apart from the inconvenience to passengers, these upheavals were expensive as shelters were often left unused on what became the wrong side of the road. Often they were not replaced because of lack of funds. These difficulties would have been fewer if the elevated walkways advocated by MALTS had been built.

The most persistent cause of city centre traffic congestion was Mersey Tunnel traffic and the traffic engineers worked towards the separation of tunnel and other city traffic. The afternoon problem was the tunnel queue as every vehicle had to stop to pay toll. After years of inconvenience the problem was solved very simply by moving the toll booths to Birkenhead so that the queue was in the tunnel where it taxed only the ventilation system.

A one-way traffic scheme in the Ranelagh Street and Clayton Square area, introduced on 28th February 1960, imposed a flow identical to that dictated by the original tramway layout before tracks were doubled in 1930. All the south end services via Church Street travelled outward via Clayton Square and Lime Street and, while there was a

Traffic management schemes improved vehicle flow but made bus services less accessible as shown in this diagram published in connection with a scheme which came into effect on 28th February 1960. Buses used Great Charlotte Street for the first time.

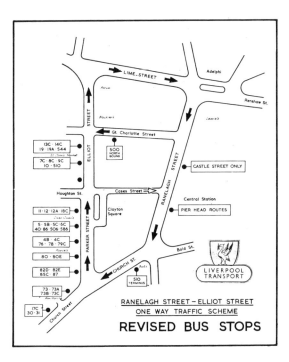

RANELAGH STREET – ELLIOT STREET
ONE WAY TRAFFIC SCHEME
REVISED BUS STOPS

great improvement in traffic flow, there was difficulty in finding enough kerb space for the many different stops, several of which had been in Ranelagh Street. Every bus passing through this scheme incurred additional mileage in one direction or the other and, whilst it amounted to only 150 or 200 yards per trip, over a year it was enormous and all of it quite unproductive.

Other measures designed to speed up traffic flow were also costly to the Transport Department. From 12th February 1962 morning peak journeys on routes 12A, 74D and 75 terminated in Whitechapel in lieu of Sir Thomas Street, adding to the mileage but reducing Tunnel Entrance traffic congestion by making their way back to depot by way of Paradise Street and Duke Street. Traffic schemes were not confined to the central area of the city. A continuous island constructed in Queens Drive between Allerton Road and Childwall Five Ways in 1964-65 was broken only at the intersection of Woolton Road so buses could no longer cross Queens Drive at Dunbabin Road, resulting in some loss of facilities and 22,000 additional unproductive miles per annum on route 73 alone. There had been another scheme for a gyratory arrangement at the foot of Everton Valley which the General Manager successfully opposed, pointing out that a roundabout would produce the same effect without buses incurring the extra wasted mileage which the scheme would entail. None of these schemes gave public transport any priority.

The first stage of an overall traffic management scheme for the city centre was brought into operation on 2nd August 1965. It had far-reaching effects on the city's bus services. The main theme of the scheme was to make London Road one-way inward and Islington one-way outward. St. Anne Street, Norton Street and Boundary Place became north to south streets while Commutation Row, Christian Street and Daulby Street became south to north. Whilst doubtless having a beneficial effect on vehicle flow, from the point of view of bus passengers, the arrangements were disastrous as the then important shopping area of London Road had virtually no outward bus connections whatsoever. The subsequent decay of this once thriving shopping street might be attributed to its conversion to a four-lane one-way street. Wavertree Road and Edge Lane services were diverted via Islington, Norton Street and Pembroke Place and it was originally intended that Prescot Road services should be similarly routed, rejoining their routes by using Daulby Street but at the last minute they were diverted to use the full length of Islington and then Moss Street. The intended arrangements would have served the London Road shops better but increased the number of conflicting traffic movements which the scheme was designed to eliminate.

All the north east services used William Brown Street or Commutation Row and Islington outward and Moss Street and London Road inwards. The Bootle joint services and the ex-tram services 23, 24 and 28 came in via Norton Street and London Road and out by Commutation Row, Islington and Christian Street. Ribble independent services to and from Skelhorne Street were obliged to conform to this pattern though this caused every bus to use London Road between Norton Street and Commutation

Row in the same direction on both the inward and outward journeys. Inward buses used Norton Street, London Road, Lime Street and Skelhorne Street whilst outward buses followed St. Vincent Street, London Road, Commutation Row, Islington and Christian Street. Although the diversion measured no more than 250 yards, the extra mileage run added up to tens of thousands per year and the inward route was changed on 12th September 1966 when Seymour Street and Copperas Hill replaced London Road and Lime Street. After suffering severely from traffic congestion in Lime Street, the Corporation diverted their London Road-Church Street services together with routes 3 and 500 southbound over the same route from October 1967. The original route was rejoined at the foot of Skelhorne Street. Crosville conformed to the route of the Corporation's Prescot Road services.

From 1st January 1966, Old Haymarket was closed to all but tunnel traffic and buses. There was no longer access from Whitechapel or Victoria Street and this created some new routing problems. These were overcome by diverting outward buses on 12A, 74, 74D and 75 along the northern part of Sir Thomas Street into Dale Street but the journeys from Pier Head on the Bootle joint services were obliged to go round by Church Street, Clayton Square, Lime Street and St. Johns Lane in order to reach their loading points in Old Haymarket. A positive feature of the exercise was the reservation of the northernmost lane in St. Johns Lane for buses only but many other opportunities were ignored. This was an early example of a bus lane in the north of England. Another lane enabled buses to travel against the traffic flow for about 75 yds in Canning Place. At a later date, there was a longer contra-flow bus lane in Elm Hall Drive but the police considered it to be dangerous and buses on route 80 were diverted via Allerton Road and Queens Drive in November 1969.

The second stage of the major scheme came into operation on 8th May 1966 and is illustrated in Map 49. The scheme had a profound effect on all Dale Street, Chapel Street and Sir Thomas Street routes. No buses were able to run outward via Water Street or Dale Street so all the routes affected were removed to Chapel Street and Tithebarn Street. This gave Exchange Station a magnificent array of services from the station but the only routes to the station, except from Pier Head, were the City Circle and 39. The latter had to come off Pall Mall on inward journeys in favour of Old Hall Street.

Crosville did not favour the use of Chapel Street and Tithebarn Street so while they retained the Dale Street route inward for their Prescot Road services H2-4, they decided to use Lord Street, Church Street, Clayton Square and Lime Street outward. The direction of the Sir Thomas Street terminal loop was reversed and 11's terminus had to be removed from North John Street to South Castle Street. The most extensive diversions were suffered by 20 and 26 northbound—from South Castle Street via Lord Street, North John Street, Dale Street, Exchange Street East, Tithebarn Street and Gt. Crosshall Street. Supplementary peak hour loading points for 6D, 77 and 78 were located in Queen Square which had seen no public transport since horse tram days.

The new arrangements were certainly successful in speeding up traffic flow and this helped to improve regularity of services during peak periods. Some of the worst congestion was now experienced in Lord Street and Church Street which were among the few two-way main streets in the city centre. The buses lost more short distance traffic in the city centre as it was quicker to walk from the Pier Head to say, an office between Dale Street and Victoria Street than to take a bus to Tithebarn Street and walk through. These arrangements were regarded by the City Engineer's Traffic Route Engineering section as an interim measure pending the completion of a system of flyovers designed to separate city traffic from tunnel traffic. The eastbound flyover, Churchill Way North, linking Gt. Crosshall Street and Islington was opened to traffic on 16th June 1969 whilst Churchill Way South between Islington and Dale Street at Hatton Garden came into service on 1st March 1970. All services except 72 and 85 used them, these two, being south end routes, provided a tenuous link from the Pier Head to Lime Street station without the need to cross a busy road.

A traffic scheme of major benefit to the Corporation and Ribble was the flyover at the junction of Rice Lane and Queens Drive, Walton which opened on 12th December 1968. Buses did not use the flyover itself and in fact the first bus to use it was one from the Training School but the removal of the conflict of very substantial north-south and east-west traffic volumes cut down delays to buses considerably.

Communications

From small beginnings in 1950 (See Volume Four p.90-91), the Corporation's radio control system gradually expanded and was augmented by telephones with loud bells at strategic points for use by inspectors. Their rocket shaped housing soon gained the name of 'sputniks'. In 1958, the original radio equipment was replaced by a more modern VHF installation. The growth of traffic congestion increased the need for adequate communications, and the City Engineer's department developed a computer-controlled system for city centre traffic lights. Rather than set up their own control room, the engineers collaborated with the Transport Department in planning a new joint Control at 24 Hatton Garden which was opened in 1968. Originally eight television cameras, mounted on 40ft poles, monitored about 3½ miles of city streets but the system has been several times extended.

In the late sixties, Liverpool Corporation experimented with radio on buses for traffic control purposes; they were enthusiastically welcomed by the trade unions and contributed to the rapid acceptance of one-man operation. Later, they also helped in protecting drivers and passengers against vandals and hooligans. A radio could be included in the cost of a new bus and thus ranked for capital grant and in 1970 the PTE agreed in principle to install radio in all new buses. By the end of 1971, 276 buses and 25 ancillary vehicles had been equipped and there were 14 portable handsets.

The controllers at Hatton Garden could regulate the traffic lights and in some cases prohibit right turns, except to buses. When accidents caused traffic jams, buses could be diverted before they became entangled. In January 1972, a broadcasting studio was added to enable controllers to make traffic and transport announcements on Radio Merseyside. These became a regular feature of local news broadcasts even if the message was only that everything was running smoothly. Several ladies in the Transport Department became, in turn, well-known 'voices'.

Bus Stations

The Transport Department believed that bus stations should be provided by local authorities or developers, not by bus operators and Liverpool continued to lag behind in the provision of off-street terminal facilities for buses in the post-war years. The Ribble station, on a sloping site between Skelhorne Street and Copperas Hill, which was opened in 1960, was the only bus station in the city for several years.

The three loops at the Pier Head, so eminently suitable in tramway days, were less adaptable for use by buses which required more manoeuvring space. In the early days of the tram-to-bus changeover, some buses traversed the tram loops anti-clockwise, using the kerbspace on the islands; others were banished to the windy canyons between the three great buildings of the Liverpool waterfront. There was an interim scheme using part of St. Nicholas Place as a terminus but the new plan for the Pier Head created an enormous traffic free area between Water Street and Mann Island with a bus station occupying an 'L' shaped site along the front and north side of the Liver Building.

Mann Island, which became the terminus for Crosville and the odd Ribble workers' services, became a cul-de-sac with a turning circle at the river end so that all services using the new bus station, which opened on 11th April 1965, had to approach and leave by way of St. Nicholas Place or Water Street. Twenty-three stands were provided around the inside of the 'L' and a further nine on an island in front of the Liver Building connected to a pedestrian way opposite Water Street by a subway. The stands were connected by a covered glass concourse and buses loaded head-on to sawtooth platforms. The area allotted was initially insufficient to accommodate all services but, in the course of time, the Pier Head terminus diminished in importance and became more than adequate for the smaller number of buses using it. When one-man operation became widespread and there were no conductors to help reverse buses from the platforms, the station became hazardous particularly at night and marshals were appointed to assist drivers from July 1972.

In the City Centre Plan, the land south of Lord Street between Paradise Street and South John Street was reserved for a bus station but no progress was made until 1974.

The City Circle

To improve facilities between the railway stations and the city centre shops and overcome some of the negative effects of traffic management schemes, a new City Circle bus service was inaugurated on 4th December 1965. It bore no number though was known internally as 100 and was

St. Nicholas Place, with the famous 'sailors' church in the background, accommodated several services before the Pier Head Bus Station was constructed. L143 was a Leyland PD2/20 with Alexander body while behind is L477, a PD2/1 with Roberts bodywork.

worked by five Leyland PD2 buses painted in a special reversed livery with cream as the dominant colour. In fact it bore little resemblance to a circle, the route being from Exchange Station via Exchange Street East, Dale Street, Castle Street, Lord Street, Church Street, Clayton Square, Lime Street, Islington, Norton Street and Monument Place to London Road (Anson Street) returning via London Road, Lime Street, Ranelagh Street, Church Street, Lord Street, North John Street and Moorfields. This route was slightly modified in May 1966 to fit in with the one way traffic scheme, the loop at the Exchange Station end being reversed. Such services are beloved of planners but, while perhaps helpful to passengers, in the main, they extract traffic from other services. A ten-minute service was given from 10.00am to 4.00pm (6.00pm Thursdays and Saturdays) at a flat fare of 3d, the special buses being allocated to Garston depot though no other PD2s were based there.

There was some public criticism of these buses running back empty to Garston depot at the beginning of the afternoon peak and the concept of buses which worked only at off-peak times when so many others stood idle all day would have been anathema in a commercially oriented organisation.

Experiments with One-man Operation

Following promises of co-operation from the Unions, orders were placed in 1966-67 for a total of 135 single-deck vehicles specially designed for one-man operation. The

The City Circle service, as shown above, was operated by five Leyland PD2s painted in reversed livery and with a fixed destination display, as shown below. Although the route was not circular it did set out to provide better facilities between the station and shops, improving access which had been made difficult by new traffic management schemes.

The original schematic diagram of the City Circle, later Cityride, which commenced on 6th December 1965. Traffic management schemes caused several later changes of route.

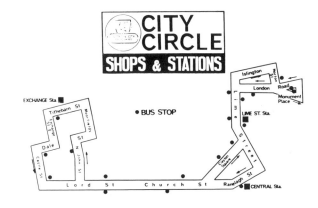

Department had been seeking an opportunity to experiment with one-man operation from the mid-fifties after Ribble had had some success with 44-seat vehicles at some of its depots. The thinking at the time from both

trade union and management was that one-man operation could be successful only on lightly trafficked routes with vehicles of low capacity. Many routes were surveyed but nearly all had some sort of peak which was considered impossible for one-man buses to handle.

In June 1955 the General Manager had wanted to run a half-hourly all-day service with 41-seat one-man vehicles on the 78 route between Hunts Cross and the city and to divert it over the full length of Woolton Road instead of via Childwall Five Ways. The all-day service was to be justified by the building activity in the Hunts Cross and Halewood areas even though there was an existing Crosville service over much the same route. The usual objections against one-man operation could not be invoked as this would have been a completely new facility and the 20-minute double-deck peak service would have continued unaltered. This proposal failed both on the grounds of trade union opposition and dubious viability and the all-day service on the direct route, using orthodox double-deckers, was not introduced until October 1962.

Experimental one-man operation was finally introduced on 9th July 1956 in off peak periods between Penny Lane and Pier Head on route 77. (See Volume Four, page 92) Only two buses were involved and difficulties arose because the public was not used to the idea and the capacity of the single-deck vehicles was too low. During 1957 further experiments were carried out on route 66 which was 'permanently' converted in February 1958 after the Garston terminus had been moved from Vulcan Street

Route 66 saw further experiments in one-man operation and this photograph shows all too clearly the price that would be paid for getting rid of the conductor. Passengers queue on-street to pay their fares to the driver whereas, of course, on a bus with a conductor they could board without delay and pay at their seat, reducing journey times considerably.

The lower picture shows passenger flow in operation, those entering queuing at the front and paying the driver, those alighting leaving via the rear exit. The driver's job must have been difficult enough coping with passengers and fares without having to supervise a rear exit through his mirrors.

to Windfield Road to avoid reversing difficulties. Route 88 between Garston and Hunts Cross was converted on the same day, the section of route along Chapel Road, Island Road and Horrocks Avenue being abandoned to supply the extra running time which was said to be necessary. At best these were half-hearted attempts at one-man operation and these services all went back to crew operation with double-deckers in March 1960.

Before any progress could be made, the life of the city was disrupted by an 11-week long municipal bus strike which started without warning on 11th March 1968 (see Chapter 55). Ribble and Crosville buses ran normally with some picking up restrictions except for a token strike called by the local Trades Council and Labour Party on 1st May. To avoid incidents, however, Ribble withdrew from the Bootle joint services. Great hardship was caused throughout the city and coach owners from as far away as Blackpool and Wigan had an unexpected off-season boost to their trade by hiring vehicles to local operators who had obtained temporary contracts to ferry workpeople and school children. T. J. Hughes department store organised a free coach service for customers, using Sunniways vehicles between their London Road store and the associated Owen Owen premises in Clayton Square and Freeman's of Wavertree Road provided free coaches from several points.

British Rail introduced extra stops at Kirkby and Fazakerley on trains between Wigan and Liverpool Exchange and this apparently brought them permanent new patronage as they were retained after the strike ended. In other cases, as far as limited resources would allow, multiple unit train sets were doubled up to provide additional accommodation.

When bus services were resumed on 27th May, 17 routes remained suspended as many men, unable to withstand the financial hardship, had resigned and found other work. Services 6D, 33, 39 and 77 were resumed only at Monday to Friday peak hours whilst 6C, 30, 40, 68, 71, 79B, 80, 81 and 93 were operated at wider headways, in some cases only every 30-40 minutes. As anticipated, traffic fell by 15% though some of this loss was later regained.

Considering the magnitude of the cuts, traffic was absorbed very well—some of it, of course, by the bus companies and British Rail in the fringe areas. While the missing services remained 'temporarily suspended' it soon became apparent that some would never reappear. Route 24 was reintroduced, apparently after Litherland depot staff threatened to strike if it were not. Number 13C also reappeared only to be eclipsed by a new version of 17C in due course. The City Circle (100) was first reintroduced on Saturdays only but of all the limited stop services only the 544 resumed operation until 500 was brought back on a reduced frequency in 1969.

The first of the new generation of one-man single-deckers had been delivered in April during the strike, and they entered service on 1st July 1968 on route 68 between Aigburth Vale and Seaforth, followed by routes 46 and 99 on 3rd September. The General Manager, Albert Burrows, had been involved in conversions to one-man operation using two-door single-deckers with Ultimate ticket

Some of the large department stores in the city hired private coaches to provide transport for their customers during the eleven week long municipal bus strike. A Crosville Lodekka passes a Bedford coach outside Owen Owens in Clayton Square, above, whilst in the lower picture an LUT Guy double-decker has just passed two coaches bringing customers to Freemans in Wavertree Road. Business seems to be brisk.

machines whilst at Portsmouth and had followed the same pattern at Lancaster and Chesterfield. He drew on this experience in planning Liverpool's initial conversions. A distinctive livery with cream as the dominant colour was adopted and eleven routes had been converted to this type of operation by mid-1969. Meanwhile further negotiations with the unions had resulted in an Agreement in 1969 for working one-man double-deckers which had been legalised in 1966 and had already been successfully introduced at Manchester and Birmingham.

The biggest hurdle to be surmounted when negotiating conversion of a route to driver-only operation was the additional running time to be allowed. In the early stages, there was little or no use made of off-vehicle fare payment and it was essential to allow extra time for cash handling and ticket issue. Management had to be careful not to dissipate the potential savings by granting concessions

The 'mini' and 'maxi' styles of conversion of Leyland Atlanteans for one-man-operation are contrasted in these views of L781 (top) with single door and L864 (lower) with central exit door and repositioned staircase. Both conversions were carried out by Pennine Coachcraft of Oldham and, in practice, the centre exit proved to be unnecessary. Note that L864 had not been modified to include the supplementary route indicator over the route number.

which created an inherently wasteful situation with excessive running and layover times, leading to bunching of buses. Journey times were based on a joint survey by management and trade unions. Time spent at stops en route was logged and 50% of this time was given as additional running time. As drivers being surveyed often 'drove to rule', the unions accepted that a downward correction was sometimes necessary. After initial reservations had been overcome, the unions co-operated fully and eventually conversions depended solely on the supply of suitable vehicles. The additional journey time proved to be insufficient on some routes, and adjustments to running times and terminal arrangements were made in the light of experience. Route 500 between Speke and Kirkby was the first double-deck route to be single-manned, on 9th November 1969, during the last month of Corporation operation.

Examining a group of 46 services on which meaningful comparisons are possible, it is found that increased running time conceded varied considerably, the original single-deck changeovers being relatively low from 3.8% on route 99 and 4.8% on route 68 to 9.1% on route 1 and 12.9% on 85. But by 1974, the average for all the services was 14.0%, some of the largest increases being given to the limited stop services — 20.7% on the 510 and 19.4% on the long cross-city 500 between Speke and Kirkby. However, running times alone are misleading as it is the length of the operating cycle — the time taken to perform a round trip plus the layover time at both ends — which needs to be compared. On the more frequent services it is

A brief ceremony marked the handing over of the first Leyland Panther bus, specially designed for one man operation, at the Pier Head bus station on 12th July 1968. The bus is standing behind the centre loading island and the old lady appears to be bewildered by the whole affair.

impossible to calculate this from the published time tables but the real increase on the 500, where the cycle lengthened from 2½ to 3 hours, was 20% whereas the 510 where the cycle lengthened from 80 to 90 minutes for a slightly longer route, showed a real increase of 12.5%.

The services which slowed down most were Edge Lane routes 6C and 40 on which journey times increased by 25% but there were other factors such as diversions in Edge Hill and allowance for works in connection with the construction of the M62. A strange phenomenon was the retention of variable running times on the Prescot Road group of services, (the only one to have this feature), but with the underlying principle reversed. Originally, because of the minimum fare and limited stop arrangements, less time had been allowed in peak hours; under driver-only operation more time was given.

A lengthened operational cycle meant more buses if the frequency was maintained and on relatively infrequent services, if the headway did not divide economically into the cycle time, there was excessive layover and waste. Whilst no extreme cases are known in Liverpool, in Wirral there was an instance where additional running time led to one bus, two drivers and two conductors being replaced by two buses and four drivers!

The conversion to one-man operation was not without its difficulties, one of which was the unreliability of the Leyland Panthers. In the early days of omo, on route 68, 16 buses were being used to maintain a 10-bus service and many vehicle defects were recurring. On routes 46 and 99 there were persistent problems caused by schoolchildren working the emergency door handle which immobilised the vehicle until reset. One bus lost 29 minutes on a single journey from this cause. An Omo Liaison Committee met regularly to analyse problems and find solutions and matters usually settled down within a week of a changeover. Another problem was the need to provide a turning circle at places where buses had habitually reversed. This sometimes involved altering or extending the route slightly and in one or two cases, land was acquired for purpose-built termini.

Two Panthers, 1023 on route 99 and 1062 on route 46 stand at Penny Lane terminus in October 1968 soon after conversion to one-man operation. Both these services had been busy tram routes worked by high capacity cars. Compare this view with the pictures on page 53 of Volume Four.

Municipal operation came to an end on 30th November 1969 after sixty-two years and three months but the next morning the same buses, still bearing the city coat-of-arms and other identifying insignia, were back on the streets. Unlike some of the other PTEs who were anxious to show their flags as quickly as possible, Merseyside moved slowly, and many buses still carried the Corporation's name several months later. Despite very serious difficulties, both operational and financial, the last municipal years were very innovative and there was no free-wheeling on the part of management in the final months.

LIVERPOOL CITY TRANSPORT
STATISTICS 1949-69

Year	Revenue (£000s)			Miles (000s)			Pence (d) per car mile		
	Trams	Buses	Total	Trams	Buses	Total	Trams	Buses	Total
1949-50	1623	2062	3686	14020	19633	33653	27.78	25.21	26.28
1950-51	1297	2382	3679	11781	23058	34839	26.42	24.79	25.34
1951-52	1171	3404	4576	8986	27275	36261	31.29	29.96	30.29
1952-53	903	3968	4871	6514	29810	36325	33.28	31.94	32.18
1953-54	686	4272	4958	5046	32051	37098	32.65	31.99	32.08
1954-55	563	4525	5088	4153	34372	38525	32.53	31.59	31.69
1955-56	429	4908	5337	3293	37189	40482	31.26	31.68	31.64
1956-57	289	5686	5975	2110	38436	40546	32.90	35.50	35.37
1957-58	95×	6595	6688	545×	41156	41701	41.71	38.45	38.49
1958-59			6611			41889			38.16
1959-60			6722			41640			38.74
1960-61			6582			40501			39.00
1961-62			6819			40435			40.47
1962-63			7424			40572			43.91
1963-64			7838			39325			47.84
1964-65			7634			38151			48.02
1965-66			7829			36719			51.17
1966-67			7956			35904			53.18
1967-68			7726			32440			57.15
1968-69	× 5½ months only		7106	× 5½ months only		24729			68.96

48 THE YEARS OF CHANGE

The legislative changes of the late sixties and early seventies, which so profoundly changed the macro-infrastructure of public passenger transport, were rooted in the political events of 1964 when 13 years of Conservative government came to an end. The incoming Labour administration regarded its nationalisation programme of 1945-51 as incomplete and sought a new transport policy which would achieve both the party's political aims and alleviate the practical difficulties flowing from the new circumstances of the times. Hence the spate of local surveys and plans, described in the previous chapter, was parallelled at a higher level by government action spearheaded by a forceful Minister of Transport, Mrs Barbara Castle.

The Transport Act 1968

This important legislation was intended to resolve the problems of public transport in the light of its current economic circumstances caused by loss of traffic and greatly increased costs. The passing of the Act was preceded by much public discussion, the Minister having visited Liverpool in January 1967 to talk about the formation of what were then called 'conurbation transport authorities' but were eventually termed Passenger Transport Authorities. The Minister was given powers to designate Passenger Transport Areas and initially proposed that there should be four, of which Merseyside was one. In each area there were to be an Authority (PTA) and an Executive (PTE). The former was political, comprising appointees of the local authorities within the Area and of the central government while the latter consisted of professional transport men who were responsible for implementing the policy laid down by the PTA and operating the transport undertaking on a day-to-day basis.

The potential relationship between the conurbation transport authorities and the company-owned bus undertakings had been the subject of much speculation, discussion and, indeed, anxiety especially by the BET Group and the few substantial independent undertakings such as Lancashire United Transport. The companies feared fragmentation of their operating territories and acquisition by the PTEs of the remunerative urban routes, leaving them in possession of the rural services which declined in prosperity every year. In November 1967 the Transport Holding Company, the statutory body set up by the Transport Act 1962 to hold the shares in state-owned bus companies such as Crosville, made an offer of £36,560,000 for the BET bus interests which was accepted

on the 22nd of the same month. The 1968 Act then established the National Bus Company to control the THC and ex-BET companies and on Merseyside, both Crosville and Ribble were therefore state-owned.

The Merseyside PTA was constituted from 1st April 1969 and the PTE from 1st November. Eighteen local authorities, including two County Councils, were represented and some shared a representative to prevent the PTA becoming too unwieldy. Nevertheless, there were 29 members including four government nominees. The PTA had powers to precept on the rates of the constituent authorities. The extent of the original Passenger Transport Area is shown in Map 48.

The statutory duty of the PTA and PTE together was to secure or promote the provision of a properly integrated and efficient system of public passenger transport to meet the needs of the Area. This duty encompassed all services including those provided by bus companies and the railways where such services were considered essential for local journeys.

Vesting

The fleet acquired by the PTE comprised 1,297 buses and seven ferry vessels. Liverpool contributed 1,001 buses, Birkenhead 223 and Wallasey 73 but 65 were non-runners and were scrapped in the first month, leaving an effective fleet of 1,232. For operational purposes the Area was split into three divisions, North, South and Wirral. Operations commenced on 1st December 1969.

The PTE also inherited the losses of the three municipal undertakings incurred since the date of the PTA's incorporation — 1st April 1969. These amounted to £418,842 and there was also a statutory obligation to compensate the three authorities to the extent of £163,895 for the increased burden of central administration charges which they could no longer allocate to their transport undertakings. The total of £582,737 was capitalised and written off over two years. Responsibility was assumed for loans totalling £5,007,106 of which a little more than half were repayable within five years.

Immediate financial needs were met by a fares increase in Liverpool and by a precept of 4½d in the £ on the rates of the 18 constituent authorities, measures which were decided at an urgent meeting within days of Vesting. This was a new experience for the ratepayers of such towns as Bootle, Crosby and Huyton whose councils had been so loud in their criticism of the transport operators over the years but who paid nothing towards transport in their rates.

Under new management . . .

The vehicles which passed to the newly formed PTE acquired new logos and liveries, though not immediately of course. It was a simple matter to apply the new logo over the top of the City Arms, as in the case of 97, above. L862 carries the new livery and Merseyside Passenger Transport Executive as the legal owner but the logo has yet to make its appearance.

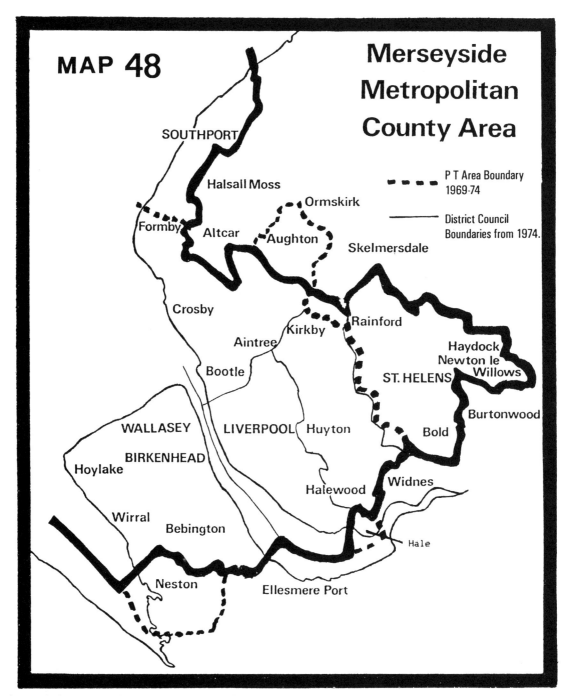

MAP 48

Merseyside Metropolitan County Area

SOUTHPORT

Halsall Moss

Ormskirk

Formby Altcar Aughton

Skelmersdale

- - - - P T Area Boundary
1969-74

———— District Council
Boundaries from 1974.

Crosby

Kirkby Rainford

Aintree

Bootle

Haydock
Newton le
Willows

ST. HELENS

Burtonwood

WALLASEY LIVERPOOL Huyton

Bold

BIRKENHEAD

Hoylake

Wirral

Bebington

Halewood Widnes

Hale

Neston Ellesmere Port

Conversely, it was a relief for those of Wallasey, who had been paying three times as much.

These were not the first financial and management links between Liverpool's transport and its neighbours. Bootle, for example, had long contributed members to Liverpool Corporation's Tramways (later Passenger Transport) Committee but did not share in the profits, although they did charge a rent for the track. Such arrangements came to an end with the tramways. The age of subsidised, rather than profit-making public transport made it necessary for all ratepayers to share the burden.

The new undertaking was much more than an amalgamation of three municipal transport departments as it now had to create an organisation to perform the functions previously carried out by the Town Clerks, Treasurers and other officials of the local councils. This took time and it was necessary to continue using some municipal facilities for over a year. Accounting was

amalgamated from 1st April 1970 and integrated management systems were progressively put in place, usually by extending well-tried Liverpool practices to Wirral. Considerable advances were made in assigning costs to individual routes and depots and budgetary control was applied at all levels. The PTE's own computer in Hatton Garden was brought into use in 1972. While there was much new blood in the organisation, the petty jealousies which surface in the course of welding together three very individualistic organisations into a cohesive whole, had to be overcome. Big fishes in small pools do not readily adapt to being small fishes in large pools but Burrows was a dedicated manager and much of his time was spent in suppressing anachronistic loyalties and developing team spirit.

After the initial financial problems had been solved, the PTE had a good year in 1971, resulting in an operating surplus of £1,742,000 on the buses. With ferry losses deducted, there was a revenue surplus of £488,000. The precept was almost halved to 1p. However, the Annual Report made it clear that this state of affairs was unlikely to continue as provision had to be made to meet the net deficit on Crosville and Ribble services from 1972, concessionary fares had to be paid for out of the precept instead of by local authority grants and the problem of railway support had yet to be faced.

Government Grants

During the fifties, all transport operators had lobbied more or less continuously for relief from the taxes on petrol and fuel oil which the government, seeing the growth of private motoring as a lucrative source of revenue, imposed on several occasions. These pleas fell on deaf ears until 1964 when the new Labour government imposed an additional tax of 6d per gallon with the proviso that stage carriage services would be exempt and subsequent tax increases were made on the same basis. In 1971 the PTE paid £550,000 in tax and received £697,000 in rebate (4.9% of revenue). As a result of the fuel price increases following the 1973 energy crisis, the government decided to refund all fuel tax to bus operators and the fuel rebate was thereby increased from 12½p to 22½p per gallon in February 1974.

Section 23 of the Transport Act 1968 empowered the Minister to make grants of 25% of the cost of new vehicles which conformed to certain specifications. The grant scheme was designed to enable hard-pressed operators to modernise their fleets with vehicles suitable for one-man operation and the salient features of the specifications were suitability for this purpose and the provision of a heating system. Because of the long lead time for delivery of new buses, all vehicles ordered before 8th July 1968 were grantworthy if they satisfied the main objectives even if they did not conform to the exact specification.

The scheme was originally scheduled to end on 31st August 1975 but in November 1971, the rate of grant was increased from 25% to 50% and the scheme was extended to 31st August 1980. Bus grants were certainly successful in achieving the government's aims on Merseyside. At an operators' conference in 1972, Mr J. Brooksbank, Director of Finance and Administration, revealed that if all MPTE buses had been financed with the benefit of the 50% grant, depreciation and interest charges in 1971 would have been lower by £366,000, equivalent to 2.57% of bus revenue in that year. Other operators produced similar figures to persuade the government to retain the grant.

Other forms of aid authorised by the Act were Rural Bus Grants to ensure the survival of unprofitable but essential services in country areas and subsidies for specific railway services. Responsibility for these grants within the PT Areas was transferred from the central government to the PTEs by the 1968 Act and to the new metropolitan counties by the Local Government Act 1972. Infrastructure grants were available for major capital works and the railway extensions on Merseyside were to a large extent financed from this source.

A new government grant structure took effect from 1st April 1975 whereby Transport Supplementary Grant replaced the Rural Bus and Ferry, railway and infrastructure grants. Counties were required to submit Transportation Policy and Programmes (tpps) annually and grants were authorised for the items approved by the central government. At the end of 1979, the new Conservative government announced the phasing out of bus grants in three stages and they ceased on 31st March 1984.

New Policies

In March 1972, the PTA and PTE published their Corporate Plan and submitted it to the Minister as the 1968 Act directed. 'A Transport Plan for Merseyside' set out the intended strategy towards an integrated bus and rail system as described in Chapter 51, the modernisation of the fleet and 100% conversion to one-man operation. It was realised that there were parts of the PT Area which could never be adequately served by development of the rail network and a cursory glance was given to rapid transit alternatives, possibly using the wide dual carriageway reservations previously used by the tramways. However, these were rejected in favour of 'Rapidride' express bus services.

The Rapidride services were designed to get people to and from work as quickly as possible. Homegoing passengers board Alexander-bodied Leyland Atlantean 1219 outside Exchange Station while Wirral Division Atlantean 195 overtakes on the New Brighton service, the first local service to use a Mersey Tunnel all day.

Bus grants made new buses more affordable, particularly when grants were doubled in 1971. As far as the staff were concerned, the ground rules had already been set by the previous undertakings as both Liverpool and Birkenhead had done their first double-deck conversions just before the PTE took over. Progress could have been faster but the supply of buses was slowed down by the economic and social conditions of the times. By the end of 1972, 57.1% of all mileage was one-man operated; a year later it had risen to 85.5% However, the basic programme in Liverpool was not completed until November 1975 (See Appendix 45) and it was January 1977 when the last crew-operated bus was withdrawn. Even then, some Ribble buses carried conductors until September 1981.

During the transitional period, optimal use was made of the fleets taken over from the previous operators as described in Chapter 53. The last rear platform buses to run in Liverpool were former Birkenhead and St. Helens vehicles.

By 31st December 1973, when the first period of the PTE's history was drawing to a close, the bus fleet total had grown to 1,396 of which 83% were suitable for one-man operation. The number of employees had decreased since Vesting Day from 6,165 to 5,275 and the ratio of staff to buses had decreased from 4.75 to 3.78.

Subsidiary Company

The PTE formed a subsidiary company, Merseyside Passenger Transport Services Ltd, on 9th August 1972 to provide services including asset leasing to operators. This gave certain tax advantages and, in due course, revised arrangements for leasing buses at an advantageous rate were made in co-operation with two other PTEs. The subsidiary company became a general member of two partnerships promoted for the specific purpose of leasing plant and equipment. The Limited Partners, who contributed 97% of the capital, were able to claim a high rate of income tax allowance and the partnerships were thus able to lease the vehicles at a rate of interest below the normal market rate. All future PTE buses were leased in this way, a practice which was to have unforeseen consequences many years in the future.

The PTE also became a shareholder in National Transport Tokens Ltd., a company which grew out of the North West Token Bank, an informal arrangement inaugurated in 1970 jointly by Merseyside and SELNEC PTEs. Aluminium tokens were minted for sale to local authorities who issued them to senior citizens. The tokens were then tendered in lieu of cash in payment of fares.

The company was owned jointly by the PTEs, National Bus Company, London Transport and British Rail. Merseyside PTE initially subscribed for 10,000 £1 shares at 10p but the share capital was later increased. Although the system was little used on Merseyside, by the end of 1974, National Travel Tokens had a turnover of £5,920 million, tokens being used by 261 local authorities and accepted by 214 operators nationwide. Liverpool's traditionally generous attitude to free travel for the elderly meant that local pensioners had no need of the few pounds worth of tokens doled out by most authorities.

Local Government Reorganisation

The Local Government Act 1972 created a number of Metropolitan Counties and merged smaller authorities into larger boroughs or districts. Merseyside became a county containing five second tier authorities—Liverpool, Sefton, Knowsley, St. Helens and Wirral. Because of changes made to the Local Government Bill during its passage through Parliament, Skelmersdale-with-Holland was excluded from the new county as were a few areas which had been in the PT Area—the parishes of Hale, Aughton and Altcar and, in Cheshire, the Urban District of Neston. The Merseyside County Council replaced the PTA as the Transport Authority from 1st April 1974 on which date the municipal bus undertakings of St. Helens and Southport were absorbed by the PTE, becoming districts under the South and North divisions respectively. The County Council had a duty to plan the development of a co-ordinated and efficient system of public passenger transport to meet the needs of the county.

The new county's neighbour to the east was another Metropolitan County, Greater Manchester, which absorbed the Wigan transport undertaking. To the south-east, a large tract of territory which included Widnes (now merged with its cross-river neighbour of Runcorn to form the Borough of Halton), and Warrington, was transferred from Lancashire to Cheshire.

With the creation of the Merseyside County Council, the political nature of the Authority changed, as the council's Passenger Transport Committee assumed the function, and the nominees of the Minister of Transport and 'shire' counties disappeared. Their restraining influence was therefore lost.

Despite the fact that high inflation was pushing up costs at an alarming rate, the County Council rejected the PTE's proposal for a fares increase estimated to produce £800,000 during the remainder of the 1974-75 financial year. The original transport deficit had been set at £8.3 million to which had been added £2.1 million of unbudgeted wage awards and various price increases. The loss of the revenue from the fare increase now made it likely that the PTE's deficit would be £11.0 million by March 1975 and £13.5 million the following year.

The undertaking was entering a very difficult time but the seriousness of the situation did not seem to be recognised by the County Council. The Passenger Transport Committee was politically a more cohesive body than the former appointed PTA. It was subject to the confirmation of its decisions by the full Council and showed greater exasperation with the independence of the Executive. Even at officer level, some feelings arose between County Council officials, steeped in local government procedures, and directors of the PTE with their wider statutory powers. Fortunately these differences never became personal and were offset to some extent by the role of the Joint Transportation Unit (JTU), a body under the administrative control of the City Planning Officer with the County Engineer, Treasurer and Solicitor and the Director General of the PTE as members.

The latter often complained of being outvoted by the others but many transportation and planning matters were happily resolved and agreement reached on the annual allocation of the County's available finance of which the PTE was a major recipient. However the JTU could not overcome the political differences. A serious rift developed between the Authority and the Executive which now felt like the meat in a sandwich, between the politicians who declined to support them, and the unions who flatly refused to discuss the economies which were essential to balance the budget.

The PTE wanted to bring the service levels into line with the current demand and exploit the potential for integrating the Ribble and Crosville services, as had been demonstrated in a relatively small way by the Huyton scheme of October 1973. It also wanted to achieve 100% one-man operation and take full advantage of road-rail co-ordination.

The main Labour objective, especially in the stark reality of the Merseyside situation, was the retention of jobs but each step of PTE policy would result in fewer jobs for busmen. Furthermore, the policies were divisive within the ranks of Labour as the interests of those who still regarded themselves as municipal busmen were at variance with those of the company busmen and the railwaymen. The fact that the latter were now nationalised made no difference; membership of a different Union seemed to aggravate such 'territorial' attitudes. The dilemma of those members of the Authority who espoused the objectives of the Labour party can be well imagined.

It was 1975 before the PTE's economies began to bite. Although there were no redundancies, a scheme to rationalise all PTE and NBC services in Liverpool met massive Union opposition, though Phase I of the plan was reluctantly agreed with a saving of 58 buses and £600,000 per year. However, new Ribble services L22-23 between Crosby and Fazakerley and Walton Hospitals sparked off further trouble as penetration of red buses into 'green' territory was seen as the thin end of the wedge. Peace was restored only when L22-23 gave way to Ribble 29 to Fazakerley and the extension of PTE 30 to Crosby. It seemed that red buses in green areas were alright if there was a quid pro quo but the trade unions would not accept that the NBC entitlement to a fixed proportion of mileage (see Chapter 49) gave their company members adequate protection.

In 1976 the Council made representations to the government, through the Association of Metropolitan Authorities, advocating the winding up of the PTEs and direct control of transport by the County Councils. In the meantime, it vetoed the introduction of zone tickets and no-change fare boxes and cancelled the 1976-77 vehicle replacement order.

Although they had several months' warning of his departure, the Committee did nothing to appoint a replacement for the PTE's Director of Operations and, when he retired on 30th June 1976, the PTE strictly became illegal as there were then only two directors. This arose because the former Director of Planning and Development, who left at the end of 1974 to take up an appointment in Australia, had not been replaced. Perhaps the Committee thought this would prevent the Executive from making legal decisions. At the end of August 1976, the Director General, Arthur Moffatt, gave six months' notice of his intention to retire when he reached the age of 60 and he duly left the PTE on 28th February 1977. As soon as he was a free agent he attacked the political direction of transport on Merseyside. 'The PTE is always in a crisis situation', he said, adding that the constant battle between the councillors and the Executive was creating major inefficiency. He spoke of irrational behaviour and said that the question of his resignation and replacement was handled in a deplorable way. It had taken the Committee six months to appoint a successor, their ultimate choice being the Director of Finance, L. W. Latter, a man with no transport background prior to his joining the Executive.

Liverpool Corporation sponsored Cityride as a free service at off-peak times in 1974-75. Here, Alderman W. Sefton, leader of the City Council and F. A. Moffatt, Director-General of the PTE, are seen boarding Panther 1069 upon the inauguration of the service

Following County Council elections and the advent of many new Committee members, the PTE was reconstituted by appointing three new Directors, for Service Operations, Service Planning and Co-ordination and Finance. Two part-time members, the County Solicitor and Secretary, and the County Treasurer also joined the Executive, a precedent for appointments of this kind having been made by Greater Manchester PTE. Perhaps the Council felt that Latter, as a municipal accountant of long standing who had spent only three years on Merseyside, would be less likely to take up a strong position on transport issues and by loading the Executive with senior county officials, they would create a more compliant body. This certainly seemed to be the case as there were no public disputes for some years.

The Reconstituted Executive

The new team settled down to preparing a Corporate Action Plan which was approved in two stages by the County Council during 1978. The three major objectives were:

- to maximise passenger mileage, subject to meeting any social, economic and financial targets which might be defined by the County Council.
- to develop means to achieve the above objective e.g. service costing and management systems and restructuring the Executive.
- to proceed with bus/rail rationalisation plans for 1978-79 and initiate a capital programme for investment in bus garages, bus stations, bus replacement, railway stations and rolling stock, with emphasis on proper maintenance and renewal of public transport infrastructure.

The techniques of allocating costs correctly and gathering information about travel habits were refined by the system dubbed SCRAM (Service Costing and Route Analysis and Monitoring System), which was fully operational by 1980. A permanent team of operatives, engaged on continuous survey work in the field was augmented from time to time by the County Council's Joint Transportation Unit, using people from the Job Creation Scheme to carry out field work.

Lengthy public sittings before the Traffic Commissioners, to consider the PTE's revised service proposals, started in March 1978 and continued for several months while difficult negotiations with the trade unions went on simultaneously. Substantial service reductions and alterations came into effect in September and October 1978 in Liverpool and Sefton and, together with similar drastic changes in St. Helens and Wirral early in 1979, they reduced bus requirements by 150 and annual bus miles by five million.

A New Council

Early in 1981, the County Council approved reductions in early morning, evening, Saturday and Sunday services in an attempt to reduce the subsidy on bus services. However, after the May 1981 elections, the new Council undertook a planning review and abandoned the service reductions, following up this action by adopted the Cheap Fares policy described elsewhere. A year later, despite support payments to the PTE buses in 1981-82 of £24 million (plus a further £5 million to the NBC companies), the Council decided to retain fares at their current levels and to base service reviews on 'good housekeeping', whatever that meant.

Government Action

The government's response to Cheap Fares policies on Merseyside and elsewhere was to pass the Transport Act, 1983, which required the PTE to produce each year a 3-year Transport Plan for submission by the County Council to the Department of Transport, setting out alternative options. The Act empowered the Secretary of State to issue guidelines specifying the maximum amount of revenue grant which it was appropriate for the County Council to make each year. In its first Plan, the PTE recommended fares increases of 39% over three years and service reductions of 10%. Revenue support of £63.8 million was proposed in 1984-85 but the government's support guidance was only £43.0 million. It envisaged fares covering 36% of costs with a further 17% from concessionary fares.

The County Council declined to increase fares but ordered a review of all services covering less than 40% of costs. In 1984-85 total support, including rail, was £66.0 million.

The conflict between the County Council and the central government and the financial consequences for the ratepayer are outside the scope of this work. The Council's policy was pure Socialism and aimed as much at job preservation as at providing transport services. However, this should be viewed against a background of over 100,000 unemployed on Merseyside — over 14% against a national average of 7.8%.

Other government measures included the drafting of new regulations to bring PTE accounts roughly in line with Companies Act requirements, proposals to abolish the Metropolitan Counties and publication of the White Paper *Buses*. This outlined its proposals for the deregulation and privatisation of bus services and for tendering for subsidised bus services.

End of the County Council

Both deregulation and the abolition of the Metropolitan Counties were fiercely opposed by the councils concerned, all of whom mounted expensive campaigns against the government's actions. The Merseyside County Council used the transport undertaking in this campaign in several ways. A number of buses were painted in a special livery and emblazoned with anti-abolition slogans.

Merseyside County Council conducted a vigorous campaign against the government's policy of abolishing the metropolitan county councils and 1971, a 1982 Alexander-bodied Atlantean, was one of five buses given a blue and yellow 'protest' livery. It is seen climbing St. John's Lane in 1986 on the Netherton via Southport Road service 56.

Metropolitan 4068 became the 'Cowboy bus' and was individually painted and manned by trade union volunteers. It toured the area as part of the campaign against deregulation and eventually went to London complete with busmen dressed in cowboy outfits. 'The Get Rich Quick Cowboy Bus Co.' was signwritten on the front with 'Going Nowhere' on the destination indicator.

The cruise ship *Royal Iris*, decorated with slogans against abolition, sailed down the west coast and up the Channel to the Thames. Perhaps someone had hoped this epic voyage would end opposite the Houses of Parliament, where Members and Ministers were lobbied, but of course the vessel was not designed to pass the bridges above the Pool of London. Special newspapers were printed and distributed door-to-door throughout Merseyside.

Merseyside County Council ceased to exist on 31st March 1986 and the PT Authority was now re-constituted with 18 appointed representatives of the five District Councils, reflecting both the per capita proportions and the political balance. Once the operating function was passed over to a company, the role of the PTE would be confined to the administration of tenders, the concessionary travel scheme, multi-journey ticket schemes, the railways and ferries, marketing, publicity and the gathering of statistical information. An Order made by the Secretary of State for

Transport prohibited the PTE from being a bus operator after 25th October 1988.

Among the last acts of the County Council's passenger transport committee was the ending of the Cheap Fares Policy and a substantial fares increase, ranging from 15% on the buses to 40% on the railways, came into effect on 27th April 1986. There was also to be a 10% cut in services, most of which was implemented over the weekend of 27th-29th June though a few changes were held over until various dates in July. This involved the abandonment of a number of services (see Appendix 48), withdrawal of others at weekends or during the evenings, and frequency reductions from 5 to 7½ minutes, 10 to 15 minutes, and 15-20 to 30 minutes. Half-hourly frequencies generally prevailed in the evenings except on the busiest routes such as 14C, 26/27, 78 and 86 which had quarter-hourly services. Three Rapidride services, 412, 478 and 479, were included in the total withdrawals. A large number of the older Atlanteans were parked out of service in July but several were reinstated two months later so that certain types of vehicle which the new company did not want to take over could be withdrawn and disposed of. All this sounded very much like the PTE's 1983 plan except, of course, that it was done all at once and thus hurt all the more.

Prelude to Deregulation

The Transport Act 1985 received the Royal Assent on 30th October and bus operators got down to the job of deciding just what needed to be done in practical terms. It was a time of frantic activity for the bus operating industry as, for the first time for some years, the financial success or failure of the undertaking would depend on the decisions made. For the first time since 1931, operators could decide exactly what routes, time tables and fares should apply without first running the gauntlet of a public hearing before a quasi-legal tribunal. In Liverpool, there was an enormous store of statistical information gathered by the PTE which proved invaluable to the principal operator when deciding what level of service was likely to be commercially viable.

The Department of Transport defined a 'transitional period' (6th January-25th October 1986) and an 'initial period' (26th October 1986-25th January 1987). Operators had to decide what local services they wished to run commercially from 26th October and register them with the Traffic Commissioners by 28th February 1986. A local service was defined as one upon which journeys of less than 15 miles as the crow flies could be made. The Commissioners had a duty to publish these registrations by 1st April so that county councils and PTAs, knowing what services would be run on a commercial basis, could decide what additional facilities were necessary and then invite tenders from operators. Within certain parameters, mainly concerned with the suitability and past record of the tendering operator, lowest tenders had to be accepted. Subsidies could become payable only after a contract had been awarded.

The second pillar of the deregulation process was the conversion of municipal transport undertakings and PTE bus operators into private companies, and schemes for achieving this had to be submitted to the Secretary of State by 31st March. All traditional operating areas and zoning agreements were swept away and there were no territorial restrictions on commercial operation except that the routes of PTA companies had to have at least one end in the area. Before the 1985 Act joint working agreements between operators had been exempted from the provisions of the Restricted Trade Practices Act 1976. They lost this exemption and any agreement in which operators accept restrictions on their competitive ability must be 'registered' with the Office of Fair Trading. However there is always the risk of an adverse judgement in the Restrictive Practices Court and no such agreements were retained or made anew on Merseyside. In some cases this was going too far as sensible, economical arrangements of long standing were set aside and replaced by erratic, competitive rat races.

The third pillar was the proposed sale of the NBC but, in the view of the government, before that could be done, the very large companies had to be broken up into units of saleable size. Both Ribble and Crosville fell into this category as, together, they covered the whole of western Britain from the Solway Firth to Cardigan. Ribble reorganised its operating areas from four to six late in 1985, Merseyside becoming a separate entity instead of part of the South Lancashire area. The company's Cumbrian region with 71 buses was amalgamated with Cumberland Motor Services Ltd. from 22nd February 1986 while Merseyside, together with Skelmersdale and Wigan, was to be the basis of a new company so that Ribble territory would be limited to Preston, Lancaster, the Fylde, Chorley, Bolton and East Lancashire. Crosville was divided into

English and Welsh companies, the latter known as Crosville Wales.

In weekday peak hours 84% of the mileage was registered commercially, between the peaks 86% but in the evenings only 65% and on Sundays 50%. The overall weekly total was 77%. The PTE used a micro-computer based management information system which involved the division of the county into 523 areas for analysis purposes. Socio-economic and travel data was then used to establish the relative dependence of each area on public transport. A parallel exercise then compared the commercial and existing networks to identify unserved or poorly served neighbourhoods.

Tenders were then invited to provide subsidised services and initially 56 operators requested tender documentation. Most got no further than this and contracts were awarded to only six. Of the 453 contracts awarded first time round, the PTA's operating company secured 347. The last few weeks before deregulation were very hectic with contracts being awarded weekly, leaving the operators very little time to prepare.

Merseyside Transport Ltd was registered as a private company owned by the PTA and adopted the fleet name 'Merseybus'. The PTE's marketing name became 'Merseytravel', a name previously used for the booking and enquiry offices. Ribble's Merseyside operations were transferred on 7th September 1986 to a dormant company which resurrected the name of North Western Road Car Co Ltd, formerly a BET company based at Stockport which had been absorbed by the SELNEC (Manchester) PTE, Crosville and Trent in 1972. It was an apt choice, even though the territory served was initially quite different.

Meanwhile momentous decisions were being made. Merseyside Transport Ltd established its head office at Edge Lane Works, much of which was converted into a running shed as described in Chapter 54. It was essential for the company to reduce its overheads and it was decided not to acquire the Prince Alfred Road and Wallasey depots and to close Litherland as an operating centre. A number of vehicles, in particular the Daimlers and Bristols were left in PTE ownership and subsequently sold. Much of the resultant redundancy was absorbed by an offer of early retirement on generous terms to all staff over 50 years of age. Such a high proportion of those eligible accepted that the new era commenced with a serious shortage of staff in certain occupations, particularly drivers.

Much midnight oil was burned by the scheduling staff and a mountain of paper was consumed in the preparation of hundreds of new time-table leaflets and other publicity handouts. Although some were not available on D-day, the few slip-ups were due to the many last minute changes.

Over the weekend of 24th-26th October there was frantic activity relocating buses and removing the PTE's insignia and name as legal owner from the fleet. They were replaced by 'Merseyside Transport Ltd, Edge Lane, Liverpool L7, 8LL' as the statutory owner's name and large 'Merseybus' decals on each side.

On Sunday 26th October, the vanguard of a somewhat reduced fleet ventured forth into a new world.

LIVERPOOL CORPORATION FARE SCALES
1951—69

18th March 1951

1½d	2d	3d	4d	5d	6d	7d

7th October 1951

1½d	2½d	4d	5d	6d	7d	8d

12th November 1956

2d	3d	5d	6d	7d	8d	9d

15th October 1961

2d	3d	4d	5d	6d	7d	8d	9d	10d	11d	1/–

30th September 1962

3d	5d	6d	7d	8d	9d	10d	11d	1/–	1/1d

19th September 1965

3d	4d	6d	7d	8d	9d	10d	11d	1/–	1/1d	1/2d

10th December 1967

3d	6d	9d	1/–	1/3d	1/6d

```
0    . 1  .  2 . .  3  . . 4  .  5 . .  6  . . 7 . .  8  .  9  .  10  .  11  .  12
                              M I L E S
```

Fares

One of the first tasks of the PTA was to consider what steps were necessary to put its finances in order. Whereas a municipal undertaking could retrospectively apply rate aid to cover losses already incurred, the PTE needed to apply for increased fares and/or precept on the rates of the constituent local authorities well in advance.

The PTE's bus fare scale was influenced in the earlier years by the historical fares policy of Liverpool Corporation and it is of interest to examine this from the time of the final tramway abandonment in 1957.

Although operating costs continued to rise inexorably, fares were maintained unchanged for almost six years,

mainly at the expense of Liverpool ratepayers. From 15th October 1961 the fare stage structure was revised on the basis of half-mile instead of three quarter-mile stages but the new stages were fixed as far as possible at traditional traffic points. The Corporation had asked for a 3d minimum but the Traffic Commissioners would not grant this. The 2d fare was retained for the first half mile and then there were 1d progressions up to 11d. Fares were increased three times during the sixties using the same stage structure with the results shown in the table.

It will be seen that the longer distance passenger suffered a much lower increase than the short distance rider, reflecting the Council's social policy. Between 1962 and 1967 the two-stage passenger's fare doubled while the

NO.OF STAGES	MILES	FARE 15.10. 1961	RATE PER MILE	FARE 30.9 1962	RATE PER MILE	% INC.	FARE 19.9 1965	RATE PER MILE	% INC.	FARE 10.12 1967	RATE PER MILE	% INC.	CUM. % INC. 1961-7
		d	d	d	d		d	d		d	d		
1	0.5	2	2.0	3	6.0	50.0	3	6.0		3	6.0		50.0
2	1.0	3	1.5	3	3.0		4	4.0	33.3	6	6.0	50.0	100.0
3	1.5	4	2.6	5	3.3	12.5	6	4.0	20.0	9	6.0	50.0	50.0
4	2.0	5	2.0	6	3.0	20.0	7	3.5	16.7	9	4.5	28.6	80.0
5	2.5	6	2.4	7	2.8	16.6	8	3.2	14.3	9	3.6	12.5	50.0
7	3.5	7	2.0	8	2.3	14.3	9	2.6	12.5	1/-	3.4	25.0	71.4
9	4.5	8	1.8	9	2.0	12.5	10	2.2	11.1	1/-	2.7	20.0	50.0
12	6.0	9	1.5	10	1.7	11.1	11	1.8	10.0	1/-	2.0	9.1	33.3
15	7.5	10	1.3	11	1.5	10.0	1/-	1.6	9.1	1/3	2.0	25.0	50.0
22	11.0	11	1.0	1/-	1.0	9.1	1/1	1.2	8.3	1/3	1.4	15.4	36.4
23+	11.5+	1/-	1.0	1/1	1.1	8.3	1/2	1.2	7.7	1/6	1.6	22.2	50.0

12-stage passenger's fare rose only 20% from 10d to 1/-. The very coarse fare structure introduced in 1967 with 3d steps was the first move towards adapting the tariff to decimal coinage due to be introduced three years later. This resulted in a very uneven distribution of the burden as indiscriminate increases of 1d, 2d and 3d were inevitable. A further objective was the simplification of the fare tables to ease the changeover to one-man operation. The accompanying table shows the various municipal fare scales between 1951 and 1967 in relation to distance.

Having considered its financial position, which was parlous, the Authority decided to apply immediately for an interim blanket fare increase of 3d on all Liverpool fares and this was implemented on 16th March 1970. A further substantial increase on the majority of bus fares in all the divisions was brought into operation on 22nd November 1970. This was a step towards greater equality between the scales of alternative modes of transport which was necessary for any co-ordinated scheme to be workable. The largest proportionate increases were made on long distance fares thus reducing both the Liverpool taper and the big step at the PT Area boundary. The resultant coarse fare structure with 3d steps from 6d to 2/6d set the stage for the changeover to decimal currency which was made on the buses on 21st February 1971, one week after its general introduction. The scale was then 3p, 4p, 5p, 6p, 7p, 10p and 13p. The PTA then decided that bus fares would not rise again until, at the earliest, the second anniversary of the November 1970 increase.

Crossley-bodied Leyland Royal Tiger SKB 172, new in August 1956, had a long and varied career. Originally a dual-purpose 40-seater with fixed 'Private' indicator display, it was used for charter work and on the Mersey Tunnel night service. In 1970 it was reseated to 38, renumbered 98 and crossed the river to become a one-man bus working out of Laird Street depot, Birkenhead in the blue and cream Wirral livery. Withdrawn from passenger service in 1972, it was painted red and converted into a Ticket Sales office which stood in Clayton Square until June 1975, when the Williamson Square office was opened. After sale to Liverpool Community Transport for spares, the remains were scrapped in 1976.

The Bus Economy Ticket (BET)

These very steep increases were softened by the progressive introduction of Bus Economy Tickets (BET) which had been planned by Liverpool Corporation but could not be brought in until after the PTE took over. Faced with some residual resistance to one-man operation and demands for more running time on converted routes which threatened to cancel out the savings, means were sought to speed up passenger loading and unloading and eliminate cash handling on the buses for regular passengers.

The method adopted was a series of 10-journey tickets (not a weekly ticket as the publicity matter was at pains to point out) which were available for all fare values and sold at a large number of tobacconists and similar shops all over the city. Tickets were validated at the point of sale on a desk top machine developed jointly by the Corporation and T.I.M. Ltd, the ticket machine manufacturers, of Cirencester. The latter hoped for a nationwide development but were disillusioned. A short vertical arrow on a yellow background was adopted as a marketing symbol. It was displayed at all sales points and on the front of each bus equipped with a canceller.

A busy scene at Waterloo Place, Church Street, in October 1972, a place now inaccessible to buses following pedestrianisation. Wirral Division Atlantean 193, with dual-door Northern Counties body, loads for Wallasey on the first regular cross river local service while 1965 Atlantean L753 with Metro-Cammell body overtakes en route from Huyton to the Pier Head. Behind, another Atlantean is loading on the limited stop service to Prescot.

On boarding the bus, the passenger inserted the ticket in a slot in a canceller mounted on a stanchion to the right of the entrance door. The date and an identifying number was printed on the ticket so that an inspector would know that it had been cancelled on that trip. One ticket could be used for two or more passengers travelling together, the ticket being inserted in the slot once for each person. Once the ten journeys were used up, the canceller rejected the ticket.

Those readers familiar with urban transport in continental Europe will recognise a system widely employed even down to the sale of tickets by tobacconists but this was the first time it had been used in Britain.

BET's were sold at a discount of 20% and were introduced progressively on a corridor basis, a method

The BET canceller was painted a bright yellow and mounted just inside the doorway so that passengers using it did not obstruct others paying fares to the driver.

designed to minimise the frustrations of a ticket holder who found a mixture of buses on the same section of route, some fitted with cancellers and others not.

The scheme was launched on the Aigburth Road routes on 5th January 1970, cancellers being fitted to buses working services 82, 85, 87 and 500; it was extended to routes 3, 20 and 25 on 2nd February. Progress was then relatively slow being governed by the supply of cancellers and the rate at which they could be fitted. All the work was done at Gillmoss.

1970

4th May	Walton Road, Rice Lane — 22, 30, 92, 93, 592
22nd June	Prescot Road — 9, 10, 510
28th Sept.	Wavertree, Smithdown Road etc. 66, 71, 72, 73, 77, 80, 88
19th Oct.	Utting Avenue — 17C, 17D
2nd Nov.	Breck Road, Townsend Avenue, 14, 15
14th Dec.	Aigburth-Old Swan-Seaforth — 61, 68

1971

28th Feb.	West Derby Road 12, 18, 75, 99
12th Apr.	Halewood, Belle Vale — 76, 78, 79
10th May	Walton Hall Avenue — 19, 44 (also 11 new)
17th May	Sheil Road Circular — 26, 27
14th June	Queens Drive — 60, 81
5th July	Docks — 1 and industrial services
6th Sept.	Bootle — 16, 24, 28 and 48-59 (PTE buses only)

1972

30th June	Ribble buses on joint services 48-59

1973

22nd Oct.	Crosville buses between Huyton area and city.

Somehow, despite the generous discounts, the scheme never took off. Market research had indicated that its use by 25% of all passengers and 60% of peak hour passengers was needed to make it viable. The costs were formidable — a 20% reduction to the passenger, a commission to the agents, capital cost and maintenance of the cancellers, expensive coated tickets and administration and replenishment of agents of which, by May 1974, there were 217.

The slow spread of the BET scheme which prevented it being launched with a big publicity bang was probably a prime cause of its failure as, so long as there was less than universal coverage, there was always the possibility of a passenger boarding a bus and not being able to use his ticket. Ribble was a reluctant participant as it reduced the fleet flexibility which was so much a part of its operating methods and, while conductors were being carried, there was no advantage.

More Fare Increases

The very high inflation experienced in 1972 made it essential to obtain more revenue to cover steeply rising costs and it was proposed to apply a further increase as soon as possible after the two year moratorium expired in November 1972 but the government imposed a prices and incomes freeze which gave the PTE no alternative but to defer a proposed 5% rise in bus fares until 20th May 1973.

With the absorption of the Southport and St. Helens undertakings, there were seven different fare structures and a four-phase plan was drawn up with the aim of standardising fares throughout the PT Area. The Authority considered this at a meeting on 2nd January 1975 and approved Phase I which reduced the seven scales to four and came into effect on 23rd March 1975. The scale was now 5p, 10p, 15p, 18p, 20p, 25p, 30p and 35p for 1.5, 3, 6, 9, 12, 15, 18 and 21 miles respectively.

Phase II was applied outside Liverpool only and Phase III was calculated to achieve parity of bus fares throughout the Area after allowing for the 20% discount which the BET system gave in the Liverpool divisions. It was proposed to abolish this scheme which had still not reached the 25% penetration considered necessary before it justified its costs. This phase was implemented on 2nd November 1975, BETs being accepted for a further two weeks. The new scale rose in 6p steps from 6p to 48p and, apart from one or two temporary anomalies, the standard scale had been attained.

Phases I and II produced very little passenger resistance but the Phase III measures, which were designed to increase revenue by 20%, met with 13.1% resistance on both PTE and NBC buses. Passengers were understandably angry and resentful of such frequent, heavy increases. The resultant shortfall in revenue of £2 million provoked a major crisis and serious friction between the Authority and the Executive (see Chapter 55).

The enlargement of the PT Area brought problems with concessionary fares. Liverpool had granted free travel to senior citizens off-peak but the PTE, mindful of the cost of extending this arrangement to the whole county, sought to limit this concession to half fare. This was political dynamite and the Committee would not approve it. A costly situation arose as on fine summer days, several duplicate buses had to be run between Liverpool and Southport to carry non-farepaying passengers using their free travel passes. The problem was eventually solved by extending the facility to the railways.

The Traveller Ticket

While the BET scheme, having been the brainchild of Liverpool Corporation, was available only in the Liverpool area, a new kind of universally available weekly ticket, known as the Traveller and costing initially £1.95 was first introduced on 8th January 1972. The objectives were to reduce cash handling on buses, make it easy for passengers to transfer between bus and rail and give a large enough discount to attract passengers to public transport. There was always the possibility that on recreational journeys the Traveller Ticket holder would be accompanied by a fare paying passenger thus attracting additional revenue. The Traveller was a true 'anywhere' ticket, available for unlimited travel on PTE and NBC buses, ferries and local railway services throughout the PT Area and proved sufficiently popular to justify the introduction of a Monthly Traveller from 7th August 1972, priced at £7.20, a discount of about 15% compared with the weekly ticket.

The passenger's first Traveller ticket had to be purchased at one of three special offices where a polaroid photograph was taken and an Identity Card and plastic wallet issued. Subsequent renewals could be made at a large number of

The Zone ticket was an effective answer to the trade union refusal to issue through bus and rail tickets at least as far as regular passengers were concerned. The 'Z' symbol soon became a familiar sight at sales outlets all over Merseyside.

suburban outlets but the ticket was not valid without the identity card and photograph.

The enlargement of the PT Area in 1974 called for revised rules to be introduced as, to have extended the Traveller's validity to cover the enlarged area without an additional charge was economically unjustifiable but, conversely, to increase the validity and cost to include the added territories would have annoyed hundreds of regular passengers who had no wish to travel in St. Helens and Southport. So two series of Traveller tickets were made available, an Inner Area Traveller corresponding to the original area and a Merseyside County Area Traveller at an additional cost of about one third, valid anywhere in the new county. This took the Traveller's validity on to Lancashire United and Greater Manchester PTE buses.

Zone Tickets

Fares were twice increased in 1977, on 6th February and 2nd October. In the latter case, the Traffic Commissioners thought that the PTE's application was excessive and reduced the proposed fares from 32p upwards by between 1p and 6p. The County Council now accepted the principle of fares rising annually, geared to average earnings but the next increase, on 29th October 1978, retained the 8p minimum but for two stages instead of three, and introduced 3, 4 and 6-stage fares to ease the burden at the lower end of the scale. At the upper end, the maximum fare of 70p was 2p lower than had originally been applied for in 1977.

Introduction of the new fare scale was synchronised with the launch of the PTE's Zone Ticket scheme, the result of two years of planning and development work. The county was divided into four areas and 37 zones, with overlaps in town centres. Season tickets were issued for one week, one month, three months or a year for any number of zones. A one-zone ticket for a week cost £1.60 while an all-Merseyside ticket cost £274 per annum, but only £70 if restricted to the off peak. It was claimed that the average passenger would save at least 10%. Zone tickets were the first of their kind in Britain and replaced Traveller and rail season tickets within the county area. They were available on all bus and most rail services and were obtainable at over 200 offices, railway stations and agents.

A tremendous publicity effort preceded the launch. Every bus stop had its zone number displayed and television and radio advertising campaigns were augmented by the door-to-door distribution of half a million broadsheets. The scheme gained in popularity and in the first seven months, 45,000 were sold. The annual off-peak zone ticket was used by the County Council as a free travel pass for the over-68s. The zone structure was used as a basis for other off-bus ticket schemes, in particular the one day Saveaway, which was launched in 1979, available for one area or all zones and sold at all railway stations and post offices. This was linked to various promotional offers, discounts at restaurants and reduced admission charges at theatres. The Take Two Saveaway

The Piggy Bank sign was used to market the money saving qualities of the popular Saveaway, an off-peak anywhere ticket sold either for one zone or all zones. The Take Two ticket covered unlimited travel for one adult and two children.

enabled two children to accompany the holder and became very popular, 28,000 being sold in four weeks in the summer of 1982. By 1984, the PTE claimed that 7.5 million Saveaways were being sold annually.

The October 1979 fares increase of 12.8% brought a 10p minimum fare which, a year later, rose to 12p but the 1980 increase (11.8%) introduced the idea of a maximum off-peak fare, fixed originally at 40p. To reduce the work involved in preparing an application to increase fares, the Traffic Commissioners agreed to the principle of a 'trigger mechanism' whereby, if it could be proved that costs had increased by a specific amount, the trigger was activated and fares could rise accordingly.

In 1981, Merseyside was one of several county councils to come under Labour control on election promises of cheaper bus fares. A warning by the Secretary of State for Transport that fares must not be reduced at the ratepayers'

expense was ignored and Merseyside announced a Cheap Fares Policy with reductions of 10% per annum until free transport was achieved. Reductions of from 10% to. 50% were applied from 4th October 1981, the maximum peak bus and rail fares being respectively lowered from 90p and £1.25 to 54p and 90p. The top off-peak fare came down from 40p to 36p. The Authority's objective was to stem the 6% annual traffic loss which it seems to have achieved as the 12.9% gross reduction gave only a 9% drop in revenue.

The idea of a free transport service comes up from time to time and it is of interest to review the results of an experiment financed by Liverpool Corporation in 1974-75 when the City Circle (by then restyled 'Cityride' for fear of offending the Trades Descriptions Act) was operated free during off peak hours and all day Saturdays as 'Freeride'. The City Council's objectives were 'to give equal opportunity to all sections of society and to attract passengers to public transport and thereby reduce the need for major highway construction hence providing financial, environmental and social benefits'. The experiment was discontinued in March 1975 when a flat fare was introduced and the results showed that the number of passengers more than doubled, from 8,000 to 18,000 per week, but many were short distance riders who would otherwise have walked and others were abstracted from the normal services on which fares were still charged. The Executive was cautious in its report stating '.... unless the journey to work modal split can be changed by such a pricing experiment, there can be little effect on related highway, parking and social costs'.

Despite the political controversy over the Cheap Fares Policy, it was taken a step further from 9th October 1983 when further selective reductions were made and the off-peak minimum fare became 30p. Reductions in Saveaway tickets were accompanied by an increase in sales outlets from 280 to about 600. Off bus sales were already 4.7% and there were more than 70 discount offers at stores and places of entertainment. Post office sales were much higher than expected — almost £1.5 million in 1983-84. Zone and Saveaway tickets from all outlets in the area brought in more than £10 million in 1984-85. The PTE claimed an increase in passengers on all services of 22% between 1981-82 and 1984-85; on PTE bus services the rise was 28% and 38% at off peak times on weekdays.

The inevitable consequence of the policy, which continued into the deregulation era, was that the proportion of the PTE's revenue obtained directly from the passenger decreased steadily from 72% in 1975 to 59% in 1979 and to 34% in 1984-85. After deregulation, the PT Authority decided to retain a lower fare scale on subsidised services, resulting in different fares at various times of the day on the same service and a complex route numbering system.

Reduced Fare Experiments

The PTE, usually at the behest of the elected representatives, engaged in a number of fare experiments. Off peak fares on route 11 were reduced by 25% from

November 1971 and in December 1976, there was a half-fare off peak experiment on routes 14C/14D for four weeks. Other more wide-ranging experiments were tried in St. Helens and Southport at various times. All resulted in more passengers but less revenue.

THE PTE AT WORK

City Centre Problems

The PTE frequently complained that the County Council's Joint Transportation Unit attached more importance to cars than buses and little or no attention was paid to its plea for bus priorities. The one-way systems introduced in the sixties had improved traffic flow and the loss of city centre and other jobs reduced the volume of traffic at peak hours. The opening of the flyovers in 1969-70 and the first tube of the second Mersey Tunnel in 1971 solved the problems stemming from cross-river traffic.

The Executive was concerned with the reduced accessibility of the buses. A substantial flow of bus traffic was banished, in one direction, to the Chapel Street-Tithebarn Street 'office expansion area' axis which generated little off peak traffic and even less after 1977 when Exchange Station closed. The next stage in the City Centre Plan, the pedestrianisation of the Church Street shopping area and adjoining thoroughfares, was effected on 17th March 1974 and took the buses away from kerbsides which had accommodated some of the most

Leyland Panther 1018, operating the former City Circle, in the green livery, loads in the embayment in Elliot Street, outside St. John's Precinct. The whole of the area behind the bus is now pedestrianised.

intensively used stops in the central area. In their place was created the clumsily named Hood Street Gyratory, formed by opening out Hood Street and Roe Street and bulldozing most of Queen Square. The forbidding, crescent shaped dual carriageway was spanned by two uncovered footbridges, connecting a line of continuous bus shelters with the new St. John's Precinct shopping centre. For others wishing to approach a bus stop from street level, there were steep stairs or lengthy ramps to negotiate. A better recipe for driving passengers away from the buses could hardly have been devised.

Buses running on what had been the Church Street services were routed from Lord Street into Hood Street by way of Whitechapel and many shoppers in Church Street preferred to walk back to Lord Street rather than cope with the physical obstacles in Hood Street.

A further planning absurdity was the virtual elimination of the limited bus-rail interchange at Central Station as the buses were now on one side of the pedestrianised area and the trains on the other. The only service terminating there, the limited stop 510 from Prescot, was moved to South Castle Street. So much for an integrated network but the PTE could not be blamed as they were entirely in the hands of the city's planners.

The entrance to Pier Head Bus Station with the Royal Liver Building and Water Street in the background. A subway passed beneath the roadway to enable passengers to reach the centre island (left) in safety.

Bus Stations

The original City Centre Plan had envisaged a busway to replace pedestrianised streets (the 'Strand-Paradise' development). The 1963 plan would have cost £1 million but it was scaled down on financial grounds to a bus station located between South John Street and Paradise Street. The Passenger Transport Department considered that the station should be regarded as a civic amenity rather than their financial liability and eventually the City Council agreed that they would have to pay only part of the cost. The structure was combined with a multi-storey car park and the opening coincided with the Church Street pedestrianisation. PTE services 11, 26/27, 87 and 544 (and 73 and 80 at peak hours) were moved from adjoining streets, together with St. Helens services 39, 317 and 320. In relation to its cost and the value of the prime site which it occupied, the station was a complete white elephant but the planners' contention was that it was designed as a busway replacement for Lord Street when the latter was pedestrianised. The majority of services continued to run to the Pier Head which generated fewer and fewer passengers as the ferries continued to decline.

There was further talk of bus stations in 1980 when new uses for the Exchange Station site were being discussed. The seven acre site had been proposed for decentralised government offices but the scheme was scrapped by the new administration which was trying to reduce public spending. A new headquarters for Merseyside County Council was next suggested and then a bus station and sports centre. The Council bid £400,000 for the site and now proposed to build a £500,000 bus station, a holding area for 50 vehicles and a giant multi-storey car park. A pedestrian tunnel would have linked this complex with Moorfields Station. The Director of Service Planning and Co-ordination explained the current thinking which echoed that of the immediate post war years (see Volume Four, pages 33-34). Three bus station sites were envisaged—Moorfields, Lord Street and a Pier Head terminal reduced in size. Lord Street was to be pedestrianised though the PTE alone asked for the retention of a bus lane. In the economic conditions of the times, no money was available for such ambitious schemes.

A further city terminal was lost to the PTE from 1st September 1980 when Derby Square (South Castle Street) was closed for pedestrianisation in connection with the new Crown Court and routes 10 and 11 were moved to the Pier Head, incurring thousands of additional unproductive miles per year.

Changes in traffic volumes and flows enabled some of the route contortions caused by traffic management schemes to be ironed out. After many years of pressure, the lower part of London Road again became two-way for buses in 1983 and Norton Street was similarly derestricted the following year, enabling Ribble buses from Skelhorne Street to revert to their original outward route and saving thousands of miles annually. But a new tunnel entrance plan precluded the continued use of Old Haymarket as a terminus from March 1986 when routes 39 and 320 (and 57 at certain times) were moved to a stand in Whitechapel. The Clayton Square redevelopment closed Parker Street to traffic in the same month, the midibus service 100 which alone served Central Station, being obliged to travel the length of Hanover Street to Canning Place to turn round.

Lord Street between Whitechapel and North John Street and part of Whitechapel were eventually pedestrianised on 24th July 1988 but there was no facility for buses which were banished to North John Street, Victoria Street and Sir Thomas Street.

Public Relations and Marketing

The techniques of marketing had not consciously been applied to public transport before the seventies and, indeed, many experienced marketing people had difficulty applying their methods to a service industry. In 1970, Liverpool University was persuaded to commence a two-year programme of research in public transport marketing at the end of which recommendations would be made on an optimum marketing strategy.

The PTE appointed Public Relations consultants in 1970 and the first steps were taken towards establishing a corporate identity. Without being too specific, the Transport Plan submitted to the DoT in 1972 outlined marketing policy based on the projection of a favourable corporate image, good quality publicity and concentration on particular projects from time to time, such as tendering the correct fare.

In view of the frequent service changes, the PTE issued separate leaflet timetables for individual routes or groups of routes though some combined timetable books containing details of PTE, NBC and rail services in specific areas were also produced. The PTE undertook publicity for all services in the area and some elaborate leaflets and booklets were produced in connection with the numerous schemes of rationalisation. Indeed, they were criticised for profligacy as some brochures were printed on good quality art paper with coloured maps. However, the PTE's publicity was of a high standard and, in addition to the general timetable leaflets, special lines were done such as pocket timetables in plastic and area booklets.

On 12th May 1975, a fully equipped enquiry office was opened in Williamson Square, adjacent to Hood Street Gyratory, with a view to later upgrading to full travel agency status. In July 1975, a Customer Relations Section was created under the control of R.S.McMillan, OBE, Senior Assistant (Traffic); its task was to co-ordinate publicity and associated matters previously undertaken by the Divisions, foster public relations and take control of enquiry offices and communications. Route maps were produced for each operating area. Three years later, the Marketing and Customer Relations functions were combined under the control of the Marketing Manager.

In the late seventies and eighties, the PTE's marketing effort became more sophisticated with a strong projection of the image through major events. The Big Bus Show, commemorating the 50th anniversary of Edge Lane Works, unfortunately had to be postponed at short notice from May to 29th September 1979 because of industrial action. Several buses were painted in the old liveries of the constituent undertakings and 20,000 people visited the Works. Another mammoth event was the 10p Flat Fare Day on Sunday 3rd July 1983 when any journey within

Merseyside county cost only 10p. The transport system was almost overwhelmed by its success as the weather was fine and five times the normal number of people travelled by bus, train and ferry. The scene at Southport railway station was reminiscent of pre-war days. This was the opening event of Transport Week. The newly-refurbished Southport garage was open to the public on Sunday and there were cavalcades of vehicles and 'Transport Nights' in Liverpool, Wirral and St. Helens during the week. The Garston-Hunts Cross Merseyrail extension was ceremonially opened on Tuesday 5th July when free Saveaway tickets were handed to rail travellers. The 10p flat fare day was repeated on 1st July (though the special facilities for the Garden Festival were excluded) and on 16th September, 1984 for the People's Festival organised by the County Council.

An enormous marketing effort went into publicising the International Garden Festival of 1984. A special range of Saveaway tickets, which included admission to the festival, was priced so that travel to and from the exhibition grounds was free.

Door-to-door distribution of broadsheets, a staff newspaper Merseylink, opening of depots to the public, radio and press advertising, were all designed to create an awareness of the PTE's role on Merseyside. Children's characters, Barney the Bus, Tommy the Train and Freda the Ferry featured in cartoon strips and on promotional drinking mugs. Special holiday offers, discounts and cheap admissions to holders of Saveaways flowed in a

Metro-Cammell-bodied Atlantean 1789 was allocated to Seaview Road, Wallasey depot and painted in the former Wallasey Corporation primrose green and cream livery with a white roof in June 1979. It managed to retain these colours until 1984, long after the other buses painted in old liveries had been repainted. In this view it is operating the cross-river service 31 to New Brighton in March 1982.

The PTE's publicity was eye-catching and effective as demonstrated by these two 1980 leaflets for the new community services 100 and 101.

continuous stream from the fertile minds of the marketing team.

On the more formal level, three Transport Users' Advisory Committees brought together many representative bodies on Merseyside and facilitated two way exchanges of views.

Shelters

The PTE adopted a progressive policy towards the provision of shelters, recognising that their non-provision was a negative marketing factor. Additions were made annually. For example, between March 1983 and March 1985 the number increased throughout the area from 1,538 to 1,736 (13%). About half were owned by the PTE, many having been manufactured at Edge Lane Works and, of the 1,020 in the Liverpool Divisions in 1985, 504 were owned by advertising contractors. Vandalism took its regular toll and even the use of security glazing, steel roof sections and heavy duty concrete panels did not entirely solve the problem. In the year 1984-85 the advertising people gave up the fight at 20 sites and removed their shelters altogether.

Shelters were seen as an important amenity in order to attract passengers but the Corporation, and later the PTE, fought a losing battle against the work of the vandals. The upper picture shows a concrete shelter built at Edge Lane but even these were sometimes smashed; centre is the Abacas shelter, as erected on the Churchill Way North flyover, with Gt. Crosshall Street in the background while below is an Adshel shelter, as erected by advertising contractors with work-weary Scousers waiting in Tithebarn Street for the bus home.

49 THE COMPANY BUSES

The bus companies suffered the same adverse social and economic factors as the Corporation but in different degrees. Television and the increase in car ownership affected the companies more than the municipalities because the profitable leisure-time traffic was important to them; company wages and conditions had lagged behind municipal rates but were catching up and there was no rate fund to share the burden with the passenger. As there was no social policy, the taper on the company fare scales was less marked and consequently the longer distance passenger's fares tended to rise commensurately with those of the short rider. Whilst the Corporation complained that the reduction of the differential between their fares and the minimum fare on company buses tended to encourage passengers to ride on company buses within the city boundary, in time the companies complained that the municipal social policy, with its tapering fares which favoured the longer distance passenger, kept fares down and caused a sudden jump in the fare table at the places just beyond the Corporation's area of influence.

This was particularly true of Crosville who were obliged to keep fares to Hunts Cross, Huyton etc. down to the municipal level. On the 1966 Crosville scale, the minimum fare on Prescot Road was 9d and that to points between Green Lane and Page Moss was only 1d more than the Corporation fare. Beyond Page Moss the fares were equal and 1/1d took one into Prescot. However on the parallel Crosville service via Huyton Lane—not a particularly indirect route—municipal influence ended at Huyton Church (1/-) and the fares beyond bounded ahead in 2d and 4d leaps to give a through fare of 2/- to Prescot,

11d more than on the main Prescot Road. Beyond Halewood there was a 6d jump which could be partially avoided by rebooking and saving 1d. Huyton was particularly prone to these absurdities. The 1/- fare from the city to Blacklow Brow was followed, along Tarbock Road, by 2d jumps to each succeeding stop resulting in a 1/6 fare to Meadow Drive, less than a mile further on. It was small wonder that the councils and public alike were loud in their condemnation of the luckless bus companies who had no rate funds to carry their constantly increasing costs. In due course, the formation of the Passenger Transport Authority solved these problems in the PTA area but, as the social policy was extended to embrace the satellite authorities, the jump in the fare structure moved further out and the vociferous authorities had to contribute to revenue support from their own rate funds.

By the sixties, the workmen's fare—a social anachronism whereby the operator charged the passenger less at the times when it cost him more to provide the service—had gone and the return fare (a device originally designed to ensure that the passenger travelled back on the same operator's bus and not with a competitor) was becoming rarer, being confined mainly to the higher values.

Ribble Services

The Crosby services had experienced several years of stability but housing was springing up on the eastern boundary of the town near the canal. New ground was

Number 239 was a Bristol RELL6G with 41-seat dual-door Eastern Coach Works body and is seen, when two months old, crossing the railway bridge after leaving Skelhorne Street. Routes L1 and L8 were converted to one man operation on a part-limited stop basis in September 1968. The bus was withdrawn in 1981. These were the first Tilling-style vehicles to join the Ribble fleet.

broken from 31st May 1958 with a peak hour service, L80, between Chesterfield Road (Hillary Drive) and Seaforth Sands, with journeys to and from Linacre Lane when starting and finishing service. The route was similar to L8 and then followed Brownmoor Lane to the new terminus; there was a half hourly service at weekday peak hours and on Saturday afternoons. This service remained in operation until 31st May 1961 when most Monday to Friday and all Saturday journeys were withdrawn upon the introduction of a new hourly service, L85, between Liverpool and Thornton (Nag's Head) via Kingsway, Brownmoor Lane and Chesterfield Road. There was considerable opposition from residents of Chesterfield Road who did not want the calm of their residential district disturbed by buses but the licence was granted after the Traffic Commissioners had inspected the route. The service was numbered L85 because it combined some of the features of L8 and L5 and it was, in fact, provided at the expense of hourly journeys on L5. L80 was reduced to five Monday to Friday peak hour trips but some of these now ran to and from Liverpool.

The new combined depot, bus and coach station built by Ribble on land between Skelhorne Street and Copperas

Hill was brought into operation in stages from 11th April 1960. Local buses were transferred from their street stands in three groups during June.

Other Ribble service developments were associated with Kirkby and the growth of housing estates on and east of the A59 in Maghull. A workers' service, W1, was introduced between Ormskirk and Kirkby Trading Estate on 3rd November 1958 but traffic was very poor and scarcely justified continued operation. In 1961 the Army Ordnance depot at Burscough was closed and its functions transferred to Deysbrook Barracks, West Derby. Ribble was asked to transport civilian employees from the Burscough and Ormskirk areas to Deysbrook on a guaranteed revenue basis. This started on 20th February 1961, as W3, originating at Burscough Bridge, calling at Ormskirk, Westhead and Skelmersdale, over the 201 route to Melling then via Kirkby Station, Moor Lane, Stonebridge Lane (for the Napier factory), Lowerhouse Lane, Dwerryhouse Lane, Muirhead Avenue East, Almonds Green, Town Row

A number of these Leyland PD1s with 56-seat Burlingham highbridge bodies worked on the Bootle joint services during the 1950s. Number 2467, new in January 1947, was withdrawn in 1958 but others of the class ran until 1961.

and Melwood Drive to Deysbrook Barracks. Service W1 was withdrawn for, although W3 did not serve Kirkby Trading Estate, adequate connections were available by Corporation services. The whole service was available to the general public and continued running at least until 1969. So, too, did the curious W12 which followed a most tortuous route from Crossens through Southport, Birkdale, Halsall, Maghull, Melling, Kirkby and Fazakerley to the Napier Works at Gillmoss.

There were other developments along the A59 Liverpool-Preston road. An operational link-up between Liverpool, Ormskirk, Chorley and Blackburn which had been running since June 1956, was licensed and operated as a through service (311) from 6th December 1958. This had little value as a through facility but was an example of efficient bus utilisation which Ribble had developed to a fine art. Eventually this and many similar link-ups had to be broken up because traffic congestion on individual sections passed on delays and caused disruption many miles from the source of the trouble. Blackburn depot usually allocated one of their two PD2s to this route as, if anything newer was sent into Liverpool, it was liable to be 'borrowed' by Aintree depot. Atlanteans, in particular, would disappear for weeks after Blackburn had put them on this service.

The spread of housing in the area between Aintree and Maghull caused routes 305 and 307 to be taken off Melling Road in May 1959 and rerouted via the Old Roan and Altway. At the same time a number of local journeys were put on between Liverpool and Altway (Bullbridge Lane) so that there was a combined half-hourly service to this point by three routes, 201 via Aintree Lane, 305-7 via Altway and 301 via Melling Road. Extensive housing development in Maghull and Lydiate resulted in the introduction of three new services, 340, 341 and 361 from September 1963. The former combined with 310 to give a half-hourly service into the estate immediately to the east of the A59 whilst the others served the area to the north of Maghull. Unusually, their terminus was situated on a roundabout at Robbins Island.

From 1st June 1963 a completely new one-man operated service (303) was introduced between Kirkby, Melling, Maghull, Downholland, Halsall, Shirdley Hill and Southport. Commencing at the Admin. Gate and calling at Kirkby bus station and railway station, this service operated at approximately two-hourly intervals and gave connections at Lydiate for Ormskirk. It absorbed most of the 300 service between Shirdley Hill and Southport and a few journeys taking a different route into Southport were later renumbered 203.

The Hall Road service (L7) was the only Crosby route without a direct Liverpool connection and, following some housing development in the north of the town, a link up was arranged in 1964 with the half-hourly L4. Two hourly services resulted; one, routed through the town centre completely absorbed the L7 and carried the number L47 (L4 plus L7). The other, which ran via Seaforth Sands instead of Litherland, showed L48 and used Oakland Avenue, avoiding the town centre.

The intricate scheduling of the Crosby services made it difficult to reduce the excess of buses along Stanley Road (31 per hour off-peak) without a major reorganisation but this was eventually accomplished by bringing all the company's management trainees to Liverpool as a special

Pictured during the years when the lower part of London Road was a one-way street are Leyland PD2/13 1408 with MCCW open platform body and PD2/12 1473 with enclosed platform Burlingham body. The buses date from 1955-56 and were withdrawn in 1971.

scheduling team and new timetables were introduced on 30th September 1968. Advantage was taken of the agreement of Bootle depot staff to co-operate in the extension of one-man operation. At the same time some purely local facilities were introduced in Crosby thus reducing the number of through buses to and from Liverpool without reducing the number of journeys inside Crosby itself. The accompanying table shows how off-peak departures were reduced from 31 to 22 and more or less equally balanced via Seaforth Sands and via Litherland. The comparison of departures from South Road, Waterloo towards Crosby centre by all routes, however, shows that hourly departures were increased from 31 to 32. Frequencies on almost all services were reduced considerably during the evenings.

The detailed scheme is shown in Map 51 but some new features are worthy of special mention. The Crosby-Thornton 'circulars' C1 and C2 operated at a flat fare of 6d using Bristol-ECW one-man single deckers with front entrance and centre exit. A number of new direct facilities and road-rail links at Waterloo station were established. L1 and L8 were unchanged in route but became limited stop services using orthodox one-man operated Leyland Leopard vehicles but they were replaced by two door Bristols when a second batch arrived in 1969. Running time was reduced to 33 minutes — a saving of four minutes. Hourly L35 was the first attempt to provide a dockside route to Crosby since horse bus days. The L3/L30 services were reduced overall from a six to a ten minutes' frequency and one L30 journey each hour diverted over the new route which covered Church Street, Lord Street, James Street, Strand, King Edward Street, Gt. Howard Street and Derby Road. For the first time direct facilities were given between the city shopping area, the Pier Head and Crosby. A summer extension of L30 to Freshfield (L33) operated only during the 1969 and 1970 seasons.

Services 391 Crosby-Maghull and 392 Bootle-Maghull were completely new. The Crosby version was a Monday to Friday peak hour service whilst 392 operated daily throughout the day until about 7.30pm. These routes

Departures from Liverpool (Skelhorne Street) for Crosby and Beyond		
Monday to Friday Afternoon Off-Peak		
September 1968 — 5th December 1975		
Minutes past the hour	via Litherland	via Seaforth Sands
0	L1, S2	L30
5		L15
7	L47	
10	L3	
15		L8, 381/2
20	L3	
25	L2	L85
30	L1 S1/2	L35
35		L25
37		L48
40	L3	
45		L6, L8
50	L3	
55	L2	L85

provided a wealth of cross-country facilities and enabled direct journeys to be made which formerly required one or two changes of bus. They cut across the hitherto accepted operational boundaries and special financial arrangements were made as explained below.

Ribble's Liverpool-St. Helens group of services continued undisturbed throughout the sixties with a combined quarter-hourly service from South John Street to St.Helens for most of the day, made up of a half-hourly service to Wigan (320), hourly departures by Lancashire United buses alternately to Tyldesley and Salford (39) and an hourly short journey to St.Helens.

The Burlingham-bodied Leyland PD2s were familiar performers on the Liverpool-Crosby and Southport services for many years. Number 1453, new in 1956, like most of its class, was fitted wih two-piece sliding doors. It is seen in Southport on the stopping service S2 on 17th May 1967.

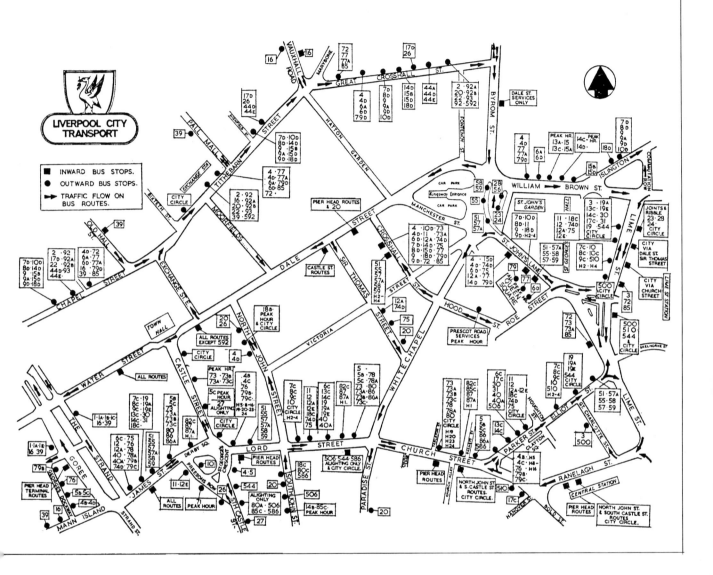

REVISED BUS ROUTES AND STOPPING PLACES
IN THE CITY CENTRE FOLLOWING THE ONE-WAY
TRAFFIC SCHEME INTRODUCED ON 8th MAY 1966

MAP 49

In the course of the build-up of services for Skelmersdale New Town (see below), an attempt by Ribble to establish a new Liverpool-Wigan route via Skelmersdale was successfully opposed by Wigan and St. Helens Corporations and Lancashire United Transport.

British Railways, under the Beeching 'rationalisation' plan, proposed to withdraw Liverpool-Wigan stopping train services by both the ex-L&Y route via Kirkby and Rainford and the ex-LNW route via St. Helens and Garswood. Time tables were drawn up by Ribble and its joint operators for a Liverpool-Kirkby-Skelmersdale-Wigan replacement bus service, running every 90 minutes and also an express augmentation of the 320 at Monday to Friday peak hours and all day on Saturday. This would have taken 37 minutes to St.Helens and 66 to Wigan compared to 47 and 87 minutes by the limited stop 320. However, in the course of the Transport Users' Consultative Committee proceedings, the railway scheme underwent considerable modification and neither service was totally withdrawn. None of the intended bus improvements was made, therefore, until after deregulation when the Liverpool-Skelmersdale services were extended to Wigan.

Crosville Services

Crosville services in Liverpool were remarkably stable and alterations were confined to occasional frequency adjustments to keep pace with changing needs. From 30th March 1958, service 143 between Liverpool and Warrington via Cronton and Farnworth was taken off the traditional route via Overton Street, Wavertree Road and Childwall in favour of the direct route via Edge Lane with limited stops. Six minutes was saved, giving a 59-minute journey time which enabled an hourly service to be run with crew changes at the depot on every trip, instead of the awkward 75-minute frequency previously given. This was the fastest bus journey between the two towns being 11 minutes quicker than via Prescot and 26 minutes better than the 120 via Widnes.

Crosville management had for some time realised that the company's route number system, hastily and reluctantly put together in 1946 in accordance with Tilling group policy, was unsatisfactory. In particular, the arbitrary abolition of suffix letters had resulted in several services in the same districts showing the same numbers. Thus in Huyton, the services originally identified as F and F1 and then as 116, 116A and 116B, all showed 116, a source of confusion to the public. Although the general instruction seemed to involve the painting out of suffix letters on combined 'via' and number blinds, there is some evidence of reluctance to do this in Liverpool where the letters continued to be displayed long after they had disappeared elsewhere. However, when buses with separate three column route number blinds went into service, there was no provision for suffix letters. The Crosville network was so vast that it was impossible to accommodate all the routes in one series between 1 and 999 so a system was worked out whereby each area was given a prefix letter and the services were numbered from 1 with reasonable allowance made for future developments. Liverpool was allocated letter H and a new series of numbers commencing at H1 was introduced with the summer time table on 5th July 1959.

Crosville MB336, a lowbridge Bristol K6A with 53-seat Eastern Coach Works body, was new in 1949 but was compulsorily loaned to London Transport for a year by the British Transport Commission in common with many others drawn from the fleets of several state-owned operators. Despite being fitted with full destination equipment, it is displaying a typical Crosville Wid plate for route No.119 (Liverpool-Prescot-Warrington) because the blind is too long to turn satisfactorily. It has obviously been in violent collision with a high vehicle or object.

The eastern extremity of Crosville's Lancashire service network was Warrington (Arpley Station) where connections were made with the routes of many operators. This 1968 picture shows Lodekka DFG258, a new FLF on the service to Liverpool via Prescot and DLB919, a 1958 LD6B on a Runcorn workers' service, against a background of the buses of five other operators. Left to right are seen an Atlantean of Salford Corporation, an AEC Bridgemaster of Leigh Corporation, a Guy Arab of LUT, an unidentified single decker (almost certainly North Western), a St. Helens Corporation PD2 and a North Western AEC Renown.

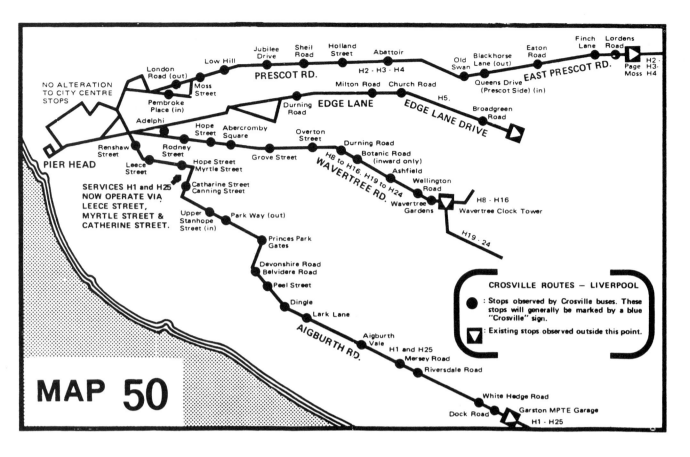

CROSVILLE LIMITED STOPS FROM JANUARY 1972

The settled pattern of company services in South Liverpool was shattered on the afternoon of Friday 21st July 1961 when the long awaited Widnes-Runcorn high level bridge was opened. The opening ceremony was at noon but the new bus services were not started until 6.00pm. The new bridge enabled Crosville to integrate their virtually detached Lancashire services with the main network on the Cheshire side of the Mersey and a complex pattern of routes, demanding a masterpiece of scheduling, was devised to link Liverpool with Chester via Widnes and Runcorn as follows:-

H20   Liverpool-Hunts Cross-Halewood-Halebank-Widnes-Runcorn-Frodsham-Chester (former H20 extended from Hunts Cross)

H21   Allocated for former H20 extension to Carr Lane via Higher Road and journeys terminating at Hunts Cross

H23   Liverpool-Tarbock-Widnes-Runcorn-Rocksavage-Frodsham-Chester (former H23 extended from Widnes)

H24   Liverpool-Gateacre-Halewood-Widnes-Runcorn-Frodsham (with peak hour journeys extended to Helsby Cable Works) (former H24 extended from Widnes)

H25   (commenced 24th July) Liverpool-Garston-Speke-Widnes-Runcorn (peak hour extension of short journeys on H1)

The return trip between Liverpool and Chester occupied 4 hours 20 or 25 minutes including lie-over, so a 12 hour operational cycle was devised for the greater part of the day, each bus performing the following journeys successively:-

Liverpool-Chester	H20)	
Chester-Liverpool	H23)	4hr 20min
Liverpool-Chester	H23)	
Chester-Liverpool	H20)	4hr 25min
Liverpool-Frodsham	H24)	
Frodsham-Liverpool	H24)	3hr 15min

Departures from Liverpool, Pier Head were co-ordinated at:-

H24 to Frodsham at 00 minutes past the hour
H20 to Chester at 15 minutes past the hour
H23 to Chester at 35 minutes past the hour
H19 to Halewood at 45 minutes past the hour.

In the evening the cycle was broken and only one hourly journey was provided to Chester thus:-

H24 to Frodsham at 00 minutes past the hour
H19 to Halewood at 15 minutes past the hour
H23 to Chester at 30 minutes past the hour
H21 to Hunts Cross at 45 minutes past the hour.

The value of the new services did not lie in their usefulness as direct facilities between Liverpool and Chester as it was still very much quicker and cheaper to go by ferry or rail to Birkenhead and use the Chester direct bus service (running time 55 minutes) from there. But the acceleration of journeys across the Mersey at Runcorn was very substantial and facilities between (a) Liverpool, Runcorn and Frodsham and (b) Chester, Widnes and the southern suburbs of Liverpool were of considerable value.

The new scheme brought Crosville buses from their depots at Chester (one bus) and Runcorn (six buses) into Liverpool for the first time and a few wrong turnings were taken until the drivers became thoroughly accustomed to the new routes. A further peak hour facility, H6, was introduced on 1st October 1962 between Liverpool and Runcorn (ICI Offices) via Bowring Park, Roby and Huyton. H19 and H20 were rerouted via Leathers Lane to serve the new Halewood housing estate from 5th September 1965.

In 1966, when British Rail proposed to truncate the Hooton-Helsby passenger service at Stanlow and Thornton, Crosville devised a scheme to extend alternate Liverpool-Frodsham trips on H24 to Birkenhead (Woodside), creating an almost circular route occupying 2½ hours with each terminus within sight of the other but separated by the River Mersey. However, the train service was retained and now prospers.

This group of routes was partially converted to single-deck one-man operation in 1970. There was a low bridge at Halebank which could be negotiated by a Lodekka but not by a VR and this hindered conversion to double-deck one-man operation. When Runcorn Shopping City opened in October 1971, these services were revised and fully converted. H20 was used for short journeys between Liverpool and Runcorn and also between Runcorn and Chester and, with H23 and H24 continued to serve the old town centre; H21 and a new H22 (via Tarbock) were routed through the new shopping centre.

The growth of population in the districts served by Crosville to some extent counteracted the depredations of the motor car so that widespread reductions in frequencies were not necessary. As Rainhill became built up, a further joint service (79) with St. Helens Corporation was commenced between St. Helens and Rainhill Stoops via Thatto Heath from 25th April 1965. A half-hourly service was provided by one vehicle of each operator, the Crosville bus being worked between Liverpool and Rainhill Stoops as an H3. One-man operation was introduced by Crosville on this service in 1969, using Bristol REs.

AEC Regent V 58 of 1967 had a MCCW 65-seat Orion style body and was the last new double-deck bus to join the St. Helens Corporation fleet, subsequent additions being AEC Swifts. The scene is High Street, Woolton in March 1970 on the Speke-St. Helens service then run jointly with Crosville. Number 58 was in the PTE fleet from April 1974 to December 1980, the last few months as a driver-training vehicle.

The Zoning Agreement

Talks on modifications to the 1938 Agreement had been going on sporadically for several years. That Agreement had established three zones, the inner or 'A' zone which was the responsibility of the Corporation, the 'B' zone, a small area of Litherland and part of West Lancashire Rural District which was jointly served by the Corporation and Ribble and the outer or 'C' zone which consisted of everywhere outside the 'A' or 'B' zones, which was company territory. Prescot Road was the boundary between Ribble and Crosville and could be used by both and there were a few 'free trade' roads such as Ormskirk Road between Park Lane and Old Roan and Archway Road, Huyton. The category of the service was determined by the zone in which the outer terminus lay. There was also provision for the carriage of passengers within the 'A' zone on 'C' zone services on payment of a toll to the Corporation. During the fifties, some bilateral concessions had been made to accommodate the changes which flowed from the conversion of tram routes in Bootle to bus operation and the closure of the Overhead Railway. However, the contentious area was the status of Kirkby which had clearly been in zone 'C' in 1938 but, of necessity, had been served by the Corporation by both buses and trams during the war.

At a meeting in November 1956, Ribble undertook to submit a proposal but none of the parties showed any great urgency and it was February 1958 before the new document was received. One of the clauses on which agreement had been previously reached read as follows:-

'It is recognised that in a developing area such as is dealt with by the terms of this Agreement, problems may arise by reason of the need for the Corporation and the Company adequately to serve the growing or changing traffic requirements of the area having regard to previously established independent traffic interests of the parties.

It is agreed that the guiding principles of permitting a settlement of such problems which may arise shall be that neither operator shall be called upon to surrender previously existing established rights either to the other or to the joint service interests without, as nearly as may be, the award of compensating benefits in any new operation.'

The Corporation complained that in the new draft this clause had been rewritten to apply only to the joint services and certain other sections had been reworded to their detriment. As this new document did not appear to meet the earlier concepts of full co-ordination it was not followed up and lay in abeyance for six years until 1964 when Ribble revived it. By this time Horace Bottomley, Ribble General Manager since 1945, was dead and most of the company's senior officers had changed. The Corporation pointed out the changes which had been made in 1958 and offered to reopen negotiations or alternatively to talk about a simpler document which would have the effect of bringing the 1938 agreement up

to date. Ribble agreed to the latter course and submitted a new draft in September 1965 which provided the basis for further informal discussions over the next three years.

The continuing informality of the relationship between the Corporation and Ribble encouraged development and new services were put on by both parties, any exceptions to the basic principles of the 1938 agreement being agreed by a simple exchange of letters. For example, from 24th July 1961 Corporation service 95B between Netherton and East Lancashire Road (Gillmoss) commenced. This was an extension of joint route 53A over the Corporation route 95 and arrangements were made for the receipts and mileage operated in the joint area to be pooled. In 1964 the parties came close to falling out over a new workmen's service W11 which Ribble wanted to provide between Lydiate, Maghull and Seaforth Sands. This covered almost the whole of joint route 54 and introduction was delayed from 30th June to 5th September when it started, with full protection between Switch Island and Seaforth. However, in 1968 a formula was devised whereby W11 was treated like 95B, mileage and local receipts between Copy Lane and Seaforth being pooled. In return Ribble agreed to Overhead Railway replacement service 1E being extended from Litherland to Netherton under similar arrangements.

From 1st May 1965 Ribble service L25 started running between Skelhorne Street and Fleetwoods Lane. This was without precedent as it started in zone 'A', passed through zones 'B' and 'C' and then back into zone 'B'. In accordance with the 1938 Agreement such a service was entitled to be jointly operated, its passage through zone 'C' being irrelevant, but such a route was never envisaged in 1938. The section of route in zone 'B' was not competitive with the joint routes so it was disregarded and L25 (which was an extension of L5) was still regarded as a 'C' zone route. In return, Ribble agreed to the Corporation running to the Tower Hill Estate, Kirkby which, being north of the railway line, was undisputedly in the 'C' zone. A similar dilemma arose in 1968 when Ribble introduced services 391/2 between Crosby, Bootle and Maghull. On Crosby journeys both termini were in the 'C' zone with intervening sections in the 'A' and 'B' zones and local traffic was carried throughout. After a period of indecision it was agreed that the 'B' zone should be treated as if it were 'A' zone and 15% of the local revenue paid over to the Corporation.

During the sixties the transfer of government offices to Bootle and building of the New Strand centre created conditions in which local services made more sense and the Bootle Circular (48-49) was put into operation on 9th September 1968. This was a weekday morning and afternoon service based on New Strand off peak but extended to the Balliol Road office complex at peak times. It required three buses, two Corporation and one Ribble, but each operator had an equal share, the mileage being put in a separate pool from the other joint services to avoid adjusting the pool proportions.

During 1968 talks were held between Liverpool Corporation, Huyton UDC and Crosville with a view to liberalising the rigid observance of the 1938 Area

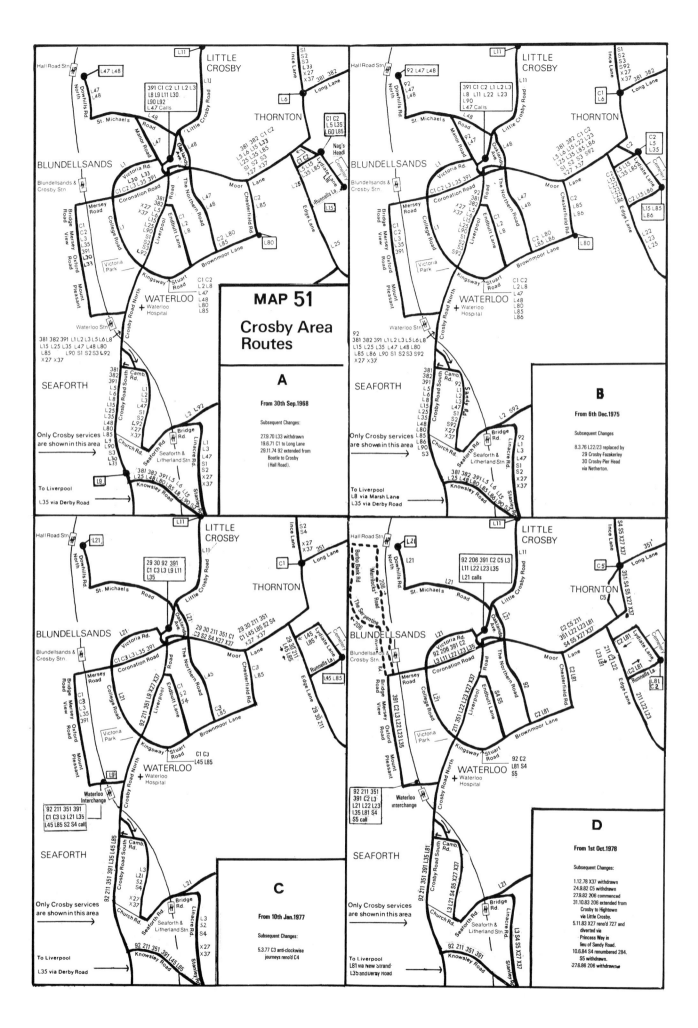

MAP 51

Crosby Area
Routes

A

From 30th Sep.1968

Subsequent Changes:

27.9.70 L33 withdrawn
19.6.71 C1 to Long Lane
29.11.74 92 extended from
Bootle to Crosby
(Hall Road).

B

From 6th Dec.1975

Subsequent Changes

8.3.76 L22/23 replaced by
29 Crosby-Fazakerley
30 Crosby-Pier Head
via Netherton.

C

From 10th Jan.1977

Subsequent Changes:

5.3.77 C3 anti-clockwise
journeys reno'd C4

D

From 1st Oct.1978

Subsequent Changes:

1.12.78 X37 withdrawn
24.9.82 C5 withdrawn
27.9.82 206 commenced
31.10.83 206 extended from
Crosby to Hightown
via Little Crosby.
5.11.83 X27 reno'd 727 and
diverted via
Princess Way in
lieu of Sandy Road.
10.6.84 S4 renumbered 284.
S5 withdrawn.
27.6.86 206 withdrawn

Agreement boundaries within Huyton-with-Roby. As successive housing schemes had grown up, Crosville had been obliged to provide new facilities serving the Mosscroft Farm and Elizabeth Road areas and almost the whole of their Huyton group of services was losing money. At the same time, the agreement prevented the Corporation services from passing beyond Huyton Railway Station. This meeting was convened at the request of the operators as Huyton Council, at that stage, was unconcerned about the viability of services. Ideas put forward included the extension of service 40 from Huyton Station to Elizabeth Road to permit the withdrawal of Crosville H16 and the extension of Corporation 10D to Mosscroft Farm via Longview Lane. In view of impending political developments, no agreement was reached at this time but a very similar scheme was eventually implemented in October 1973.

Accord on the final amendments to the draft Agreement was finally reached in March 1969, over 21 years after the 1938 Agreement had expired. A final draft involving Ribble, Crosville and the British Railways Board was prepared and dated 14th April 1969. This designated a new zone 'AK' to cover the Kirkby situation and recognised the right of the Corporation to run services between zones 'A' and 'B' over former tram routes (covering 23 and 24) and to operate Overhead Railway replacement services without reference to zone boundaries. The Bootle joint services pool proportions were formally amended in accordance with a formula which had been used in practice for several years. Using the revenue for 1954 as a base, the first £528,640 was to be divided as to 61.46% to the Corporation and 38.54% to Ribble, all additional revenue to be divided equally.

A formula was attached whereby the amount of £528,640 was increased proportionately as fares were increased. The toll payable by the companies to the Corporation in respect of local traffic carried within and between zones A and B on independent services remained at 15% but no new services were to be permitted to carry local traffic without the express permission of the Corporation. This went some way to alleviating the Corporation's fears of a continuing erosion of their revenue as the differential between Corporation fares and the minimum fare on company buses diminished. Originally the protective fare had been double the tram fare — 4d as against 2d, but successive fare increases had made it impossible to maintain the differential without creating cross-boundary anomalies. A method of commuting the payment such as had been agreed with Crosville in 1942, had been devised in 1956 when Ribble converted from the preprinted Willebrew to the Setright ticket machine system and this was brought up to date and expressed in the new agreement as percentages of the total revenue of groups of routes as follows:-

1.700 % of the total revenue of the Crosby group of services (including L9, L11, L60, C1 and C2 which operated wholly within Crosby, and 391-2)
1.423 % of the total revenue of the Ormskirk Road group of services

0.4918% of the total revenue of Service 39 Liverpool-St. Helens-Salford
1.000 % of the total revenue of Service 89 Speke-St. Helens
2.9865% of the total revenue of Service 317 Liverpool-St. Helens
1.1361% of the total revenue of Service 320 Liverpool-Wigan

Meanwhile, in 1967 the British Electric Traction Co Ltd disposed of its bus interests to the Transport Holding Company (the successor to the British Transport Commission, set up by the Transport Act 1962) and thus Ribble came under state control. The Transport Act 1968 then created the National Bus Company to hold shares in the subsidiary operating companies on behalf of the government and geographical groups of companies were formed with common boards of directors. Crosville and Ribble, together with the original North Western Road Car Co Ltd of Stockport (which is not the same as the present company of that name) and Cumberland Motor Services Ltd, made up the North Western region under the chairmanship of George Brook, who had been general manager of Ribble since the death of Horace Bottomley. The change of ownership had little immediate effect. The Tilling Group was notoriously more bureaucratic and centralised than the BET but local Ribble management suffered no loss of local autonomy.

With the impending formation of the Merseyside PTE, a question mark stood over the future of both municipal and state-owned buses so the Agreement, reached after almost 20 years of discussions, was never signed. Its provisions were meticulously observed by all the parties until completely new arrangements were concluded between the PTE and the companies in 1972.

The PTE's Agreement with the Companies

Talks between the PTE and the National Bus Company went on throughout 1971, the object being to sweep away, once and for all, the territorial boundaries of the past so enabling bus services to be integrated without waste and overlapping. The protective arrangements of the past were designed not only to protect the rights of individual operators but to ensure that the longer distance passengers were not crowded out by local riders. These needs had largely fallen away as the same buses could comfortably accommodate all the traffic on offer..

Ribble had followed a policy of co-operation with most of the operators in its huge operating territory for many years and the joint working agreement with Liverpool Corporation had stood the test of over 30 years of working together. Some of the remaining barriers had been broken down in 1968 but Waterloo and Crosby remained a Ribble stronghold. As the port declined, Seaforth became less of a traffic objective and some of the traditional local routes could be merged with those bound for places further afield.

Historically, relations between Liverpool Corporation and Crosville had been less flexible especially in Huyton

Leyland PD3 1706 was numerically the first of the MCCW 72-seat forward-entrance Ribble double-deckers. It entered service in April 1961 and is seen in September 1974 in the NBC poppy red livery turning from Water Street in front of the Liver Building. Note the 'BET' sign on the front, indicating that it is equipped with a canceller for multi-journey tickets. Number 1706 was withdrawn in 1977 and dismantled for spares at a Barnsley scrapyard.

where the boundary between the two operators virtually passed through the town centre. Many Crosville routes in Huyton were making losses and a previous attempt at rationalisation in 1968 had failed. At Halewood, PTE service 78 and Crosville service H19 were almost identical though the usefulness of the latter was hindered by the minimum fares which still prevailed on some sections of the route.

The new Agreement was negotiated against the background of the statutory duty of the NBC to collaborate in securing an integrated transport system, an objective which was attained in different ways in the various PT Areas. In the West Midlands, the PTE simply purchased the relevant routes and assets of the Midland Red company thereby literally tearing the heart out of what had been the largest of the BET bus companies. A similar solution was reached in Manchester, the old North Western company being apportioned between the PTE and other neighbouring NBC companies. The independent Lancashire United company was subsequently acquired by the Greater Manchester PTE.

On Merseyside, however, the companies retained their identities but lost their traditional operating areas. The extent of their interests in the PT Area was quantified and expressed as a percentage of the total operations in the Area. Crosville, which had extensive networks on both sides of the river, was guaranteed 13.402% while Ribble was allocated 13.074%. All revenue for journeys wholly within the Area was to be held in trust for the PTE, a formula for handling revenue from cross-boundary riders being worked out from data collected during an extensive census. A complex schedule defined the operating costs which would be met by the PTE. The mileage entitlements were altered to 11.16% for Crosville and 12.89% for Ribble when local government reorganisation changed the PT Area boundaries in 1974.

Determination of the pattern and standard of services and the fares to be charged was the prerogative of the PTE but the routes on which the mileage shares were to be run off were to be mutually agreed. Theoretically, the companies could be allocated work on any route but Union opposition to change tended to keep company buses on their traditional routes. It seems certain that the companies delayed making cuts until after the terms of the Agreement had been settled so as to secure as large a share of the mileage as possible. The document was signed on 29th January 1972 and came into force the following day.

A New Agreement

The PTE had never been happy with the Agreement. In 1974, a spokesman said that in 1973-74 the cost of paying the NBC to run certain services would be £1.5m and owning the services outright would release a portion of that revenue for other purposes. One wonders if the interest on the capital sum necessary to buy the companies out had been taken into consideration. In 1978 the PTE gave the necessary one year's notice to terminate the Agreement as it believed that putting the companies in the role of agents, with a guaranteed revenue, had induced a complacent attitude. It was felt that the companies had not tackled the conversion to one-man operation with sufficient vigour and that labour problems which had bedevilled performance, particularly by Crosville, had been allowed to drift with little serious attempt being made to reach lasting solutions. However, there was nothing in the Agreement about one-man operation and the companies cannot be blamed for giving economies in their own operating territories priority over Merseyside where their costs were guaranteed. On the other hand, there were those in the companies who believed that the PTE had given too much away in order to achieve their goal of 100% one-man operation quickly.

The PTE told the County Council that it should seek a new Agreement which ensured that the Executive had adequate operational and financial control of company activities and a system of payment towards company overheads should be established which was more equitable to both parties. A sensible basis for interworking of personnel was also needed. No doubt the Executive looked with envy at Manchester and Birmingham where there were no such problems, but the NBC was not prepared to sell the Merseyside area services. An interim continuation Agreement was signed when a solution had not been reached as the period of notice expired.

Negotiation of a new Agreement was a long, drawn out process and it was eventually signed on 20th June 1984 but backdated to 17th May 1981. It could be terminated with two years' notice but not before five years. There was provision for establishing a Bus Council, comprising senior members of the PTE and company staffs, to meet three times a year to consider the general state of the 'county services'. A budget had to be submitted by each company to the PTE by 30th November each year in respect of the next financial year. There were somewhat vague provisions for interchangeability of labour. There were very complex costing arrangements which recognised that certain services were more expensive to run than others; every service was listed together with its costing group. The PTE now had much better cost control, as the SCRAM methods (see Chapter 48) applied equally to company services.

The Agreement addressed the problem of backlog depreciation which became an accepted cost. The companies, on their part, had an incentive to keep their costs as low as possible.

Payments to the NBC during the eighties were substantial, ranging from £5 to over £7 million annually but they did not increase at the same rate as support to the PTE buses.

In Liverpool, labour inflexibility and jealousy made the agency agreement difficult to administer economically as any proposal to put the buses of a company operator on a traditionally municipal route or vice versa was immediately opposed. This made it difficult to allocate the mileage in the agreed proportions and accounts for Ribble and Crosville buses being used on the Garden Festival services in 1984. In Wirral, matters went more smoothly and by 1979, after long and difficult negotiations, an integrated network was achieved.

Crosville under the PTE

Minimum fares were immediately abolished on all Crosville routes in Liverpool but, to avoid having to allow additional running time, Crosville buses ran limited stop over the inner sections of route. (See Map 50). The facility for using Crosville buses for local journeys at ordinary fares was marketed under the name of 'Merseyfare' which was shown on the stops which they observed. When services were altered or rescheduled, running times were increased so that all stops could be served. The only other immediate change was the abandonment of the traditional company route for services H1 and H25 along Upper Duke Street and Canning Street in favour of the old tram route along Leece Street, Myrtle Street and Catharine Street.

The PTE soon complained about the use of the Johnson Farebox without tickets on the H12-13 Pier Head-Prescot via Windy Arbour Road services which had been converted to single deck one-man operation in June 1971. The fare box was really suitable only for flat fare routes as foolproof control of revenue or over-riding was impossible. The Setright register was duly restored and BET cancellers fitted.

The first major rationalisation scheme was delayed until 22nd October 1973 when PTE routes 11 and 40 were extended from Huyton Station to Pluckington Farm and Elizabeth Road respectively. Crosville H16 to Elizabeth Road was withdrawn whilst H14, Pier Head-Prescot via Huyton Lane, was renumbered 76 and diverted over the route of the former PTE service 76 via Brownlow Hill, Wavertree Road, Thingwall Road and Rocky Lane. Along Wavertree Road, the use of the PTE number 76 indicated that these particular Crosville buses observed all stops while, for the time being those with the 'H' prefix stopped only at places with the 'Merseyfare' sign.

Crosville was an early user of the Leyland National and SNL822 was a dual-door 44-seater placed in service late in 1972. The all over, unrelieved leaf green livery was dictated by the NBC's corporate image policy.

New services were put on to serve the new Lickers Lane estate at Whiston. An hourly shuttle, H18, between Prescot and Huyton Station, was at first supplemented by the diversion of the Windy Arbour Road service H12 but there were so many complaints from the public that it reverted to the original route within two weeks. A few peak hour trips between Prescot and Pier Head or the Crosville garage were numbered H15 and routed via Lickers Lane, Edge Lane and Brownlow Hill. H11 was renumbered H7 to avoid confusion with route 11 in Huyton. The mileage saved in the first year was 170,000.

In Hunts Cross and Halewood, Crosville's presence was reduced to two buses per hour off peak on H21 and H22; H19 was withdrawn and H20 diverted via Gateacre and Hough Green and curtailed at Runcorn Shopping City instead of running to Runcorn bus station. This eliminated the problem with the low Halebank bridge. These services together with H1 and H25 were further reduced in frequency on 23rd November 1975. Liverpool depot buses ceased running through to Chester in 1980 though one trip reached Helsby Grammar School during term time until deregulation. Runcorn Shopping City attracted people from south Liverpool and, in 1980, a daily service was introduced on H25 from Pier Head via Speke and Hale, marking the gradual decline in importance of H1 to Warrington which was abandoned for a time after deregulation.

The services along the A57 to Rainhill and Warrington (H2-3) were converted to one-man operation in December 1976, the H4 route via Manchester Road, Prescot, being abandoned as the Bristol VRs were too heavy to cross the railway bridge in Bridge Road. One peak hour short journey, worked by a Lodekka, continued for a time. H2 was now interworked with H5 via Cronton.

The Huyton-Prescot services (H6-9) underwent many minor changes with some emphasis on reducing the number of trips running through to and from Liverpool. They were all converted to double deck one-man operation on 21st June 1978, four days later than announced, because of a labour dispute. H12-13 were changed from single-deck to double-deck operation as they were now interworked with H7-8. On the same day, Crosville buses on 89/89A, St. Helens-Speke or Halewood, went over to driver only operation. The PTE buses on the route, all from St. Helens depot, had changed over six months earlier, necessitating an increase from four to five buses. The continued participation of Crosville on this route was an absurdity as it could have been worked much more economically from Speke depot, while Crosville could have continued to participate in the Pier Head-Halewood service. Crew changeovers on 89 were done at Archway Road, Huyton. The crew would take a bus from the company's Edge Lane garage and, if they liked it better than the one which came along, the unfortunate passengers would be transferred.

Matters came to a head when Crosville moved their depot to Love Lane as the dead mileage to and from Archway Road could no longer be justified, so the Crosville share of 89 was transferred to Ribble who worked it from Wigan depot. Reasonable economy of operation was achieved by working the bus to St. Helens 'live' on the 342/352/362 Wigan-Billinge-St. Helens service, the bus arriving on the 89 carrying on to Wigan in its place. The only problem was that the last duty at night finished at Halewood from where the bus had to run empty to Wigan. This strange state of affairs lasted from 2nd June 1985 to 24th October 1986 when the companies withdrew from the route.

Crosville finally achieved 100% one-man operation at Liverpool and Warrington depots on 29th March 1981 when H1 and 76 were changed over and the last Lodekka was withdrawn from the area. This also marked the last instance of limited stop 'Merseyfare' operation.

Ribble under the PTE

Whereas Crosville services in the south of the city were well integrated with the PTE's own services and the Huyton problem was relatively easily solved, Ribble's position was rather more complex. In Waterloo, Crosby, Thornton and along Ormskirk Road there were large tracts of well-populated Ribble territory where the residents had been accustomed to having direct services to and from the city centre. As most Ribble-served suburbs were adjacent to the Southport or Ormskirk railway lines, they were prime targets for bus-rail co-ordination projects.

There was an obvious over-supply of buses between Liverpool, Bootle and Crosby. The changes brought in in September 1968 had slimmed down the Crosby services but, despite the gradual decline in patronage, the same time tables were still in force in 1972 and there had been no extension of one-man operation. Ribble pointed to the large fleet of Leyland PD3s in the area which could not be adapted for driver only operation and still had some years of useful life. In October of that year there were thus 22 off-peak buses per hour running between the city and Crosby (including one trip via Derby Road). Between the city centre and Stanley Road/Marsh Lane junction there were 39 buses per hour comprising 21 to Crosby etc., 2 route 24, 4 route 28, 6 route 55/55A and 6 route 58/59 (subsequently reduced to 4).

Furthermore, the network showed distinct signs of the shortcomings of the old zoning agreement, the most obvious of which was the concentration of all Liverpool-Crosby routes through Seaforth or Litherland, whereas improvements to highways made an alternative route through Aintree and Netherton a practical proposition. The only concession in this direction had been the hourly L25 to Fleetwoods Lane.

March 1975 saw a little progress with one-man operation in the course of the reduction of services in the Ormskirk Road corridor. The last through journeys (on weekday evenings) on the 101 Preston-Ormskirk-Liverpool stopping service disappeared in favour of separate services either side of Ormskirk; many of the Ormskirk-Liverpool journeys were routed through Town Green under route No. 331. Routes 310 and 340 were interworked, both running to Moss Side Hospital which was always euphemistically styled 'Park Lane Lodge' by Ribble, presumably because of its associations with the criminally insane. They were both converted to one-man operation and withdrawn on Sundays when a hybrid 350, with some characteristics of both, was operated. Route 307 was extended extended from Melling Rock to Green Park estate, Maghull while 301, Liverpool-Ormskirk via Waddicar and Melling was rerouted through Kirkby Town Centre on most journeys which were numbered 306. A new facility was given by diverting Maghull-Liverpool service 341 via Hornby Road, Marsh Lane and New Strand. The frequency of the local service 321 between Lydiate and Liverpool was reduced. From 23rd March 1975 local passengers were carried on Ribble buses between Rotunda and Black Bull except at peak hours.

The extension of PTE route 92 to Hall Road, Crosby in November 1974 (see chapter 50), was clearly a political gesture designed to show the PTE flag in this Ribble stronghold as none of the existing facilities was withdrawn. An interim scheme for Crosby, pending the opening of the Link railway extension, was put into effect on 6th December 1975 and included the opening up of all Ribble services along Stanley Road (except X27 and X37) to local passengers at ordinary fares. Route 24 was withdrawn and L1 and L8 lost their part limited stop status, the latter being rerouted along Marsh Lane to replace 24.

The combined Liverpool-Crosby off-peak frequency was reduced from 22 to 12 buses per hour, of which two served the Derby Road route. Freshfield received an improved service by extending many L6 journeys from Long Lane, Thornton as S3. Many buses were withdrawn on Sundays when L11 and L48 did not run at all.

However, the most controversial innovation was Ribble service L22/23 between Crosby and Walton and Fazakerley Hospitals, via Netherton which replaced and extended many journeys on L25, and threatened to spark a serious labour dispute, based on the erroneous contention that Ribble men were taking over PTE work. As a compromise, after three months, L22/23 was replaced by a less efficient arrangement with Ribble buses running a new service 29 between Crosby and Fazakerley Hospital while half-hourly journeys on PTE service 30A were diverted from Netherton (Northern Perimeter Road) to Thornton and Crosby as 30C.

The major upheaval in Crosby was timed for 10th January 1977, four months before the opening of the Link. Most of the established services were withdrawn and replaced by a new layout with many buses curtailed at Waterloo Interchange or Bootle, New Strand. All the main road routes were diverted via South Road to serve the railway station and the local Circulars were revised with emphasis on making all parts of Crosby accessible to rail.

It was expected that the scheme would initially lead to complaints but the financial situation was so serious that it could not be delayed until the railway extension was opened. There were several controversial issues which are explained in Chapter 51.

The Liverpool-Crosby-Ormskirk route 381/382 was replaced by a new 351 between New Strand and Ormskirk via Town Green, the direct route into Ormskirk being abandoned. A new hourly 211 between New Strand and Kirkby Trading Estate combined with 351 to give a half-hourly service between Bootle and Maghull but by different routes between Thornton and Sefton, 211 via Buckley Hill Lane (where it replaced 52) and 351 via Lunt. In due course these routes were extended into Liverpool to improve the frequency between the Knowsley Road area and the city centre.

Some aspects of the reorganisation proved to be unsatisfactory but the PTE waited for the full effect of the opening of the Link and the introduction of Zone tickets to be felt before making any changes. It was not until 1st October 1978 that further major revisions were made. The most significant of these was the total withdrawal of the through service S2 between Southport and Liverpool, overlapping routes between Freshfield and Liverpool (S4-5) and Formby and Southport being substituted. This was a consequence of the validation of old age pensioners' and other concessionary passes for rail travel.

Some routes, which were new in 1977, were replaced by yet more new routes with unfamiliar numbers adding to the public's confusion. Agreement had been reached with the union for the reintroduction of L22-23 which reappeared with the addition of a long loop from Crosby to Waterloo; 29 and 30C were withdrawn, the latter being cut back to Aintree. The new Circulars, C1, C3 and C4, which were part of the 1977 scheme, all disappeared and the original C2 came back. More evening and Sunday buses were withdrawn. The Crosby services now became more stable, though mention should be made of service 206, a circular route between Crosby Bus Station and Blundellsands via Mersey Road, Warren Road, The Serpentine, Burbo Bank Road North to Hall Road, returning via Merrilocks Road and Agnes Road. Between Warren Road and Agnes Road 'hail-and-ride' conditions applied. There were four trips on Mondays to Fridays with a 10p flat fare. A bus was made available by withdrawing C5, also a four journey service between Crosby and Thornton (Long Lane) via Quarry Lane which had been devised so that pensioners would not need to cross the busy main road, but was not well supported. The 206 was likewise little used but was retained as a social service and extended to Hightown in October 1983. This was the first time that Hightown had ever had a bus service.

There was further progress with one-man operation. Routes 391-2, L3 and L21 were converted during 1977, 57A, 300, 302 and 341 in 1978, all remaining Aintree depot workings in November 1980, 211, L35, L81, S4-5 in June 1981 (bringing Bootle depot up to 85%) and, finally, 58 and 351 on 26th September 1981.

The Skelmersdale Services

Ribble became deeply involved with the Skelmersdale New Town project which was one of a number of Liverpool overspill schemes. A two-hourly Liverpool-Skelmersdale service via Waddicar and Melling (201) had started as long ago as April 1951, before the New Town was established and it was not until the mid-sixties that additional services

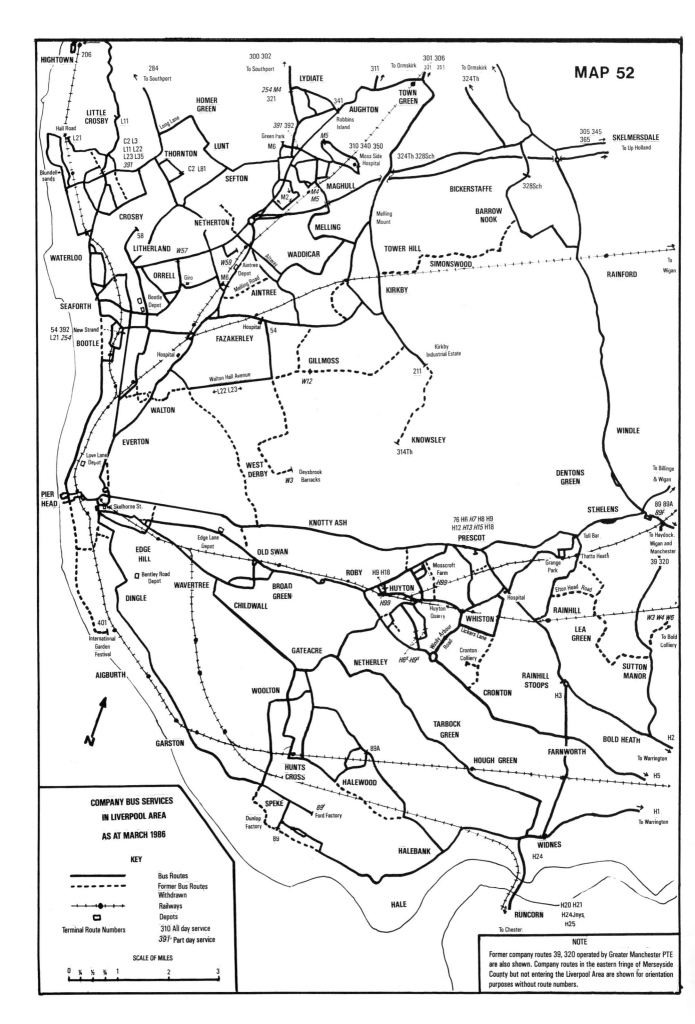

MAP 52

HIGHTOWN

206

284
To Southport

300 302
To Southport

LYDIATE

311

To Ormskirk

301 306
331 351

To Ormskirk

324Th

305 345
365

SKELMERSDALE
To Up Holland

HOMER
GREEN

254 M4
321

TOWN
GREEN

LITTLE
CROSBY

L11

Hall Road

L21

C2 L3
L11 L22
L23 L35
391

Long Lane

THORNTON

LUNT

SEFTON

391 392

Green Park
M6

AUGHTON

341

Robbins
Island

M5

310 340 350
Moss Side
Hospital

324Th 328Sch

BICKERSTAFFE

328Sch

BARROW
NOOK

Blundell
sands

C2 L81

MAGHULL

Melling
Mount

CROSBY

58

LITHERLAND

W57

NETHERTON

M2

M4
M5

MELLING

WADDICAR

TOWER HILL

SIMONSWOOD

RAINFORD

To Wigan

WATERLOO

ORRELL

Giro

W59

M6

Aintree
Depot

Melling Road

Altway

AINTREE

KIRKBY

SEAFORTH

Bootle
Depot

Hospital

54

Kirkby
Industrial Estate

211

WINDLE

54 392
L21 254

New Strand

BOOTLE

FAZAKERLEY

Hospital

GILLMOSS

W12

Walton Hall Avenue
L22 L23

KNOWSLEY

314Th

DENTONS
GREEN

To Billinge
& Wigan

WALTON

EVERTON

Love Lane
Depot

WEST
DERBY

W3

Deysbrook
Barracks

ST.HELENS

89 89A
89F

PIER
HEAD

Skelhorne St.

KNOTTY ASH

76 H6 H7 H8 H9
H12 H13 H15 H18

To Haydock,
Wigan and Manchester

39 320

EDGE
HILL

Edge Lane
Depot

OLD SWAN

PRESCOT

Toll Bar

Thatto Heath

Bentley Road
Depot

WAVERTREE

ROBY

H9 H18

HUYTON

Mosscroft
Farm

H99

Grange
Park

Elton Head Road

RAINHILL

W3 W4 W6
To Bold
Colliery

DINGLE

BROAD
GREEN

CHILDWALL

H99

Huyton
Quarry

WHISTON

Lickers Lane

Hospital

LEA
GREEN

401

International
Garden
Festival

GATEACRE

NETHERLEY

H6ˣ H9ˣ

Windy Arbour
Road

Cronton
Colliery

CRONTON

RAINHILL
STOOPS

SUTTON
MANOR

AIGBURTH

N

WOOLTON

TARBOCK
GREEN

H3

BOLD HEATH

H2

GARSTON

89A

HOUGH GREEN

FARNWORTH

To Warrington

H5

HUNTS
CROSS

HALEWOOD

89ᶠ
Ford Factory

H1
To Warrington

SPEKE

Dunlop
Factory

89

WIDNES

H24

HALEBANK

COMPANY BUS SERVICES
IN LIVERPOOL AREA
AS AT MARCH 1986

HALE

H20 H21
H24 Jnys
H25

RUNCORN
To Chester

KEY

———	Bus Routes
- - -	Former Bus Routes Withdrawn
+++	Railways
▭	Depots

Terminal Route Numbers

310 All day service
391 Part day service

SCALE OF MILES

0 ¼ ½ ¾ 1   2   3

NOTE
Former company routes 39, 320 operated by Greater Manchester PTE
are also shown. Company routes in the eastern fringe of Merseyside
County but not entering the Liverpool Area are shown for orientation
purposes without route numbers.

were needed. In 1965, a limited stop service 211 ran between Liverpool and Pimbo Industrial Estate via Fazakerley and Kirkby. This was essentially a shift workers' service for Dunlop's 6.30am, 2.30 and 10.30pm shifts with one Saturday afternoon trip from Tawd Bridge, timed to make it possible to go shopping or attend a football match in Liverpool.

As the town spread, 201 was extended first to Tawd Bridge in 1966 then to Hall Green, Up Holland in 1968. A limited stop version of 201, numbered 221, ran at weekends from August 1967 to April 1968 when it was withdrawn for want of sufficient patronage. In May 1972, the Skelmersdale services were again recast, 201 being diverted through Gillibrands Industrial Estate on Mondays to Fridays as 205 with an additional hourly service, 245, running via Altway and Tanhouse. At weekends 201 was retained and 245 was replaced by 241 which followed the same route but ran non-stop between Melling and the outskirts of Skelmersdale, saving five minutes. Together, 201/241 or 205/245 provided approximately a half-hourly service throughout the day.

At the same time, 211 was renumbered 265 and another limited stop variant, 266, appeared, operating between Liverpool and Tanhouse once on Mondays to Fridays and four times on Saturdays. This service left the normal Ribble route at Walton Church and ran via Queens Drive, Walton Hall Avenue, East Lancs Road and Kirkby town centre. It was one-man operated from the start.

On 20th October 1974, Ribble closed its Ormskirk premises and moved into a new depot at Skelmersdale which now had a network of local services.

It is not known if the PTE played a part in the decision to renumber the Skelmersdale services in the 300 series. At this time, the planners wanted to get rid of the L-prefixed numbers and favoured a series starting at 201 (see Chapter 51). According to the 'rules' of the Ribble route number scheme when it was devised in 1938, 200+ numbers had no place in Liverpool, their rightful place being East Lancashire.

On 2nd March 1975 all these services were renumbered as follows:-

205 to 305, 245 to 345, 265 to 335 and 266 to 336 and two-

hourly 345 journeys were rerouted via Fazakerley and Kirkby as 355. The limited stop weekend journeys (241) were discontinued.

Services now remained undisturbed until the great economy drive in October 1978 when 336 and 355 were withdrawn and replaced by 395-6 between Skelmersdale and Kirkby Town Centre, and extra journeys on 345. This attempt to divert passengers to rail failed as there was very little time saved. In fact, following the opening of the M58 motorway, some trips on 305 and 345 were replaced, in September 1980, by a new 'Timesaver' 705 on which some trips continued beyond Skelmersdale to Parbold. Less than three months later, 395-6 and most journeys on 305 were withdrawn and a new 365 commenced running between Liverpool and Skelmersdale via Aintree village, Fazakerley and Kirkby, this being made possible by the strengthening of Wango Lane bridge over the canal.

Service 705 suffered various changes; it reached Blackpool via Chorley in the 1981 season and had a Pier Head extension for a time. However, it became a permanent part of the network with a normal terminus at Ashurst, on the northern perimeter of the New Town, and peak hour trips to Parbold and, in due course, received revenue support from the PTE.

The underlying trend was for the ties between Skelmersdale and Liverpool to diminish; it was much nearer to Wigan which had an attractive market able to satisfy most of the needs of the inhabitants.

Lancashire United

On 27th April 1974 there was a tripartite regional exchange of routes. Ribble gave up its share in the Liverpool-St. Helens routes 39, 317 and 320 in favour of Lancashire United in return for the latter's interest in several express

The changing face of the inner city suburbs is typified by the new University buildings in Oxford Street beneath which passes Lancashire United Guy Arab V 163 with 73-seat forward-entrance Northern Counties body *en route* from Wigan in May 1969.

services. Ribble contracted to run certain journeys on 317 and 320 on behalf of LUT in order to balance mileage worked on other joint services but these ceased about the end of 1974, the Ribble licence being surrendered early in 1975. Crosville took over a group of local routes in Warrington which could be worked much more economically from their depot in the town than from LUT's Atherton depot. The LUT mileage on the St. Helens routes in the old PT area was deemed to be part of Ribble's share of the Area services as the transfer had been foreseen at the time the 1972 Agreement was drawn up.

With the inclusion of an enlarged St. Helens in Merseyside from 1st April 1974, the county boundary extended to Newton-le-Willows and a number of Lancashire United local services came into the Passenger Transport Area. Most of these crossed the county line into the neighbouring Greater Manchester PT Area so the situation was complicated. Eventually an agency agreement was made with Lancashire United Transport Ltd. on 31st December 1975 but in this case there was no guaranteed mileage clause.

Meanwhile the St. Helens group of routes underwent many minor changes. In 1973 the traditional 'back street' route along Oxford Street, Chatham Place and Jubilee Drive was replaced by a better route along Brownlow Hill, Edge Lane and Holt Road, returning via Towerlands Street and there were other small alterations to fit in with traffic schemes.

When the new Central Bus Station opened in Liverpool on 17th March 1974, all three services were moved there from neighbouring South John Street which was due for eventual closure to make room for the new law courts. They remained there until 1st June 1980 when stands in the bus station had to be found for the new Kirkby services.

For one day only, 2nd June, they went back to South John Street and then moved to a new stand in Old Haymarket. At first they left via St. Johns Lane but were soon diverted to call at Hood Street Gyratory. In March 1986, in furtherance of another traffic management scheme, Old Haymarket ceased to be used as a terminus and 39 and 320 were moved to Whitechapel though the following year they were back in the Central Bus Station.

The 317 Liverpool-St. Helens time-tabled journeys were withdrawn in January 1979 in the face of declining traffic and competition from the half-hourly dmu rail service and thereafter there was a basic hourly service to both Wigan and Manchester. The various colliery workings had been converted to contracts and the need for them gradually diminished as the St. Helens pits ran down. W3 may have run until 15th March 1986 when Bold Colliery closed. The number was still to be seen on a stop sign at Mann Island until around that time.

The day after the Merseyside PTE's agreement with LUT was signed, the company became a wholly-owned subsidiary of Greater Manchester PTE and on 1st April 1981 Lancashire United was completely absorbed. In the St. Helens district, this resulted in one PTE giving revenue support to the buses of another PTE in its own area but the routes to and from Liverpool were not in this category.

Wigan Corporation 130, a Leyland PD2A/27 with 64-seat forward-entrance Northern Counties body, awaits departure time in South John Street, Liverpool. The livery was light maroon and white and the two green lights either side of the destination indicator were reminders of the days when such distinguishing features were used to identify buses of competing operators. In 1974 this bus became No.3248 in the Greater Manchester PTE fleet.

THE COMPANY BUS FLEETS

Ribble

Up to 1955, Ribble's double-deck fleet consisted predominantly of low height vehicles with a side gangway and rows of four seats on the upper deck. Some highbridge buses had been bought in the immediate post-war years and older buses had been rebodied in a similar style by Burlingham about the same time. Many of these were used on Merseyside. The lowbridge policy had been dictated by a number of low bridges at strategic places on the company's route network, together with Ribble's practice of devising long stage carriage routes which took buses far from their home depots. The most troublesome bridges were at Preston, Garstang and Coppull but none of these affected the majority of Merseyside services. Experience of the post-war buses had emphasised the greater comfort of the highbridge bus, the improvement in the speed of fare collection and faster loading and unloading times. Many disused railway bridges were being demolished and the company's policy changed to providing lowbridge buses only on routes that needed them. However, there were still hundreds of lowbridge buses in the fleet, mainly all-Leyland PD2s with 53-seat bodies of which 80 had platform doors. By 1962 only three, all without doors, remained at Aintree. Rebodied pre-war TD4s and TD5s with Alexander and Eastern Coach Works bodies remained in service until 1961 and the general type was not extinct until 1967.

In 1955 Ribble took delivery of 120 Leyland PD2/12s (1381-1500), the body order being split between Burlingham and Metropolitan-Cammell Carriage and Wagon Co. All seated 61 passengers and, in each case, there were open back and enclosed platform versions though only five of the Burlinghams lacked doors. The all-metal Metro-Cammell bodies had very clean lines externally, though the interiors lacked trim; the doors, where fitted, were of the four-leaf folding type. By contrast, the composite-bodied Burlinghams had a rather fussier appearance, their doors being of the two piece sliding type whereby the rear section travelled at twice the speed of the front part. Doors could be controlled from the platform or the cab. A large part of the Merseyside fleet was made up of buses of this type from mid-1955 onwards.

Following the relaxation of regulations in 1956 to permit 30ft long double-deckers on two axles, Ribble saw an opportunity to increase its load factor and reduce duplication by adopting a 72-seat vehicle with a fully fronted forward entrance body to facilitate supervision of loading by the driver. Ribble general manager Horace Bottomley was so confident of the success of this type of vehicle that he ordered 105 on Leyland PD3/4 chassis. The Burlingham bodies seated 41/31 and were fitted with a one-piece sliding door which opened and closed with a resounding thump. They had sliding windows and 27 of the batch were equipped for illuminated offside advertisements though, like many other operators, the company had difficulty in selling all the space available. The first (1501), which arrived in September 1957, was

Ribble 2569, an all-Leyland PD2/3 was one of a large batch of lowbridge buses placed in service in 1948; they were the first 8ft.-wide buses in the Ribble fleet. By the time this picture was taken in Aintree depot yard in November 1957 there were very few lowbridge vehicles at work in Liverpool. No.2569 was withdrawn in 1962 and sold for further service in Scotland. The train on the embankment behind has just left Aintree station for Ormskirk and Preston.

Ribble Leyland PD2/12 1497 with MCCW 61-seat body, leaves Carisbrooke Road, Walton on the joint service 52 to Sefton whilst Corporation Regent A244 prepares to depart for Penny Lane on ex-tram route 46 in July 1966. The Ribble bus was already ten years old but continued in service for another five years. The office block is part of the rebuilt Corporation Walton garage. Compare this picture with the photograph on page 67 of Volume 4.

inevitably tested on the busy L3 route and from the end of that year the 72-seaters started to replace the PD2s on the Crosby and Ormskirk Road routes but not on the Bootle joint routes which retained their 61-seaters until the Corporation was in a position to contribute vehicles of equal capacity. Perhaps each party was waiting for the other as rear entrance buses remained on these routes until PTE days. By January 1962, there were 51 PD3s on Merseyside — 15 at Aintree, 26 at Bootle and 10 at Liverpool; this increased to 25, 56 and 14 respectively by July 1966.

Ribble's next double-deck deliveries were PDR1 Atlanteans (1606-1705). Number 1630 was sent to Aintree depot in February 1960 and was soon joined by 1629 but the company decided to standardise on PD3s on Merseyside and the following year further PD2s were displaced by a batch of PD3/5s with Metro-Cammell bodies. These were to the same layout as their predecessors except that they had Pneumocyclic gearboxes, as fitted to the Atlanteans and the emergency door was at the offside instead of centrally at the rear; they were also 8ft. 2½in. (2m) wide, the extra width being given to the gangways. The reversion to PD3s was influenced by the teething troubles with the first Atlanteans and there were never more than three PDR1s at Aintree.

A combination of examples of the two batches made up most of the Merseyside area fleet until the seventies, the 1501 class being withdrawn between 1971 and 1976. The last Burlingham-bodied PD2 was not withdrawn at Bootle depot until the end of 1974.

Few single-deck buses were needed on Merseyside, though the weight restriction on Ledson's Bridge at Waddicar meant that routes 201, 301 and 307 were single deck for many years though Ormskirk depot contributed at least one vehicle. Two of Ribble's standard all-Leyland 44-seat Leyland PSU1 Royal Tiger buses, based at Aintree were the only single-deck service buses working from the Merseyside depots until the early sixties when the 36ft.-long Marshall-bodied 53-seat saloons on PSU3 Leopard chassis started to come into the fleet. They were little used on Merseyside and, nationwide, the Transport and General Workers' union refused to accept them for one-man operation, saying that their capacity was equal to many lowbridge double-deckers still in the fleet. Some buses had eight seats removed to bring them down to the 45-seat limit imposed by the unions but in 1966-67 the company purchased 55 PSU4s which were 30ft 10in long and had

Ribble took delivery of 100 Leyland PDR1/1 Atlanteans between November 1959 and April 1961, all with 78-seat MCCW all-metal bodies. Seen in Skelhorne Street in February 1960, 1630 had been delivered only the previous month and was one of only two to be permanently based on Merseyside. The first generation Ribble Atlanteans were rarely seen in Liverpool. Bus 1630 was sold to a dealer in 1973.

Service L3 between Liverpool and Crosby via Litherland and Waterloo was reputed to be one of the busiest on Ribble's vast network which, at that time, extended from the Solway to the Mersey. The Leyland PD3/5s with 72-seat full-fronted MCCW bodies were 8ft. 2½in. wide and worked the route almost exclusively for several years. No.1764 is seen in Linacre Road soon after delivery in 1962. It had obviously been used for express duplication the previous weekend, (probably to Blackpool), as the running number label with Bootle depot code CL is still affixed to the windscreen. The bus was withdrawn from service in 1973.

only 44 seats in a Marshall body of very similar appearance to the 36ft long PSU3s. They were equipped for one-man operation with a small reversing window in the centre of the rear panel. One (645) replaced a Royal Tiger at Aintree in 1966 and by 1970, there were five PSU3s and one PSU4 in the area. Many PSU4s were withdrawn early from Ribble service when larger vehicles could be used for driver-only operation; some went to Cumberland and others to the Isle of Man.

As Ribble staff would not at first agree to work one-man buses with more than 44 or 45 seats, the company bought 55 short Leyland Leopard PSU4s of which Marshall bodied 645, new in June 1966, is seen two years later turning from Skelhorne Street into Bolton Street, beside the bus station. These buses were specially equipped for one-man-operation and had a small window in the rear panel to assist reversing. No.645 was burnt out in 1971.

Ribble placed 108 of these all-Leyland Royal Tiger 44-seat buses in service in 1952 and sufficient of them were based at Aintree depot to supply the routes which crossed the weak canal bridge at Waddicar though, as shown here, they sometimes strayed on to other routes too. Bus 390 was withdrawn in 1966 and sold to the Ulster Transport Authority together with several others of the same type. After passing into the fleet of Ulsterbus upon its formation the following year, it became a towing vehicle in 1971 and was finally scrapped in 1973.

The NBC Era

Following the renewed availability of the marque on the open market, 10 Bristol RELL6Ls with Leyland engines and dual-door Eastern Coach Works bodies, entered service at Bootle in September 1968 for use on routes L1 and L8 and the newly introduced Crosby internal circulars. They had 41-seats and, when new, were licensed for 31 standees though this was later reduced to 25. Ribble's one-man operation agreements were based on five standing passengers so these capacities were irrelevant at that time. A few of the short length Bristol RESLs with 47-seat Eastern Coach Works bodies were stationed at Aintree; they worked various duties including the Maghull locals and were still in service on route 54 in 1984. This was the only restricted headroom route with low bridges at Old Roan Station and Irlam Road. The same type of vehicle worked locally in Formby but from Southport depot. The order was placed in the BET era as, following a share exchange with Leyland, Bristol/ECW products had been available outside the nationalised Group since 1965.

Ribble and Crosville were among the first NBC operators to acquire Leyland Nationals, the characteristics of which are described in Chapter 53. The majority were of the 11.3m length and the early models (some of which arrived in Ribble cherry red but were repainted poppy red before entering service) had twin doors. They arrived with 44 seats but were quickly reseated to 48. However the company, like the PTE, decided that two doors were unnecessary and contributed to boarding and alighting accidents, and there was soon standardisation on 49-seat single door bodies. Ribble used few Nationals in Liverpool, two National 2s arriving at Bootle about 1981.

No two-door double-deckers were acquired, the first one-man double-deckers being Bristol VRs with 70-seat Eastern Coach Works bodies, delivered in 1972. Some of the older Atlanteans were converted for one-man operation but in Liverpool, progress awaited the arrival of AN68/1R Atlanteans with Park Royal bodies to NBC specification, numbered from 1301. By early 1975, there were 43 of these in service — 14 at Aintree, 26 at Bootle and three at Liverpool. At this time, Ribble had 162 vehicles (excluding coaches) at the Merseyside depots (Aintree 52, Bootle 93 and Liverpool 17), compared to 135 in 1962. The fleet was again reduced to the latter figure by 1981.

With a length of 30ft. 9in., the AN68s were of four-bay construction with 43 seats on the upper deck, 30 below and provision for 20 standees. The usual side seats inside the door were replaced by a luggage pen with another in the stairwell and the rear wheelarch seats were back to back as on PTE buses. The interior sides, ceilings and seat backs were covered with plastic laminates while the forward ascending staircase, driver's cab and side panel were structurally integrated in one prefabricated unit. The driver's position was 10in. higher than normal, the gearshift being pedestal-mounted on the left side. Inward opening weatherproof tilt windows provided adequate ventilation and there was a cab periscope. Externally, the double curvature windscreen was of Alexander pattern; the lower front square cut panels were detachable. There

were black masked destination glasses and a mixture of large and small route numbers within batches.

As these buses arrived, there was a massive clear-out of PD3s and the final PD2s from Merseyside, sufficient being retained for working the remaining crew-operated routes though some AN68s ran with conductors towards the end of crew operation. The numbers reduced gradually until final withdrawal of the last six PD3s at Bootle depot on 26th September 1981 when routes 58 and 351 were converted. A batch of 30 AN68Bs (1486-1515) replaced the PD3s during 1980-81.

Later Atlanteans had the full height version of the standard five bay Eastern Coach Works bodies fitted to the Bristol VRs of which only two ran on Merseyside, 1972 examples 1986-7 being chosen as Ribble's contribution to the Garden Festival bus services in 1984.

Ribble's share in the joint St. Helens-Speke service 89 when it first started was 8% and it was never anticipated that it would ever operate on it. Leyland National 716 with 49-seat single-door body was ten years old when seen in Grange Park, St. Helens in March 1986 after Ribble buses from Wigan depot had replaced Crosville on the service.

(Lower left) Some of the Park Royal-bodied Ribble Atlanteans were equipped with the large route numbers which had been in use for many years and were much more visible from a distance. Bus 1384 and another of the same type are dwarfed by the Dock Office and Cunard Building whilst taking lie-over at George's Dock Way in June 1984.

(Below) Ribble 1421 was one of the 32 Atlanteans with five-bay Eastern Coach Works 74-seat bodies delivered in 1976. It is passing Lime Street Station, carrying both NBC and PTE logos, having just left St. Johns Lane for the Old Roan in 1984, though the driver has forgotten to set the indicator.

North Western

In August and early September 1986 there was a considerable movement of vehicles between Ribble depots in order that the buses should be in the right places when the company was split. The fleet allocated to the Merseyside depots of North Western more than doubled on deregulation as shown by the following 'before' and 'after' figures:-

	Before (as at 5.10.86)	After (as at 2.11.86)
Bristol REs	5	1
Leyland Nationals & 2s	6	14
Leyland Atlanteans	34	66
Leyland Olympians	9	19
Mercedes Benz minibuses	-	20
TOTAL	54	120

By April 1990, the total had further increased to 159.

Crosville

Unlike the BET companies, which were free to develop their own vehicle policies, Crosville, as a member of the nationalised Tilling group, was governed by the centralised policies of the British Transport Commission. The days of second-hand vehicles and extensive rebodying, though never very noticeable in high-profile Liverpool, were also over and Crosville used the products of Bristol Commercial Vehicles and Eastern Coach Works, both members of the group and prohibited by the Transport Act 1947 from selling their products to outsiders. The K type double-deckers of orthodox layout remained in the company's fleet in diminishing numbers until the late sixties but were rarely seen in Liverpool where the Lodekka, with its 13ft 2in overall height and roomy upper deck layout, became the standard workhorse. It was a rugged, durable and economical bus with a good standard of interior finish and examples of the type in standardised liveries could be seen all over the country quite literally from the Scottish border to Penzance. With few exceptions, Crosville Lodekkas were powered by the Bristol BVW or Gardner 6LW engine and batches were frequently mixed.

In 1958 both the fleet and route numbering systems were changed, the latter influencing the destination equipment layout. The new fleet numbering scheme adopted elements of systems used by other ex-Tilling companies, comprising a three letter prefix and a number. There were two numerical series, one for single-deckers and one for double-deckers; the first prefix letter indicated the type of vehicle, the second the chassis and the third the engine. Thus all double-deckers were D (until 1980 when H was introduced for highbridge), but single-deckers were sub-divided into S (ordinary bus), E (express bus or dual purpose) and C (coach). Thus, when a vehicle batch included buses with different engines, the prefixes would vary e.g. DLB—a Lodekka with a Bristol engine or DLG with a Gardner engine. If a single-deck vehicle was downgraded, the first letter would change but the remainder would not. thus CMG to EMG.

The 1958-59 vehicles were fitted with two-leaf hand operated doors and thereafter rear platform doors became universal on all new deliveries. The last LD6s, which entered service in 1960, were the first with hopper windows and the Cave-Brown-Cave heating system, with which Crosville had been experimenting since 1957. It was a forced air system, the radiators being fitted between decks on either side of the front destination indicators with exit vents in the side panels. Some buses had no dummy radiator grille in the conventional position but these were later fitted for purely cosmetic reasons.

In 1960, the LD series of Lodekkas gave place to the FS series ('flat-floor short') which externally differed little from the LD. However, the transmission was modified to give a completely flat floor on the lower deck instead of just a sunken gangway, and air suspension was fitted. Crosville's classification was DFB or DFG. The range was augmented in 1961 by the FLF ('flat floor long front entrance') which had a noticeably more upright front. It was 30ft. long and had a forward entrance with four-part power operated doors. The ECW body seated 70, 38 of them on the upper deck, and Crosville continued to take delivery of both types until 1966.

Variety was provided by Lodekka coaches for the North Wales coast services. Periodically, as a new batch arrived, the older ones were downgraded to express buses and Liverpool depot had examples of both LD and FLF models in this category. They retained their coach seats and exchanged Huyton and Prescot for Llandudno at weekends.

A fleet of new FLFs with semi-automatic transmission replaced some of the older Lodekkas in Liverpool in 1968 and these were the last new front-engined buses to enter service locally until the PTE's Volvo Ailsas in 1982. In the same year, Crosville's vehicle policy changed to single-deck only though there was little demand for such vehicles in Liverpool. In 1971-72 the company purchased 100 Gardner-engined Seddon RU single-deck buses with bodies by the manufacturer of which half were 45-seat dual door (SPG class) and half were 47-seat dual purpose (EPG class). Seddon, which had a substantial export market, enjoyed brief popularity on the home market but its products did not have a long life in the Crosville fleet, many being withdrawn in 1980-81. The EPGs were used for the conversion of routes H12-13 to one-man operation and were initially fitted with Fare Boxes though these were eventually replaced by Setright machines after the PTE complained of poor revenue control with this ticketless system on multi-fare routes. Standard Bristol REs were also used on one-man operated routes.

During 1972, three Bristol SC4LK forward-engined, full fronted 35-seaters (SSG class), purchased in 1957 for lightly trafficked routes, ran in Liverpool with full crews.

Roby still had the air of a tranquil village in September 1964 when these two Crosville Lodekkas were photographed. The Liverpool-bound bus on route H12 from Prescot is DLG789, an LD new in 1956 while DFG26, en route to Warrington via Cronton, is a 1960 FS6G, fitted with the Cave-Brown-Cave heating system. Note the blanked out rear destination box on the LD.

In 1960, the LD series of Lodekka gave way to the first of the FS series with completely flat floor in the lower saloon. DFG37 was fitted with the Cave-Brown-Cave heating system, the vents for which are visible alongside the destination display and on the front of the upper-deck side panels but this one was unusual in having practically no radiator grille. Note the illuminated advertisement panel. The vehicle of almost identical appearance behind is a 1959 LD6G, DLG4.

Bristol Lodekka FLF6B DFB149 was the first of five 55-seat double-deck coaches which entered service in 1964 for express services to the North Wales coast. They were downgraded and repainted green and cream in 1968, retaining their coach seats, and used on local services during the week. Note the illuminated fleet name and the disused advertising panel. The lower-deck seated only 18 passengers with plenty of luggage room at the rear. The bus was parked in Mann Island above the workings of the Loop line, as indicated by the Merseyrail Underground signboard.

These had very economical 3.8-litre Gardner 4LK engines but were quite inadequate for Liverpool traffic. Their presence was due to a top management directive to several depots to lend double-deck buses to handle the summer traffic at Rhyl. The SSGs were used indiscriminately on double-deck duties in Liverpool but the exercise was not repeated in subsequent years. On Route H5, Warrington depot occasionally supplied one of the vehicles transferred from the old Stockport-based North Western Road Car Co Ltd when that company was broken up in 1972. Thus a Park Royal-bodied AEC Renown or an Alexander-bodied Daimler Fleetline would occasionally appear in the city.

While the Lodekka was a trouble free vehicle, it was unsuitable for one-man operation and, after the signing of the PTE/NBC agreement in January 1972, the PTE showed increasing signs of impatience at Crosville's lack of progress in the one-man double-deck field. Several Leyland Nationals entered service, Crosville passing through the same cycle of experience as Ribble, rejecting two-door 44-seaters in favour of single-door 48 or 49 seaters. The 1973-74 orders included many dual purpose vehicles, several of which ran on service in Liverpool, mostly from Runcorn depot, giving a very comfortable ride. Finally, in the second half of 1974, in response to PTE pressure, nine rear engined Bristol VRs were temporarily diverted from Potteries Motor Traction Co. (PMT) to Crosville. They arrived new in Crosville livery but with PMT as the legal owner and were given the temporary fleet numbers DVG610-8. In March 1975 the first Crosville VRs arrived, being shared by Liverpool, Warrington and Heswall depots and, following a fire at PMT's Newcastle depot, their nine buses were hastily recalled being partially replaced by Ribble 1301 and 1369 on hire. Typically, Crosville produced a new class designation and renumbered them DAL701 and 769.

The Bristol VRT was the NBC's answer to the Atlantean and Fleetline. It had a 74-seat Eastern Coach Works body and rear mounted transverse engine, the early in-line version (VRL) having proved troublesome. Like all rear-engined buses, it had its idiosyncrasies but, because of its single-deck policy, Crosville missed many of these problems, the first of its vehicles being Mk IIs. The 1975 VRs (DVG class) had Gardner 6LX or 6LXB engines but, from 1976, the Leyland 501 was fitted (DVL class). Following the big one-man conversion programme of 1979, most of the Lodekkas in Liverpool were replaced by VRs but seven remained until March 1981 to work H1 and 76.

In 1980, Crosville purchased a number of second-hand VRs and Fleetlines of which a few operated in Liverpool. One of six VRs with East Lancs bodies, bought from South Yorkshire PTE and three of 30 Fleetlines from Southdown, were used on a contract service between Lime Street Station and the Dublin steamers and also, after the move to Love Lane, to ferry drivers to and from Mann Island. Two ex-Southdown Fleetlines with 71-seat Northern Counties bodies (HDG910/4), dating from 1970, were used as Garden Festival buses in 1984, with ex-South Yorkshire VR HVG933 as standby. Immediately prior to

The Bristol SC4LK 35-seat vehicles with 4-cylinder Gardner engines were purchased in 1957 for use on rural routes in Wales. In the summer of 1972, several Crosville depots were instructed to lend double-deckers to Rhyl for the summer traffic in exchange for these small buses which, nevertheless, were used on double-deck duties. SSG606 (originally SC6), seen at Mann Island in July 1972, was one of three operated in Liverpool. Note the lower case fleet name.

Dual-purpose Leyland Nationals were favoured by Crosville for one-man operation and ENL827, with 48 coach seats, is seen leaving Mann Island when new in October 1973, *en route* to Prescot via Windy Arbour Road, though the H prefix to the route number is missing. The dual-purpose livery was a great improvement on the plain green bus livery.

On a busy day extra buses were provided for the Garden Festival services and HVG931 is seen at the Festival exit on 8th Sept.1984. This was one of six 1972 Bristol VRs with 73-seat East Lancs bodies, new to Sheffield Transport Dept. and purchased third-hand from South Yorkshire PTE in 1980.

deregulation, the fleet at Love Lane comprised 65 vehicles of which 50 were VRs. This was destined to be substantially augmented but, sadly, only briefly, as related in Chapter 56.

In the mid-eighties, Crosville embarked on a major programme of replacing the Leyland engines in the early Nationals with Gardner 6LXBs, thereby extending the vehicle life.

Lancashire United

The jointly licensed services to Wigan and Manchester were dominated by Lancashire United buses after the territorial exchanges in April 1974 and, from time to time, there was a strange mix of coaches and double-deck buses on the 39 route. SELNEC PTE lent a batch of Eastern Coach Works bodied Leyland Leopard coaches (86-91, KDB 673-8P) to LUT in November 1975 for use on the 39 and associated routes. They had two-leaf doors with sensitive edges so that they opened if anything was trapped. A conductress was thrown against a door and fell out and the whole batch was withdrawn while centre stanchions were fitted. LUT's own Plaxton-bodied Leopards with 48 bus seats also saw service on the route from the late seventies and all the Northern Counties bodied Guy Arabs had gone by 1980.

LUT Fleetlines carried on the Northern Counties tradition, the later models being Leylands rather than Daimlers and, after the merger with Greater Manchester PTE in April 1981, the same vehicles were used for a time being gradually superseded by standard PTE Atlanteans in the orange and brown livery with the 'M' logo.

Lancashire United Leyland Fleetline 575, with Northern Counties body, new in 1979, bears the Greater Manchester PTE 'M' logo when seen at Old Haymarket in July 1980. Less than a year later, it was to become 6952 in the GMPTE fleet when the company was finally wound up.

Leaving the Central Bus Station in March 1979, Lancashire United 460, a 1976 Leyland Leopard with Plaxton 48-seat bus body, is working one of the two-hourly intermediate trips to Tyldesley on the Manchester stopping service No. 39. Its livery is red and grey and it is carrying the company's red rose emblem on the front panel.

50 THE SERVICE PATTERN

When viewed in retrospect, the period between the withdrawal of the last trams in September 1957 and the end of Liverpool Corporation operation in November 1969, a time during which passengers carried declined annually, is remarkable for the lack of change to the basic route network. Outer suburban development, as described in chapter 47, added relatively short extensions to established routes but a 1968 route map, confined within the boundaries of Liverpool, Bootle and Litherland, would have differed little from a map drawn 20 years earlier. In the fifties, much departmental time had been devoted to devising various north-south links across the city centre to avoid the need for a central bus station but traffic congestion, scheduling difficulties and minimal passenger demand resulted in their rejection.

Perhaps discouraged by the events of late 1957 when an apparently beneficial simplification of routes turned sour, the Passenger Transport Department showed no inclination to 'test the network' to see if it still met the needs of a rapidly changing situation. Techniques for origin and destination surveys were crude and unreliable, a complete network change across the Mersey at Wallasey in 1967 having had disastrous results. The government's plan to set up conurbation transport authorities was sufficient excuse to adopt a laisser faire attitude.

The reduced passenger demand and introduction of large capacity buses resulted in wider headways but it was the 11-week strike in 1968 which enforced the trimming of the services to a level which the professionals had often seen as feasible but the politicians found unacceptable. Much of the lost demand was in the inner suburbs where residential density had fallen. Routes such as the Wavertree-Smithdown Road circular 4B/5B, rooted in early tramway days, had had several longer routes superimposed and their 'temporary' withdrawal, which became permanent, caused little public inconvenience. However, many short peak hour duplicates remained.

It took some time for the nature of the changes which were taking place to be understood and analysed. The passenger demand on traditional high-frequency trunk services consisted of a multiplicity of individual desires many of which were only partially satisfied by the service. The growth of personal transport and changes in social habits removed some of these demands and, at the same time, expectations increased. These were manifest in insistence on heating and an improved interior environment but there was also a reluctance to accept a service which entailed a long walk to reach the destination. If the service could not be improved, it was often rejected altogether.

A decline in the traditional port activities and cessation of such old-established industries as sugar refining,

reduced the travel demands at all times of the day in the districts adjoining the docks. Thus between 1969 and 1975, all the former tram routes between the city centre and Seaforth disappeared in favour of diversions of longer Ribble routes. Service 16 between Pier Head and Seaforth via Vauxhall Road and Linacre Road, (which was the former Litherland tram route extended), still had a 15-20 minute frequency from 5.00am to midnight in 1974. It was reduced first to a peak hour service in 1978 and then to only two trips each way in January 1981; it disappeared completely together with the remnants of 33, Everton-Seaforth (also a former all-day tram route) in the run up to deregulation in 1986.

One-man Operation

During the seventies, the policy with the most far reaching results was undoubtedly the conversion of services to double-deck one-man operation. Each changeover involved an enormous amount of work behind the scenes — agreement on running times and terminal arrangements, application to the Traffic Commissioners for new time tables, conversion of buses, training of drivers and compilation of new schedules and publicity matter. The availability of staff and vehicles were the limiting factors but, in retrospect, the conversion was carried out remarkably quickly, as shown in Appendix 45. From 13th May 1973, the only PTE-operated all-day two-man services were the Bootle service 24 and the Ribble joint routes 55 and 56. To avoid possible conflict arising from Ribble's slow progress with one-man conversions, the pooled routes were shared out between the two operators. Thus 55/55A joined 28, 53/53A and 56 as exclusively PTE routes whilst 51, 57/57A, 58 and 59 became Ribble operated as 54 had always been.

All off-peak buses were conductorless from the changeover of 55/55A on 28th September 1975 and the remaining industrial routes were converted as staff and buses came available. At peak hours many duplicates were worked by two-man rear-entrance double-deckers, many of which had been transferred from Birkenhead, St. Helens and Southport as explained in Chapter 53. The last of these was withdrawn on 8th January 1977. One Atlantean, the experimental E2, was never converted to one-man operation and remained in service until 1978.

Inter-suburban Facilities

The orbital routes 26/27,60,61,68 and 81 continued to provide invaluable inter-suburban facilities and they

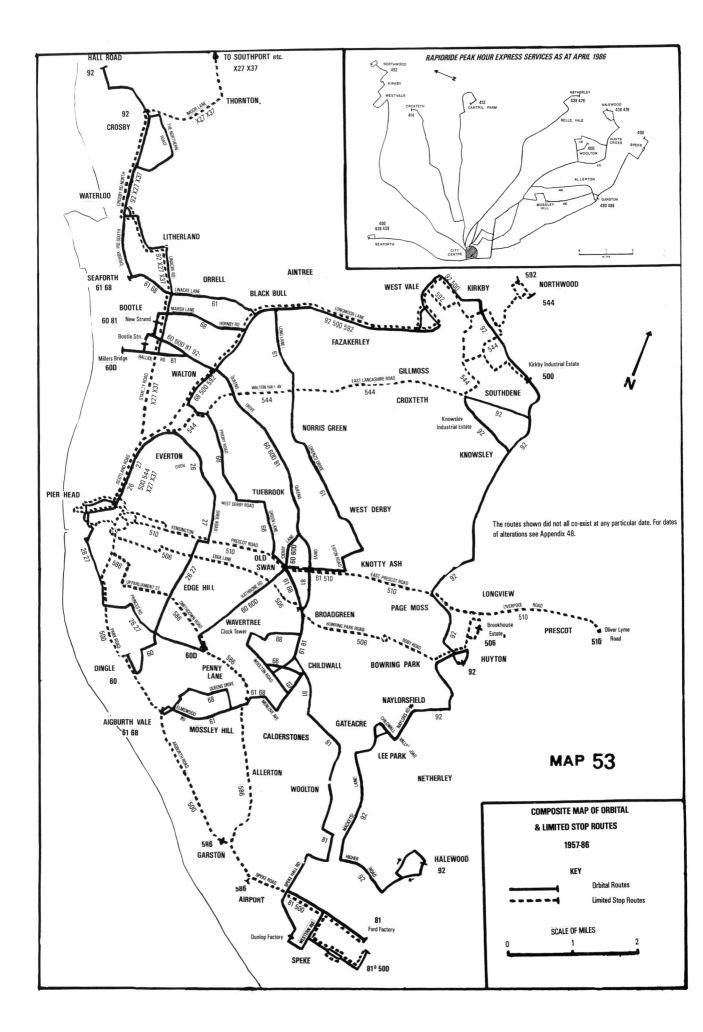

HALL ROAD
92

TO SOUTHPORT etc.
X27 X37

THORNTON

92
CROSBY

MOOR LANE
X27 X37

THE NORTHERN
ROAD

WATERLOO

CROSBY RD NORTH
92 X27 X37

LITHERLAND

92 X27 X37
61 X37

CROSBY RD SOUTH

LINACRE RD

SEAFORTH
61 68

61 68

ORRELL

AINTREE

WEST VALE

92 500

KIRKBY

592

NORTHWOOD
544

LINACRE LANE

BLACK BULL

61

LONGMOOR LANE

592

92

BOOTLE
60 81   New Strand

MARSH LANE

68   HORNBY RD

92 500 592

544

SOUTHDENE

Bootle Stn.

60 60D 81 92

LONG LANE

FAZAKERLEY

Kirkby Industrial Estate
500

Millers Bridge
60D

BALLIOL RD   81

WALTON

68 500 592

QUEENS

EAST LANCASHIRE ROAD

544

GILLMOSS

544

92

STANLEY ROAD
X27 X37

544

WALTON HALL AV
544

DRIVE

CROXTETH

Knowsley
Industrial Estate

92

EVERTON

SCOTLAND ROAD

27

ROAD

26

PRIORY ROAD
68

60 60D 81

QUEENS

NORRIS GREEN

LORENZO DRIVE

61

KNOWSLEY

92

500 544
X27 X37

PIER HEAD

26

TUEBROOK

WEST DERBY ROAD

SHEIL ROAD

GREEN LANE
68

WEST DERBY

KENSINGTON

27

510

506

PRESCOT ROAD

510

EDGE LANE

OLD SWAN

ABBEY ROAD
60 60D

DERBY

EATON ROAD

DRIVE

KNOTTY ASH

EAST PRESCOT ROAD

92

26 27

586

UP.PARLIAMENT ST.

26 27

EDGE HILL

RATHBONE RD

60 60D

61 68

81

61 510

510

PAGE MOSS

LONGVIEW

LIVERPOOL   ROAD

510

PRESCOT

Oliver Lyme
Road
510

PRINCES RD

586

SMITHDOWN ROAD

506

BROADGREEN

BOWRING PARK ROAD

506

ROBY ROAD

Brookhouse
Estate
506

DINGLE
60

500

PARK ROAD

26 27

60

60D

596

WAVERTREE
Clock Tower

68

68

61 68

81

CHILDWALL

BOWRING PARK

92

HUYTON

92

AIGBURTH VALE
61 68

AIGBURTH ROAD

586

ELMSWOOD RD

61

PENNY LANE

QUEENS DRIVE

68

MOSSLEY HILL

WOOLTON ROAD

MENLOVE AVE

61

61 68

81

GATEACRE

NAYLORSFIELD

CHILDWALL   VALLEY ROAD

NAYLORS RD

92

CALDERSTONES

500

586

ALLERTON

WOOLTON

81

LEE PARK

NETHERLEY

MAP 53

586
GARSTON

500

81

MACKETS   LANE

92

HIGHER   ROAD

92

HALEWOOD
92

SPEKE ROAD

586
AIRPORT

81 500

WESTERN AVE

81
Ford Factory

Dunlop Factory

SPEKE

81 9 500

COMPOSITE MAP OF ORBITAL
& LIMITED STOP ROUTES
1957-86

KEY

Orbital Routes

Limited Stop Routes

SCALE OF MILES
0   1   2

The routes shown did not all co-exist at any particular date. For dates
of alterations see Appendix 48.

RAPIDRIDE PEAK HOUR EXPRESS SERVICES AS AT APRIL 1986

NORTHWOOD
492

KIRKBY

WESTVALE

CROXTETH
414

CANTRIL FARM
412

NETHERLEY
439 479

HALEWOOD
438 478

BELLE VALE

HUNTS
CROSS

SPEKE

400

436
405
WOOLTON

478

ALLERTON

488

MOSSLEY
HILL

480

GARSTON
480 486

400
438 439

SEAFORTH

CITY
CENTRE

MILES

N

94

Prototype Atlantean E2 was the only one of its type in the Liverpool Corporation fleet to carry the standard Metropolitan-Cammell-Weymann body. It is seen at Trafalgar Dock augmenting the regular buses used on the Irish boat feeder service. Note the nineteenth century road surface in the foreground.

underwent only minor changes, such as the diversion of 60 and 81 from Bootle Station to New Strand, described elsewhere. The growth of a ring of new outer suburbs created a demand for new links even further out from the city centre. The long route 92, Pagemoss, Knowsley, Kirkby, Fazakerley, Walton and Pier Head, was curtailed to run between Pagemoss and Walton (Spellow Lane) only, in September 1971. Its variants, 92A, 92B and 93, continued to run through to the city but at peak hours only and simultaneously the limited stop 592 was abandoned in favour of Rapidride 492.

In May 1973, 92 was diverted at Queens Drive to run to New Strand at first via Merton Road but within two months this was changed to Balliol Road. On 29th November 1974, in an extraordinary act of empire building, the 92 was extended at both ends to run between Crosby, Hall Road and Huyton Town Centre, without any corresponding reduction in existing services. The decision to run to Hall Road, situated in an exclusive district with high car ownership, rather than terminate in Crosby bus station, was probably taken in order to avoid any confrontation with Ribble crews as was the retention of the existing Crosby-Hall Road facilities given by Ribble routes L47-48 which were more than adequate for the district. But the half-hourly 92, the PTE's longest route, had a running time of exactly 1 hour and no canteen facilities at either end. Furthermore the residents objected to Atlanteans being parked outside their highly-rated properties for the official 16-minute lie-over period, which was often unofficially extended.

The PTE would send out an elderly PD2 with a tea-urn and park it outside the railway workshops, to the west of Hall Road level crossing, where the lie-over was taken. Matters were made worse when the residents of the various council estates *en route* discovered that there was a seaside promenade close to the end of the 92 and travelled

in large numbers at summer weekends in 1975-76. Sometimes there were three Atlanteans at the Hall Road terminus simultaneously. The canteen problem was solved by the PTE presenting a refrigerator to the railway canteen in return for allowing the bus drivers to share the facilities.

The 92 route was diverted through the Knowsley (South) industrial estate in December 1975 and curtailed at Crosby Bus Station in the big upheaval on 10th January 1977. At the same time it was rerouted via Knowsley Road instead of Bridge Road and Linacre Road and diverted via Waterloo Interchange; it was further rerouted in Crosby via The Northern Road in October 1978. A supplementary service (92C) between Huyton and Bootle doubled the frequency over this section at busy times. From 2nd June 1980, hourly journeys were extended from Huyton to Halewood via Gateacre, Woolton and Hunts Cross and this was to be the 92 route's fullest extent as, after deregulation, it was split into two sections, the northern part combining with the former 99 to give a Crosby-Penny Lane service (92) and the southern half running as a subsidised route 192 between Kirkby and Halewood.

The PTE's continuous systematic analysis of passenger demand, particularly after the development of the SCRAM techniques, and the detailed surveys of specific areas, resulted in several major revisions, details of which will be found in Appendix 48.

There was a tendency to create longer routes which, in general, use crews and buses more efficiently. Thus in a major rescheduling exercise from 4th September 1978, two ex-tram routes, 3 Dingle-Walton and 85 Garston-City via Mill Street were merged as 85 Garston-Walton and 11 was extended from Huyton back to Cantril Farm to form a curious question mark shaped route.

The PTE endeavoured to negotiate productivity deals with the staff but was successful only at Green Lane depot. Under one of these deals, from 7th October 1984 two new circular services were formed by joining the outer termini of routes 12 and 12C and 17D and 18D. The Lowerhouse Lane circular was numbered 7D clockwise (via Scotland Road, Everton Valley, Utting Avenue. Townsend Avenue, Lowerhouse Lane, Muirhead Avenue and West Derby Road) and 8D anti-clockwise., On Saturdays the service ran via Lord Street instead of Dale Street/Tithebarn Street as 7 and 8. The Cantril Farm (later Stockbridge Village) circular was formed by linking the Pagemoss terminus of 12/12A with the Cantril Farm terminus of 12C; this produced a somewhat complex arrangement with clockwise buses numbered 12 (via Deysbrook Lane) or 12A (via Leyfield Road) with anti-clockwise buses showing 13 or 13A. Sir Thomas Street was abandoned as a terminus, routes 12A and 75 being extended to the Pier Head. The 7D/8D circular was withdrawn entirely at the end of June 1986 when the 12A/13A circulars experienced some unsuccessful rerouting via Queens Drive. Eventually they were withdrawn on weekday evenings and all day Sunday being replaced at these times by 22A/23A, operating via Muirhead Avenue, Queens Drive, Alder Road and Honeysgreen Lane. This arrangement ceased on deregulation day.

Community Services

The concept of services designed to penetrate deeply into residential areas instead of keeping to the main arteries had been developed in Wallasey in the sixties, using vehicles with 13-19 seats and the PTA explored the idea as a means of improving the amenities of some of the less favoured residential districts. In 1980 the Vauxhall Community Council suggested a route and after discussions, the PTA instructed the PTE to provide experimental services for both Vauxhall and Toxteth. Midibuses seating 27 were at first hired, and later purchased, from West Yorkshire PTE and the first circular service, 101 between William Brown Street and Silvester Street, outward via Gt. Homer Street and Lambeth Road and inward via Boundary Street and Vauxhall Road, started on 6th May 1980. The inward route was soon amended to take in Latimer Street and Burlington Street. Route 101 was marketed as 'The Round-a-bout' and ran half-hourly from about 9.30am to 3.30pm on weekdays with a 10p flat fare and regular drivers. It was joined on 1st September by 'The Link-Up', running between Central Station and Grafton Street (Beresford Road) via Royal Liverpool Hospital, Hope Street, Windsor Street and North Hill Street, with a half-hourly weekday service between 8.30am and 7.30pm. This took over the route number 100 from 'Cityride' which had been withdrawn on 30th August as much of its original purpose had been frustrated by one way streets and pedestrianisation.

After careful monitoring and some changes, 100 and 101 were adopted as a permanent part of the network in 1982. On 3rd March 1983, the County Council issued a directive to the PTA to provide a certain level of bus service between Croxteth and Fazakerley, Walton and Alder Hey Hospitals, to operate as a circular service via Rice Lane, Oak Lane, Croxteth Hall Lane, Princess Drive, East Prescot Road and Queens Drive. This eventually materialised as the third midibus service 102 between Walton (Spellow Lane) and Broadgreen Hospital which is described below under Hospital Services.

Dennis Lancet 7026 runs past the Royal Court Theatre to Hood Street Gyratory. Route 100, one of the two community services, penetrated deeply into a network of minor roads to the south of the city centre to reach its terminus at Grafton Street, Toxteth.

Peak Hour and Industrial Services

Peak hour traffic was in some respects especially vulnerable to competition from private cars as every worker's car tended to become a lift club. Traditionally, peak hour services had fallen into three categories—(1) augmentation of all day services, (2) additional services operated to a more or less regular headway at peak hours and (3) trips timed to meet the specific needs of individual workplaces.

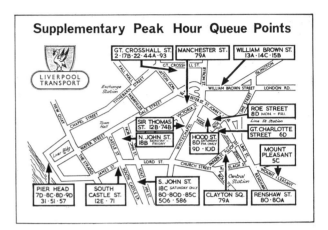

The supplementary peak hour short workings spread the load throughout the city centre and improved bus utilisation by shortening some journeys. This diagram appeared in the official guide in 1961.

When factories were built cheek by jowl with workers' housing in high density areas, there was less need to study the individual requirements of each one as many of the workers lived nearby and others could be accommodated on services in categories (1) and (2). However, the trend towards locating industry in widely dispersed trading estates accentuated the trend towards dedicated journeys for the employees of particular firms, often starting from loading points within, or immediately adjoining, the works premises. Such buses were supposed to operate as duplicates, picking up ordinary passengers en route but often failed to do so, being regarded as 'our bus' by the passengers. Trade unions frequently took a lively interest in these matters and more and more dedicated buses were scheduled following requests to the bus operators by the employers, who were constantly under pressure from the workers' representatives.

These trips were usually highly unremunerative and needed much more management than ordinary duplication as a bus missing due to staff shortages was immediately noticed and usually triggered a complaint. The absence of a bus from a frequent main line service was less obvious and usually resulted only in the queues taking a little longer to clear. The demands on the operators were so heavy at peak hours that dedicated buses were made available only by withdrawing general duplication so that the passengers employed by smaller firms with insufficient workers to justify dedicated facilities, often suffered.

Workers' special buses often started from inside the factory gates and this early seventies view shows three buses inside the confines of Jacobs' biscuit works in Long Lane. Note that while Duple-bodied Leyland PD2 L111, new in 1955, carried the PTE logo, the following bus still displayed the city coat of arms, over a year after the PTE was formed. Atlantean 1213 was new in 1971.

By the end of Corporation days, there were only seven special peak hour services running at more or less regular intervals for general passengers — 1A/1E, 6A, 33A, 50/50A, 67, 71 and 97. All other industrial services were geared to specific needs with irregular headways and one — 10B, Pagemoss-Prescot — ran in one direction only.

The planning ideal of industry with its adjacent housing estate was never entirely attained and the growth of the outer suburbs created new demands for workers' services. In May 1962, the Corporation started a quartet of new services, allocating four consecutive vacant route numbers.

62	Speke (Western Avenue)-Kirkby Civic Centre
63	Hunts Cross (Old Hutte Lane)-Kirkby Civic Centre
64	Edge Lane (Southbank Road)-Kirkby Civic Centre
65	Edge Lane (Southbank Road)-Speke (Western Avenue)

Whilst intended to combine as many diverse needs as possible, the individual trips became specialised as time went on and several branches and diversions appeared such as 62 to Dunlop Factory, 62A to Gillmoss, 63 to Ford Factory and 65A to and from Netherley and Halewood.

During the 1968 strike, there was substantial unofficial operation of coaches for groups of workers, often hired by employers and occasionally by groups of passengers. At the end of the strike, Reliance Coaches (H. F. Edwards) applied for a licence to run between Cantril Farm and Edge Lane. The Corporation objected but, in the post-strike situation, were in no position to operate the service. However, they obtained a licence and arranged for Edwards to operate it for at least a year starting in November 1968. After a time, certain irregularities in Edwards' operations came to light and the PTE took over operation on 4th June 1973 as service 43. For a short time, as a form of protest, Edwards continued to operate, charging no fares but agreement was reached with him that he would continue to run certain journeys until 30th June 1974 when the licence expired. However, Edwards seems to have ceased running on 27th September 1973. The last vehicle he used was a Bristol LS5G XHW 414, ex-Bristol Omnibus Co.

In August 1973, J & M Coaches (Joan and Malcolm Gray) started running a minibus service under a Section 30 Permit (a simplified form of licensing) between Halewood and Old Swan. There was provision in the Transport Act 1968 for services within a PT Area to be provided only by, or by agreement with, the PTE but the government did not activate these powers. However, in both the Merseyside and Greater Manchester areas, it became the practice for both factory and school services which were operated by independents, to be the subject of an agreement between the operator and the PTE and from 25th July 1975, J & M Coaches' service was operated on the PTE's route 65 licence as 65B and 65C, carrying an 'on hire' board. J & M used a 12-seat Ford Transit with Williams Deansgate body, AKA 183J.

As passengers became fewer and operation more expensive, there was a move towards contract operation or revenue support, an arrangement whereby an employer agreed to make up the revenue on a dedicated service to a minimum level. As mentioned in Chapter 49, all the colliery services were eventually run as contracts; many special trips for Littlewoods were put on a contract basis in July 1982. The last remnant of service 52, Walton-Sefton, on which the regular service was discontinued in January 1977, was one Ribble-operated journey numbered W52 which finally ceased in April 1981 when an employer at Sefton Industrial Estate declined to continue support.

The decline of the industrial services was rapid from 1980 onwards. Several factory services (13, 15D, 44A, 92A and 92B) disappeared in the Kirkby rationalisation scheme of 1st June 1980. All the former St. Helens Corporation services along the East Lancs Road to Gillmoss, Walton Hall Avenue, Melling BICC Works and Kirkby (110-114) were withdrawn in April 1981 except the Littlewoods service 113 and one or two journeys from Kirkby to St. Helens which survived for another two years or so. In November 1981, 60D, the docks extension of 60 to Regent Road, was withdrawn along with many journeys on 42, 62, 64, 65, 70 and 77. In June and July 1982, Speke, Green Lane and Gillmoss garages were rescheduled resulting in 62A disappearing entirely. Many trips on other services were withdrawn. Walton and Litherland depots were similarly treated in August, the most far reaching change being the relegation of 33, Everton-Seaforth from a 20-minute all day service to a few odd journeys, some of which were extended to the Containerbase. Minimum fares which had been in operation since the 1939-45 War, to keep short distance passengers off factory buses, were abandoned on almost all industrial services from 6th December 1982.

In October 1984, route 41 was withdrawn and 34, 43, 47, 67, 70 and 97 were reduced or retimed; three months later 67, Old Swan-Seaforth, disappeared entirely as did several more trips on 34, 43, 47, 95, 96 and 97. Finally in June 1986, 16 and 33 and Ribble 254 (formerly W54, Bootle-Lydiate) were totally abandoned.

Amid all this retrenchment, there was some expansion of industrial services particularly in Huyton where growth of the factory estate was stimulated by its proximity to the M57/M62 motorway junction. A new service 71 between Speke and Wilson Road via Hunts Cross, Halewood and Netherley, started in May 1977; it was extended to the new Lucas Aerospace factory in August 1982, as were some journeys on route 70 to and from Pagemoss. The latter also had a journey extended to Old Swan. There was a further extension in the estate to Brickfields in April 1985 and, on the same day, a new service 74 started between Pier Head and Wavertree Technology Park, situated on the site of the former Edge Hill marshalling yard.

Limited Stop Services

The origin of the Limited Stop services was described in Volume Four, the objectives being to provide a service which was more attractive to the user and to maximise bus utilisation by increasing average speeds. There was a third benefit, the reduction of wear on brake linings and tyres and the improvement in fuel consumption as a result of less starting and stopping. Route 500 between Speke and Lime Street had been inaugurated on 17th May 1954 and extended to Kirkby just over a year later; route 510 to Prescot had started in August 1955. At the time of the final tramway conversion, service 506 was introduced from 15th September 1957 between Brookhouse Estate, Huyton and South Castle Street (inward) or South John Street (outward). This was identical with service 6C except that it did not go to the Pier Head but had a minimum fare higher than the other limited stop services, probably by tacit agreement with Crosville. The 7d minimum charge was equivalent to the fare to Bowring Park and there was insufficient all-day traffic to and from Huyton to justify this facility in addition to the 6C and Crosville services. After incurring losses it was reduced to peak hour and Saturday afternoon operation in December 1958. In the meantime, on 31st March 1958, 544 between Northwood and South Castle Street made its appearance, the stopping service 44D being reduced in frequency at the same time. 544 was a faster Church Street version of the 44D with a 20-minute daily frequency increased to 12 minutes on Saturday afternoons and was destined to become one of the most successful and enduring of the limited stop services.

Route 586 between Garston and Central Station, running a 20-minute service via Mather Avenue and Smithdown Road at peak hours and on Saturday afternoons, started operating on 5th January 1959. Five months later it was extended to South Castle Street/South John Street.

In October 1963, both 506 and 586 were withdrawn on Saturdays as part of an economy drive affecting several services but in May 1966, 586 was extended to the Airport Terminal Building with a half-hourly daily service to replace the airport coach service. Off peak trips on 85, which had served the airport since May 1961, were cut back to Windfield Road, Garston at the same time.

The ex-BEA Bedfords which the Corporation had taken over on 1st October 1952, had been replaced by Royal Tigers in 1960-61 and when it was known that Liverpool Corporation would take over full control of the airport from 1st January 1961, it was decided to have them rebuilt as two-level airport coaches with enlarged luggage compartments. In 1964, BEA withdrew from Liverpool and their successors, Cambrian Airways, declined to subsidise the coach service. The Airport Committee of the Corporation bore 75% of the operating loss and, from 25th May 1964, the service was rerouted via Ullet Road and Mather Avenue with a new picking up point at Penny Lane; the frequency was reduced to 10-12 journeys daily for the 1965 summer season. It is of interest to note that in 1955, Liverpool Corporation had applied to the Traffic Commissioners for alternative terminal points at Blackpool, Birmingham or Manchester Airports or city air terminals, for use only when planes were diverted.

Whilst awaiting conversion of the Royal Tigers into airport coaches, Liverpool Corporation hired Crosville EUB329, a 1953 Bristol LS6B with 39-seat dual-purpose Eastern Coach Works body, from January to June 1961 to augment the remaining Bedfords on the Airport service. It is seen inside Dingle depot in June 1961 with a Bedford OB behind. The tall gentleman on the left is K. W. Swallow who was destined to become Director General of the PTE 25 years later.

The four dual-entrance Royal Tigers used in the early one-man-operation experiments were rebuilt in 1961 by MCCW as airport coaches. They operated between Lime Street Station and the old airport terminal building in Speke Road until 1966 after which they were transferred to the Prince's Landing Stage service, the word 'Airporter' being replaced by 'Transport'.

The gap between costs and receipts did not lessen and merger with 586 seemed to be a relatively economical method of serving the Airport. It needed three vehicles plus a spare and four Atlanteans (L763,779,783 and 788) had luggage racks built in. Evidently this move did not have universal approval; British Eagle International Airlines, the successors to earlier operators on the Liverpool-London service, who had lost much of their traffic to the electrified railway, applied to run an express service of 4-5 seat cars between their city office in Lord Street and the Airport. In December 1966 the 586 route was

extended to Exchange Station but heavy losses were still incurred and it reverted to its original route and to Monday to Friday peak hour operation from 30th May 1967. No further dedicated airport services were operated for many years.

The last limited stop service to be introduced was 592 between Northwood and Pier Head, over the 92B route through Fazakerley and Walton on 10th February 1964. The 592 was also the only such service to run to the Pier Head and had a daily half hourly service which finished around 7.00pm. The buses were found by halving the frequency of 92B, which was eight minutes slower.

After the 11-week strike of bus crews in 1968, 544 was the only limited stop service to resume immediately. 500 came back on a reduced frequency a year later, followed by 592 and 510 at the end of 1969. 506 and 586 were quietly forgotten. Numerous other limited stop services were investigated, 514 from Croxteth and 579 from Lee Park being two which almost happened, but all were discarded for want of a consistent regular through traffic flow over a substantial part of the day.

Most of the limited stop services survived the upheavals of the PTE's initial years though the all day 592 gave way to a peak hour Rapidride (492) in 1971. Route 510's city terminus had to be moved from Central Station to South Castle Street when Church Street was pedestrianised in March 1974. It lost its evening service in January 1977 and was withdrawn in its entirety on 4th September 1978. The survivors, 500 and 544 were casualties of the Kirkby scheme of June 1980, both being seen as competitive with rail. Whilst this was undoubtedly true of 500, most of 544 was a long way from the railway. There were industrial journeys on 500 for Ford Factory which showed 501 and 502 and these survived for at least three years after the demise of the main service. The number 582 was also briefly used for an accelerated shift workers' trip from the Adelphi to the Ford Factory but it failed to get the necessary support and reverted to an 82.

Rapidride

The operation of non-stop peak hour expresses, picking up passengers in a limited suburban catchment area and then running through to the city or other destination without stops, was first considered by Liverpool Corporation in 1967 but the events of 1968 prevented any progress. Traffic flows had to be carefully investigated as it was only when there was a consistent demand by through passengers at the same times each day that such services could be justified. The idea was not new on Merseyside as such services had been inaugurated by Birkenhead Corporation in 1930. The aim was to satisfy the passenger by speeding up his journey to and from work, reduce operating costs and achieve greater productivity through higher speeds.

The first service of this nature was inaugurated on 27th April 1970 as the Halewood Express (478) with two trips in each morning and two return trips in the afternoon on Mondays to Fridays. The journey to the Pier Head was scheduled to take 31 minutes, 20 minutes (39%) quicker than the parallel 78 service. It was an immediate success; taped music experiments were started in October 1970, service announcements being interspersed later. It was claimed that 82% of passengers approved of the tapes but there were many who doubted the methodology of the survey. The project was not pursued and the equipment probably broke down under constant vibration which was the usual fate of such endeavours in those days.

A second peak hour express (480) between Garston and Pier Head via Mossley Hill, started in June 1970 with three inward and two outward trips. The 480 observed all route 80 stops to Dovedale Road (Queens Drive) then took a short cut over Penny Lane bridge and along Greenbank Road, the only bus route ever to cover this section. It then ran non-stop to the Adelphi. There was a scheduled time saving of 12 minutes (32%). In 1971 the Rapidride name was introduced for this category of service, the word being displayed in the destination box in sloping letters on a striking yellow background.

Five more Rapidride services commenced in 1971 — 412 from Cantril Farm to Exchange Station (later extended to Pier Head) and 486 from Garston to Pier Head via Allerton in April; 492 from Northwood to Pier Head in September and 405, the only all-single-deck urban Rapidride service, from Woolton to South Castle Street in October. An exhaustive survey was carried out prior to the introduction of each service which was designed to meet the specific needs of the route. Thus whilst 480 served all the stops along Brodie Avenue, the parallel 486 stopped at only five points between Garston and Rose Lane, reflecting the different distribution of traffic along the two routes. Route 492 replaced the all-day 592 between Northwood and Pier Head, the survey having shown that the off-peak service was underutilised.

The network was completed in August 1972 by three routes to Seaforth, 400 from Speke, 438 from Halewood via Woolton and Smithdown Road and 439 from Netherley

Most of the Rapidride services were operated by double-deckers but in 1981 an influx of new Leyland National 2s led to their appearance on numerous double-deck routes where the loadings were not too heavy. The 'Rapidride' sign had a yellow background. Number 6147 was quite new when seen at the Pier Head on 6th April 1981 and the bulbous front of the National 2 is clearly discernible.

via Wavertree, each with one inward and one outward trip. To avoid picking up city centre traffic, the first setting down point was at Princes Dock (Bath Street). An arrangement to set down passengers at dock gates was unsuccessful and route 1A stops were soon adopted. No additional buses were employed, time tables being adjusted or duplication cancelled to provide the vehicles needed for the new facilities.

The initial Rapidride services had a flat fare of 1/3d or 1/6d; by decimalisation these had become 10p or 13p. Eventually, ordinary fares were charged over the last section of route on outward trips as was done on the 500 series of routes.

Rapidride routes were also developed in Wirral with mixed success. After the opening of the first tube of the Wallasey Tunnel on 28th June 1971, the blue Wirral Division buses ran into Liverpool city centre for the first time (except for the night service) on off-peak route 31 from New Brighton and peak hour 32 from Liscard; these were not designated Rapidride routes until after deregulation when they became 431/2. From the outset, they followed a circular route through the city centre which was shortened to save five minutes in order to serve the commercial rather than the shopping areas at peak hours to facilitate an increase in frequency. However, routes 418/9, introduced on 10th December 1973 between Heswall and the city centre ran non-stop from Pensby, using the M53 motorway for some distance and hence were given numbers in the Rapidride series. This service was run all day by Crosville buses which followed the same routes as 31/32 through the city centre. This was the only Rapidride route with a Saturday service and proved so popular that the original single-deck buses were replaced by double-deckers in March 1975.

The Rapidride services performed a very useful function while the volume of through traffic at certain times was sufficient to fill the buses but, as traffic declined, there were empty seats on both the express and stopping buses so the former had to go. The first casualties came with the major economy exercise on 10th January 1977 when 414 and 492 succumbed but all the others continued for another five years, the next cuts being in November 1981 when 439 from Netherley to Seaforth lost its afternoon journey, the same happening to 400 and 438 in June 1982.

Ribble tried a similar type of service when, in September 1980, it commenced 705 between Parbold, Skelmersdale and Skelhorne Street to replace some journeys on 305 and 345. A Saturday service was added in March 1981 between Ashurst and Pier Head but matters became a little confused in July 1981 when 705 also became part of the company's 'Timesaver' network and was extended to Blackpool for the summer season. It lost its Pier Head extension at the end of the 1982 season.

The economies of the eighties saw the disappearance of most of the Rapidride services, only an extended 405, 438 and a shortened Ribble (now North Western) 705 surviving deregulation. However, from 26th October 1986 there was a flood of new commercial Rapidride-type services through both tunnels from Wirral and as far afield as Chester, some in direct competition with the rail network.

In Liverpool there has been a minor revival with 412/3 from Stockbridge Village, 444 from Kirkby, 475 from Huyton and 482 from Norton, Runcorn and Speke. North Western 705 became hourly all day with revenue support whilst 405 reached Halewood and Runcorn. Other routes, operated by various companies, from Southport, Rainhill, Runcorn and places on he Wirral peninsula, also have Rapidride characteristics.

Shopping Services

In the days before widespread car ownership, the three or four Saturdays before Christmas warranted special traffic arrangements to cater for city centre shoppers. It was customary to assemble a pool of spare buses at Cleveland Square and establish radio links through Head Office Control to patrol cars stationed in the Lord Street, London Road and Renshaw Street shopping areas. Buses were then despatched as required. Vehicles working football specials after the match would run empty to Cleveland Square after setting down their passengers but the coming of floodlit grounds and later kick-offs upset this arrangement as buses could not reach the city centre before 5.45pm. When the climax of Christmas shopping was reached on 24th December, many industrial buses which operated their trips early due to factories closing before the normal times, were used to assist in moving late afternoon shoppers.

A park and ride service for shoppers was tried before Christmas 1973 when Liverpool Corporation sponsored 'Shopparide', a free service between the newly-opened New Quay car park, near the Pier Head, and Church Street shopping area. It was worked by a hired 8-seat Ford Transit manned by a PTE driver; it carried 1,720 passengers on 342 journeys between 3rd and 24th December. The experiment was not repeated in subsequent years.

A feature of modern life is the out-of-town shopping centre, often designed to make shopping easier for the motorist but, where it lies close to residential areas, attracts bus passengers, too. Belle Vale District Centre was a good example, being provided with a buses-only access road and, later, with its own Bus Station. Routes 66 and 79A served the centre from October 1973 when an off-peak

This Ford Transit can probably claim to have been the first minibus in Liverpool. It was hired to operate a free park-and-ride service between New Quay and the shopping centre, sponsored by Liverpool Corporation at Christmas 1973.

service 79E commenced between Pier Head and Belle Vale via Childwall Valley Road. In 1983, buses on routes 89, 89A and 92 were diverted.

New Strand was a similar centre and, as mentioned in Chapter 51, it attracted various bus services from Bootle's environs. In the eighties much of the off peak service on former joint routes 57 and 55 was curtailed at New Strand instead of running through to Liverpool.

A shopping development of a different kind was the informal Saturday market in Great Homer Street. The Pier Head-Broad Lane journeys on 17D were diverted via Great Homer Street instead of Scotland Road as 17. They were successively renumbered 117 in 1983 and back to 17 a year later. The Dingle-Walton trips on 85 were similarly rerouted in May 1984 as 85C.

Shopping services of another kind were the free promotional trips run from Croxteth Park (906) and Rainhill Stoops (907) to the Asda store at Huyton from January to April 1986.

School Services

Changes in the educational system and closure of small schools in favour of large multi-stream establishments led to many more children using public transport to travel to and from school. Whilst some lip service was paid to the idea of arranging school traffic so that it flowed against the prevailing direction, there were limits to what could be achieved. In many cases the ordinary route network was unsuitable and special routes were needed.

School services were very unremunerative as they often required special buses in the peak to carry passengers at concessionary fares. As industrial working hours were shortened, the afternoon school and industrial peaks began to overlap so that buses could no longer work a school trip followed by a factory journey. The Suez crisis of 1956-57 presented an opportunity to stagger hours but some of the measures were unpopular, especially with families with working mothers whose children attended different schools with varying hours. After much discussion, school finishing times were, in many cases, brought forward from around 4.00pm to 3.30pm.

A special series of school service route numbers starting at 601 was introduced on 7th January 1960. The idea was copied from St. Helens Corporation whose 601-up series had appeared on 22nd October 1956. The 6xx numbers were originally used by Liverpool Corporation and the PTE mainly for services to and from special schools and some Social Services establishments while a 7xx series was used for contract operation to swimming baths and playing fields. Since deregulation, subsidised 6xx services to and from ordinary schools have replaced much of the unremunerative augmentation of ordinary services.

Hospital Services

As long as the route network remained reasonably comprehensive and the services frequent, out-patients and visitors had little difficulty in reaching hospitals. The exception was the Royal Southern Hospital which had relied heavily on the Overhead Railway. It will be recalled that the condition of the road surface precluded the use of Grafton Street by buses until almost two years after the abandonment of the railway and, despite lengthy discussions, patients, visitors and staff had to endure a 400 yd walk through a rather rough area to and from Mill Street.

In the seventies the position changed drastically. Not only were services becoming less and less frequent, especially in the evenings and on Sundays when most visiting took place, but the smaller local hospitals were being closed down and replaced by enormous district hospitals, often at some considerable distance from the areas they served. Furthermore, specialist functions were often available only at certain hospitals.

These factors combined to create many new demands on the transport system and a number of service revisions were specifically geared to satisfying them. Wherever possible ordinary services were rerouted as in the case of the extension of 18C from East Lancashire Road to Fazakerley but eventually some special subsidised hospital services had to be provided. At least the transport authority was consulted and there was a series of meetings between PTE officials and the Liverpool Regional Hospital Committee in 1973.

The geography of the area lying half way up the ridge to the east of the city centre was altered by the construction of various new buildings; in particular the Royal Liverpool Hospital replaced the Royal Infirmary which stood in nearby Pembroke Place. Its use was phased in but it was officially opened on 2nd October 1978. The Royal Liverpool, being located close to the top of London Road, had few transport problems as a wide variety of city services passed close by. In addition, the long established cross-city ex-tram routes 25 and 46 ran along Daulby Street and Moss Street. However, there was one special visitors' service, 80E from Speke via Mossley Hill which had started on 1st April 1974 as a visitors' service to Sefton General Hospital, Smithdown Road and was subsequently extended to serve both hospitals. Links with the south end were further improved in 1978 when route 25 was extended from Aigburth Vale to Garston. The Toxteth Link-Up (100) midibus service, introduced on 1st September 1980, also gave a direct facility to and from the hospital. This gave rise to a dispute with drivers over running time on journeys from Toxteth where the route from Minshull Street was via Mount Vernon, Hall Lane, Prescot Street and Daulby Street. It was announced that from 1st October 1984, the bus would run direct via West Derby Street but, in fact, this had been done since 1st March as the men had taken it into their own hands to change the route in order to keep time.

Walton and Fazakerley Hospitals needed many new facilities. As long ago as 1950, the 68 route between Aigburth, Old Swan, Walton and Seaforth had been devised as an extension of route 67 at both ends to improve access to Walton Hospital and to provide connections at Seaforth for Waterloo and Crosby. The extension of the 30 (Aintree) route to Netherton and

Sefton Estate in 1971 gave the hospital its first direct link with those areas. The diversion of route 92, first to Bootle (New Strand) in 1973 and its extension to Crosby in 1974, linked the latter with both hospitals direct, access being further improved in the course of the first major revision in Crosby on 6th December 1975 when Ribble services L22 and L23 were introduced for this specific purpose. The route ran from Crosby via Thornton, Ford and Netherton to the Black Bull and then became a circular via Longmoor Lane, Lower Lane, Walton Hall Avenue, Queens Drive and Rice Lane, L22 clockwise and L23 anti-clockwise. This was a half-hourly daily service but labour troubles followed the penetration of Ribble buses so far into traditional PTE territory and after three months, it was replaced by two separate services, Ribble 29 to Fazakerley and PTE 30 extended from Netherton to Crosby.

Eventually, the problem was resolved and L22/23 was restored from October 1978. After Wango Lane bridge was rebuilt, route 54 was extended from Aintree Village to Fazakerley Hospital in 1984, improving facilities from Netherton and Aintree. When the Kirkby railway line was electrified, the hospital also enjoyed a frequent train service, Fazakerley Station being just across the road.

Another route designed specifically to serve hospitals was 102, started experimentally in 1983 as a midibus route, made permanent after a year and eventually worked by full size buses. It originally ran from Spellow Lane to Broadgreen Hospital, taking in Walton, Fazakerley and Alder Hey Hospitals, as well as Croxteth Hall, on the way but after deregulation it started at Norris Green (Broadway) before heading for Walton Hospital. Broadgreen Hospital lay on the 40 route and, being quite close to Queens Drive, it was well served by 61, 68 and 81 with a short walk. It had one other dedicated route, the 69 from Netherley via Childwall Valley Road, which dated back to 1977.

Withdrawal of evening and Sunday services after deregulation left some hospitals with limited transport services for visitors and the PTE, as the tendering authority, took the opportunity to create some new facilities. Tenders were invited for several new services which were numbered in a series commencing at 200. Of interest was the City Centre Hospital Service (200) which was short-lived but, during its brief career linked the Pier Head, Moorfields Station, Hood Street Gyratory and Skelhorne Street Bus Station with the Royal Liverpool, St. Paul's Eye Hospital and the cluster of smaller medical establishments in the vicinity of Myrtle Street. The 69 was extended at both ends and renumbered 203 to provide a Halewood-Broadgreen-Alder Hey facility. Other routes served Walton and Whiston Hospitals, the latter having previously been well served by a wide range of regular services. Many of the hospital service tenders were soon won by independent operators.

Football Services

At the time of the Suez fuel crisis in 1956, direct football specials to and from outlying areas had been withdrawn as an economy measure and the number of buses employed had been almost halved. Only two services continued to operate, one from the city centre and the other from Old Swan. Passengers from other districts made their way to these points or used ordinary services passing close to the grounds and the demand was catered for much more economically. After the match, extra buses were provided on services passing near the grounds.

In September 1958, the Department was under pressure to reintroduce the full range of special services which had embraced Prescot, Huyton, Belle Vale, Bootle, Garston and Pagemoss. The General Manager pointed out that, except in the case of some of the longer routes, the revenue from a full load just about covered the cost of operation but 25 extra buses would be needed and the question was really not one of fares but whether the manning of the extra vehicles could be justified. Sometimes full loads were not carried.

There were always plenty of volunteers to work overtime on football specials; the difficulty was in manning late evening duplicates which would suffer as a result. Discussions spread on to the subject of the general disruption of bus services in the vicinity of football grounds after a match.

As car ownership increased, the Department's ability to clear the football crowds expeditiously was further hindered. Enormous traffic jams were caused when cars and coaches emerged from the side streets where they had been parked; Cherry Lane bridge created a serious bottleneck until it was widened. The repercussions were widespread as the practice was to use a bus for two or even three trips. For example, a bus would load for the Rotunda, return to the ground, load for Lower Lane then run empty to Littlewood's, Walton Hall Avenue to pick up one of about ten loads of workers at 5.30pm. The General Manager gave

The older buses tended to be used on football specials and A526 (formerly A326), one of the original AEC Regent IIIs dating from February 1948, is seen at Pier Head in September 1966, a few months before withdrawal. These buses were the first to carry the angular four-bay Weymann-sourced bodies finished at Edge Lane works.

some specific examples of problems encountered after the department had been subjected to a barrage of uninformed criticism at the October 1958 Committee meeting.

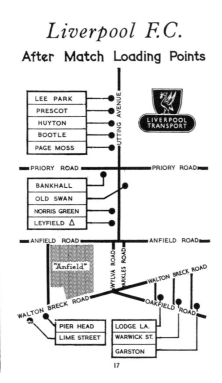

In an effort to keep buses out of the worst traffic congestion after first team matches, the loading points were relocated as shown in 1959.

'...on Saturday 18th October, for a period of 28 minutes not a single bus was able to pass under this (Cherry Lane) bridge in an outward direction. A similar situation existed last Saturday, 1st November. A line of buses waiting to proceed outwards stood perfectly still for over 15 minutes at the Cemetery Gates, Walton Lane and it was 7.30pm...before normal headways were restored.

'With a view to overcoming the particular difficulties which arise, at about 5.20pm on 1st November, an empty bus was despatched from Spellow Lane with an inspector on board and instructions to pass the football queue, thus leaving space in Walton Lane for other intending passengers. The bus passed the queue successfully, but was then held up in traffic for 20 minutes after the next stop and during this period, of course, it became filled with football passengers who were walking along Walton Lane.'

This gave the Committee some food for thought and whilst it was resolved to restore the full range of football specials, implementation was delayed until the Traffic Superintendent could consult the police about measures to minimise problems. Nothing was done that season but from 26th August 1959 special buses were operated between the grounds and Bankhall Station, Bootle Station, Roe Street, Garston, Huyton Station, Lee Park, Leyfield Triangle, Lodge Lane (Earle Road), Old Swan, Page Moss and Prescot. Loading points after the match were situated in some cases at a considerable distance from the grounds so that buses avoided some of the congestion as shown in the accompanying diagrams which embody some modifications made in the light of experience. No priority was given to buses and the services generally became less attractive.

The special services continued until the end of the 1965-66 season but, because of falling traffic, they were not reintroduced for the following season and there were no more dedicated facilities until 1972.

Soccerbus

The 'Soccerbus' park-and-ride service was an imaginative plan to take advantage of the chaotic parking conditions near the Everton and Liverpool FC grounds. It was introduced on 1st April 1972, towards the end of a football season, with a view to ironing out any teething problems before a full scale launch for the 1972-73 season. Parking areas, secure from vandals, were set aside at Edge Lane and Gillmoss garages (and later on at points in the Wirral) and special express buses ran direct to the Liverpool or Everton grounds for first team Saturday home games. Passengers were set down outside the ground and picked up there after the match. The police now promised to give priority to the buses but there was a limit to what they could do under conditions of severe congestion. The car parks were chosen for their proximity to main traffic routes and motorways; the RAC co-operated by erecting signs at strategic places.

The combined car parking fee and return bus ticket from Edge Lane or Gillmoss was initially 25p (child 15p) or 50p for car, driver and up to four passengers. Over the years these fares gradually increased until they reached 75p (child 35p) and £1.60 for a car load. In 1973, 6,504 cars were parked and 14,218 passengers carried on 296 journeys (including Wirral), an average of 48 passengers per trip.

By the early eighties, patronage was declining and for the 1982-83 season holders of Saveaway tickets could use them to travel by ordinary service bus to Edge Lane and then on the special buses to the football ground. The Gillmoss service came to an end in May 1983 and from August 1983 operations were restricted to Edge Lane and Birkenhead (Woodside). On this basis they continued until 11th May 1985 when the facility was finally withdrawn.

By agreement with British Rail and the police, other buses were operated from Lime Street and Edge Hill stations direct to the grounds with a view to keeping unruly soccer fans off the streets. Through booking facilities were given.

Landing Stage Services

Coast Lines Ltd continued to run their AEC Regals between the railway stations and Princes Landing Stage in connection with the Belfast and Dublin steamers while the Corporation fed the Isle of Man steamers using the Royal Tigers in both their original and rebuilt form, supplemented by double-deckers as necessary. The small capacity of the Regals and the need for a separate luggage van, made the Coast Lines service uneconomic as costs increased and there was doubtless some difficulty in continuing the somewhat relaxed arrangement whereby

This AEC Regal, MLV 683, with Roe 35-seat body was owned by the Belfast Steamship Co. and used on the service between the railway stations to Prince's Landing Stage. It is seen crossing an almost deserted dock road in June 1960. In the background is the branch entrance of the first Mersey Tunnel.

the buses were manned by lorry drivers employed by the associated Liverpool Cartage Co. One of the Regals was rebodied with an enormous luggage compartment at the rear but the van was still needed at busy times.

The six road service licences held in the name of the Belfast Steamship Co Ltd expired in June 1966 and were not renewed, the service probably continuing on short-period licences for the rest of that season. Arrangements were then made with a Blundell Group coach company, Lawrenson's Travel Ltd, to operate the service, substantive licences being granted to them in April 1967. Double-deckers could not operate to Prince's Landing Stage because of restricted headroom under the awning in Prince's Parade but when the terminal was moved to Prince's Dock, this problem no longer existed and Coast Lines decided that Atlanteans with luggage racks replacing some seats would be the best means of moving people to and from the steamers. After some discussion, Liverpool Corporation was persuaded to take on the work on a contract basis.

The date when the Corporation took over is uncertain and may have been delayed by the 11-week strike. Certainly L779 and 783 had the luggage racks (recently removed after withdrawal of the Airport service 586) replaced in February 1968, L763 in March and L788 in June and it seems likely that Lawrenson's continued until the summer of 1968. The luggage van was withdrawn though the Atlanteans' racks were never adequate on busy days when the extra luggage was stacked on several seats. Extra buses were also used and these had no luggage accommodation whatsoever.

In November 1981, P&O Ferries discontinued the Belfast service but this was resumed by Irish Sea Ferries on 2nd May 1982, operating from Langton Dock instead of Prince's Dock. The PTE provided a service to and from Lime Street Station running at regular intervals between 7.20 and 10.40am daily, at a flat fare of 50p.

As the docks contracted and car ferries were introduced, the ferry terminal was moved further north, first to Trafalgar Dock and then, from October 1983, to Brocklebank Dock, and the contract service was extended accordingly. However, the passenger demand had fallen as many people now travelled with their cars. From June 1984, the PTE sub-contracted the service to Crosville who used three second-hand Daimler Fleetlines and a Bristol VR.

Special Services

There were several special events for which exceptional services were required. The operations staff prided themselves on meticulous attention to detail and the provision of a high standard of service often under difficult conditions as normal service commitments also had to be met.

On 27th June 1971, the public was permitted to walk through the first tube of the second Mersey Tunnel prior to its opening and special bus services were provided between Pier Head and the Liverpool entrance in Scotland Road and between Seacombe Ferry and the Wallasey

The last buses operated by Coast Lines Ltd were three AEC Regal IIIs with Roe 39-seat bodies, delivered in March 1954. This one, PKD 590, was rebodied by Bonallack, incorporating an enormous luggage compartment. It is seen at Princes Dock in June 1960 and ran until 1966 when Lawrenson's of Bootle took over the service under contract.

In 1966, Coast Lines disposed of their own buses and arranged for Lawrenson's of Bootle to provide the link between the railway stations and Prince's Landing Stage on their behalf. Bedford SB XTC 799 with Duple body, one of two specially painted for this work, is seen in Marsh Lane, Bootle when off duty.

entrance. A total of 55,000 pedestrians walked through the tunnel of whom 11,936 purchased a combined 'walk through' ticket covering the two bus journeys and return by ferry, or vice versa. Another cross-river related service was the shuttle operated between St. Nicholas Place and Prince's Parade between 11th February and 13th April 1976 when George's Landing Stage was out of commission and the ferries sailed from Prince's Stage. Buses were brought from Southport to work this service.

The Silver Jubilee visit of HM The Queen to Merseyside on 21st June 1977 involved all the divisions as the ceremonial started in St. Helens before moving through Prescot, Huyton and Old Swan to both Liverpool cathedrals. In addition to maintaining normal services and coping with a host of diversions, the PTE provided 140 buses to convey to and from their schools, 17,000 children who presented a pageant along the route between the two cathedrals. Crowds of people were also carried to and from vantage points along the royal route. After visiting Bootle, the Queen boarded the PTE's cruise boat Royal Iris in Gladstone Dock and from it reviewed a number of ships in the river. Her Majesty's next visit to Liverpool, on 25th October 1978, was a special transport occasion, when she officially opened the Merseyrail extensions.

The visit of Pope John Paul II to Liverpool on Sunday, 30th May 1982 was highly disruptive of public transport because of the strict security measures imposed. The Pope arrived at Speke Airport at 4.00pm and drove in procession to both cathedrals. However, some services started earlier than usual so that everyone could reach vantage points. The areas around the Airport and the cathedrals were 'controlled' and closed to traffic from early morning, resulting in bus services being diverted for most of the day. Services along Aigburth Road were suspended and others diverted in the late afternoon during the motorcade. Special commemorative Saveaway tickets were issued at ordinary rates.

In the evening, the Pope's procession went from the Catholic Cathedral to an overnight stop in Calderstones and as no traffic was allowed to cross the papal route, all services using Smithdown Road and Menlove Avenue were suspended, curtailed or diverted; some inter-suburban routes were run in two parts and normal traffic was not resumed until after 10.00pm. Only one special service was operated, a shuttle numbered 50 between special coach and car parks set up on the North Docks and Old Haymarket at a flat fare of 25p.

As the following day was a Bank Holiday, the Pope's early departure via Menlove Avenue and Speke Hall Road to the Airport caused little disruption to bus services although some buses were diverted before 8.00am.

The Garden Festival

The International Garden Festival was held on 125 acres of formerly derelict land between Toxteth and Otterspool from 2nd May to 14th October 1984 and attracted considerable interest. As the site was remote from regular transport routes, two special services were provided — 401 from Pier Head via Exchange Station, Lime Street Station and Renshaw Street to the Herculaneum Entrance and 402 from Aigburth Vale via Jericho Lane to the Fulwood Entrance.

Route 401 operated at a minimum frequency of 10 minutes (7½ minutes during the school holidays), at a fare of 35p, the basic service being provided by two PTE buses from Edge Lane depot, two Ribbles from Bootle and two Crosvilles. It had been intended that all six buses should be

(Lower left) Crosville contributed two of the six specially painted Garden Festival buses in 1984 and chose two 1970 Daimler Fleetlines with Northern Counties 71-seat bodies bought second-hand from Southdown Motor Services in 1980. HDG 910 is seen loading at Pier Head in June 1984. Note that the front has been rebuilt without destination indicators. A PTE Atlantean (1014) waits to take its place.

(Below) Atlanteans outnumbered Bristols at Ribble's Merseyside depots but 1986, a 1972 Bristol VR with Eastern Coach Works 70-seat body, was one of two (1986-7) selected to work the special Garden Festival service 401 in 1984. Note the NBC and PTE logos flanking the fleet name and the special decorated yellow front.

in advertising livery with yellow fronts and Festival logos but, in fact, only the PTE vehicles carried advertising for Higson's Brewery which was adjacent to the route, though they all had yellow fronts. The 402 service, with a 10p fare, was normally run by PTE Atlanteans 1028/30 in standard livery from Prince Alfred Road.

A third service, 403, was planned to run between an overflow car park in Sefton Park and the Herculaneum Entrance but was never needed. Several streets never used by public transport would have been used as the planned route was via Mossley Hill Drive, Croxteth Gate, Ullet Road, Dingle Lane, Dingle Mount, Beloe Street, Mill Street, Harlow Street, Grafton Street, Park Street and Sefton Street, returning by this route to Harlow Street then North Hill Street, Princes Avenue, Croxteth Road and Croxteth Gate. Only passengers in possession of £1.00 parking tickets would have been carried.

Thousands of passengers were also carried by rail to and from St. Michael's Station which was specially upgraded. Marks and Spencer made a grant of £30,000 from their community programme in their centenary year, having been attracted by the appropriateness of the name. Special combined Saveaway and admission tickets were priced to give free travel from virtually anywhere on Merseyside. The public transport arrangements were voted a great success, 33% of visitors being thus conveyed instead of the predicted 20%

The Festival grounds were opened again from 23rd May to 8th September 1985 and service 401 ran on an altered route from Skelhorne Street to Herculaneum Entrance via Albert Dock, using Ribble buses.

A further event of 1984 was the Tall Ships Race which ended in the Mersey on Saturday, 4th August. Enormous crowds gathered for the event and the PTE carried thousands of people by bus, rail and ferry to vantage points in Wallasey and New Brighton. In the evening, traffic congestion was so severe that everything came to a complete standstill. It was decided to keep public transport operating all night if necessary and staff readily agreed to keep working to get everyone home. The ferries were carrying passengers at the rate of 6,000 an hour and the last buses left the Pier Head at 1.15am on Sunday.

Other Leisure Traffic

Private transport gradually took over the Aintree race traffic. For the Spring Meeting in 1957 routes 2 and 30 were cut back to the old tram terminus, itself an indication of the changed circumstances as the trams had usually had to turn back at Hall Lane. On National day, the Aintree buses forsook Warbreck Moor altogether, running via Longmoor Lane and Greenwich Road to a terminus at Wyresdale Road. In 1979, 2,000 combined travel and entrance tickets were sold for the Grand National but, by this time, congestion made rail the most effective way of handling traffic to and from Aintree where the station adjoined the main entrance to the course.

One problem which remained was that of religious processions though the buses were able to divert more readily than the trams and found themselves squeezing through streets which rarely saw large vehicles. The fervour of both Orange and Green having declined, Liverpool now sees few such processions.

Religious processions played havoc with bus schedules and delayed all traffic. The camera caught this Orange Day procession in William Brown Street on 17th July 1955 but similar scenes were to be repeated in later years. Note the tunnel beacon, long demolished.

City Tours

Despite falling patronage, the department persevered with the operation of the City Tours which had originated with the Festival of Britain in 1951. The 1958 programme offered two tours, No.1 South Liverpool and Speke Hall, featuring the Anglican Cathedral, Allerton, Hunts Cross, Speke Hall, Otterspool Promenade and Sefton Park and No.2, Dockland and the Airport which replaced the tour which had included the now abandoned Overhead Railway. Older 7ft 6in wide buses were used on the latter because of the difficulty of negotiating some of the dock bridges. Tours ran at weekends and on Bank Holidays from Whitsuntide to the end of August or early September and No.1 ran also on Wednesdays in July and August. Buses departed from the south end of the Pier Head and tickets were issued at the nearby enquiry office.

The tours were still reasonably well supported in 1962 by which time No.1 had been labelled 'Homes and Halls' and No.2 was 'Port Panorama' which had been cut by about half to 14 miles but given three departures instead of two. Litherland, Walton, Carnegie Road and Green Lane garages covered the former while Dingle and Prince Alfred Road covered the latter. The practice was to hold buses in readiness at the various garages from 40 minutes before the advertised departure times. On August Bank Holiday, 6th August 1962, 16 vehicles were scheduled and in that month the minimum number of vehicles on stand-by on any one day was eight. By 1965, the vehicle allocation was reduced to two or three and the tours ceased at the end of that summer.

Short one-hour City Tours, starting from St. John's Lane, with a fare of 45p, concentrating on the central area, were started in 1978 using open-top double-deck buses brought in from Southport. In 1981, following the deregulation of express services and excursions, the PTE joined forces with Ribble and National Travel (West) in operating various short guided tours with local themes. These included 'Mysteries of Bygone Liverpool', 'A Beatles Magical Mystery Tour' and 'Maritime Merseyside'.

From June 1984, the tours programme was stepped up in connection with the Garden Festival and supported by the Merseyside County Council Tourism Department. The tours ran daily (twice in the height of summer) until mid-October and at weekends during the winter. The demise of the County Council put an end to this but the Merseyside Tourism Board supported short tours taking in the principal places of interest in the immediate environs of the city centre. In the summer of 1989, there were six daily departures from the Maritime Museum marketed as 'City Heritage Shuttle' (service 200), worked by an open-top bus at a fare of 25p. The first £6,000 was underwritten by the National Galleries and Museums on Merseyside who wanted an unlimited break of journey facility which Merseybus considered to be impracticable.

Knowsley Safari Park

Following the establishment of a Safari Park at Knowsley, the seat of Lord Derby, special inclusive tours were operated from Pier Head, Garston, Speke, Netherton, Kirkby and St. Helens on Wednesdays during the school holidays and Sundays commencing on 8th August 1971. A 2¼ hour tour of the park was included and in the first season 11,688 passengers were carried on 206 journeys. The tours did well for a few years until the novelty had worn off; the starting points were progressively reduced in number until, by 1975, only the Pier Head and St. Helens departure points remained, the latter being cancelled for the 1978 season. The following year 2,000 passengers were carried from the Pier Head.

The popularity of the city tours gradually waned during the sixties as car ownership opened up new horizons. AEC Regent III A693 of 1951 is seen awaiting passengers at the Pier Head before the terminus was remodelled in 1965. Its Weymann-framed body was finished by Davidson and it was withdrawn in 1966. The width of dock bridges still dictated the use of elderly 7ft. 6in.-wide buses on this tour.

Private Hire and Coaching

During the sixties, private hire was a minor activity of the transport undertaking consisting mainly of local jobs within the city and its immediate environs and summer weekend hire of buses to Crosville on the North Wales express services.

Occasionally there would be a big job such as the Church Rally held at Southport football ground on 23rd May 1964 which involved a convoy of double-deck buses starting from many different points in and around the city. In the winter there would be the late dance specials like Waterworths' Annual Staff Dance held at the Grafton Rooms, West Derby Road on 10th November 1964 and repeated the following year. This involved the midnight departure of 19 buses to all parts of the city. There were many similar events and in July 1984, the Loyal Orange Lodges were conveyed to Southport in 62 buses; this trip had been traditionally made by train. There was also the contract work taking schoolchildren to swimming baths and playing fields which was fitted in between the peaks.

Unless they had specific powers, municipal transport undertakings were restricted to running private hire in their own operating areas unless they were on hire to another operator. There was a gentlemen's agreement between the three Merseyside corporations for running into the areas of the others from their own home town and this enabled Liverpool buses to reach New Brighton, Thurstaston and Eastham. The PTE was not inhibited in this way and was able to take on jobs to more distant places such as Blackpool and Morecambe, provided the hirer would accept a service bus or one of the ex-airport coaches.

In the early years, staff shortages restricted the work that could be done and it was not until 1974, when absorption of the St. Helens fleet brought with it a second-hand Bedford coach, that thoughts were turned towards developing the private hire activities. On at least three occasions, consideration was given to buying the business of a coach operator as a going concern as Manchester's PTE had done. This was seen as the best way to gain the expertise needed to make progress in this very competitive business but such negotiations that took place were never brought to fruition.

Although revenue from private hire increased annually, it was not until the arrival of the first coach-seated Leyland Nationals in 1978 that coach work was taken seriously and a fleet of luxury coaches was ordered. Most coach work was centred on Southport and is therefore outside the scope of this work. For the record, Merseyside PTE's first full-day excursion ran from Southport to Harrogate on 23rd April 1981. There is a story, probably apocryphal, that Southport district management (who had as little to do with Liverpool as they could get away with) arranged this on their own initiative and told Divisional headquarters afterwards. The Road Traffic Act 1980 had abolished the need for a licence for this type of operation and, as soon as

This Atlantean received a special livery in March 1985 designed to boost private hire. Note the modified fleet title to make room for the slogan on the side. This was one of the final batch of Atlanteans delivered in 1984.

Seven Atlanteans operating a private hire journey, lined up in William Brown Street near St. George's Hall in September 1985. The leader is 1975 and behind it is one of the same batch painted in the Merseyside County Council anti-abolition campaign livery. The Birkenhead tunnel entrance is in the background.

more new coaches arrived, regular excursions were started from Liverpool.

The year 1980-81 was a good one for private hire as two events, the National Pastoral Congress and the 150th Anniversary of the Liverpool and Manchester Railway with the associated re-enactment of the Rainhill Trials, generated considerable work. In 1981-82 revenue exceeded £1 million for the first time.

Royal Visits demanded very special efforts and this line-up of vehicles near Grove Street on 21st July 1977 would require a high degree of organisation. Note the canteen and recovery vehicles parked in the background. A total of 140 PTE vehicles conveyed 17,000 schoolchildren on this occasion; a few Crosville buses and private coaches are also in evidence in the foreground.

The Manx Coachliner

From 30th March 1985, the long-established Liverpool-Douglas steamer service was transferred to Heysham. The PTE, with the support of the Merseyside County Council and in conjunction with Lancaster City Transport, inaugurated a daily coach service (741) between Liverpool (St. John's Lane) and Heysham from 1st April 1985. The number 741 seems to have been derived from the original Ribble X41 Liverpool-Morecambe service. The fare was £3.00 single or £3.75 return and the service was extended to Pontin's Holiday Camp at Middleton Towers on Tuesdays and Saturdays. Each operator worked one return journey daily.

As the Steam Packet Company was now aiming at the car ferry market rather than foot passengers, even this service was little patronised and from 4th October 1985 it was reduced to one trip on Fridays, Saturdays and Mondays, all operated by the PTE. These received poor support and the service was withdrawn permanently on 6th January 1986. The Leyland Tiger coaches 7011, 7017 and 7019 were normally used on the Manx Coachliner.

All Night Services

The Committee brought up the question of all-night services once more in 1959 and the General Manager drew up three alternative schemes as shown in the accompanying diagram. There had, in fact, been no request from the public for such a facility and this seems to have been a whim of the Committee. The subject had been aired many times before and, in 1924, a service of all-night trams was started and abandoned within three months due to lack of support.

Twelve buses would have been needed to run a comprehensive hourly service (Scheme A). Annual mileage would have been 250,000 at an operating cost of £45,800. Various suggestions were made to achieve some economies to offset this additional cost. Half a million miles could have been saved by terminating all main services at 11.00pm instead of midnight but there was a tradition of running until midnight in Liverpool and, during the fuel crisis of 1956-57, there had been strong resistance to an early close-down. Furthermore, buses were generally quite well patronised during the last hour. Another suggestion was to withdraw staff buses which ran about 240,000 miles annually. However, their withdrawal would have saved only £6,500 and there would have been strong employee resistance as the public night buses would have lacked the flexibility of the staff buses. There was an arrangement whereby drivers and conductors could book a special diversion in advance and co-ordination with a Ribble staff bus at Spellow Lane, where passengers were exchanged.

The truth of the matter was that whilst Manchester and Birmingham had all-night buses Liverpool had not, but the circumstances in those cities were quite different. National newspapers were produced in Manchester with workers

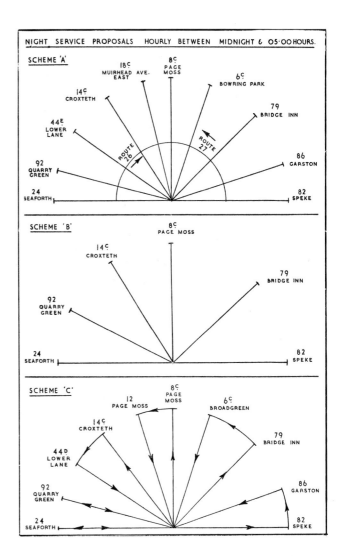

finishing at odd hours during the night and there were far more train arrivals and departures.

It was pointed out that even if double fares were charged with a minimum of 1/-, the service would incur a heavy loss as there was no hope of carrying the 2,700 passengers needed every night to break even. At such fares, two or three passengers could combine to hire a taxi more cheaply.

The only night facility, therefore, was the tunnel service to Birkenhead which was run for three-monthly periods alternately with Birkenhead Corporation, the single vehicle being supplied by Litherland depot. Originally, passengers paid their fares at the toll booths but, after the abolition of toll booths on the Liverpool side, there was difficulty in ensuring that all fares were paid and from 1st November 1969, fares were collected by drivers in the normal way.

This service continued unchanged under PTE auspices, being allocated the vacant number 94 in October 1982. Diversion of the buses to use the Wallasey tunnel was originally a temporary expedient during maintenance work but it proved so popular that it was retained, buses running outwards via Wallasey Tunnel and back by the Birkenhead tunnel. With the opening of several clubs in Liverpool, the weekend demand increased and from July 1985 the advertised frequency between 2.15 and 3.15am on Saturdays and Sundays was stepped up to 20 minutes, three trips running both ways by the Birkenhead tunnel as 94A. A number of night services were started by Amberline in 1989 using ex-PTE Atlanteans from the 1236-95 batch, fitted with wire cages to protect the drivers from attack.

Services for the Disabled

In 1984, the PTE was one of the operators chosen by the central government to operate a new type of dial-a-ride service for disabled and blind persons. It was given the name 'Merseylink' and those eligible were issued with a membership card bearing a photograph. The service was widely publicised.

A Merseylink office was opened in a shop adjacent to the St. George's Hotel and journeys, which could be made between any two points in the county, had to be booked in advance by telephone or letter. The service was available from 8.00am to 10.00pm and was initially launched on 21st May 1984 in connection with the International Garden Festival. Fares were based on the zone system, 25p for one zone and 50p for longer trips but, because of licensing difficulties, the service was provided free of charge in the early months, the vehicles not being licensed as PSVs at the time.

The Quest 80 midibuses intended for use on this project failed to arrive in time and four vehicles were hired for Merseylink comprising 101-2, diesel Ford Transits with 6-seat Mellor bodies and a tail lift from Chalfont Line of Perivale; 103, a Renault Trafic with 7-seat Taurus body from Hadfield Motors of Stockport and a prototype Carbodies CR6 taxi numbered 104 which was replaced in June by another identical vehicle which bore PTE livery but no number. The PTE bought a petrol-engined Ford Transit with a 16-seat Mellor body which was reseated to six with a tail lift; this became No. 105. It was soon realised that smaller vehicles were more suitable for this work as they could penetrate the residential areas better and six Mercedes L307Ds with 8-seat Taurus bodies with tail lift were in service by late summer as 110-115.

At first the Traffic Commissioners granted a licence only on condition that an attendant was carried in addition to the driver, basing this decision on a code of practice which recommended that stage carriage vehicles carrying wheelchairs should not be one-man operated. However, the PTE successfully appealed against this decision as the code applied only to vehicles with 17 seats or more. It was while this case was being decided that the free service operated.

At deregulation, the six Mercedes minibuses were retained in PTE ownership but, to circumvent restrictions imposed by the 1985 Act, their operation was contracted out, at first to Crosville, then to Amberline and eventually to Merseybus; they were theoretically renumbered 8201-6 in 1987 but the old numbers remained on the vehicles. They were replaced by Omni minibuses during 1990. The service could only scratch the surface of the demand and was well over-subscribed and the PTE decided to supplement Merseylink with groups of fixed route services, operated by wheelchair-accessible buses.

Ford Transit 105 originally had a 16-seat Mellor body but was equipped with a tail-lift and altered to seat six passengers and accommodate wheelchairs. It was the first petrol bus in the PTE fleet but was not licensed as a public service vehicle.

Number 110 was the first of six Mercedes L307Ds with 8-seat Taurus bodies and tail-lifts, bought in 1984 for the 'Merseylink' special service for the disabled whereby individual journeys could be booked in advance. These vehicles remained in PTE ownership at deregulation but were run by contractors; they were not PSVs.

Renault Trafic No. 103 with 7-seat Taurus body was hired with other vehicles to start the 'Merseylink' dial-a-ride service for the disabled. It is seen outside the 'Merseylink' centre by the St.George's Hotel in Roe Street in June 1984.

Merseybus converted five Leyland National 2s to 'Mobility Buses' with 23 seats and a Radcliffe lift for wheelchairs positioned where the centre exit door would be on a two-door bus; some of the conversion work was done by MCW but all were finished off at Edge Lane. These conversions were done speculatively and, their tender for the Merseylink services being unsuccessful, the buses stood idle except for the occasional private hire. The contract for the initial Mobility Bus service, in north Liverpool and south Sefton, was won by C & M Travel, employing two rather similarly converted Nationals with accommodation for 22 passengers and five wheelchairs. At the PTE's request, they were painted in a special Merseytravel livery of white, grey, yellow, blue and black, hitherto used only on letterheads and publicity matter.

After deregulation, the PTE sponsored several timetabled services for the disabled to augment the 'Merseylink' facility. Although Merseybus converted some Nationals to load and carry wheelchairs, they failed to get the contract which went to C & M Travel. This Leyland National, WFM 810L, which was new to Crosville in 1972 as SNL810, is seen in Hood Street in May 1989.

Taxis

Passenger resistance to the substantial fares increases of the seventies brought competition from an unexpected quarter — the meter cabs, for long a familiar sight in the city but restricted in both number and clientele. When it was realised that four or five people could get together and ride in relative luxury virtually door-to-door for less than the bus fare, taxis became a familiar sight in the suburbs at peak hours, even in the low-income council estates. The habit spread to shopping expeditions, women without the use of a car being able to indulge in volume shopping and carry it home in a taxi. Another spur to the growth of the taxi habit was the fear of rowdyism and violence which regrettably became an increasing facet of life, especially at night.

The Transport Act 1985 legalised the widespread practice of charging separate fares and, prior to deregulation, four taxibus services were registered but none got off the ground. However, by this time taxis were well-established in their traditional role but substantially increased numbers were working from numerous additional ranks including places such as New Strand, Bootle and Kirkby Railway Station where, twenty years earlier, taxi traffic would have been almost non-existent.

51 BUS—RAIL INTERCHANGE

The Rail Policy

As a legacy of its pre-eminence as a port in the nineteenth century, Liverpool was particularly well endowed with railways which, by the sixties were either abandoned or under-utilised. Some lines had been planned and built primarily to handle freight traffic to and from the docks, although many of Liverpool's docks were not laid out with direct rail transhipment in mind. As much traffic was carted to and from warehouses, the railway companies had built a number of goods stations adjacent to the dock road to give adequate coverage within the limits of horse haulage. In pre-grouping days the territorial companies, the LNW, successor to the original Liverpool and Manchester Railway and the Lancashire and Yorkshire Railway, had been joined by the Cheshire Lines Committee thus giving improved dock access to the city for its three constituent owners, the Great Northern, Midland and Great Central companies.

Liverpool had also been a pioneer in electrified suburban passenger railways, with the building of the Liverpool Overhead Railway (opened 1893), and the electrification of the Mersey (1903) and the L&Y Southport line (1904). Thus in Edwardian times, the city already possessed three electric passenger railways, one underground, one overhead and one on the surface. The two survivors were important factors in the City Planning Department adopting a pro-rail policy for local transport; another was the dreadful traffic congestion in the city centre which developed in the sixties and perhaps the policy was underlined by the lengthy bus strike of 1968 which drove many passengers to use the railways for the first time.

There had long been enthusiasm in various quarters for creating a unified rail network in the city from the still largely separate nineteenth century systems and when the ideas were revived in the course of the MALTS Study, they were eagerly supported by the City Planning Department.

A scheme dear to the planners, and perhaps the most controversial among transport men, was the Outer Rail Loop, a circular railway route to be formed by joining a proposed underground extension of the Southport/Ormskirk line across the city centre with the former Cheshire Lines route from Central (High Level). This line was to be followed through St. Michaels, Garston, Hunts Cross and Gateacre and over the CLC North Liverpool lines through Knotty Ash and Fazakerley Junction. A short connection with the Ormskirk line near Kirkdale would have completed the circle into the city centre. A somewhat similar plan which involved linking the CLC with the Overhead Railway had been mooted early in the century. The planners' idea was that the outer suburban bus services would terminate at the loop line and all

passengers would continue their journeys by rail. The scheme had three weaknesses: (a) an existing five mile direct road journey would, in some cases, have been replaced by a 12 mile indirect rail journey, (b) buses would still have been required to serve the area between the Outer Rail Loop and the city centre and (c) there was no suitable infrastructure at any of the proposed interchange stations though the planners envisaged a ring of District Centres along the line.

Whilst there are considerable advantages in handling heavy commuter traffic by rail in suitable cases, the benefits to the passenger must be more than marginal and the service must be convenient and direct. This was confirmed by the results of an interesting road-rail co-ordination experiment carried out between 12th December 1966 and 11th March 1967 when special buses showing No. 900 were operated between Northwood and Aintree Station during the morning and evening peak hours. These buses, which followed the 92B route to Hall Lane and then ran along Hall Lane, Warbreck Moor and Ormskirk Road into Aintree station forecourt, carried special indicator displays in blue with 'Kirkby Rail Link' and the British Railways double arrow motif. Aintree station, rather then Kirkby, was chosen because of the frequency and available capacity of the service. Only special through return tickets at 2/-(2d less than the return bus fare) were issued but the time saved was only marginal and insufficient to overcome passengers' resistance to a change of vehicles; the maximum number of passengers carried was about 140 on any day. This represented a mere £14 in revenue to be divided equally between the Corporation and British Rail and most, if not all, of this was absorbed by the costs of supervising the interchange at Aintree.

The Gateacre Line

Preoccupation with the Outer Rail Loop led to a long drawn out struggle between the Corporation and British Railways which started when the latter announced its intention to close Liverpool Central High Level station and withdraw the local service between Liverpool and Gateacre. Through trains from Manchester were to be diverted through Allerton and Edge Hill to Lime Street. The Corporation objected to this and under the procedure laid down by the Transport Act 1962, the proposed closure had to be considered by the Transport Users' Consultative Committee. Having noted this body's observations, the Minister of Transport agreed to the closure in April 1966, provided that the lines be retained intact for the time being in view of the Outer Rail Loop proposal. The Minister also

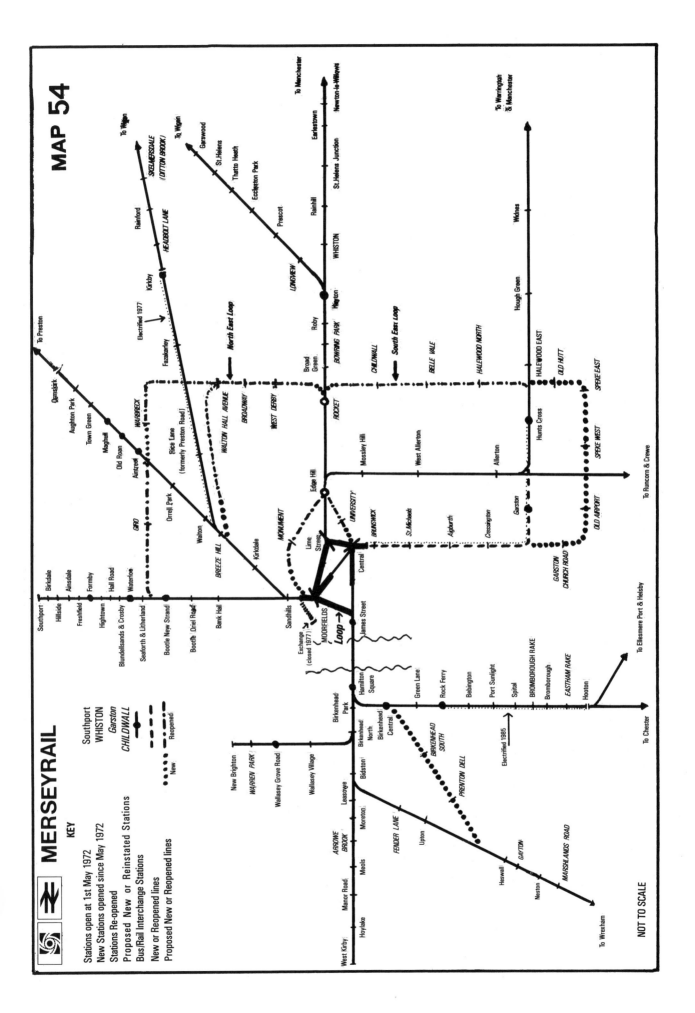

specified that at least five additional bus journeys be provided from Garston to Liverpool in the morning peak and vice versa in the evening peak on Mondays to Fridays. Three months later, the Corporation Passenger Transport Committee, having noted the decision 'with regret', agreed to provide the additional buses if crews were available but the City Council referred the decision back. 3rd September 1966 was fixed as the date for closure of Central Station but, as there was still no sign of the extra buses being provided, British Rail was obliged to retain the hourly service to Gateacre whilst diverting the main line trains into Lime Street as proposed.

In November the Council endorsed a subsequent decision of the Passenger Transport Committee not to provide the additional buses, which could be done only at the expense of facilities elsewhere in the city. The Minister intervened and suggested that as Liverpool was so anxious to retain the service, they should relieve the Railways Board of the annual losses incurred in its operation, variously quoted as between £60,000 and £120,000. The Corporation was naturally reluctant to do this and finally, in February 1968, the British Railways Board itself applied to the Traffic Commissioners for a road service licence to provide the additional buses, with the proviso that it would be pleased to surrender it if Liverpool Corporation could take over. The Corporation objected on the grounds that the desire to close the line was inconsistent with plans for setting up a Passenger Transport Authority contained in the Transport Bill. Furthermore, there was already heavy traffic congestion on Aigburth Road. British Railways proposed that Crown Coachways should operate the service on their behalf and, in a reserved decision, the application was granted. British Rail undertook not to withdraw the trains during the 11 week Corporation bus strike and the Corporation, still undaunted, lodged an appeal to the Minister of Transport against the grant of the licence. The appeal hearing was fixed for 28th June 1968 but the railway announced the closure of the line would take effect from 15th June, a decision which gave rise to such howls of indignation that the closure was deferred at the eleventh hour. It was now the turn of the railways to suffer from labour troubles and the Gateacre line closed down for two weeks because of the work-to-rule and overtime ban by NUR and ASLEF members. At the appeal, the Corporation put forward the view that closure of the line should be deferred until the establishment of the proposed Passenger Transport Authority and the report of the Land Use/Transportation Study. It offered to share the losses equally with British Rail if the line could be kept open for one more year and in January 1969 the Minister of Transport announced a grant of £60,000 under section 39(1) of the Transport Act 1968 to be matched by a similar grant from Liverpool Corporation. The line, and Central High Level station, were eventually closed on 17th April 1972.

The Loop and the Link

MALTS recommended that priority be given to two city centre rail schemes both of which had been proposed in one form or another at various times in the preceding century. The first, known as the Loop, was the diversion of the under-river Mersey Line over a clockwise single track loop with new stations at Moorfields, (near Exchange), Lime Street and at Central (Deep Level) below the existing Low Level platforms. The line was then to be continued, joining the existing alignment at Paradise Junction before carrying on to James Street. On the Birkenhead side, a burrowing junction at Hamilton Square was planned to eliminate conflicting train movements where the line diverged into two branches.

The second part of the priority plan was the closure of Exchange Station and the projection of the Southport and Ormskirk lines underground, using part of the right of way of closed goods lines to Great Howard Street and then by tunnel to Paradise Junction from where the existing Mersey Line was followed to Central Low Level. This was christened the Link.

The use of the physical connection at Paradise Junction, which took its quaint name from the street above, was to be limited to the exchange of rolling stock. Nevertheless, it was seen as a source of great economies as the Southport and Ormskirk Line rolling stock was already being maintained at Birkenhead North, necessitating a long diesel-hauled journey via Warrington. The Loop and burrowing junction were authorised by a British Railways Act, the Mersey Rail Extension Act, 1968 and the Link by the British Railways (No.2) Act, 1971.

A Co-ordinating Committee on rail matters had been formed by Liverpool Corporation and was formalised by the PTE, other members including representatives of the Department of the Environment, British Railways Board and others co-opted from local authorities as necessary. A Technical Team reported to the Co-ordinating Committee.

The Rail Policy was attractive to the Authority and the Executive for its unifying role as it fused together the operating areas on either side of the Mersey in a way unequalled by any other mode. In the course of compilation of the PTE's Transport Plan, several additional rail schemes were drafted with purpose-built road-rail interchanges. The planners, whilst clinging to their Outer Rail Loop panacea, were persuaded to modify the scheme into North-East and South-East Loops converging on a new station near Broadgreen named The Rocket after the public house at the junction of Queens Drive and Broadgreen Road. This was part of a plan to re-electrify the Bootle-Aintree branch (using second hand materials), reopening part of the Victoria freight tunnel to join the ex-LNW Manchester line with the Link and a new tunnel between Central Low Level and the ex-CLC line last used by the Gateacre service, a link originally authorised by Parliament in 1888. The PTE paid the North West Road Construction Unit to make the M62 motorway foundations deeper so that the future South-East Loop would not interfere with them. Electrification to Wigan via both Kirkby and St. Helens and to Hough Green and Hooton was envisaged.

Powers for most of these schemes were included in the

Merseyside Metropolitan Railways Bill, promoted in 1973 but, because of various delays and two Dissolutions, not passed until 22nd May 1975. Major work on the Loop and burrowing junction and preparatory work on the Link commenced in 1972. Considerable government financial aid was given but both schemes suffered from the ravages of inflation and the Loop was dogged by labour disputes and materials shortages.

Lack of money and Local Government reorganisation led to a gradual whittling down of the grand design. Electrification to Wigan via Kirkby was abandoned in favour of a simpler plan to electrify to Kirkby where there were to be separate lines divided by buffer stops back-to-back; a dmu service was to connect Kirkby with Wigan and beyond. There was a somewhat similar layout at Ormskirk with a connecting line for emergency and departmental use only. The Wigan via St. Helens electrification was shelved in favour of a regular interval dmu service which was very successful. Following the success of the interchange at Hunts Cross between Merseyrail and the main BR network, plans for electrification to St. Helens and construction of the Edge Hill-Central connection were unsuccessfully revived in 1985. As the 1984-85 Report stated 'If finally found feasible and justifiable, the scheme could add a catchment population to Merseyrail equivalent to the Southport, Ormskirk and Kirkby lines and greater than the whole of Wirral'. The only further tunnelling scheme to survive was the southward extension of the Link to join the ex-CLC line. The Outer Rail Loop plans were a long time dying but were ultimately abandoned as official policy.

Sec.20 of the Transport Act 1968 was applied to the PT Area from 1st January 1972 and, in due course, agreement was reached with the British Railways Board on which services would be supported and on what basis, this being put into effect from 1st January 1973.

Interchange Experiments

Having accepted the MALTS recommendations for the development of the railway system, the PTE was receptive to any measures likely to result in a a transfer of traffic from road to rail. During 1970, the Ministry of Transport conducted a series of car/rail and bus/rail experiments nationally and, towards the end of that year the PTE, jointly with the central government, appointed consultants to design a series of projects. The aims were to ascertain to what extent existing car or bus users could be persuaded to transfer to rail for at least part of their journeys thus relieving pressure on the highway system and city centre parking facilities. Over distances beyond four or five miles from the city centre, rail travel could offer time savings and if patronage could be increased sufficiently, operating costs by rail could be less than by road.

There had been a few earlier experiments including the three-month trial in 1966-67 between Northwood (Kirkby) and Exchange Station via Aintree Station and the Ormskirk line. In August 1967, Ribble introduced three local circular services in Formby with a flat 6d fare but, although the bus passed the railway station on certain circuits, the network was not specifically rail-orientated. It is said that some local residents would give their children 3d to ride round all the circulars while they enjoyed an hour's peace and quiet.

The first major revision of services in Crosby in September 1968 had greatly improved connections with

The Kirkby Rail Link experiment of 1966-67 involved running peak hour buses between Northwood and Aintree station. Duple-bodied Leyland PD2/20 L96 of 1955 is seen in Longmoor Lane displaying route number 900 which was specially added to all stop signs *en route*. Blue cards bearing the LCPT and BR logos and 'Kirkby Rail Link' filled the destination screen apertures.

Maghull station's road-rail links were worked entirely by Ribble buses and three Bristol RESL6L 1972-built vehicles with ECW 47-seat bodies are seen in the station yard. Note the PTE and BR logos and the lower case fleet title which preceded the NBC corporate style.

trains at Waterloo Station by the introduction of the so-called circulars C1 and C2 but, again, road-rail connections were not the primary objective. The same could be said for the small network of local services put on by Ribble in Maghull in June 1970.

The attraction of the rail routes terminating at Exchange Station was restricted by the location of the station, far away from the shopping area, resulting in very low off-peak usage. Experience elsewhere suggested that, if a change of vehicle or mode is necessary, passengers preferred it to be at the origin end of the journey rather than at the destination end. Consequently, passengers from the Crosby area preferred a slower bus journey into the heart of the city if the bus terminus was within walking distance of their ultimate destination. It was reasoned that completion of the Link would remedy this defect, which was well borne out by later events but there had to be improved access to the rail system at the origin end. Monitoring techniques were devised to measure public reaction to various facilities and to forecast the likely outcome of a particular course of action.

The consultants' first report, published in October 1971, recommended 16 experiments centred on 13 railway stations but, as certain of the schemes had more than one option, 28 different experiments were conducted between 6th December 1971 and 4th June 1973. Some of these were in Wirral and therefore outside the scope of this work. In the meantime, the national scheme had adopted a Formby rail feeder as one of the Ministry's projects and the existing Formby local bus network was revised in November 1970 so that the town circulars operated only from 8.40am to 4.45pm, a special rail feeder taking their place during peak hours. This experiment was specifically designed to test the effect of the provision of a convenient bus-rail feeder service in an area of very high car-ownership. The service was successful and continued beyond the experimental period.

Car-rail experiments, which were conducted at eight stations, resulted in a recommendation that all station car parks more than four miles from the city centre should be free to rail users and this was put into effect in June 1974.

The bus-rail demonstration projects were, by their very nature, more complicated as, to judge the extent to which people could be persuaded to change their travel habits, it was essential that the experimental services should be superimposed upon an unchanged network. Fare scales had to be carefully examined so that bus-rail interchange would not be ruled out on grounds of expense. As conventional fare scales made short distance bus rides relatively more expensive than long ones, through bus-rail tickets had to be made available at fares below those applicable to the sum of the separate bus and rail journeys and the mechanics of ticket issue had to be taken into consideration. 'Ultimate' ticket dispensers were used for all through tickets, taking advantage of the double-ticket facility of that machine.

The projects were preceded and accompanied by publicity campaigns — house-to-house leaflet distribution, posters at stations, press advertisements and the issue of pocket time tables. 'Mersey Interchange', accompanied by the PTE and BR logos, was adopted as the 'brand name'. Slogans such as 'The fast new way to work', 'Gives you a longer lie-in every morning' and 'Try Interchange and enjoy a shorter working day', became familiar on Merseyside.

In most cases, the demonstration projects were conducted on a stage-by-stage improvement basis so that the effect of each new benefit could be carefully recorded. Progressive improvements comprised frequency increases, fare reductions and connectional timing improvements. The various projects in the Greater

Liverpool area are described below.

1. Hillside

This Southport suburb was outside Merseyside at the time the experiment was conducted but is of interest as PTE Panthers 1100 and 1101 were used on hire to Southport Corporation. The buses worked a tortuous route numbered 6 from Scarisbrick New Road/Balfour Road and passing through the eastern part of Birkdale. It was a dismal failure, the number of interchange passengers on a typical day being only 15. Strangely, more purely local passengers were carried. The service was withdrawn early in March 1974 but, in view of the imminent absorption of the Southport undertaking, the Panthers remained there.

2. Aintree

A feeder service (A1) ran right through the Netherton estates and along Park Lane to Aintree Station. On the return journey it diverted via Bridle Road to serve the Giro, providing a distributor in the reverse direction. It was deemed a success, generating about 130 interchange journeys in each direction and about as many local passengers. It was retained after the experiment ended.

3. Huyton

Worked by one Crosville bus, H99 linked the Mosscroft and Pluckington estates with Huyton Station via Seel Road. About 65 interchange passengers and slightly more locals were carried during each peak period on this 10-minute journey and the service was made permanent.

4. Maghull

This scheme which was operated by Ribble buses was created by modifying the existing network of local services. Two connectional services, M4 and M5, were established. Route M4 from Lydiate via Maghull centre was relatively infrequent with only two or three journeys in each direction and was not well patronised. Route M5 covered a seven-minute local route from Dodds Lane with a quarter-hourly service. During the experimental period, traffic was insufficient to satisfy the set criteria for retention but the services were continued and, by the autumn of 1974, patronage of M4 had doubled to 160 interchange journeys in each direction while M5 had increased by 78% to 178.

5. Waterloo

This experiment, also operated by Ribble, comprised time table alterations and through ticket facilities on the local service C2. A second stage increased the frequency so that a bus met every train. This was not very successful mainly because of operational difficulties as large numbers of school children making very short journeys resulted in poor timekeeping. However its situation at the southern end of the Crosby and Thornton residential area obviously gave it great potential. The defect was in the design of the experiment and much more attention was to be given to Waterloo as an interchange station in the future.

Leyland Panther 1100 was one of two lent to Southport Corporation to work an experimental interchange service between Blowick and Hillside station in 1972-73 before Southport joined the PTE. Note the various logos and stickers and the BET symbol.

North Western Leyland National 2 305 (formerly Ribble 853) at Maghull Station with 1972 Bristol RE 358. The National is still in Ribble livery with North Western vinyls applied.

The programme was completed well before the Link and Loop railway extensions were opened so the effect of these could only be estimated. A peak hour service on the Cityride service between Exchange Station and Lime Street had been introduced as a stop-gap measure in January 1972 but this did not have the same appeal as a through rail service.

Taken as a whole, the programme suggested that bus-rail interchange was attractive in a belt between four and ten miles from the city centre. Beyond that limit passengers were generally unwilling to undertake through bus trips because of the lengthy journey time and, for less than four miles, bus-rail offered no time-saving advantage over through bus travel. Through tickets were essential to avoid the tapering effect of individual fare scales. Purpose designed bus feeders had a high degree of reliability and were preferred to connections using multi-purpose bus services passing railway stations on which priority very often had to be given to non-connectional factors, a truism well known to busmen for many years but rarely recognised by enthusiastic planners. The reluctance of the travelling public to make long walks at the destination end of the journey was again demonstrated.

Waterloo Interchange, though by no means elaborate, was the largest purpose-built bus-rail interchange on Merseyside. It is seen during its last month of full operation with three ex-Ribble Atlanteans still in NBC poppy red but carrying North Western decals. The two on the right are from the 1486-1515 batch of 1980-81 with Eastern Coach Works bodies while that on the left is an earlier Park Royal vehicle. The ECW buses are both on interurban services, the 284 (formerly S4) between Liverpool and Freshfield and the 351, Liverpool-Crosby-Ormskirk. Both have deviated from the main road to call at the Interchange, a practice which ceased after deregulation.

A previously unsuspected discovery was the lengthy time that the public can take to change its travel habits. This was demonstrated by the increase of almost 40% in bus-rail transfers on the routes recommended for retention in the year after the end of the experiments and particularly by the experience at Maghull, mentioned above.

These conclusions were accepted by the PTE and, following the approval by the PTA of railway electrification to Kirkby and Garston, rationalisation schemes were designed with bus-rail as an essential element. At this stage, the busmen's trade unions began to sit up and take notice, fearing that there would be serious job losses. Non-cooperation in all rail related schemes became union policy and, in particular, busmen refused to issue or handle through bus-rail tickets.

Waterloo Interchange

Despite the failure of the Waterloo demonstration project and a fall in the number of interchange passengers in the year following the experiment, a detailed report was drawn up in 1976 on the potential of this station as an interchange as many more rail passengers were expected after the opening of the Link. It was also influenced by the urgent need to reduce bus mileage and the Crosby corridor undoubtedly had the greatest off-peak over supply, a legacy of the previous 40 years. The planners were obviously offended by the non-standard L prefixes to the Crosby area route numbers as their proposed network was presented as follows:-

30C   Crosby-Aintree-Liverpool (30C)

201	Crosby-Liverpool via Oxford Road and Derby Road (L35)
202	Crosby-Liverpool via Oxford Road and Linacre Road (L3)
203	Crosby-Waterloo-Crosby via Oxford Road and Chesterfield Road (C2)
204	Runnells Lane-Liverpool via Chesterfield Road and Knowsley Road (L85/86)
205	Runnells Lane-Liverpool via The Northern Road and Knowsley Road
206	Southport-Formby-Liverpool via Endbutt Lane and Linacre Road (S2)
207	Freshfield-Waterloo Interchange (Liverpool at peak) via Endbutt Lane & Linacre Rd.
208	Crosby-New Strand or Balliol Road via Liverpool Road and Knowsley Road (L90)
209	Hall Road-Huyton via Liverpool Road and Knowsley Road (92)
210	Crosby-Waterloo via Liverpool Road (L9)
211	Kirkby-Maghull-New Strand or Balliol Road via Liverpool Rd. & Knowsley Road
212	Crosby-Netherton-Fazakerley (29)
351	Ormskirk-Maghull-New Strand or Balliol Road via Liverpool Rd. & Knowsley Rd.(381/2)
391	Waterloo-Maghull via Marsh Lane (391)

The nearest equivalent route at the time is shown in parenthesis. Number 204 was to have an additional service to Waterloo Interchange at peak hours while 205 was a combination of L85/86 and L48. The diversion of 206 and 207 via Endbutt Lane had no equivalent while the desire to renumber 92 as 209 showed a lack of appreciation of this long route's functions in other parts of the area.

Whilst some detail changes were made, the scheme was accepted in principle and work commenced on an interchange station on the north side of South Road, opposite Waterloo Station. The full plan envisaged the construction of a roof over the station platform to form a car park and the replacement of the South Road frontage by a bus turning circle surrounded by new commercial development. A new booking office was planned with direct access from the bus station but lack of funds ruled this out and resulted in all interchange passengers having to cross South Road. A new covered footbridge costing £71,000 was eventually installed. It was decided that all buses running along Crosby Road North would call at the

Interchange and, because of the lack of suitable bridges across the railway line, there was no way of routing the main road services other than by making a double run along South Road. On the inward journey this involved two right turns and added at least five minutes to the journey time.

Financial considerations dictated that the rationalisation of the Crosby services should be done before the Link was opened as part of a massive reduction of services all over the area. The scheduling and administrative work involved was enormous and could not reasonably be repeated so a new, rail-orientated network was scheduled to commence on 10th January 1977. The Ribble crews at Bootle depot registered their disapproval by staging a one day strike. There were long queues for railway tickets on the first day and some public disquiet at the withdrawal of many through facilities. The fare tables in Crosby were distorted to give a 6p fare from any point in Thornton or Crosby to the Interchange in order to compensate for the lack of through tickets. Much of this disappeared when the Link opened in May 1977 though, in the early stages, there were serious operational problems on the railway. Details of the final service changes will be found in Appendix 48 and it is of interest to note that only one of the new 200 numbers was used — 211 for the Bootle-Kirkby service — and several new 'L' numbers appeared. Happily, the PTE put public familiarity before administrative tidiness.

Before deregulation, 29 buses per hour used Waterloo Interchange; afterwards there were only four. Off peak 18 used it, after deregulation none, though numerous trips used South Road.

Railride

Progress on the Link overtook that on the Loop and the Wirral line between Central Low Level and James Street was closed to traffic on 18th July 1975 to enable the connection at Paradise Junction to be constructed. A free bus service for rail passengers described as 'Railride' was provided with buses advertised at three-minute intervals in the peak, five minutes off peak, ten minutes in the evening and quarter-hourly on Sundays. The buses described a loop via Hanover Street, Canning Place and Strand Street into James Street, returning via Lord Street and Church Street. A number of ex-Birkenhead and St. Helens single deck buses were deployed but eventually ex-Liverpool Panthers took over.

(Right) Leyland Panther 1104 in green livery turns from Strand Street into James Street in August 1975 while working the Railride service. The step in the waistrail became more prominent with the reversal of the original livery.

(Right upper) AEC Swift 223 with Marshall 44-seat body was new to St. Helens Corporation in 1971. It was still in the St. Helens livery when pictured outside Central Station on the Railride service in July 1975. It was soon returned to St. Helens and replaced by a Panther.

The Leyland Atlantean was rare as a single-decker but 95 was one of a pair with 40-seat Northern Counties bodies ordered by Birkenhead Corporation though delivered to the PTE. It is seen emerging from Hanover Street during its brief time on the Railride service before transfer to Southport in 1975.

121

Opening of New Railways

The extensions and re-openings were brought into use in several stages as follows:-

2nd May 1977	The Link opened. Southport and Ormskirk trains diverted to Central Low Level and Kirkby-Liverpool Central electric service commenced. Moorfields station access restricted to Old Hall Street.
9th May 1977	The Loop opened but with no intermediate stations.
30th Oct. 1977	Lime Street Low Level station opened on the Loop.
3rd Jan.1978	Central Low Level-Garston electric line opened with through service between Kirkby and Garston. St. Michaels, Aigburth (formerly Cressington) and Garston stations reopened.
8th May 1978	Moorfields Wirral Line (Loop) platform opened.
31st July 1978	Full Moorfields concourse opened.
25th Oct. 1978	Official Merseyrail opening by HM The Queen.
5th July 1983	Garston Line extended to Hunts Cross.
30th Sept. 1985	Rock Ferry line extended to Hooton.

Following experience of the extended railway services and lengthy bargaining with the Unions, some further changes were made to the Crosby network on 1st October 1978. Local services C1, C3 and C4 were withdrawn and replaced by the reinstatement of C2 extended to Runnells Lane. The Unions agreed to the withdrawal of Ribble 29 and PTE 30C and the reintroduction of L22-23 which were diverted via Waterloo Interchange. L9, L45 and L85 were all withdrawn, The Northern Road being served by rerouting 92. However the most important event was the withdrawal of the Liverpool-Southport through service S2 and its replacement by local services between Freshfield and Liverpool and Formby and Southport. Since the extension of availability of old age pensioners' passes, buses had been thronged by free riders between Liverpool and Southport on fine days. Now that availability of these passes had been extended to rail, it was desirable to transfer this traffic to rail where there was off-peak capacity. The local services also improved internal facilities within Formby and gave rail interchange options at both Formby and Freshfield stations.

As the railway journey time was half that of the buses, there were few complaints and the peak hour limited stop service X37 was discontinued on 1st December leaving the two-hourly X27 as the only road service between Liverpool and Southport on the coast road. The introduction of zone tickets on 29th October 1978 effectively overcame most of the through ticket problems for regular passengers.

OTHER INTERCHANGES

Trade union opposition continued to hamper progress on adjusting the bus network following electrification of the Kirkby and Garston lines and there was substantial duplication of facilities while long and difficult negotiations dragged on.

HM Queen Elizabeth with Counc. Mrs Jean Leech, OBE, Chairman of the Passenger Transport Committee and Director General Leslie Latter, at Kirkby on the occasion of the official opening of the Merseyrail extensions on 25th October 1978.

Kirkby

Two years and one month elapsed between the introduction of a 20-minute train service to Kirkby and the reshaping of the bus network on 2nd June 1980. A number of Panthers had been overhauled and had their centre exits removed for use on a local network as single-deck buses were considered to be less prone to the vandalism prevalent in that town. They were augmented and eventually replaced by Leyland Nationals.

The Kirkby line passed through no traffic centres of importance as the positions of the intermediate stations at Sandhills, Kirkdale, Preston Road (later renamed Rice Lane) and Fazakerley had been determined in the previous century by main road crossings. Kirkby station was near the northern edge of the town and the Industrial Estate and the residential areas of Southdene and Northwood were remote from the railway. Much of the bus traffic was destined for parts of the city without any rail connection so it was obvious that the potential for transfer from bus to rail was limited. However, the through journey time to Liverpool Central of 17 minutes was attractive compared with about 40 minutes by limited stop bus and therefore Kirkby railway station was given interchange facilities. In fact, an additional station was built west of the original structure which now served only the Wigan dmu service. The building was notable for its vandalproof features.

The need for a revised bus network was emphasised by the extent to which taxis were being used for local journeys within Kirkby. A new series of route numbers from 151 to 159 was allocated. There were three local services within Kirkby all of which fed the railway, three services to Liverpool city centre, one to Walton and one to Norris Green on Saturdays. The use of the numbers 13, 15D, 44A, 92A and 92B ceased so 19 was the only original Kirkby number to remain. Both limited stop services, 544 to the city centre and 500 through to Speke were withdrawn. The latter was closely duplicated for much of its length by the through train service to Garston with a journey time of 29 minutes compared with 50 by bus between the closest equivalent points. Both had a 20-minute frequency which was the most the railway line, which had been singled beyond Fazakerley, could accommodate. In 1985, when a standard 15-minute headway was adopted on all the electrified lines, double track was restored for a quarter mile. The full integration planned was not achieved in the absence of through ordinary tickets but zone tickets now accounted for a high proportion of journeys.

Prior to the introduction of the local bus network, there was an attempt to make Kirkby the railhead for Skelmersdale where the railway had closed just as the town was being expanded to house Liverpool's overspill. On 1st October 1978 Ribble routes 336 and 355 from Liverpool to Skelmersdale were replaced by routes 395-6 to and from Kirkby Station (later extended to the Industrial Estate) which gave approximately a one hour trip time from Skelmersdale to Liverpool Central. This was no better than the through limited stop bus services which were restored in December 1980. In 1982 the evening rail service between Kirkby and Wigan was withdrawn and eventually, under pressure, the County Council instructed the PTE to provide a bus service between Kirkby Station and Rainford. Numbered 50, it ran from 11th April 1983 until 28th January 1984, having carried little more than empty seats in the intervening months.

Bootle New Strand

New Strand was typical of the off-street suburban centres with built-in car parking and bus loading facilities which were springing up in the late sixties. Much of the area adjoining it had been devastated in the air raids and it was an important step in the urban renewal process. Strand Road, the eastern end of which was to be straddled by the new buildings, was closed to traffic from 1st May 1967, route 23 being withdrawn and replaced by the diversion of 24 via Marsh Lane instead of Knowsley Road. Under the original plan, a section of Stanley Road would have been pedestrianised but this was not proceeded with as the alternative routes were not fully developed.

Marsh Lane and Strand Road station which lay directly to the west of the centre was renamed Bootle New Strand and if the full railway plans had come to fruition there would have been a covered pedestrian way between the platforms and the bus station, shopping mall and car parks. However, the attraction of the interchange was diminished by the need to negotiate precipitous stairways and cross a busy road.

The public library and other official buildings were moved to adjacent sites. Bootle at last had a viable town centre instead of being a dependent satellite of Liverpool. The town's prosperity was boosted by the government's policy of moving whole departments away from London; the National Giro with its huge clerical staff was soon to become an important generator of bus traffic.

From August 1968 the orbital routes 60 and 81/81D were diverted at Stanley Road to New Strand instead of Bootle (Oriel Road) Station which was left temporarily without buses until June 1969. Both routes then reverted to Merton Road and Oriel Road and continued along a new street, Washington Parade, made possible by the elimination of a low canal bridge. A month later, a Bootle circular service (48/49) was started jointly by the Corporation and Ribble, linking New Strand at off-peak times and the government offices at Balliol Road at peak hours, with Orrell, Ford and Netherton and to this was added a new Ribble off-peak service 392 to Maghull.

Despite the inadequacies of its infrastructure, New Strand became a useful interchange and there has been a gradual tendency for city routes from the north to be curtailed there, in whole or in part. In more recent times, the virtual demise of Seaforth as a bus traffic centre has led to the further rerouting of old established trunk routes such as 61 and 68 to serve New Strand.

Garston and Hunts Cross

When electrification reached Garston in May 1977, a

modern station building and ramped footbridge were built and the approach road was upgraded to make a bus terminus. But the familiar staff problems prevented a feeder bus service being introduced until 4th September 1978 when route 84 commenced running between Garston Station and Speke as part of a big package of service reductions. The lack of through ordinary tickets was a handicap as the sum of the rail and feeder bus fares exceeded the through bus fare. Nevertheless, a substantial volume of interchange traffic developed though this reduced when the trains were extended to Hunts Cross in 1983. At Hunts Cross there were no terminal facilities but several bus services passed nearby and these were suitable as feeders to Halewood and Speke. Route 81 was retimed to connect with the trains. If plans to extend electrification beyond Hunts Cross mature, it will be possible to increase direct rail service to the large residential area of Halewood where a new station has already been opened. Hunts Cross also acts as a rail-to-rail interchange as the local Liverpool (Lime Street)-Warrington-Manchester trains on the ex-CLC line were cut back to this station and there is a substantial cross-platform traffic. During the Liverpool Garden Festival in 1984, a spare electric train was kept at Hunts Cross to move passengers arriving on British Rail excursions.

Aintree, Old Roan and Maghull

Serving a lower density of population, the Ormskirk line did not attract large volumes of bus-rail passengers. Reasonably free flowing traffic between the outlying areas and the city boundary made car commuting attractive and Aintree station was developed for park and ride. This car-rail traffic was of some importance and, on two occasions during rail strikes in 1982, Ribble opened its parking ground at Aintree garage, offering a £1.00 park and ride ticket by bus to Liverpool and return.

Ribble M3 and M4 local peak hour services which had originated during the experiments, continued as subsidised services and, in 1980, route 307 from Liverpool to Maghull (Green Park) via Aintree village, Waddicar and Melling Rock was replaced by a truncated version, M6, between Old Roan and Green Park only. Its principal role was for shoppers but it passed close to Maghull station and terminated at Old Roan station. The latter, accessible also from parts of Netherton by routes 54 and 59, was not popular as an interchange because it is perched on a high embankment with many stairs to climb to and from street level so, in October 1981, M6 was extended to Aintree station where there was better access.

Meanwhile in March 1983, the Aintree feeder peak bus service A1 was renumbered and extended back to Aintree from Sefton Estate as a circular, a move made possible by road improvements. It continued to serve the Giro, working clockwise in the morning as route 29 and anti-clockwise in the afternoon as 29A. However, at the time of the interchange experiments in 1972 there had been no through bus service from Netherton to the city via Park Lane and Walton, joint services 53/53A terminating at the

Lime Street Merseyrail station subway with British Rail and PTE logos prominently displayed. Little bus-rail interchange was possible at this point as traffic conditions required many buses to drive in the outer lane prior to turning right into St. John's Lane. The bus is 1157, a 1971 Leyland Atlantean PDR2 with Alexander dual-door body.

Black Bull. Since 1974, route 30 had worked through from Sefton Estate to Pier Head and, for many passengers, a transfer to rail gave little or no time advantage. For those who wanted to make the transfer, the combined frequency of 30, L22 and L23 made a dedicated feeder from Netherton redundant and 391-2 linked the Giro with Aintree station. Route 29/29A was withdrawn altogether in September 1984.

Huyton

Whilst the half-hourly St. Helens-Lime Street dmu service was popular, it did not have the appeal of the electrified network with its high frequency services and more modern image. The main line terminus at Lime Street was connected with the shopping area and the Hood Street bus stops by grimy pedestrian subways, haunted by undesirables, which many people were loth to use.

Nevertheless the line had its adherents. The station at Huyton, being adjacent to the town centre was served by numerous bus services which were not specifically rail-orientated and the H99 continued to run in the peaks. With each service revision, the PTE endeavoured to steer more traffic to the railway and the Crosville Prescot-Liverpool group of routes was the obvious target.

In the big scheme of 1973 the new Lickers Lane estate at Whiston had through direct buses to Liverpool only in the peaks, the all day service H18 running to Prescot and Huyton centres. In the course of the 1977 economies, H6 from Prescot was curtailed at Huyton though it reverted to running through to Liverpool in 1978 when H9 took its place as an off-peak and evening service between Prescot and Huyton station via Whiston Hospital and Huyton Quarry. In 1980 H7, the Cross Lane service, was changed to the direct route into Huyton town centre via Seel Road, forsaking the traditional Crosville route via Tarbock Road which avoided the station. A completely new railway station opened at Whiston in October 1990.

Consolidation

Once the problems of through ticketing had been more or less overcome by the use of zone tickets, the speed and convenience of the Merseyrail network attracted new passengers without the need for any more demonstration projects and over the next two or three years the PTE found itself forced to adapt the bus network to suit various patterns of bus/rail interchange established by the public by trial and error.

Between 1969 and 1976, rail traffic into the city declined in parallel with bus traffic. In the two years beginning March 1977, rail passengers entering the central area on weekdays increased from 27,000 to 34,000 (26%) and by November 1979, to 41,000 (52%). However, off peak daytime passengers, which had declined from 7,500 to 7,100 between November 1976 and March 1977, (perhaps reflecting the closure of Liverpool Central Low Level station), rose to 11,000 (55%) by March 1979 and 14,600 (106%) in November 1979. The steep rise during 1979 was mainly the result of extending concessionary travel, in particular senior citizens' passes, to rail and, of course, much of this traffic was transferred from the buses.

Organised bus-rail interchange increased more slowly and periodic surveys gave the following results:-

	Passengers
Autumn 1977	1,166
Spring 1978	1,386
Autumn 1978	1,327
Spring 1979	1,348
Autumn 1979	1,646
Spring 1980	1,637

By 1980-81, Merseyrail patronage overall had increased by 27% since the opening of the Link and Loop. Forty per cent of all rail traffic was carried on the Northern Line (Southport, Ormskirk, Kirkby and Garston) on which traffic had almost doubled. The effect of the Hunts Cross extension was also dramatic as the average 430 journeys made daily to and from Hunts Cross in May 1983 had increased to 2,850 one year later.

Whilst there is some unreliability, due largely to staff and recruitment difficulties, the railway network has been welcomed as a stable factor contrasting with the constant changes in the bus route network, a source of much confusion to the older people who make up much of public transport patronage.

Much of the expansion of rail traffic has been at the expense of the buses even though the network is far from perfect. Being based on lines with origins far in the past, there are none of the ideally planned interchange stations which one meets in many continental cities where passengers emerge from stations directly to street transport without the need to cross a road. None of the city centre Merseyrail stations is conveniently located for transfer to and from buses, a state of affairs made worse by the large scale pedestrianisation of the shopping area.

The rail network is unable to serve several important traffic corridors where buses are left to compete only with the taxis and private cars. Having backed heavy railways rather than 'light rail', Liverpool was able to make to make some progress in public transport during the difficult seventies and eighties when so many other changes were negative. By not participating in the still-promised new era of Light Rail, Liverpool cannot extend electric traction into wide areas of the city, for the Inspecting Officers forbid the inter-running of light and heavy rolling stock. But it is worth noting that Tyneside, where the Victorian railway network has been resuscitated with rolling stock which in continental Europe would be classified as trams, has still failed to run them on the streets. Ironically, Liverpool's suburban roads still show evidence of many miles of central reservations where trams once ran.

Detailed plans were made for electrifying the St. Helens line and joining it to the Link, but no work was done beyond making provision for a junction near Central Low Level station. Modern diesel railcars, not without their problems, have at last replaced the first generation stock and services improved, but the line, though well used, has not reached its full potential. Among the constraints on the PTE, who were of course financing British Rail, were the cost of electric rolling stock and the need to avoid further investment. Thus the Hooton extension was possible with the available fleet but not St. Helens.

The PTE encouraged the marketing of the network as 'Merseyrail', a name coined by Mr R. Cotton, a former BR Divisional Passenger Manager and the name and PTE logo appeared on the dc electric trains. Unlike other PTEs, the bus livery was not extended to railway rolling stock nor did diesel trains carry PTE markings.

Merseyside PTE developed a close and fruitful relationship with British Rail which, despite problems, made good use of otherwise wasted or underused railway assets. Contrary to the general drift of those years, the PTE was able to combine bus and rail to give a better level of service and retain substantial traffic for public transport.

52 THE BUS FLEET 1957-72

The evolution of a standardised fleet based on AEC and Leyland chassis had its origin in 1953-54. Earlier, opportunistic purchases had been made in an endeavour to overcome arrears of replacement of second-hand buses during the war years and, simultaneously, provide for expansion of the bus route network and the early stages of tramway abandonment. These events were fully described in Volume Four.

Standardisation extended to body design and, although this policy was firmly in place by the last tramway year, 1957, there were still five makes of vehicle on the road at the beginning of that year when the bus fleet numbered 1076. With the exception of 11 single-deckers (one AEC Regal, four Bedford coaches and six underfloor engined Royal Tigers), the whole fleet comprised orthodox rear entrance half-cab double-deckers with open platforms. None was equipped with interior heating; the equipment added weight which increased fuel consumption and, in any case, the average urban journey was considered to be too short to justify the expense.

The ultimate in Liverpool Corporation body design for orthodox rear platform double-deck buses had been reached in 1956. This was a 62-seat vehicle, 33 on the upper deck and 29 in the lower saloon with a rear-facing seat for five passengers against the front bulkhead. The body was of four-bay all-metal construction but, despite the extent of standardisation, Liverpool followed its own ideas to a remarkable extent in regard to full-width bonnets, concealed radiators and 'tin fronts'. There were, in fact, five variants, all but one peculiar to the fleet. First was the style used on A1-100 of 1953-55 which had almost the same radiator grille used by Crossley on various Regent III models, in particular the last 100 of a large Birmingham order. However, Liverpool's buses had a true full-width bonnet. Next came the 'standard' Leyland version on L61-170, of which L61-90 were the first production batch of the PD2/20, the front end of the chassis being based on a modification of the PD2/12 specified by Midland Red. Ironically, the curved contours of the Leyland body, which

Two of the Royal Tigers, with Crossley frames finished at Edge Lane, retained their original bodies and were never used on ordinary service in Liverpool, having fixed 'Private' destination displays. SL176, seen in St. Nicholas Place North in June 1961, in company with a Coast Lines AEC Regal, was destined to become a one-man bus in Birkenhead after transfer to the PTE and was scrapped as No. 97 in 1973.

The Bedford OB airport coaches B1-4, acquired from British European Airways in 1952, were Liverpool Corporation's last petrol-engined buses. B1 is seen in Dingle depot just before withdrawal in June 1961 with its replacement, XL172, a rebuilt Royal Tiger behind.

One of the last surviving 1939 AEC Regals (A178) is undergoing steam cleaning before submission for MoT inspection. It carries the last paint scheme which, unlike the double-deckers, extends round the front of the bus.

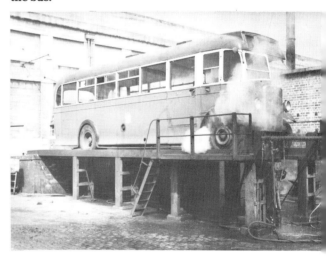

Leyland PD2/1 L484 with Roberts bodywork is seen emerging from Barrington Road on a diversion of route 60 due to roadworks in Gainsborough Road. The bus was new in 1951 and standardisation on four-bay bodywork had already commenced.

The essential narrow lines of the 7ft. 6in.-wide AEC Regent III are emphasised by this head-on view of A670 operating the Lime Street Station to Princes Landing Stage service. A side entrance to the station has now been made at this point in Skelhorne Street.

Few remnants of rural Kirkby remained by the 'fifties but hedgerows still lined Kirkby Row when Daimler CVA6, D591, with Weymann-framed Edge Lane body was caught by the camera en route from Page Moss to Pier Head. The parish church, now close to the town centre, is in the background.

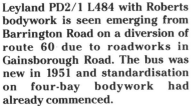

AEC Regent V with Crossley-framed body, finished at Edge Lane, is seen at Fazakerly when new. Note the custom-built bonnet with built-up nearside front wing and original three-line intermediate indicator.

Leyland PD2/20 L190, with Weymann body, was chosen to work the No. 90 service from Southdene to St. Helens on 26th November 1956 when St. Helens played Halifax in the Rugby League final at Wembley. Many of the staff wanted to attend and St. Helens Corporation prevailed upon its joint operators to cover as many of its duties as possible. As far as is known, this is the only occasion that Liverpool Corporation operated a service to St. Helens town.

Leyland TD7 L205X, with Leyland body, was one of three buses 'unfrozen' and released to Liverpool Corporation in 1942. Liverpool was fortunate in being able to have its standard destination equipment fitted. Note the radiator casing painted black and the typical Leyland waistband.

The pre-war AEC Regent Is had long lives and A167X, a bus which took the road in 1940, is seen at Edge Lane shortly before withdrawal in 1958. Note the complete removal of the beading which formerly enclosed the upper-deck cream band.

had ceased production in 1952, were built in to the front end, virtually forcing bodybuilders to use a similarly bow-fronted upper deck which was probably irksome to Liverpool's designers. Both Duple and Alexander (especially the latter) were prepared to vary their established designs to meet Liverpool's very detailed specification.

Thirdly, the front end of the Regent V was modified for Liverpool to the extent of omitting the chromium plated semi-traditional AEC grille. Although broadly similar, the Liverpool version had numerous minor differences including square-cornered bonnet opening and mudguard fairing and, even though the grille was of the same style as one adopted by Glasgow, it lacked blank areas for badges at top and bottom.

Fourth was perhaps the most intriguing of all, the Leyland style used on L177 and subsequent Titans with a cab front designed to be flush with the windscreen and quite unlike any other concealed radiator style for a PD2. The fifth variation was the revised Regent V style on A168 upwards described later.

In 1957, there were still 39 vehicles of pre-war design although, because of wartime circumstances, 19 of them had not entered service until 1940-42. Several of the AEC Regent Is and the sole survivor of the trio of 'unfrozen' Leyland Titan TD7s (L205) had had X suffixes added to their fleet numbers as the numbers of replacement vehicles caught up. These old vehicles had been retained as a consequence of the decision to abandon the Overhead Railway at the end of 1956 and all were withdrawn during 1958-59. No fewer than 138 new buses entered service during 1957, providing generously for replacement of the last trams and of 20 pre-war buses. In 1957 the Committee agreed that vehicle life should be increased from 15 to 18 years and in April 1958 it was advised that current deliveries would allow all pre-war buses to be scrapped. Thereafter, no replacements would be needed until about 1964. Eighteen years was unusually long as an 'official' life and, in the event, was not achieved.

The tramtrack and overhead wires are still in position at Kirkby as a Leyland PD2/20 with Crossley bodywork heads for the City Centre on tram-replacement route 44D. There was great criticism of the changeover to buses during the Suez fuel crisis of 1956-57.

Daimler CVD6 D547 with Northern Counties body and another of the same type, stand, bereft of indicator blinds, at Edge Lane just after withdrawal in 1961 after less than 12 years service. D547 was one of ten Daimlers with Daimler CD 8.6-litre engines, the remaining 80 being powered by AEC 7.7-litre units. Note the variation in liveries.

Among the non-standard vehicles were the 50 Crossley DD42s dating from 1948-49 and working from Garston (and later Speke) depot; the bodywork of these vehicles made a better impression than the chassis. There were also the 80 Daimler CVA6 and 10 CVD6s of 1949-50 operating on north end routes; the majority of these having AEC power units, deviated rather less from Liverpool's standard practice. There were also the four Bedford petrol-engined coaches taken over from British European Airways which survived until 1960-61 and then saw further service with other operators.

As a result of changes and decline in dockside traffic, the bus fleet needed to replace the Overhead Railway was grossly over-estimated and by 1958 the Corporation found itself with a surplus of buses. Thirty chassis, complete with body frames, were stored for almost four years, placing a financial strain on the undertaking which would have been considered intolerable in almost any well-managed enterprise.

Bigger Buses

The growth of industrial estates in Kirkby, Speke, Huyton and Netherton helped to provide a balance of traffic in both directions on certain routes but empty running in one direction at peak hours remained a grave problem for all operators. Since the war, during which several oversize vehicles, originally intended for export, had operated without difficulty, both manufacturers and operators had campaigned for revision of the PSV (Construction and Use) Regulations and as a result of these efforts, the immediate post-war dimensions for a double-deck bus on two axles were increased gradually from 26ft. long by 7ft. 6in. wide to 36ft. long by 8ft. 2½in. wide. In more recent times the length has been further extended to 12m (about 39ft. 4in.). So far weight restrictions have resulted in few double-deck buses on two axles (as distinct from coaches) being built to the maximum length but these

changes have meant that the pre-war maximum of about 56 seats has risen to over 80 and, because of the increased width, buses are more roomy. Ribble was quick off the mark in taking advantage of the increase in length to 30ft. which came into effect in July 1956 but had been announced by the Minister some months previously. In October 1956 an experimental rear-engined Leyland bus—the prototype of the Atlantean—was operated on Crosby routes L3 and L30 from Bootle depot being followed by similar experiments with an AEC Bridgemaster. Pending further development of the rear engine principle, an order was placed by Ribble for 69 Leyland PD3 double-deckers with 72-seat front entrance Burlingham bodies. The first of these entered service on 4th September 1957 (though not on Merseyside) but eventually considerable numbers were put to work in the Liverpool area.

While the layman may criticise the wisdom of running enormous vehicles with only a handful of passengers at off-peak times, in practice, the cost of running a large vehicle is only marginally greater than a smaller one and enormous benefits are obtained at peak times when the large capacity buses mop up traffic for which extra vehicles and crews would otherwise be required. These extra vehicles might only be used for about 15 hours a week but at least a proportion of their crews would need to be paid a full week's wage. The use of large capacity buses helped the operators to meet the constantly increasing costs of operation and reduced the effects of the chronic labour shortages. They also smoothed the worsening effect of the peak caused by the reduction in industrial working hours and the consequent overlap between the afternoon school demand and the evening peak.

Although one-man operation of double-deckers was unimaginable in the late fifties, the development of the rear-engined Leyland Atlantean obviously opened up new possibilities. The first production Atlantean in municipal service took to the road in Wallasey in December 1958 and Ribble adopted the chassis fitted with

The first experimental rear-engined double-decker and predecessor of the Atlantean was a Leyland demonstrator, chassis number 530001, registered STF 90. The O350 turbocharged engine was mounted across the rear platform. The light-alloy 61-seat body, built by Saunders Roe, had an overall height of only 13ft. 3in., achieved by using a drop centre rear axle and offset differential. The bus was tested in service by several operators, from 1954 onwards, including Ribble in whose service it is seen in Old Haymarket, operating on joint service 58 to Litherland.

the more powerful O.680 engine for express services to London, Bristol and Glasgow. It was not long before operators were seeking dispensations to experiment with one-man operated double-deckers at off-peak times with the upper deck closed off and this was obviously the thin end of the wedge. Southport was one of several which tried this with forward-entrance PD2s. Pressure from the operators for the extension of single manning was met by union demands not only for more money but for greater sophistication in vehicle design. Greater power was needed to make up time lost at stops, as passengers now had to file slowly past the driver's desk rather than board as quickly as possible. Semi-automatic or fully automatic gearboxes reduced driver fatigue in the more demanding driving conditions of the late fifties and sixties. Sophistication itself brought consequential problems as removal of the engine to the rear eliminated the traditional 'feel' by the driver for engine performance. This and changed attitudes increased driver abuse of machines on which there was already more to go wrong than on the older vehicles. Reliability suffered and more spare vehicles were needed.

Thus the trends of the fifties towards lightweight vehicles with low fuel consumption were completely reversed towards the end of the following decade when heavier, more powerful buses with larger and more thirsty engines were entering service. In 1950 a 45-seat bus with a 10.45 litre engine would have been considered a fantasy but such buses were entering municipal service in Liverpool 19 years later. Vehicle weight was, and is, the main culprit.

Attention to both driver and passenger comfort figured largely in body design and development. Platform doors have already been mentioned and heaters were introduced on experimental buses placed in service in 1959. Company buses, whose passengers tended to travel longer distances than city bus riders, had had heaters in pre-war days and the need for them on urban routes on which passenger journeys had lengthened with population dispersal, was now recognised. However, it could not be claimed that the quality of the ride was maintained.

The Last Half-Cab Double-Deckers

The Leylands.

Delivery of the last Titan PD2/20s commenced in November 1956, side by side with the stragglers of the previous (SKB) batch (L230-44) which were completed at Edge Lane on Crossley frames.

The VKB batch numbered 100 chassis of which 76 were PD2/20s and 24 were PD2/30s, the differences between the variants being minimal. Seventy had complete Crossley bodies while 30 had Crossley frames intended to be completed by local labour at Edge Lane. This order introduced the 62-seat layout with rear facing lower deck seat previously described. The first 35 (L245-79) were all running by January 1957 and they were followed by L310-44 between February 1957 and February 1958.

Leyland PD2/30 L347 carried one of the last Crossley bodies built and ran from 1958 to 1972. An unusual feature was the front windscreen which fitted flush with the full-width radiator grille.

A body combining a Crossley frame and Metro-Cammell finish was carried by L302, seen at Pier Head in February 1962. This was one of the 30 buses stored from 1957 to 1961. Note the full version of the cream window surround livery. The bus behind is 1948 Regent III A570.

The next 30 chassis, which included the last six on PD2/20 chassis, were all of 1957 manufacture but were fitted with body shells and delivered in 1958 by which time it had already become apparent that they were not needed. They were allocated the missing fleet numbers L280-309 and VKB numbers which followed on the earlier 35 buses but remained unlicensed and were put into store at Edge Lane works. Unfortunately, the design was dated and therefore less likely to find a buyer. If the Department did try to dispose of them, no record has been found.

The final batch of rear-entrance Leylands were PD2/30s, again with Crossley bodies — L345-69 — and these entered service between March and October 1958. They were also the last Crossley-bodied buses to join the Liverpool fleet. Although Crossley Motors had been taken over by AEC in 1948 it had continued to enjoy a measure of independence for some years. Liverpool had been one of

Crossley's largest bodywork customers, 346 bodies and frames having been purchased between 1951 and 1958.

By September 1960, because of labour shortages and the demands of the overhaul programme, Edge Lane had done no work on the 30 partly built vehicles and the Committee agreed to invite tenders for their completion. The contract went to Metropolitan-Cammell Carriage and Wagon Company, Birmingham (MCCW) whose work incorporated some new features. There were two additional upper-deck seats, bringing the capacity up to 64, and heaters were installed on both decks, the first example of this refinement in the Liverpool Corporation fleet except for the experimental buses described below. The depth of the destination indicator apertures was reduced to suit more economical blinds which eliminated spaces between names and which required indicator boxes of the old dimensions to be partially masked. Strangely, the original booked registration numbers VKB 736-65 were retained which caused some raised eyebrows as Liverpool had changed over to reversed registrations in 1958. These buses took to the road between October and December 1961 and had the distinction of being the last half-cab open rear platform buses to enter service for Liverpool Corporation. They must also have been the last basically Crossley bodies to be placed in service anywhere, as Crossley had ceased production while they had been in storage.

The AEC Regent Vs

As the Leyland Titans described above came into service, 125 AEC Regent V D3RV chassis with Metro-Cammell Orion style bodies were simultaneously delivered. As with the Leylands, 30 were supplied with body frames to be panelled and generally finished at Edge Lane works. These final Regents were powered by A218 9.6 litre engines though some received A208s in the course of normal engine changes. The difference between the two designs was mainly that certain water passages in the earlier version were found to be 'stagnant'; to cure a tendency to overheat, an external pipe delivering more water to the rear of the engine was a feature of the A218. Possibly Liverpool modified the A208 in this respect. The radiator grilles were of a specific Liverpool design and the nearside front wing was built up to accommodate the parking light. The seating layout was similar to that of the contemporary Crossley bodies.

Fleet numbers were A168-292 with A203-32 allocated to the vehicles for completion at Edge Lane. As the new buses came into service, any remaining pre-1946 buses with the same number individually received the X suffix. In January 1957, all 200 of the AEC Regents delivered between 1946 and 1949, which carried fleet numbers A225-424, were renumbered by adding 200 to their existing numbers.

Delivery started in November 1956 and continued until March 1958 with the exception of the Edge Lane batch. Eleven of these were ready for the final tramway conversion in September 1957 but only six more were completed during the next 13 months after which production ceased altogether for a time and the final 13 entered service only in September and October 1959. Five were unpainted and some if not all of these had moquette upholstery on the upper deck instead of the usual brown leather-look.

In the event, these were the last bodies to be completed at Edge Lane on bought-in frames. The practice had originated before the 1939-45 war and 151 vehicles had been completed since 1946.

One of the surplus 30 Leyland PD2/30s with Crossley frames which were stored at Edge Lane Works for three years before being completed by MCCW in 1961.

Tower blocks dominate the skyline as unpainted AEC Regent V A228 (left) negotiates Netherfield Road on the inter-suburban Walton-Penny Lane route. The unpainted buses took on a very dilapidated appearance when dirty and scarred by minor accidents as exemplified by A221 (right) pictured at Speke depot in June 1971. Note that although it had been owned by the PTE for nineteen months, it still carried Liverpool City Transport as the legal owner and the City's insignia.

The Experimental Buses E1-3

The Corporation's capital estimates for 1958-59 included a sum of £18,000 to cover the purchase of a number of experimental buses. Bus manufacturers had been working on new designs, some of them revolutionary in concept, to take advantage of the new regulations. Two-axle double-deckers could be 30ft. long with effect from July 1956, though Liverpool was by no means alone in having no such vehicles until some years later. As no replacement vehicles would be needed until about 1964 there was ample time to consider the various types available and decide on a prototype for the fleet of the future. Three different vehicles were ordered and the first arrived in Liverpool on 5th December 1958. This was one of six AEC Bridgemasters built for demonstration purposes and was hired from ACV Sales Ltd (the sales organisation embracing AEC, Crossley, Maudslay and Park Royal), with an option to purchase at any time. It arrived in full Liverpool Corporation livery except for crests and was numbered E3, although its demonstrator status was underlined by the Middlesex registration 116 TMD.

The Bridgemaster's main attribute was its ability to negotiate low bridges. Its overall height was 13ft. 5in., about normal for a low-height double-decker, but its interior layout was orthodox with pairs of seats and centre gangways on both decks instead of the awkward side gangways and rows of four seats traditionally associated with the type. This was achieved by chassisless construction with a completely flat lower deck floor, level with the rear platform; the transmission line was moved to the side. The idea had originated with the Bristol company in 1949 whose 'Lodekka' could be sold only to other nationalised bus companies, because of restrictions on

trading in the Transport Act 1947. However, the Bridgemaster had coil-spring suspension, independent for the front wheels.

Although Liverpool was not much troubled by low bridges, the low, flat floor helped loading and unloading. The Bridgemaster was 30ft. long and its Park Royal body seated 76, sometimes quoted as 43/33 but certainly 45/31 for most of its time in Liverpool. It was powered by the AEC AV590 9.6 litre engine and had heaters on both decks with the air intake of the heating system beneath the front destination indicator. Rexine seats were fitted and the interior was finished in an attractive green and cream colour scheme.

The low height of the AEC Bridgemaster, E3, is clearly shown by comparison with the following bus in this 1960 photograph. Despite its unorthodox design, E3 remained in service for 14 years, being sold for preservation in 1973.

The bus entered service on 10th January 1959 but was withdrawn after two days when the staff decided that no standing passengers would be carried. There was some controversy over high-capacity buses in various places at that time, the TGWU tending to do battle in suitably militant areas. Vehicles of similar capacity were in service all over the country without restrictions of this kind, so the dispute was referred to the National Joint Industrial Council for the Road Passenger Transport Industry. The bus did not run again in Liverpool until 26th October, the NJIC having ruled that standing passengers should be carried normally. In the meantime, E3 had been demonstrated in Bolton and Bury and perhaps elsewhere, still in Liverpool colours. Liverpool was sufficiently confident, despite the dispute, to order one AEC Regent V with forward entrance Park Royal bodywork (E1) and one of the first production Leyland Atlanteans with Metro-Cammell bodywork (E2). E3 was finally purchased for £3,657 in 1961, this representing the initial cost less hire charges between October 1959 and the end of 1960. It was prone to gear selector problems and on one occasion, when working route 60 in Bootle, its driver took a wrong turning. Reverse gear was found to be unobtainable and the conductor had to ask some of the passengers to alight and help push the bus back to the corner.

The Regent V (E1) arrived in August 1959 and, despite its capacity of 72 (40/32), was accepted by the staff without restriction as its forward entrance made it easier for the driver to watch loading and unloading if the conductor was not on the platform. It also had the AV590 engine but with semi-automatic transmission of the Monocontrol type, a feature not available on the Bridgemaster. Both models had air-pressure brakes. It was full-fronted, had power-operated doors and a sliding cab door, the body design being very similar to those supplied to the East Kent Road Car Co Ltd.

The revolutionary rear-engined Atlantean PDR1/1 entered Liverpool service in December 1959, a year after the first municipal example had appeared across the river in Wallasey. It had semi-automatic transmission but the power unit was the familiar 0.600 engine as used in the PD2. It originally seated 44 upstairs and 34 in the lower saloon but one seat was later removed from the staircase area on each deck and back to back seats were placed over the rear wheel arches instead of the more usual inward facing seats. This layout was to become standard on Liverpool Atlanteans.

By the end of 1960, E1 had worked from every depot except Prince Alfred Road and E3 had been at Garston, Speke, Dingle and Edge Lane. E1 eventually found a regular niche on route 88 from Garston. In April 1961 the Council decided in favour of the Atlantean and placed an order for 200 to be delivered over a period of three years at a cost of £1,436,646.

All three experimental buses were still in the fleet in 1969 but only Atlantean E2 was in regular service and surprisingly survived until 1978, though it was never equipped for one-man operation. It was sold for use as a playbus-cum-caravan and stood in a garden off Huyton Lane until eventually bought for preservation. E1 and E3

AEC Regent V E1 was distinctive with its full-width cab and forward-entrance door. It was similar in general layout to Ribble's PD3s but it remained the only one of its type in the Corporation fleet.

Experimental Atlantean E2 was to all outward appearances a standard Metro-Cammell-bodied bus but it was, in fact, the test bench for the large fleet built to Liverpool specification in the 'sixties.

were withdrawn in 1973; E1 served with the driving school for two months in 1974 before sale to T. Hollis, a Queensferry operator who also collected old vehicles and ensured the vehicle's preservation..

Trials were also carried out with vehicles hired from other operators. London Transport RMF 1254, a front entrance Routemaster used as a demonstrator by AEC, ran for a time on route 27 from 29th October 1962, whilst a Manchester Corporation Daimler Fleetline (4606) ran on routes 79C/79D in March and April 1963. An AEC Renown, 7552 MX, was also tried on 79C/79D in the same year, this last-mentioned being a successor to the Bridgemaster, with a separate chassis and conventional front suspension.

The First Production Atlanteans (L500-879)

Although the Metropolitan-Cammell Carriage & Wagon Co secured the order for the bodies on the 200, E2 was to be the only Liverpool Corporation Atlantean to carry what at first sight appeared to be a standard Metro-Cammell body. The vehicle was used as a mobile test-bed and various modifications were made to it, many of which were incorporated into the bulk order. The Liverpool Atlantean body was among the first to depart from Metro-Cammell's standard style, derived from the Orion body for front-engined chassis. Its design was unusually imaginative, reflecting what were then the latest car styling ideas. It is not known who was responsible at Edge Lane. The conventional front and rear domes gave way to a full-length roof line with 'peaks' at each end; the rear end of the upper deck had less overhang than the standard model. A polished aluminium decorative panel ran all round the body to blend with the front and rear bumpers. The fibreglass engine cowl was in three parts, the side pieces being quickly detachable and the centre part hinged.

Inside a level floor, 2ft. 4½in. high with one step from the platform, replaced the ramped floor of Liverpool's original specification, reducing the staircase steps from eight to seven. This allowed a more compact staircase, a wider landing at the top and a more spacious lower saloon. For an even roomier platform, the steering wheel and pedals were moved four inches to the offside which helped the driver to lean out when reversing. The driver's instrument panel was moved to form part of the cab ceiling.

The interior colour scheme was grey and red with white ceilings and chocolate brown floors. Leather-look seats and fluorescent lighting completed the interior equipment. There were 45 upper-deck and 33 lower-deck seats, those over the wheel arches being arranged back to back, thus eliminating the unpopular inward facing seats. The two-passenger seat behind the staircase was replaced by a single seat while the three-passenger seat opposite was replaced by a double seat, making room for a clothing locker for the crew and a detachable used-ticket box. The nearside front corner was modified with a pillar set in by about 6in. thus placing the entrance doors at a slight angle to the body and providing a slightly wider entrance. A distinctive external feature was stainless steel trim at the bottom of the bodywork which extended right round the vehicle. It was an impressive and carefully detailed design.

The first 200 Atlanteans were given fleet numbers L500-699 with matching reversed KD registrations. They comprised the first production run of what Leyland termed the MkII Atlantean though the original type designation PDR1/1 was retained, 'MkII' merely indicated the incorporation of most of the Liverpool features as standard. L501 was exhibited at the Commercial Motor Show at Earls Court in September 1962 and attracted considerable attention. It had a modified rear end with a deeper panel between the emergency window and the lower deck. All 200 originally had the O.600 engine but in course of normal engine changes, some eventually received O.680 units. The transmission was by semi-automatic

Much thought went into the design of the Atlantean's entrance. The step from the platform into the lower saloon enabled a flat floor to be used. The driver's position was moved further over to the offside to improve his rearward vision and make a roomier platform.

Pneumocyclic gearbox and the accelerator pedal was hydraulically operated. Buses from L560 upwards incorporated the modified rear end design of which L501 had been the prototype.

The Atlanteans started arriving in Liverpool in November 1962 when one or two isolated sorties were made by L500-1 on routes 27 and 87. However, in December, when the introduction of the first batch was imminent, the staff demanded extra pay for working large capacity vehicles. The Passenger Transport Committee was sympathetic but the National Conditions Agreement which governed working conditions in municipal transport undertakings nation-wide, precluded any such agreement so a draft resolution was submitted to the National Joint Industrial Council and the buses remained in store until it was considered. After the NJIC had again declared that no additional payment should be made, the first batch of Atlanteans entered service on the Garston Circular 86/87 on 4th February 1963, followed by the Childwall Valley Road routes 79C/D three weeks later. It had been calculated that, theoretically, the fleet of 1108 which existed at the time the order was placed could be reduced to 950 by the introduction of high capacity

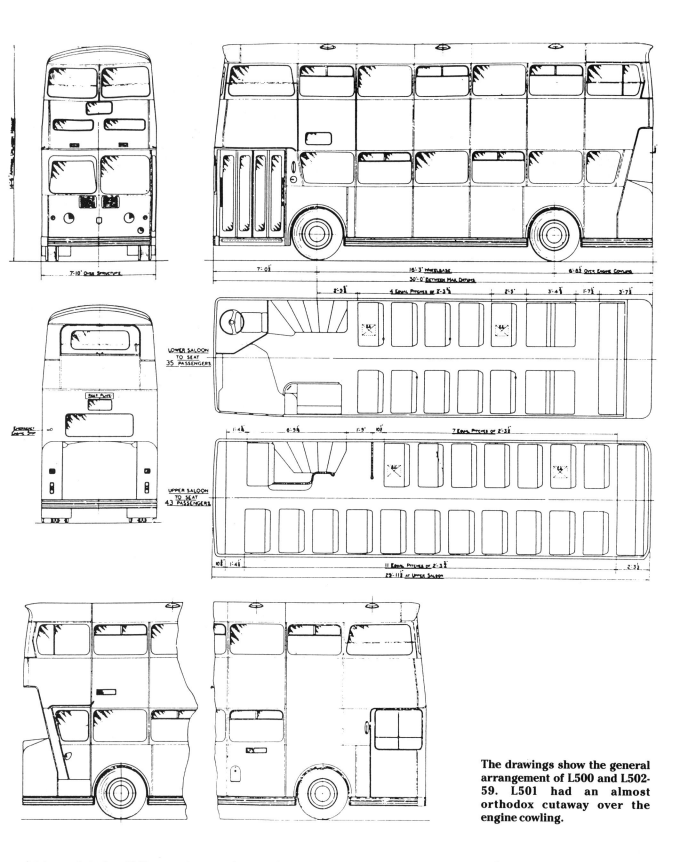

Lower saloon to seat 35 passengers

Upper saloon to seat 43 passengers

The drawings show the general arrangement of L500 and L502-59. L501 had an almost orthodox cutaway over the engine cowling.

vehicles and during 1962 several applications had been made to the Traffic Commissioners for new time tables which reduced frequencies.

In July 1963 it was decided to purchase 120 more Atlanteans over the two financial years following completion of the current order and it was originally proposed that 40 should be completed at Edge Lane on Metro-Cammell frames. However, when the order for L700-819 was placed in March 1964 it was for complete Metro-Cammell bodywork as the Edge Lane body men were already working four hours overtime per week to cope with existing work. The unit price for the chassis was £3,022 compared with £3,365 for a Fleetline. Six bodybuilding firms submitted tenders ranging from Willowbrook at £3,775 to Strachans at £4,594. Metro-Cammell at £4,350 was slightly lower than Park Royal and Alexanders.

The Leyland PDR1 Mk II Atlantean with Metro-Cammell bodywork was undoubtedly Liverpool's bus of the sixties and these views of L503 and L518, both of which went into service in February 1963, show the first version of Liverpool's distinctive body design; the back-to-back seats over the rear wheel arch are clearly visible. L500-59 (except L501) had this rear-end arrangement; from L560 the rear 'peak' was all but eliminated.

The last vehicle of the first order, L699, entered service on 8th September 1964 and, although Liverpool vehicle licensing office had changed over to the suffix letter system on 1st May 1964, it retained its booked registration 699 KD. L695 went over to Dublin as a demonstrator for a time before entering service in Liverpool.

Buses of the second batch were 30ft. 9in. long, nine inches more than the first order, the limit having been increased by the time this batch was designed. Such increased body length became quite common but, for Liverpool, the wheelbase was extended to 16ft. 9in. compared with the normal 16ft. 3in. This was a variation from the Leyland specification not normally available but justified by the size of the order. Unusually, they did not receive a special type number being designated PDR1/1 like their predecessors. The extra length was used to provide more platform space, a tip-up conductor's seat and two extra lower-deck seats. The rear end was again redesigned, the upper-deck overhang being eliminated altogether, thus avoiding dirt traps and facilitating mechanised cleaning. Ventilators were fitted to the front upper-deck windows. The first units, L700 amd 710 went into service on 1st November 1965 but the Council had already decided in the previous June to extend the order by a further 130 (L820 onwards). However, in September 1966 this supplemental order was changed to 60 Atlanteans and 70 single-deck Panthers because of the impending introduction of one-man operation which, at the time the specification was drawn up, had not been approved for double-deckers. Tenders were also invited for a further 65 single-deckers for 1968-69.

Deliveries of Atlanteans up to L879 were completed on 3rd April 1967 and, with their introduction on the Aintree routes 2 and 30 on 24th of that month, the 50-month

programme was completed. Over half the vehicles in all day service and one third of the total fleet were now Atlanteans, working from all garages, except Litherland. In May 1967 the allocation was as follows:-

Edge Lane	20
Garston	27
Gillmoss	55
Green Lane	106
Prince Alfred Road	51
Speke	64
Walton	48
Total	371

Several were fitted with illuminated offside advertisement panels. L724, L763, L779, L783 and L788 were originally fitted with additional luggage racks behind the stairs for use on service 586 when it ran to and from the Airport but were returned to a normal configuration in December 1967. The racks were put back in the following year and again removed in PTE days. L724 erroneously carried registration number CKF 724C instead of 724D but it was eventually corrected. L760-819 had the O.600 engine when new whereas L820-79 had the O.680. However there was considerable intermingling of engines in later years. L749, L780, L806, L809 and L826 had step-counters, actuated by passengers boarding and alighting, for census-taking until 1972.

Although the law was changed in July 1966 to allow one-man operation of double-deckers, general agreement was not reached with the Trade Unions throughout the country until 1968. It was believed that the slower boarding of omo buses would necessitate separate entrances and exits to avoid too much time being taken up at stops. L749 was experimentally rebuilt at Edge Lane to incorporate a central exit, central staircase rising forwards, periscopes and simplified destination display mounted immediately above the windscreen to facilitate easy changing from the driving position. The lower-deck seating capacity was thus reduced from 35 to 27 — making a total of 70 instead of 78. It was repainted in the reversed livery of cream with green trim, which was proposed for all one-man operated vehicles at this time, and exhibited at Liverpool Show in July 1968. However, when it re-entered service in May 1969 it had been restored to normal livery. Subsequently, starting in April 1969, 50 of the first batch of Atlanteans were similarly treated at Edge Lane and a further 50, L830-879, were converted by Pennine Coachcraft at Oldham with the loss of seven lower deck seats. This dual-door design was known internally as the 'Maxi' or the 'Jumbo'. Ironically it was found in Liverpool, after some experience of one-man double-deck operation, that the central exit made very little difference to the time spent at stops and invited fare evasion, particularly by children, and this expenditure could therefore have been avoided. Many considered the centre door to be the cause of boarding and alighting accidents. The remaining Atlanteans were converted by Pennine for one-man operation without loss of seating by merely fitting a periscope and repositioning the indicators but this operation was spread over five years, being completed in October 1974. Inevitably this simplified design was soon labelled the 'Mini'. The driver's interior door was designed internally and patented. It incorporated a pivoted cash hopper, change-giving machine and ticket storage cupboard. Manually operated 'Ultimate' machines were used.

Although the MkII modifications had improved performance, the PDR1/1 Atlantean proved to be a troublesome vehicle. Units which performed satisfactorily in vehicles of traditional design were in trouble on the Atlantean, a factor being that components designed for a 10½ ton gross weight were expected to handle 14 tons with only marginal redesign. The remoteness of the engine from the driver meant that he could no longer rely on hot smells and the appearance of steam as signs of impending trouble. There was a concentration of heat at the rear of the vehicle, not just the engine but rear brakes and exhaust, leading to overheating even when radiator calculations were alright. Brake compressors became coked up and a hot engine, oil or fuel leaks and a chafing cable were a recipe for fire. The starting pinion frequently failed to engage with the starter ring on the flywheel and this required some grovelling under the rear bustle with a long screwdriver. Some staff would be happy to do this but others would be content to await the arrival of the engineering staff. The failure rate of front shock absorbers was very high. Unreliability called for over 20% spare vehicles, a highly uneconomic rate which would not have been tolerated by any commercial undertaking or in earlier municipal days. Leyland's preoccupation with the ailing car industry diverted expertise which should have been able to solve these problems as, eventually, a careful fresh look at the Atlantean, involving no very dramatic changes, transformed the model into a highly reliable bus.

The first Atlanteans were withdrawn in 1975—so much for the planned 18 year life—L503, 514, 520, 541, 620 and 692 being the first six to be delicensed and parked. L677 had an unfortunate encounter with a low bridge in 1974 and was permanently converted to an open topper, re-entering service at Southport in July 1975. This mishap was to prolong its life and it became the last of its class,

Atlantean L749 was the first to be converted for one-man operation in 1969 and was finished in this reversed livery which was proposed to be used by all one-man vehicles. However, the idea was abandoned and L749 was repainted before re-entering service. The only feature retained was the repositioned coat of arms and title.

The last survivor of the Liverpool Corporation Atlanteans was L677 (latterly 0677) which, having lost its roof in a low bridge accident, was rebuilt as an open-top bus for seaside work in Southport. It eventually received the Southport red and cream livery and was withdrawn in 1984.

surviving until 1984, with a slight change of number to 0677 to satisfy the computer when all the other prefixed buses had gone; towards the end of its life it was used as a treelopper.

Early in 1976, a decision was made by MPTE to curtail a current Atlantean order from 100 to 60 and to rehabilitate 40 of the early batch including several vehicles which had stood unused for several months. The first six vehicles were back in service after a full overhaul at Edge Lane by April 1976, the stainless steel trim having been replaced by steel painted to match the green of the lower panelling.

L508, L515, L533 and L623 were overhauled at Laird Street, Birkenhead and on completion went into service for the Wirral division. L515 had been only partially converted for omo six years earlier, having retained a full indicator display and the conversion was at last completed on overhaul. Soon after re-entering service, L508 and L515 dropped their L prefixes as there was confusion with 1508 and 1515 which were also based at Laird Street. These buses remained on the Wirral until shortly before withdrawal in 1981 when they saw further brief service in Liverpool.

A few of the buses originally selected to be overhauled and refurbished were found to need too much spending on them and returned to the so called 'reserve fleet'; L536 and L538 were two of these. Withdrawals during 1976-77 totalled 126 and several saw service elsewhere, L554 and L607 turning up in Australia where they operated for several more years. Five went to Fylde Borough Council and several vehicles were used by the driving school before ultimate disposal.

Withdrawal of the second batch of Atlanteans started in 1978 and continued until 1981 though most had gone by 1980. Fourteen went to the Isle of Man for further service while L737 sailed further to Northern Ireland to join the fleet of the Londonderry and Lough Swilly Railway. L720 and L793 became mobile libraries in Liverpool, painted in multi-coloured liveries and labelled 'The Book Bus'. The last to go out of service was L749, the prototype one-man double-decker though L815 and L850 remained in the driving school until 1982 and L832 and L878 went to the

St. Helens driving school. One went to Fylde to provide spares for their earlier acquisitions.

The refurbished buses remained in service until 1981 and early in that year L500 and L501 were the oldest buses in service in the PTE fleet. Apart from L677, already mentioned, the last survivors were L509 and L510 which ran until December. Local enthusiasts arranged a farewell tour on L510 on 27th December 1981 to mark the end of a significant era in the evolution of buses in Liverpool.

Atlantean L848 with Metro-Cammell dual-door body was one of the last batch delivered to Liverpool Corporation, entering service in 1967. It was modified for one-man-operation by Pennine Coachcraft in September 1969 and is seen in East Prescot Road, Knotty Ash on a depot journey from Green Lane to take up service on the 97, Page Moss-Kirkby industrial route. Elimination of the cream window surrounds at the front made for a very bland frontal appearance.

Atlanteans of the first batch being fitted with centre exit and revised front indicator layout at Edge Lane Works in 1969 prior to re-entering service as one-man-operated buses.

The Leyland Panthers

The choice of the Leyland Panther PSUR1A/1 for single-deck one-man operation was influenced by the interchangeability of many components with the Atlanteans. The Panther had much greater success overseas than at home and the total UK sales were insignificant. It suffered from the same defects as the Atlantean and many operators preferred the underfloor engined Leopard with its more orthodox transmission line. Liverpool, with 110 Panthers, was Britain's biggest user of the model. The Panther standard bus chassis had a wheelbase of 18ft. 6in. but Liverpool opted for a non-standard 17ft. 6in. The vehicle had a stepped chassis over the rear axle, was powered by the 0.680 engine and the 'rationalised' Pneumocyclic gear-box (as officially described by Leyland) and air brakes were fitted.

Liverpool's Panthers were bodied by Metro-Cammell with 47 seats and optimistic provision for 24 standing passengers. They seemed to owe some of their design features to the AEC Merlin 'Red Arrow' buses which had recently been introduced to central London, the curved windscreen being identical. A front entrance and centre exit layout was selected but the position of the radiator at the front was criticised as it caused a slight internal bulge which restricted passenger circulation. In December 1966, a councillor moved that Leyland Motors be requested to move the radiator to the rear 'and..if this is not possible..the whole of the order for 70 single-deck buses be given to AEC Ltd for the supply of their Swift chassis which has the radiator at the back.' There had been some discussion with Leyland which, by that time controlled AEC; they were quite prepared to supply Swifts in place of Panthers and at one time it was suggested that the order be split into 50 Panthers and 20 Swifts in order to make comparisons. However, the motion was defeated 5-10 which was probably just as well. The Swift did not have the same advantage of interchangeability of components and, in any case, it was not a particularly popular model with those operators who bought it. The initial order for 70 Panthers was followed by a repeat order for 40.

The bodies had a stepped waistrail and hopper windows were fitted. The rear engine layout facilitated a very low

This frontal close-up view of Leyland Panther 1041 shows the very low floor level of the first purpose-built one-man-buses. Liverpool became the largest operator of Panthers, a breed which were not favoured by many operators.

floor level and these vehicles had a rather attractive, slinky appearance similar to the later Mercedes Benz 0305 model which became a familiar sight in city service in many parts of the world. The interior trim was much the same as the Atlanteans' with the added refinement of a formica covering on the interior panels and seat backs. Double-tier racks for prams and luggage were placed near the centre door. At the rear there was a 'Reversing' warning sign alongside the number plate. An interlocking device prevented a gear being engaged while the centre door was open.

These buses were finished in cream with green window surrounds, a reversal of the normal livery, although the intention to paint all one-man operated vehicles in this

The sleek lines of the Leyland Panthers is apparent from this view of No. 1007 on route 68 in Childwall. Note the 'City of Liverpool' fleetname adjoining the City coat-of-arms.

style was dropped. Normal livery was applied in later years. The Panthers introduced a new style of fleet numbers on metal plates without the prefix letter indicating the make, probably a concession to data processing needs. The system emerged as 1001—Leyland, 2001—Bristol. The Panthers were numbered 1001-1110 and were allocated to Edge Lane, Garston, Green Lane and Prince Alfred Road. During the last week of June 1968, Panthers were put on display at the Pier Head and Paradise Street and on 1st July the first examples entered service on route 68. Routes 46 and 99 were converted to Panther operation on 3rd September. For some years routes 1/1A, 4, 5, 11, 17C/17D, 46, 66, 68, 88, 99 and 100 were run exclusively by Panthers and Bristols. At the time the second batch from 1071 were being placed in service early in 1969, bus 1035 had still not appeared as it was retained at Edge Lane Works for various experiments. When it did eventually take to the road, it had only 45 seats.

After double-deck one-man operation became widespread, the Panthers were an embarrassment. Their full standing capacity was rarely used and many of the routes on which they were employed needed double-deckers at peak loading times. Furthermore they had a poor reliability record.

Between 1971 and 1973, 79 of them were repainted in the normal Liverpool green livery with cream window surrounds but by mid-1975 over 30 were parked up awaiting certification. At that time shortages of spare parts kept large numbers of vehicles off the road.

In 1972 Panthers 1100-1 worked in Southport on a rail feeder demonstration project, being based at Southport Corporation's Canning Road depot. When the Southport undertaking was absorbed into the PTE on 1st April 1974, a further 22 Panthers were taken over and it was decided to complete the changeover of Southport routes to one-man operation the same month by transferring sufficient Panthers. Southport became the first district of the PTE to achieve 100% driver only operation on 22nd April 1974. After overhaul 1001-7, 1010, 1016, 1026 and 1072 went to the seaside permanently between February and August 1975.

Several Panthers had their nearside route number indicators removed at overhaul; others had them painted over. Between 1975 and 1977 several out of service Panthers were parked at St. Helens where there was room for them. In January 1977 the first three Panthers were withdrawn (1033, 1044 and 1048) and it was decided to sell surplus Panthers and rehabilitate the remainder; A total of 53 were sold during 1977-78 including 19 to Chesterfield Corporation and seven to the Peak District operator, H.Hulley and Sons for further service. During 1977-78 24 were rebuilt to single-door layout by removing the centre exit doors and installing luggage racks though 1082 was converted by just sealing the exit door. A few ventured across the Mersey on a temporary basis. Buses 1018, 1024, 1039, 1041 and 1042 were in the Wirral in 1979, probably while delivery of Leyland Nationals was awaited. The remaining Panthers were gradually withdrawn, the last to go being 1019 and 1065 in October 1981.

Similarities and differences are notable in these contrasting photographs of Metro-Cammell-bodied Leyland Panther 1093 and Park Royal-bodied Bristol RELL6G 2017. Both had rear engines but the Panther had a much lower floor level in the front section. The cream livery was originally intended for all one-man-operated buses but no double-deckers ran in this colour scheme.

The Bristols

The supply of Bristol chassis and Eastern Coach Works bodies had been restricted to the nationalised company operators since 1948 but in 1965, Leyland acquired a 25% interest in Bristol Commercial Vehicles and ECW. In return, the government-controlled Transport Holding Company, (by then the parent company for the entire Tilling Group as well as BCV and ECW, among other state-owned road transport undertakings), took a stake in the bodybuilders Park Royal and Charles H. Roe, both of which were by then in the Leyland Group. Bristol and ECW products then became available to all and Liverpool was one of the first large non-THC operators to place an order for Bristol chassis.

Simultaneously with the delivery of the later Panthers in 1969, 25 rear-engined Bristol RELL6Gs with 45-seat Park Royal bodies arrived and were numbered 2001-25. Liverpool had never previously patronised Park Royal. These buses, which were allocated to Litherland, were powered by the 10.45-litre Gardner 6HLX engine. These were almost the last buses to be delivered to Liverpool Corporation before the transport undertaking was merged into the Merseyside PTE.

The general arrangement of the bodywork on the Bristols was similar to that of the Panthers but a straight waistrail gave them a better overall appearance. Hopper ventilators were fitted to all the windows behind the centre exit. The Bristol RE was generally regarded as an

Like the Panthers, the Bristol REs' appearance was changed when the green livery was applied. Bus 2007 stands in Mann Island in September 1973, ready to depart on a short working of the No. 1 Line of Docks service to Seaforth.

Painted in green livery, Leyland-engined Bristol RE 2088 is seen at Crosby Bus Station whilst conveying participants in the Omnibus Society Presidential weekend on 20th June 1971. The NBC style Eastern Coach Works body identifies the bus as one diverted from PMT.

The dual-door Bristol VRs of 1970 had the angular appearance of all the East Lancs vehicles, not enhanced by the lowered window over the nearside wheelarch. Bus 2029 arrives at Pier Head from Aintree on 17th April 1971.

excellent vehicle; it gave good service in Liverpool and proved much more reliable than the Panther. Bus 2017 was withdrawn prematurely and cannibalised after a serious accident in 1970 and 2022 was withdrawn in February 1977. The remainder were overhauled and about 20 were transferred to St. Helens where they remained until withdrawn in 1982. Latterly seven operated from Litherland, the last to go being 2018 and 2024 in December 1982.

Sixty 33ft.-long double-deck Bristols had also been ordered by Liverpool Corporation for delivery in 1970-71, the body order being placed with East Lancashire Coachbuilders at Blackburn. The chassis of what would have been 2027 was written off after a fire at the bodybuilder's works and the first batch became 2026-49, number 2050 remaining unused. These buses were model VRTLH6G, powered by Gardner 6LXB engines. Although this model in NBC fleets is associated with a straight rear end profile, the Liverpool examples had an upper deck overhang and bustle, a feature which had been eliminated from the earlier Atlanteans both on aesthetic grounds and to facilitate mechanical cleaning. There was seating for 80 passengers (49/31) in the double-door bodies and accommodation for 18 standing. The centre exit was situated immediately behind the front axle and the waist level of the smaller window above the nearside wheel was lower than that of the rear section of the saloon which had three and a half wide bays. They were very impressive if angular vehicles. The first six entered service at Walton on 17th August 1970 and worked on routes 3, 20, 25 and 30, the latter being still two-man operated at that time; others went to Garston for 86/87.

The fire at the bodybuilders interrupted production and 35 chassis were in store at various Liverpool depots in the spring of 1971 but all were completed and in service by October. The nominal standing capacity of these buses, which were numbered 2051-85, was 21 bringing the passenger carrying capacity up to 101.

In the meantime 10 single-deck Bristol RESL6L buses with standard Eastern Coach Works 44-seat front entrance bodies with alternate sliding and hopper windows (2086-95), had arrived. These had Leyland O.680 engines and had originally been intended for Potteries Motor Traction Co. Ltd. The destination indicators were modified to Merseyside's standard and the batch was allocated to Green Lane and Gillmoss. The first three joined Panthers on the revived and extended route 11 when it commenced on 10th May 1971.

The Bristol double-deckers could always be distinguished from other makes by the front radiator grille. They gave good service but nevertheless had relatively short lives by modern standards. The Bristol VRT was not as well regarded as the RE. In municipal and PTE service the VRT generally gave less satisfaction than when working for NBC companies where operating conditions were usually easier. Seventeen were withdrawn in 1982 and all had gone by early 1985, the last three in service being 2026, 2028 and 2043. Crosville bought two for spares. In 1979, following serious transmission problems, Fidus Overspeed Protection units were fitted to prevent

The single-door East Lancs-bodied Bristol VRs were no less massive in appearance than their dual-door predecessors. They lacked the front upper-deck ventilator windows and 2133, seen in Old Haymarket in August 1975 with Atlantean 1607, sported an unusual frontal livery. Note the flyovers in the background, designed to separate city and tunnel traffic.

The revised Verona green livery, with brown window surrounds and skirt, improved the appearance of the 1970 dual-door East Lancs-bodied Bristol VRs, the eye being drawn away from the broken nearside waistline.

abuse by drivers changing down at the wrong speed. Similar equipment was later fitted to some Atlanteans. The first single-door 44-seater to go was 2088 in April 1982 and 28 more were withdrawn that year. Latterly 2094-5 and possibly some others had seen service in St. Helens but were loaned to Garston more than once for service on route 100 still carrying St. Helens orange fleet names. Bus 2091 became a towing vehicle at Laird Street, Birkenhead depot and all had gone by the spring of 1984.

The Second Generation Atlanteans

The final bus to be delivered to the Corporation, though it did not enter service until after the PTE took over, carried the striking fleet number 1111 and was the first of a batch of 40 Atlantean PDR2/1 buses with bodies by W. Alexander and Sons (Coachbuilders) Ltd of Falkirk.

At 33ft. (nominal), the PDR2 Atlantean was longer than its predecessor and had a wheelbase of 18ft. 6in. There was seating for 79, 47 upstairs and 32 inside, with a front entrance and centre exit. It was clear that the smooth rear end design feature of the original Atlanteans had been abandoned in favour of the more usual bustle but those who blame the PTE for this backward step do so in error as the specifications for these vehicles had clearly been drawn up by Liverpool Corporation. Many features of their forebears were retained by the new Atlanteans and the Liverpool peaks were combined with the Alexander roof. The all-round metal skirt, the off-set driving position and the back to back seats over the rear wheel arches were incorporated into the design. However, the driver's windscreen was higher and slightly V-shaped as were the front upper deck windows. The Alexander bodies were similar to their East Lancs. contemporaries on Bristol chassis being built to a similar customer specification. The reduced number of window pillars gave an impression of great length.

This was the first order Alexander's had obtained from Liverpool since 1954 but the Scottish factory was destined to share a large portion of the PTE's body requirements with East Lancs. during the next decade. The PDR2 Atlanteans were powered by the Leyland O.680 engine and fitted with the rationalised Pneumocyclic gearbox. The batch was numbered 1111-1150 and 1111, 1112 and 1114-6 entered service on 15th December 1969 from Green Lane depot on the newly revived limited stop service 510 between Prescot and Central Station; the whole batch was operational by March 1970.

Two further batches of Alexander-bodied Atlanteans were delivered between April and December 1971. The first 25, Nos. 1151-75, were identical with 1111-50 but, following experience with the Bristols (2028-49), the layout of the final 60 (1176-1235) was changed to place the centre exit immediately behind the front axle and the staircase behind the cab's bulkhead. This increased the seating layout to 49 on the upper deck and 31 inside and completed the orders placed by Liverpool Corporation.

These vehicles ran throughout Liverpool until 1982 when all of the first 40 (1111-50) were withdrawn, three going to the Isle of Man for further duty. 1151-75 were taken out of service in 1982-83 and 1176-1235 in 1983-84, 32 going to the Isle of Man though six of these were shipped partly dismantled for spares. The last two-door buses in service were 1208 and 1226.

Mention should perhaps be made of the 13 twin-door Atlantean PDR1A/1 buses with Northern Counties bodies which had been ordered by Birkenhead Corporation but were delivered to the PTE in late 1970 and early 1971. They were painted in the Wirral division livery of blue and cream and received their planned Birkenhead fleet

(Above) Leyland Atlantean PDR1A/1 185, seen passing Lime Street Station in May 1979 on route 31 to New Brighton, was one of a batch of 13 ordered by Birkenhead Corporation but delivered to the PTE in 1970; it had 71 seats in its dual-door Northern Counties body and spent the whole of its working life in the Wirral Division. It is seen in standard livery and the lower front and side indicators have been blanked out.

(Right) Although still carrying city insignia over a year after the formation of the PTE, PDR2 Atlantean 1111 was appropriately the first new bus to enter service with the PTE. Despite its twin-door layout, it seated 79 passengers, exceeding by one the seating capacity of the largest trams of the thirties. This represented the ultimate in Liverpool municipal bus design though buses ordered by the Corporation continued to be placed in service until January 1972.

numbers 183-195. Numbers 190-195 were based at Wallasey from mid-1971 and equipped for carrying 'Cross River Express' boards. From June 1971 they were to be seen in Liverpool city centre on the Wallasey tunnel services 31-32.

Rebuilds and Withdrawals.

The traditional half-cab rear platform double-deck bus continued to dominate the Liverpool scene until 1963-64 when Atlanteans in large numbers took over many all-day duties. In the years between 1958 and 1963 the fleet was mainly static. As already stated, the last pre-war and wartime buses were withdrawn in 1957-58 and in 1959, with traffic declining and 25 part-built buses in store, there were neither additions nor withdrawals.

The phasing out of the buses placed in service between 1946 and 1949 was spread over several years. The first casualty was A429 in 1960 but the last eight of the 26 1946 AEC Regent IIs continued in service until February 1966, longer than the official 18-year life span. Similarly, withdrawal of the 1947 Regents up to A524 was spread over six years from 1961 to 1966. Most went to scrap dealers but 20 of the 1946-47 Regents were retained by Liverpool Corporation Works Department to carry workers or act as mobile site offices. A507 and A509 stood for years awaiting conversion and passed into PTE ownership but were scrapped immediately together with A717 and L396 which had inexplicably escaped the torch.

The 1948-49 Regent IIIs (A525-624, originally A325-424 until renumbered in 1957) were being taken out of service at the same time as the earlier AECs; 41 went in 1963 but the last survivor, A536, was still plodding along in 1968. A606 was taken by the City Engineer for conversion to a gritting lorry while A617 became treelopper LR2 in which role it served until September 1969. The PTE sold it for scrap in February 1970.

The ten Leyland PD2s allocated to Liverpool after the Green Lane tram depot fire in 1947 (L425-434) went out in 1963-64, five each year but the later PD2s were spread over a longer period between 1964 and May 1967 as some had not been put on the road until 1951. Of the L435-484 batch, some outlasted the 1952 Leylands with Weymann bodies (L807-866) withdrawal of which had been spread over almost four years — from February 1966 to December 1969. These buses had been renumbered L370-429 in February 1966 as their numbers were needed for new Atlanteans. At least three—L836, L837 and L844—had been taken out of service and never carried their new numbers.

Of the non-standard makes, the Daimlers, most of which had AEC engines, lasted longer than the Crossleys, C622 and C630 having been scrapped in 1961; ten more went in 1962 and the remainder, 37 vehicles in all, were withdrawn in 1963, only C636 surviving until the early days of 1964. Oldham Corporation took two—C626 and C632—as spares for its own Crossley fleet. The 90 Daimlers gradually diminished in numbers between 1960 and 1966. After 37 buses had gone in 1960-61, there was a lull as only one was

Relatively few of the AEC Regents were sold for further service with other owners but showmen took several. The former A19 was photographed on a fairground at Norris Green after its new owner had lowered the roof by removing the top deck window pillars.

AEC Regent I A9 was one of the first of the new generation of Liverpool buses placed in service in 1935. After withdrawal from passenger service it was converted to a departmental lorry, in which guise it is seen at Edge Lane Works.

scrapped in 1962 and two in 1963. A further 14 went went to dealers in 1964 and 35 followed in 1965 leaving one solitary Daimler, D600, to survive into 1966. Bus D563, withdrawn in 1961, saw further PSV service with J. Lloyd of Nuneaton and later with Shirley's Garage of Meriden until December 1965.

Airport Coaches

The four ex-BEA Bedfords were withdrawn in 1960-61. Being standard Duple-bodied coaches of a type which enjoyed enduring popularity with independent operators, all saw further service, three as PSVs and No. B4 with the Lockheed Sports Club, Speke. They were replaced by four of the Royal Tigers, SL171-4. Two, SL172-3, were rebuilt at Edge Lane from 40-seat dual-entrance to 36-seat front-entrance layout in 1960 but in 1961 all four were completely transformed by MCCW to '1½-deck coaches'. The rear half of the 44-seat front-entrance bodies was raised to accommodate a large luggage compartment; there were 21 seats in the elevated compartment. The finished job was very similar to airport coaches in use at Manchester and elsewhere. They were painted in two shades of blue and inscribed 'Liverpool City Airporter'. Oil burning heaters and fluorescent lights were installed and they were renumbered XL171-4.

There is some evidence that the Liverpool coaches were influenced by American practice as a picture of a Flxible touring coach in the service of Gray Line has been found with 'Airport Coach' annotated in Hall's handwriting. They worked out of Garston depot and, after the demise of the airport service in 1966, they were transferred to the summer Lime Street-Isle of Man steamer service as one-man vehicles. For this duty the word 'Airporter' was replaced by 'Transport'. They were completely overhauled and fitted with higher ratio differentials to make them suitable for long distance private hire work. After withdrawal in 1973-74, they were sold to various social service groups in Liverpool.

Between the withdrawal of the first of the Bedfords and the completion of these rebuilds, Crosville coach EUB329 (SFM 6), a Bristol LS6B with Eastern Coach Works 39-seat body, was hired. From January to June 1961 it was based at Dingle to assist on the Airport service. Dingle's association with this service ended when the little Bedfords were sold, and the fleet became all diesel once more.

A Shrinking Fleet

The composition of the fleet changed radically in 1966-68 in which years 120, 80, and 130 vehicles were respectively withdrawn. By the end of this period the fleet had reduced in numbers from its peak of 1236 in 1959 to just below 1100. In truth it could have fallen much more as, inexplicably, delicensed but serviceable buses were allowed to stand about at Edge Lane and any depot which had the space, for months and occasionally years before they were scrapped. These vehicles were termed the 'reserve fleet' but for what contingencies they were in reserve was not clear. It had been the same with the trams in 1946-53 but for different reasons; in those days the cars were desperately needed but were slow to be repaired. At a time when traffic was falling and one-man operation was spreading, there was no market for time-expired rear entrance double-deckers.

One of the first rebuilt Royal Tiger airport coaches, XL171, awaits passengers near the old side entrance to Lime Street Station in Lord Nelson Street. Below is an interior view showing the individual seats and raised floor to accommodate a vast luggage boot.

The majority of Liverpool buses went to one of three scrap dealers at Barnsley and a typical transaction in 1966 produced an average price of £83-16-0d for 29 buses. The lowest price (£21) was for A710, probably minus engine, whilst A549, A668 and A671 went for £110-10-0d each. Cannibalisation was widely practised and when withdrawal of a batch was protracted, bodies were sometimes exchanged before disposal. Numerous vehicles continued to be seen about the streets of Liverpool for some years as personnel carriers for other Corporation departments; others went to the driving school which had a continuous turnover of vehicles for many years. In the late sixties the Road Transport Industry Training Board had a policy of paying grants only in respect of dedicated training vehicles which changed the time-honoured practice of using the ordinary fleet for training purposes off-peak.

All but one of the 7ft. 6in. buses had been taken out of service by 1968 and none of the first batch of eight-footers (A757-806) passed to the PTE. A717, withdrawn from service in October 1969, was the last 7ft. 6in.-wide bus in the fleet and the last with a preselector gearbox. Of the 100 last Regent IIIs, dating from 1953-55, 51 were transferred to the PTE but 36 were immediately scrapped. Two were still in stock in 1974 (A39-40) and happily, the latter, the first unpainted bus, was preserved. The contemporary Leyland PD2s (L61-90) had a more varied career. Five of the Alexander bodied PD2/20s (L80-84) had been rebuilt by S. H. Bond of Wythenshawe in 1959, L80 having been fitted with a very ugly sloping radiator grille and a pillar at the nearside front corner. The reason why these five consecutively numbered buses were selected for attention is not known but no more were done as the work was considered to be too expensive. These buses were the first to have the new reduced size destination and route indicators.

Several from this batch and the next one had their wheel arch seats replaced by luggage racks for use on the Isle of Man steamer feeder service. Most, if not all, seem to have been converted back each winter. L111-112 served in both 1962 and 1964; L61-63, L80, L116 and L121 were done in 1964 and L61-64, L93-94 and L96-97 in 1965.

Another five (L79, L158, L161, L164-165) were converted for use on the so-called City Circle which started on 4th December 1965. They were painted in reversed livery, fitted with static one-piece destination displays and ran in that condition until converted back to a normal state in December 1969.

Fifty-one of the first batch went into the PTE fleet but 24 were already 'in store' and all but L28 soon took the road to Barnsley. Eighteen of the second batch (L91-170) had gone in Corporation days and one (L121) was in reserve at the time of transfer. Most were disposed of in 1971-72 though L113 lasted until 1974 when it was 19 years old.

Only a few individual vehicles had been withdrawn from the remaining batches of rear entrance buses before the PTE was formed, mainly as a result of accidents. To sum up, the PTE took over 542 vehicles of this type from Liverpool Corporation of which at least 66 were already 'in reserve'. Forty-three were scrapped immediately, 39 in 1970, 93 in 1971, 126 in 1972, 112 in 1973, 67 in 1974, 47 in 1975 and 14 in 1976. Some of their duties were taken over by similar but younger buses from Birkenhead, St. Helens and Southport as described in Chapter 53 and of the last 41 traditional double-deckers which operated on 10th January 1977, the last day of two-man operation in Liverpool, only one (L227), a 1956 Leyland PD2, was an ex-Liverpool Corporation vehicle. The only bus of this type to be repainted in the Verona green livery of the PTE was L220 which became a towing vehicle in January 1976 and was repainted after its passenger carrying days were over.

During the sixties a number of buses were fitted with illuminated offside advertisement panels. The first was A102 in 1960 and, unlike BET and Tilling practice, the advertisements were silk screened on the inside of toughened glass. This was a passing fad which was abandoned by most operators by the end of the decade when advertising agencies realised that changing social habits resulted in diminished exposure during the hours of darkness. All these panels had been removed before the PTE took over.

Leyland PD2 L80 as rebuilt by Bond of Wythenshawe with the unusual support between bonnet and canopy. No more were done.

53 THE BUS FLEET 1972-86

Vehicle orders in the seventies and early eighties were strongly influenced by the government's bus grant policy and by the time the vehicle orders placed by Liverpool Corporation had been fulfilled in 1972, the PTE had evolved a fleet policy which differed very little from that of its principal predecessor. Once it had become clear that successful one-man operation of double-deckers could be achieved without the refinement of a separate exit door, most PTE orders were for single-door buses on shorter length chassis seating 43 on the upper deck and 32 below and this layout remained standard for the next decade.

An opportunity arose to take over an order for 60 Atlanteans with Alexander bodywork originally destined for the Birmingham and Midland Motor Omnibus Co Ltd (Midland Red) which no longer required them following the sale of its Birmingham and Black Country services to the West Midlands PTE. There was time to change the specification to meet all normal Merseyside PTE requirements except power steering. These buses were 30ft.-long PDR1A/1s and took fleet numbers 1236-95, Nos. 1271-95 being allocated to the Wirral Division and painted blue and cream. These buses had a long life, some having been put back in service on contract work at St. Helens by Merseybus early in 1990. An order was also placed for 50 Daimler Fleetlines all of which entered service at Birkenhead in 1973. Twenty Metro-Scania single-deckers, delivered in 1972, were followed by 20 double-deckers from the same source in 1974 and another 40 in 1975.

The existing Liverpool fleet number system was developed as follows:-

1000	Leyland (but later for Atlanteans only)
2000	Bristol
3000	Daimler
4000	Scania

Later additions were:-

5000	Intended for Leyland Titans but not used
6000	Leyland Nationals
7000	Coaches
0000	Experimental vehicles

In 1972 orders were placed for 250 Atlanteans, 200 with Alexander 'AL' and 50 with East Lancashire bodies; these were delivered between 1972 and 1976. In effect delivery of 40 was deferred, the same number of PDR Atlanteans being overhauled and returned to service. A further order for 50 Bristol double-deckers specified the shorter VRTSL6G single-door model with the standard East Lancs bodywork; these came into service in 1974-75. Ten Bristol single-deck REs with MCW bodies were ordered for service in St. Helens after acquisition of that undertaking in 1974.

The Metropolitan double-deckers were quite eye-catching with their asymetrical screens 4021 is seen when new participating in a local government rally at Southport on 31st March 1974, the day before the Merseyside County Council came into existence. Note the square logo and the radiator ahead of the rear axle.

The Metro-Scania saloons had a refreshingly different look, the eye being immediately drawn to the curved roof profile and asymmetrical front windscreen. Note the radiator grilles behind the rear axle on both sides and the uncluttered rear end compared with many rear-engined vehicles. Unfortunately, however, operators found the Metro-Scanias very thirsty, and also extremely expensive when spares were needed. Bus 4013 had been decorated for a visit to Brussels in 1974.

East Lancashire-bodied Atlanteans 1426 and 1435 were painted with whole bus advertisements from new 1973 but received the standard livery the following year. In the case of 1435 the advertiser's needs have been met to the extent of dispensing with the front fleet number plate. Note the lowered first nearside window to accommodate the route indicator below upper-deck floor level and the offset front number plates necessitated by the split front panel.

Orders placed from 1973 onwards underwent many alterations because of production problems within the Leyland Group. A further 110 Daimler Fleetlines ordered in 1973-74, 50 to be bodied by Metro-Cammell and 60 by Alexander, would have been 3051-3160 but delivery was still awaited in 1977 when the order was cancelled and replaced by one for 110 AN68 Atlanteans. It was then altered to 100 Atlanteans and 10 Leyland Nationals—subsequently five of the AN68s were replaced by five Leyland Titan B15s. The order was further reduced to 89 and five Metrobuses and one Leyland National Suburban Express were added.

Alexanders were also experiencing difficulty in meeting their orders on time so 44 of the 89 AN68s to be supplied with their bodies were changed in 1978 to 22 AN68s with East Lancs bodies, 20 Leyland Nationals, and two Suburban Expresses, the other 45 AN68s taking Metro-Cammell bodies.

By 1979-80 it had been decided that no second generation double-deckers would be ordered until evaluation of the five Metrobuses, five Titans and five Dennis Dominators was complete. The 1979-80 orders were for 30 AN68s and five Dominators with Willowbrook bodies and 35 Leyland Nationals. Production problems at Park Royal caused the five B15s to be replaced in 1980 by six National 2s, the final product of the 1973-74 orders. One Titan B15 was subsequently taken on long term loan from Leyland.

Five second-hand Bristol midibuses were purchased from West Yorkshire PTE for the Toxteth and Vauxhall services and, for 1980-81 the PTE decided to order 59 Leyland National 2s, a Leyland Leopard coach and 40 Alexander bodied AN68s. It was provisionally agreed to order 65 similar AN68s for delivery in 1981-82; this was subsequently reduced to 55 and an intended order for 35 National 2s was also cut down to 25. The difference of 20 was intended to be made up of five Scania/Alexander BR112s, 10 Leyland Olympians, five with Alexander and five with ECW bodies, four Suburban expresses and one more Leopard coach but the Scania order was cancelled and replaced by two more Metrobuses and two more Dominators with Alexander bodies. The Olympians were all delivered with ECW bodies due to output problems at Alexanders. More Nationals were ordered and eventually 75 Mk Is and 98 Mk IIs were owned, including eight inherited from Southport Corporation.

In 1982, 24 more Alexander-bodied AN68s brought the fleet numbers up to 1991 at which point there was a reversion to 1001 for the 70 similar vehicles placed in service in 1983-84.

Following the hire of two Volvo Ailsas from Derby in 1982, two Alexander-bodied Ailsas were ordered for 1982 followed by 13 in 1984 but these were all stationed in Wirral and were rarely seen in Liverpool. Ten dual-purpose Dennis Lancet midibuses completed the orders in 1983 while the final deliveries to the PTE were the six Quest 80B buses for the disabled with Locomotors bodies which appeared in 1984-85.

The orderly numbering of PTE vehicles with matching registration numbers was upset following the Ministry of

Bristol LH MUA 44 stands at the William Brown Street terminus of the 101 Vauxhall Round-a-bout community service in July 1980. It was still in West Yorkshire PTE livery with their fleet number 44 but was soon to become 2159 in the PTE fleet.

The Eastern Coach Works-bodied Leyland Olympians, delivered in 1982, were fitted with electronic destination indicators. The small route numbers drew strong criticism as they were hard to discern, particularly in bright sunlight. They were eventually superseded by a larger type mounted above the destination.

Transport's insistence on certain prefixes being used with specific year letters and registration numbers became jumbled when vehicles were delivered out of sequence or across the registration year end on 31st July. Many booked registration numbers were surrendered unused.

The first and last production Leyland Atlanteans were posed side-by-side on the occasion of the handing over of the final vehicle of the last batch, in September 1984. Wallasey Corporation No. 1, restored to original condition by the PTE, was reputedly the first of the type to enter service while 1070 was the last. The officials are (left to right) Colin Watters, Leyland Bus Sales and Marketing Director, W. Gwyn Thomas, Director of Operations and L. W. Latter, Director General, Merseyside PTE and Wesley Keys, Managing Director of W. Alexander, Coachbuilders.

The Electric Bus.

In 1972 the Department of Trade and Industry sponsored the development of battery-electric buses. Liverpool, of course, had had such a thing as early as 1925 (see Volume Two page 289). A consortium known as Crompton Leyland Electricars Ltd. was formed by the Hawker Siddeley Group and British Leyland, and two prototype vehicles were manufactured at Tredegar. They had Willowbrook bodies with nine seats, five along the back and two inward facing seats over the rear wheel arches. There was a small luggage rack and room for 17 standing passengers.

Power was derived from lead-acid traction type batteries 110 cells (220v) with 376Ah capacity at the five hour rate. Propulsion was by a DC series-wound motor continuously rated at 24 hp at 1350 rpm driving through a conventional propellor shaft and differential to twin rear wheels. Speed was regulated by a low-loss thyristor controller. The vehicle, which bore Morrison Electric badges, had a range of 35 miles per battery charge in city centre service and 70 miles on a continuous non-stop run. Top speed on the level was 25 mph and the vehicle could, in the jargon of the day, only just claim to be 'traffic compatible'.

The vehicle which came to Liverpool (CWO 600K) was based on a modified Leyland 900FG chassis. It was 22ft. long, 8ft. 0½in. wide and 9ft. 6in. high with a wheelbase of 13ft. 4in. and was given the fleet number E4 by the PTE. It was operated on the City Circle, but as an extra vehicle because its low seating capacity was a great disadvantage. It was in Liverpool from 7th June to 26th

September 1972, departing then for Bournemouth. It subsequently moved around the country until 1974 and, after a period of inactivity, joined the fleet of South Yorkshire PTE in 1976. Its seating capacity was increased to 21 and it operated alongside a number of other battery-electric vehicles but the project was abandoned and it went for scrap in July 1979. The solid-state control system did save power but the trial confirmed that such vehicles were constrained by the limited capacity and great weight of lead-acid batteries.

The AN68 Atlanteans.

Meanwhile, the PDR range of Atlanteans which had been in production for 14 years was replaced by a new version known as the AN68. There were initially two versions, the AN68/1R with a length of 30ft 10in. and a wheelbase of 16ft. 3in. and the AN68/2R which was 32ft. 9in. long with a wheelbase of 18ft. 6in. Subsequent minor technical improvements have produced the AN68A, B C and D. The AN68 was a long overdue but thorough redesign of the PDR series Atlanteans with very little in the way of radical change but intended to overcome the various problems, notably overheating. Considerable development work had gone into the detail modification of the chassis and running gear and there is no doubt that Liverpool's 1962 specification, having proved superior to that of the standard PDR Atlantean, and field work by SELNEC PTE, London Country and other companies had been strong influencing factors. The three-piece engine cowl and

One of two prototype battery electric buses with Willowbrook body which ran on the City Circle as an additional vehicle for three months in 1972. There were nine seats and room for 17 standing passengers on the vehicle. The Department of Trade and Industry's name and logo can faintly be discerned on the panel immediately behind the door.

stainless steel hose clips were good examples of detail changes. The extra 10in. of length were added to the rear overhang to facilitate a more roomy seating layout at the rear of the lower saloon.

The fluid coupling, which took the place of a clutch, had been in a sealed unit on the PDRs but on the AN68 it shared the same oil supply as the gearbox and angle drive thus giving much better cooling. The engine cooling system was also improved and audible and visible warnings of overheating were installed in the cab. Shields were placed round the engine compartment to keep dirt out and protect the drive belts and propellor shaft from accident damage. Several other components were repositioned in the chassis with the same objective.

One of the problems associated with the original Atlanteans was that a loss of air immobilised the whole vehicle as gears, brakes and doors all became inoperable. Tales are told of the door operating lever being blown out followed by all the air; resourceful drivers would replace the lever and build up the air supply with the conductor sitting on it until the bus reached the depot. The AN68 had dual line air supply and fail-safe spring parking brakes were fitted as standard. Batteries were repositioned to give easier access by lifting a hatch in the saloon floor.

The frame was designed to accept a passenger entrance 4ft. 4¼in. wide, the layout of the controls was improved and power-assisted steering, a statutory requirement on 10 metre double-deckers since 1968, was fitted. Finally, exhaust noise was reduced in accordance with the trend towards quieter vehicles. Between 1972 and 1977, the PTE placed 470 of the AN68/1R model in service of which 340 had Alexander bodies and 130 had very similar bodies

by East Lancashire. Fleet numbers ran from 1296 to 1765.

The first batch, 1296-1345 with Alexander bodywork similar to that fitted to the last PDRs, commenced delivery in August 1972 and was complete by the end of the year. These and all subsequent Alexander bodies supplied to Merseyside until 1984, with the exception of the experimental buses, were of aluminium alloy construction of type AL, modified to the PTE's specification. This affected the window pans and the front end arrangement. Visually, the windows lost depth compared to the standard AL. All went into service from Liverpool depots. No fewer than 200 AN68s (1346-1545) were delivered to the PTE in 1973 including 50 with East Lancs bodywork (1396-1445). All but 1542-45 were in service by the end of the year. However 82 vehicles went to the Wirral Division (Nos. 1356-70, 1446-93, 1506-16 and 1535-38). Pneumocyclic gearboxes were normally fitted but three buses were equipped experimentally with various types of fully automatic transmission, 1375 by Leyland, 1389 by Self Changing Gears and 1391 by CAV; all were removed in 1974-75. At least 1375 had the letters 'AT' on the sides near the Merseyside emblem.

A further 10 AN68s with Alexander 45/29 two-door bodies were delivered to Southport Corporation (Nos.81-90) and entered the PTE fleet in April 1974; they remained in Southport.

The 1974 order comprised Nos. 1546-1625 but ran well over into 1975. All had Alexander bodywork of the now standard pattern. Deliveries started in April 1974 but had reached only 1570 when the year letter changed. The 1975-76 Alexander order was originally for 100 vehicles (1626-1725) but 40 were deferred on economy grounds, a

The East Lancs-bodied Atlanteans had a rather angular but nevertheless businesslike appearance though the nearside lines were spoilt by the lowered waistline over the front wheel. Bus 1747 entered service in 1977 and is seen in Lime Street in May 1979 against a background of some of Liverpool's finest public buildings.

similar number of the ex-Corporation Atlanteans being overhauled and retained in service as described in Chapter 52. Numbers 1673-85 were not delivered until 1976. This was the first batch to have 5-speed gear boxes though 1640-43 were fitted with automatic transmission. Several buses from this delivery were fitted with Autofare ticket equipment for use on routes 26/27 from Edge Lane garage.

The next batch, which was model AN68B/1R with East Lancs bodies was already arriving by April 1976. These were numbered 1686-1765 and the order was not completed until late 1977. There were detail differences front and rear in the bodies of 1726-65. Numbers 1695, 1705, 1728, 1734 and 1738 went to Southport, but the majority went to Litherland to replace Bristol REs transferred to St. Helens and Gillmoss.

The 1978 Atlanteans comprised 45 AN68s with attractive Metro-Cammell-Weymann four bay bodies (1776-1820). They had very smooth lines with deep windscreens and upper deck windows.

Atlantean bodywork for 1979 reverted to East Lancs but with many differences. The batch consisted of only 22

buses (1821-42) but delivery was spread over more than a year. These vehicles were the first to make use of 'Warerite' decorative laminates for the exterior panels surrounding both the upper and lower-deck windows in a dark brown colour which was also used for the window rubbers. Many interior panels were fabricated of the same material, all but the seat backs being bonded to aluminium and marketed as 'Melaminium' which was claimed to be fire resistant. Interior lower-deck cove panels featured the Liverpool skyline in silhouette. The skirt panels, also in brown, were in plastic covered 'Lamiplate' which was easy to replace if damaged. The first to arrive in January 1980 was 1840 which retained the standard Merseyside 43 over 32 seating arrangement but all the others were 45 over 33.

There were five vehicles with non-standard features. Numbers 1822/4/8/30/34 had HELP energy absorbing bumpers while 1824/8 had new heating systems with larger front grilles; Nos. 1822/8/30/34 also had 'glued-in' floors. 1828 alone had a Leyland National-style cab layout and modified electrical equipment including additional direction indicators. These special features delayed delivery of some buses in the batch which was to have been registered RBG821-42T. Bus 1834 had two registration numbers allocated, RBG834T and TWM218V before finally appearing as WWM917W. This batch was the first to have four track route numbers at the front to enable three-digit numbers to be displayed with suffixes but there were no nearside number indicators.

The next Atlantean batch carried bodywork by Willowbrook, a builder usually associated with luxury coach bodies, who broke into the double-deck business around this time after some years' absence. Thirty five bodies were ordered, the other five being fitted to Dennis Dominators. Output was slow and delivery of the AN68Bs 1843-72 started on 25th November 1980 at Green Lane and continued into 1982. These were originally intended to be numbered 5000-29.

The Willowbrooks had a four-bay lower saloon with a sloping two-piece curved windscreen. They seated 45 upstairs and 33 down like the previous year's East Lancs bodies but were 14ft. 10in. high, about four inches more than normal; they were fitted with PLC Peters entrance doors with a unique air bleed system designed to simplify installation. They had four track route numbers at the front only and were delivered simultaneously with two further Alexander-bodied batches, 1873-1912 and 1913-67 in 1981-82. At least the first of these were fitted with the same type of entrance doors as the Willowbrooks. Numbers 1915-66 were the specially painted Garden Festival buses in 1984. They were followed by AN68Ds Nos. 1968-91, 1991 being the highest fleet number used in the Atlantean series. The 1873 batch did not have the Mersey skyline interior but the Willowbrooks did. All the Willowbrooks were advertised for sale in 1989. All the Alexander-bodied buses of these batches had three track number blinds.

Despite its many experiments with other models, the PTE decided to stay with the Atlantean as long as it was available, and two further batches of standard Alexander bodied AN68Ds were placed in service, 15 (1001-15) in 1983 and 55 (1016-70) in 1984. The first examples of the second batch had modular seats but standard moquette seating was fitted to 1025 onwards. Delivery of bus 1070 was delayed as Merseyside PTE had been promised the last production Atlantean. It was ceremonially handed over alongside the first Atlantean (or certainly the first municipal one), Wallasey No. 1 of 1958, which had been carefully restored to its original condition at Edge Lane Works. It was said that the PTE and its predecessors had bought 1,365 Atlanteans of which 724 had been bodied by Alexanders.

The first AN68, 1296, was broken up in 1986 and many others were withdrawn in 1986-87 but the majority survived to pass into the Merseybus fleet.

A number of new features were incorporated in the last batch of East Lancs-bodied Atlanteans delivered in 1979-80, and seen centre right. They had four track route numbers at the front only and the dropped nearside waistline was eliminated at the expense of the side route indicator. Number 1828 was one of five fitted with HELP energy-absorbing bumpers. Note the larger fleet number plates, repeater direction indicators and front grille for a new heating system. It also had a Leyland National cab and glued-in floor.

Willowbrook-bodied Atlantean 1845 arrives at the Pier Head on 5th January 1981, right. Some of these buses, which were four inches higher than normal, were sold prematurely by Merseybus. Note the curved, raked windscreen and the panoramic windows.

The wide windows of the Metro-Cammell-bodied Atlanteans placed in service in 1978 gave them an air of elegance compared to the East Lancs bodies which they followed. Bus 1783 is entering Hood Street Gyratory when new.

Metro-Scanias, Metropolitans and Metrobuses

About 1000 orders for Scania Vabis trucks had been placed in Britain in 1967-69 and this encouraged the Swedish manufacturer to investigate entry into the passenger vehicle market. The monopolistic situation which had evolved in British heavy PSV chassis manufacture had caused great dissatisfaction among many operators. There was a sellers' market, frequent industrial unrest and long lead times for delivery of vehicles and spares. When, in 1969, Scania announced the formation of a partnership with Metro-Cammell Weymann Ltd to produce integrally-constructed buses at MCW's Washwood Heath (Birmingham) plant, even the most diehard patriots showed considerable interest.

Two single-deck demonstration buses were built and one of these, VWD 452H, arrived in Liverpool on 18th March 1970, entering service on 23rd from Prince Alfred Road on route 99. After a week it went to Green Lane and ran on 17C/D and finally had a few days on route 1 from Litherland.

The Metro-Scania BR111MH was a fraction under 36ft. long and had a wheelbase of 19ft. 4½in. It was of chassisless construction, the body frame being built up on jigs in six sections—two side pieces, one front, one rear and two frame units which carried elements included in the chassis kit. The rear-mounted engine was the powerful Scania D11 11-litre power unit and the drive line incorporated a very smooth two-speed torque convertor; acceleration was said to be equal to that of a trolleybus. The air suspension comprised two lobe-type bellows attached to the front axle and four similar units to the rear. A distinctive body feature developed by MCW which enabled Metro-Scanias to be instantly recognised, was the lowered front windscreen on the nearside, designed to increase kerbside visibility. At 8t 1c 1lb the unladen weight was rather high for an integral saloon bus.

Impressed with the demonstrator, the PTE placed four orders for Metro-Scanias, an initial one for 20 single-deckers followed by three for a double-deck version consisting of 20 each, the last two being run together.

A new fleet number series was started from 4001. Bus 4003 was exhibited at the Commercial Motor Show at Earls Court in September 1972 in the Wirral division's blue livery. All the single-deckers were in service by November; 4001-8 were 47-seaters and were allocated to Wallasey to replace the last of their 20-year old PD2s. They spent most of their working lives there though some were transferred to Liverpool in 1980. The others were 44-seaters and finished in Liverpool green, 4009-14 going to Green Lane for routes 17C/D whilst 4015-20 were allocated to Prince Alfred Road from where they ran on two ex-tram routes, 46 and 99.

For the double-deck model, designated BR111DH, the Metro-Scania name was dropped in favour of 'Metropolitan' and there were numerous design changes, though the engine and transmission were basically unaltered. A better weight distribution was obtained and engine accessibility improved by fitting twin radiators, one each side, forward of the rear axle which may have helped to reduce the heavy rear brake lining wear experienced on the single-deckers. The engine air intake was at roof level. Whereas the interior finish of the single-deckers had been rather old fashioned, the double-decker was as modern as tomorrow. There was, however, some criticism of the intrusion of the side radiator grilles into what were generally considered to be 'body' areas and also of the extensive use of mouldings on the exterior which made panel repairs costly. Indeed, mechanical parts generally were very expensive.

The first Metropolitan double-decker to go into service anywhere, 4021, arrived on 15th March and, after attending a rally at Southport, appeared on Rapidride 412 from Green Lane. The cream relief of the window surrounds was carried round the front and rear of the vehicle on both decks and there was a wide cream band with two heavy strips of aluminium trim at waist level on the lower deck. The appearance was quite dramatically different. The wide windows had sliders not scuttles and the seating arrangement was 44 up and 29 downstairs. As before, these vehicles were divided between Green Lane and Prince Alfred Road and all 20 were in service by October 1974.

Delivery of the second double-deck order (4041-60) started in July 1975 to Prince Alfred Road. They were generally similar to the earlier models but with a ramped floor in the lower saloon and trailing edge doors. Numbers 4061-80 were brought forward, following directly on the

Leyland Atlantean 175 had carried the same number in Birkenhead where it had been new in 1969. It had a dual-door Northern Counties body and was one of 15 Wirral Division buses which worked in Liverpool between 1979 and 1981. It is seen in Lime Street in October 1980 overtaking Metropolitan 4062.

previous 20 and were divided between Green Lane and Prince Alfred Road where they remained throughout their service. In their first summer, some ran to Llandudno on hire to Crosville at weekends.The bodies were copied from Manchester's Mancunian design with near-vertical panels above the upper deck windows and a very shallow domed roof.

The Scanias were very thirsty vehicles, fuel averages of 4-5 mpg being quite common and, unlike previous generations of Metro-Cammell bodies, they suffered from severe corrosion, a particularly worrying problem in an integral construction design. But the major failing of these interesting vehicles was their fuel consumption due to losses in the torque convertor. Scania coach and lorry models with mechanical transmission did not share this problem.

The green saloons, 4009-20, were not immediately recertified when their CoFs expired in 1979, and remained in store for many months but overhauls started about May 1980 and all eventually returned to service. In 1982 their fate was in the balance. The first casualties were 4048 with accident damage and 4066 which was damaged by fire. Five saloons were withdrawn in mid-1982 including three from Wirral. Six were sold for further service with Kingston-upon-Hull Corporation in 1983 (4031-34, 4036-37), the new owner renumbering them by deleting the '0', thus retaining the matching registrations.

Further withdrawals continued during 1983-4 and by the end of the year only five Metropolitans remained (4038/42/68/69/79), all based at Prince Alfred Road. The last to go were 4042, 4069 and 4079 in June 1985. Some of the earlier Metro-Scanias survived longer, 4008 and 4016 being sold to dealers in a clearing up operation before the PTE's direct operations ceased in October 1986.

In 1979, 4050 came out in the old Liverpool Corporation maroon and cream colours, being one of several buses painted in the liveries of the former constituent authorities. Bus 4025 shared with Bristol VRT 2102 the distinction of being the last buses to wear the Liverpool green livery, being repainted only in 1981. Number 4068 was painted yellow in 1985 on behalf of the Joint Trades Union campaign against the Transport Bill.

In 1980 an order was placed for five Scania BR112DH double-deckers with Alexander bodies but this was cancelled the following year and partly replaced by Metrobuses.

The Metrobus.

The shortcomings of the Metro-Scanias and Metropolitans led MCW to terminate the collaboration agreement with the Swedish manufacturer and in March 1977 it recruited its own chassis development team. Some of the Daimler drawing office staff were engaged following Leyland's attempt to transfer them to Lancashire. The Metrobus was to be 31ft. (9.5m) long with a wheelbase of 16ft. 3in. and a height of 14ft. 4¼in. The rear engine compartment was designed to accept either a Gardner 6LXB or a Rolls Royce Eagle 220 with full noise insulation and cooling through a front mounted radiator. Air suspension, ZF power steering and low step height were further features.

Although MCW were obviously keen to supply the vehicle with their own bodywork, they saw the wisdom of making provision for other bodybuilders' products to be fitted thus potentially extending the market to those operators who had particular preferences. To this end, though generally supplied complete, the model had what amounted to a complete chassis.

MCW's design team completed its work remarkably quickly with very little publicity. Alloy bolted body construction with internal stress panels replaced the welded steel construction of the Metropolitan and the chassis was riveted, with welded sub-assemblies. The Metrobus came together much faster than the Leyland Titan and was much more successful. Pre-production models were tested in service with the West Midlands PTE and by the time the Commercial Motor Show was held in September 1978, orders had been received for over 500 vehicles. Merseyside placed a small order for five as part of its experimental vehicle programme and 0019 with Gardner 6LXB engine and Voith transmission entered service at Gillmoss in November 1979. The single-door MCW body seated 43 upstairs and 30 in the lower saloon.

MCW Metrobus 0021 was one of the five experimental vehicles delivered during 1979-80. The general lines of the Metro-Cammell body-work were reminiscent of the 1978 Atlanteans 1776-1820. It is seen at Gillmoss depot in April 1984.

Numbers 0020-23 followed early in 1980, the last two having Rolls Royce Eagle 220 engines. In their early days, three of the vehicles were spread around, 0021 at Speke, 0022 at Birkenhead and 0023 at Southport but all were concentrated at Gillmoss before very long. They had standard MCW destination apertures masked to PTE requirements.

A further 10 Metrobuses entered service in 1982 but all had the favoured Alexander 'R' type bodywork seating 45 up and 31 downstairs. 0042-3 had Rolls Royce engines but 0056-63 had Gardners and all had Voith transmissions. The Rolls Royce was a much heavier engine than the Gardner.

The Metrobus enjoyed considerable success particularly in the West Midlands but these 15 vehicles were the only examples placed in service by Merseyside PTE. Had it not been for the uncertainties which preceded deregulation, the PTE would almost certainly have placed orders for the Mk II Metrobus which was announced in 1982. This had restyled bodywork eliminating the assymetrical windscreen and a frame based on three aluminium extrusions. The stress panels were bonded with Warerite before assembly and pre-coloured and the internal finish, with exposed rivet heads, was a little austere. However, the manufacturer had serious problems due to low investment in public transport, especially on the rail side, and, in 1989, the Laird Group, parent company of MCW, decided to dispose of all its transport-related manufacturing interests, causing grave concern to those operators with large Metrobus fleets about future supplies of spare parts. Eventually, the Metrobus designs were acquired by DAF and Optare.

Merseybus took delivery of 25 Metrobus IIs with 46/31 MCW bodies (801-25) in 1989.

More Bristols

A further 50 Bristol double-deckers were placed in service in 1974-75. These were single-door buses of model VRTSL6G, slightly shorter than their predecessors, with Gardner 6LX engines and numbered 2096-2145. Numbers 2096-2103 were delivered in Liverpool green in October 1974 but 2103 was repainted Verona green before entering service and 2104 onwards were delivered in the new livery. They had standard East Lancs. bodies. The waist was lowered over the front wheel arch to keep the nearside route indicator below upper-deck floor level. They were shared between Walton and Garston which were the only depots to operate VRs.

Number 2096 was withdrawn in 1984, 2101 in 1985 and the rest, which were all allocated to Garston, in 1986. The last four were 2103, 2117, 2126 and 2136 which came out of service at the end of October, none being taken into the Merseybus fleet.

Ten single-deck Bristol RESL6Gs with Eastern Coach Works 47-seat single-door bodies (2146-55) were delivered in 1975 for service in St. Helens where they spent virtually all their working lives. They were similar to 2086-95 which had been diverted from PMT in 1971 except that they had Gardner 6LX instead of Leyland engines and their rear indicators were painted over. All were still in the fleet on deregulation day.

In April and May 1980, the PTE borrowed from West Yorkshire PTE and subsequently purchased five 1975-76 Bristol LHS6L 27-seat midibuses with front-entrance Eastern Coach Works bodies. The West Yorkshire PTE fleet numbers had been 36-8 and 44-5 and they were numbered 2156-60 by Merseyside in July 1980. The LHS was the smallest member of a family of underfloor-engined vehicles which was available in three lengths. They were 24ft. long and powered by Leyland O.400 engines. They were placed in service on the Toxteth and Vauxhall community services 101 and 100 but latterly did duty also on route 102 between Walton and Broadgreen Hospital. They were withdrawn in October 1984 when 102 became double-deck operated. The following month they were lent to Nottingham Corporation who purchased them soon afterwards.

Daimler Fleetlines

The Daimler Fleetline had entered the market in 1960 as a competitor to the Leyland Atlantean, which it closely resembled in layout and dimensions and, by 1968, when Daimler was merged with the Leyland organisation, the Fleetline was the top-selling double-deck bus anywhere, having overtaken the Atlantean. The Gardner 6LX engine, with which most were fitted, had proved more economical and, on the whole, the Fleetline was less troublesome than the early Atlanteans even though all the first generation rear-engined double-deckers had their problems. The Bristol VRT had only just gone into production and took third place, the new bus grant specification having had the effect of restricting choice to these three for a time as it had virtually killed off the surviving front-engined models.

Whereas the Atlantean's rear axle was straight, the Fleetline's had a dropped centre, enabling a flat, low floor to be used in the lower saloon. A lowbridge version was thus practicable without the sunken upper gangway of the low Atlantean, though most models were produced to more generous vertical dimensions. There was an ingenious concentric drive Daimatic gearbox incorporating a set of epicyclic gear units basicly similar to those used in most Daimler buses since 1930 but with a hollow mainshaft which allowed the drive from the engine to be taken through to the remote end. The output emerged through bevel gears at the end nearer the engine, lining up with a straight propellor shaft. In later years, a Leyland O.680 engine was offered and the 6LX gave way to the 6LXB.

Birkenhead Corporation had bought nine of these buses (101-9) in 1964 and they duly came into the PTE fleet in 1969. The PTE ordered 50 Fleetlines with Metro-Cammell bodies for delivery in 1973; they carried fleet numbers 3001-50 and all entered service at Laird Street, Birkenhead in blue livery. They never ran in PTE service in Liverpool and it may, therefore, be thought that they play no part in this story. As already mentioned, orders for a further 110

The PTE's 1973 Daimler Fleetlines (3001-50) never ran in PTE service in Liverpool, only in Wirral, and were not taken over by Merseybus. Ten of them had not long returned from long loan to Crosville, based in Heswall from where they worked into Liverpool on services 418-9 and immediately prior to deregulation, 36 were hired by Crosville from the PTE to work tendered services in Liverpool. The five seen here in Love Lane depot yard in December 1986 are in PTE livery with Crosville fleetnames. Nearest the camera are 3003, 3023 and 3036 (Crosville numbers HDG 935, 947 and 952).

Fleetlines (3051-3160) were placed but the Leyland organisation was in turmoil and the order was cancelled in 1977.

Between December 1982 and April 1983 Nos. 3011-20 were lent to Crosville who repainted them in NBC green livery but with Merseyside PTE legal lettering. They were based at Heswall and operated regularly on routes 418-9 to Liverpool city centre via the Wallasey tunnel. They were returned during 1985, being repainted in PTE livery by Crosville but without the brown skirt round the front.

On deregulation day, the Fleetlines did not pass to Merseybus but 36 were hired by the PTE to Crosville and allocated to Liverpool depot for service on tendered routes. When Crosville withdrew from Liverpool, they were returned and sold, many of them to Gold Line of St. Asaph whose associate, Busman Buses, placed some in service on various routes in Wirral in a white and blue livery.

The Leyland Nationals

The Leyland National was a joint project of British Leyland and the National Bus Company. The concept of a highly standardised single-deck bus originated in 1965 within Leyland, at that time largely on the basis that it would be a city bus, as many believed that one-man operation spelt the end of the double-deck bus. Talks with the NBC began soon after the latter became operational in January 1969. A joint company, Leyland National Ltd. was formed and a new, highly-automated factory was eventually built at Whitehaven, Cumberland, in an area where there was serious unemployment.

Seven prototypes were built and rigorously tested in places as far apart as Finland and Spain but, inexplicably,

none was evaluated under service conditions with an NBC operator. Some of the model's weaknesses might have been discovered earlier if this obvious course had been followed. One was shown to the public at Earls Court in September 1970.

The National was an integral vehicle available in 10.3 and 11.3m lengths and with single or dual-doors. All the Merseyside vehicles were of the longer version. The body modules were steel pressings built up into ring frame assemblies between bays, the panels being attached by patented rivets easily removed with the aid of a special tool. There was no welding in sensitive areas and the components were subjected to a very effective anti-corrosive process.

The power unit was the 8.2-litre 510, a turbo-charged version of the 500 series of 6-cylinder in-line Leyland engines with the cylinder head cast integrally with the block, a return to the methods of the early motor car era. The aim was to eliminate the cylinder head gasket, apt to be a source of trouble, but it presupposed that the engine would not require dismantling for long periods for other reasons. The engine was mounted horizontally under the floor at the rear and the drive taken through a charged fluid coupling which shared its oil with the gearbox. Like many rear-engined buses, where dirt and oil is liable to build up inside the engine housing, they were prone to catching fire.

Elevation of the Leyland National 2, 11.6m 49-seat dual door bus as used by Merseyside PTE. Note the bulge at the front end to accommodate the re-positioned radiator. The windscreen was that fitted to Leyland's Danish subsidiary (DAB) vehicles.

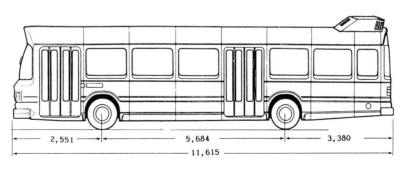

The front axle was of a new design incorporating power assisted rack and pinion steering and this was the first time rack and pinion had been used in so large a vehicle. There were wide doors and an efficient air suspension system which kept the height of the entrance steps constant. Low profile tyres permitted a low floor level with minimum intrusion of wheel arches. Ventilation and heating equipment was housed in a pod at the rear of the roof and the National became known by passengers for its ability to demist all the windows in the bus. There was also an air curtain across the doorways. However, the interior was notably austere, the overall effect having been compared to a hospital waiting room and the seating was less comfortable than Leyland's standards of 30 years earlier.

At the time the first Nationals took to the road in 1972, Ribble and Crosville being among the first recipients, Merseyside PTE had no thought of adding any to the fleet though a demonstrator came for a few days in November 1972. The PTE inherited eight new two-door Nationals (1-8) from Southport Corporation in 1974, one of which had already been on loan to St. Helens for a few weeks. These buses remained at Southport and, after being renumbered 6042-9 in May 1980, were converted to single-door 49-seat layout; the original three-track rear route numbers were either removed or painted over.

It was the long saga of the Fleetline order which never materialised, and then Alexanders' inability to fulfil their orders on time that led the PTE to substitute Nationals for Atlanteans. One advantage of the National was its availability. Production at Whitehaven never reached capacity and, in 1980, it took only seven weeks from placing the order to delivery.

The first Nationals new to the PTE, which arrived in mid-November 1977, carried fleet numbers intended for the Atlanteans for which they were substituted (1766-75) and went into service at St. Helens as did many more of those to follow, St. Helens being almost entirely a single-deck depot until the mid-eighties when school contracts required double-deckers. The next to arrive was a dual-purpose Suburban Express which differed from the standard model in having a flat floor so that all the 45 coach type seats faced forward. Its fleet number 1000 was changed to 7000 in January 1979, marking the introduction of a separate series for coaches. It was initially allocated to Southport. Crosville also received 46 of this type of vehicle, some of which were used on local services in Liverpool. The next 20 standard Nationals (1866-85) also went to St. Helens. Two more Suburban Expresses which followed them were numbered 1886-7 in error; these were quickly renumbered 7001-2, 1887 receiving its new number before entering service.

The National proved to be a very thirsty vehicle, to a large extent because of its 8½ ton weight, a ton heavier than a Bristol RE, and the 510 engine was inferior to the Gardner and prone to smoky exhausts, particularly when accelerating from rest when turbocharger lag temporarily starved the engine of enough air for clean combustion. Smaller operators disliked it because of the special tools needed to gain access to the engine. In 1976 Leyland had announced a phase II version of the National with

The difference between the frontal treatment of the 11.3m National and its successor, the 11.6m National 2, is clearly seen in these pictures of 6010 (above) at Pier Head in July 1979 on service 12 and 6084 (below) leaving the Central Bus Station a year later.

batteries moved to the front to improve weight distribution and make room for sound deadening material; brakes were modified to meet new EEC requirements, the rake of the seats was improved and the cab bulkhead integrated with the structure for greater rigidity. More important, the Leyland National 2 appeared in prototype form in 1978 and production deliveries began early in 1980. The 510 engine was replaced by the well-tried O.680 and, in due course, with its derivative, the L11, which was the unit fitted to all the PTE's National 2s. The radiator was moved to the front, involving redesigning the front to a more curvaceous profile and using windscreens from DAB, Leyland's Danish subsidiary. This operation lengthened the vehicle slightly to 11.6m. The sophisticated heating system became optional and those vehicles which had ordinary underfloor heaters had no roof pods, this being an option originally known as the Series B version that had been introduced on the previous model. However, all Mersevside PTE vehicles had pods.

The PTE now regarded the National as a replacement for the Panther, the last of which were withdrawn in 1981. All the early National 1s were renumbered 6050-79 in May 1980, their original numbers in the 1700s and 1800s being reused for Atlanteans. The first National 2s were 6035-41 followed by 6080-6163 in 1980. Numbers 6080-6138 had roof pods, rear route number indicators and Ambla seats while 6098 had a ripple destination indicator at the front only. Many of these vehicles went to Garston and Gillmoss but others went to Wirral depots and St. Helens. Four further dual-purpose vehicles arrived in 1981 (7004-7) of which the first and last went to Prince Alfred Road and Green Lane depots respectively. The final ten buses (6164-73) arrived in 1982 and most went to St. Helens which, in due course, became a National stronghold. A few buses were withdrawn in 1986 but most Nationals passed into the Merseybus fleet.

The Evaluation Buses 1980-84

The decision in 1978 to purchase small numbers of vehicles of different makes followed hints from Leyland that the Atlantean, Liverpool's standard workhorse for almost 16 years, would be phased out.

After the absorption of AEC and Daimler and various bodybuilders and the link with NBC bringing Bristol and ECW as well as the new Leyland National into the picture, the British Leyland Motor Corporation on its formation in 1968, briefly became virtually the only home source of new heavyweight buses. It was beset by many problems and the industry became very dissatisfied with long delivery times, non-availability of spare parts and general inefficiency. Inevitably other manufacturers exploited the situation and, by the mid-seventies, a measure of operators' choice had been restored.

The PTE devoted a new series of fleet numbers prefixed 00 to several experimental vehicles, all of which were to undergo a carefully planned evaluation programme. Some confusion attended the early stages of this project and the numbers 0001-18 were never used. Numbers 0001-8 were intended for eight Nationals but, as there were already 41 of this model in the fleet, the Nationals were dropped from the programme. Numbers 0014-18 were to have been Leyland Titans, of the new generation rear-engined type, originally introduced under the code B15 in 1975, a model which had a brief undistinguished career and was represented in the PTE fleet only by 0029, a demonstrator which was on loan in the Wirral division from May 1980 to March 1982. It was altered from dual to single-door layout and painted in PTE livery and did not go into service until November 1980.

The Metrobuses which played an important and successful part in the evaluation programme are described separately in the MCW section on page 155.

The Dennis Dominators

The re-entry of the Dennis name into the bus market was generally welcomed. In recent years it had become associated with fire fighting and refuse collection vehicles. Its new owners, the Hestair Group, encouraged by various operators, saw a gap in the market and recruited Bob Crouch, the man responsible for the very successful Daimler Fleetline, to produce a no-frills, no-nonsense competitor to the new, ultra-sophisticated, third-generation double-deckers. Thus was launched the Dominator double-decker, and also the Falcon and Lancet single-deckers, both being revivals of well-respected model names of the thirties and forties.

The PTE's order for five Dominators (0009-13) was at first cancelled and then reinstated with new numbers 0024-28. This was the first Dennis order since Liverpool Corporation's airport bus in 1935. Leicester City Transport lent their No. 203 with East Lancs. dual-door body from November 1978 to January 1979.

Although the Dominator was offered with either the Gardner 6LXB or the Rolls Royce Eagle 220 engine, the PTE opted for the Gardner in all its examples. The Voith D851 fully-automatic transmission, embodying a built-in hydraulic retarder was fitted. The footbrake tripped the retarder into operation down to 12mph after which the automatically adjusting Girling brakes came into use. Kunifer brake pipe tubing was guaranteed for the life of the vehicle.

Buses 0024-25 went into service in mid-April 1980 and 0026-28 from Speke in February-March 1981. The Willowbrook 14ft. 10in. bodies were similar to those mounted on Atlanteans 1843-72. The initial experience was sufficiently encouraging for a further order for 12 to be placed with much the same mechanical specification but with Alexander R type bodywork seating 45/33. The R body had deeper windows on both decks than the AL built to Merseyside specification. Both the two-part driver's windscreen and the front upper-deck windows had a slight 'vee' and were similar on both types. These arrived as 0035-36 (with electronic destination indicators and air suspension) for Gillmoss in early 1982 and 0046-53 in mid-year for service from Speke. The PTE contemplated placing an order for 80 vehicles to be split between Dennis and MCW for delivery in 1984 but this was not proceeded with.

In the slimming down before deregulation in 1986, 0024-28 were sold to dealers, 0026 finding its way to Hong Kong. The remaining Dominators passed to Merseybus.

The Dennis Lancets

The Lancet single-decker was available as a full length bus or a 8.2m (27ft.) midibus with a wheelbase of 3.86m (12ft. 8in.). Despite its relatively small dimensions, the Lancet had many heavyweight features, the front axle being the same as that used in the Dominator. The bus was leaf sprung and powered by the Leyland 402 engine mounted vertically amidships.

Dennis Dominator 0048 was one of the second batch of this make, placed in service in 1982. The pleasing lines of the Alexander 'R' body with wide windows and gentle V-front, were well suited to the Verona green, jonquil and brown livery. The small route numbers were not considered satisfactory and most were replaced by the 10in. electronic type.

When new, Dennis Lancets were used on the Toxteth community service 100. Their Duple bodies had 31 coach seats giving a high standard of comfort. Number 7024 is seen in Ranelagh Street near Central Station on 11th June 1983.

One of the first Lancet midibuses to be built, Portsmouth Corporation No. 97 with Wadham Stringer 35-seat body, visited Merseyside in February 1982; it was driven over the 100 and 101 routes in Liverpool and the 27 in Wallasey but did not carry passengers. As a result of this test, an order was placed for 10 with Duple 31-seat dual-purpose bodies (7021-30) to replace the Bristol LHLs in Liverpool and the Leyland 550FGs in Wirral.

They all arrived in 1983 and 7024/6/8 went to Garston,

7029-30 to Walton and the others to Wallasey (1) and St. Helens (3) while 7027 went on loan to Tayside Regional Council.

Although in a bus body shell, the Lancets had full coach seating and were designed for use on private hire by small parties. After deregulation, 7024-8 were at first based at Edge Lane for service 100 but eventually they were all transferred to St. Helens.

The Volvos

A Volvo B59 rear-engined single-deck demonstrator with 48-seat dual-door (plus 24 standing) Marshall Camair bodywork was on loan from February to March 1972 but, by this time, the PTE had too many single-deckers of this type.

The Volvo Ailsa double-deck bus first appeared at the Scottish Motor Show in 1973. It was evolved by Ailsa, Volvo's Scottish agents in response to Scottish Bus Group interest, early examples being sold under the Ailsa name, although later brought into Volvo's own marque name. The aim was to overcome the problems inherent in the rear engined layout. The compact turbocharged Volvo engine was located centrally at the front, making for a cramped cab and smaller boarding platform. About 400 Ailsas, made at the Volvo factory at Irvine, Scotland, entered service in 1975-77 and the makers' claims of low maintenance were well borne out.

The Volvo Ailsa had its critics, some claiming that it was noisy, ill-sprung and fierce in gearchange. Volvo evolved Mk II and Mk III versions which eliminated most of the complaints and in August 1981, Strathclyde PTE's Volvo A10 was demonstrated in Liverpool in West Midlands PTE livery, carrying WM fleet number 7053. It ran for about six weeks from Gillmoss following which an order was placed for two vehicles. Arrangements were made for two Derby Corporation vehicles to be delivered new to the PTE on trial for six months and they came in 1982 in full PTE livery numbered 0044-45. They went to Wirral Division and saw no service in Liverpool and when the PTE's own vehicles arrived later in the year, they replaced the Derby vehicles which were finally delivered to their owner. The PTE then placed an order for 13 Ailsa MkIIIs with 44/37 Alexander R bodies which also went into Wirral division service on delivery in 1984.

Volvos were well tested in Liverpool but no substantial orders were placed. An Ailsa with Alexander 'R' bodywork in West Midlands PTE blue and cream colours and showing their fleet number 7053 (above) was operated from Gillmoss depot for about six weeks in 1981 while a Citybus with East Lancs. body worked from Prince Alfred Road in 1984. The latter is seen (below) in Green Lane on route 99.

A Volvo Citybus demonstrator with 47/36 East Lancs body was on loan in November and December 1984 and ran from Prince Alfred Road depot on routes 46 and 99. Another, with Alexander body, (B108CCS), ran on route 61 from the same depot in September-October 1985. The Citybus chassis had a centrally-positioned underfloor engine.

After sampling a demonstrator and two Volvo Ailsas belonging to Derby Corporation,from January to August 1982, two (Nos.0054-55) were placed in service the same year followed by 13 in 1984. The PTE decided to concentrate them in the Wirral Division and 0055, with Alexander 'R' body, is seen leaving Crosville's Heswall bus station, reputedly the oldest purpose-built bus station in the north of England, opened in 1924.

Five Leyland Olympians joined the experimental fleet in 1984 again with Alexander 'R' bodies of which a total of 38 were commissioned for the evaluation buses. Bus 0066 turns from Lime Street into St. John's Lane in June 1984.

The Leyland Olympian

The Olympian, originally known as the B45, was Leyland's intended replacement for the Daimler Fleetline, Bristol VRT and ultimately the Atlantean. It was designed largely in response to NBC pressure for a vehicle that would replace the standard low-height VRT and did not have the Titan's independent front suspension but also because none of the other three chassis from the Leyland stable would be able to fully meet forthcoming EEC regulations. Unlike the integral-bodied and unsuccessful Titan, the Olympian returned to an all-steel perimeter frame which relied on the bodywork to give it full rigidity, as used on the Atlantean, Fleetline and VRT. The frame was swept up at the rear and the engine suspended from it. The power unit in the Merseyside examples was the Leyland TL11, a turbocharged version of the L11, updated from the O.680. Alternatively, a Gardner 6LXB or 6LXC was available and such units were in the overall majority, being chosen by most NBC fleets including Crosville and Ribble. Later on, a Cummins L10 was offered, becoming the official standard when Leyland engine production ceased.

The transmission comprised an integral, fully charged fluid flywheel and a five-speed Hydracyclic gearbox with

semi- or fully-automatic control. The intrusion of the front mounted radiator on to the platform was less than on the VRT. The rear axle was a dropped-centre unit, continuing the Fleetline practice, and the cab was identical with that of the National 2.

Ten Olympians with some of the first production Eastern Coach Works 46/31 bodies (0030-34, 0037-41) went into service at Green Lane in 1982 and another five with Alexander 'R' bodies (0064-68) joined them in October 1983. Despite serious problems with the Hydracyclic gearbox, which Leyland eventually overcame, the Olympian was accepted by the PTE as the Atlantean's successor though no further examples entered service until after deregulation.

The Quest 80Bs

Quest 80 was a new manufacturer founded by an entrepreneur, R. T. Knowles, who had a regard for the side-engined AEC Q of the thirties and the name was intended to reflect this. The firm specialised in vehicles of unorthodox layout, mainly rear-engined models based on Ford components. It was located originally at Telford but later at Andover and the firm obtained some publicity when it built a double-deck trolleybus for Johannesburg. In 1984 it became part of the UEI Group who also owned a bodybuilder known as Locomotors and the PTE placed an order for six 27ft. Quest 80Bs with Locomotors bodies, early in 1984; they were delivered late the same year.

These buses were numbered 0082-87 and had a nominal seating capacity of 23 but could be adapted to 11-seats and four wheelchairs or 15 seats and two wheelchairs. For use by the disabled, they were equipped with a kneel facility which allowed the front air suspension to be deflated, thus lowering the entrance step. There was also a hydraulically-operated ramp located below the entrance step which would extend to the pavement to allow wheelchairs to be loaded through the wide front entrance.

Bus 0083 entered service at St. Helens in mid-December and 0086 ran for a time on service 100 from Garston depot. No. 0084 was allocated to Wallasey. The vehicles were controversial as there were various switches which, if accidentally activated, led to the engine being switched off automatically, even if the vehicle was in motion. The same happened if the emergency door or access flap was opened. It seems that none was ever used on the Merseylink service for the disabled and 0084/6/7 never ran in service on Merseyside, the registration number of 0087, C844 OBG, being taken up only when it was sold. Merseybus did not want these buses which were sold by the PTE in 1987 for service in various parts of the country. 0084 and 0086 stayed fairly local with Smith's Aaron Travel of Rainhill.

Coaches

The PTE owned 32 vehicles with coach seating of which 15 had full luxury coach bodywork and 17 were dual-purpose vehicles, ie bus bodies with superior seating. The first acquisition came with the St. Helens undertaking in 1974. It was a Bedford VAM70 with Duple 45-seat body which had been bought second-hand from a dealer in 1971, having been new to N. Boyes of Bradford in May 1968. It was numbered C201 and the PTE, apparently feeling that St. Helens should not possess a coach while the big city lacked such refinement, transferred it first to Edge Lane and later to Wallasey and Southport. It was sold in 1981.

Leyland National Suburban Express dual-purpose vehicle 1000 was placed in service at Southport in 1978 followed by similar vehicles, originally 1886-7. In 1979 a new series of fleet numbers was commenced for coach-seated vehicles and these three became 7000-2 respectively. The dual-purpose National had a level floor

One of the Quest 80B Locomotors-bodied midibuses delivered in 1984-85. They were designed for use as 23-seat buses or as wheelchair carriers with reduced seating. The fork lift mechanism for wheelchairs was built into the front platform which could be extended. Only two of the six buses saw limited service and 0084, seen here whilst stored at Wallasey, was never used. Merseybus did not want them and they were all sold by the PTE in 1987.

This 1968 Bedford VAM coach (201) had a 45-seat Duple body and was purchased second-hand by St. Helens Corporation in 1971. Under PTE ownership, it was allocated to several depots in turn and was photographed in 1977 in Southport depot.

throughout as opposed to the stepped up floor at the rear on the standard bus version.

The deregulation of express services (defined as journeys over 30 miles) in 1980 enabled the PTE to run long distance excursions and most of the coach work was centred on Southport though vehicles were often brought to Liverpool for private hire work. Two Leyland Leopards with Duple Dominant I 49-seat bodies (7003, 7008) were added to the fleet in 1981 together with four more dual-purpose Nationals (7004-7) which were spread around the area, 7004 to Prince Alfred Road, 7005 to St. Helens, 7006 to Wallasey and 7007 to Green Lane.

In 1982, 12 Leyland Tigers with Duple Dominant IV 49-seat bodies (7009-20) were acquired. One went to Green Lane (7011), three to Speke (7014/8/20) and two to Walton (7017/9), the others being stationed at Southport, St. Helens and Wallasey. Numbers 7011, 7017/9 were used on the express service to Heysham which was operated in 1985. A further Tiger with Duple Laser body (7031), which had been used as a demonstrator by the bodybuilder, was purchased in 1983. The intervening numbers (7021-30) were occupied by the Dennis Lancet midibuses which have been described earlier.

The coach fleet passed to Merseybus who sold the two Leopards in 1988, acquiring two Dennis Javelin coaches (7032-3) with 57-seat Duple 320 bodies. Number 7032 was equipped to carry a demountable drinks dispenser and servery which, when installed, reduced the seating capacity to 52. The fleet name 'Merseycoach' was adopted by the new owners.

The PTE showed a preference to the Leyland Tiger chassis and Duple Dominant IV 49-seat body for its coach fleet, acquiring a fleet of 12 such vehicles during 1982. The general theme of the standard livery as applied to single-deck buses adapted well to these handsome vehicles. The camera caught 7013 in a parking ground in Skelhorne Street.

Open Top Buses

When the Southport fleet was taken over in 1974, six open-top vehicles—three double-deck and three single-deck—came into the PTE fleet. The double-deckers (184/186/187) were 1947 PD2s while the single-deckers (10/11/12) were 1950 Leyland PS2s bought from Ribble and were withdrawn in 1976 (10) and 1979 (11/12). All had originally been orthodox covered vehicles. They were used for various local tours in Southport and sometimes for a service on the beach between Southport and Ainsdale. The double-deckers would occasionally be hired for a special occasion in Liverpool such as the triumphal return

Atlantean 1551 was a 1974 Alexander-bodied vehicle which was converted to open top and repainted red and cream in June 1983. It is shown at a rally at Seacombe ferry a month later. In 1985 it was repainted in the County Council's blue and yellow livery.

Atlantean 1612 loads for a County Council sponsored sightseeing tour at Mann Island in July 1984 shortly after conversion to open top; it was painted in the blue and yellow livery. Most of the conversions were done at Southport where there were men who had done this type of work for many years but 1612 was done at Edge Lane.

Ribble 1927 was a 1961 Leyland Atlantean with Metro-Cammell open top body. It was new to Devon General in whose fleet it was named 'Sir Martin Frobisher'. It passed to Western National when that company absorbed Devon General in 1971 and then to the non-operating NBC subsidiary, APT Ltd, in 1982. After running on loan to Lincolnshire Road Car Co during the summers of 1982 and 1983, it was acquired by Ribble in November 1984 and, after being painted white with a red band and grey frontal stripes, entered service in May 1985 on service 401 between Skelhorne Street (where it was photographed) and the Festival Gardens.

of a victorious football team when the London train would be specially stopped at Allerton. The team would then ride on the open-top deck to pass through cheering crowds *en route* to the Town Hall.

In 1974 Atlantean L677 hit a low bridge and was sent to Southport to be rebuilt as an open-topper, re-entering service there in July 1975. Southport had men who were skilled in these conversions as they periodically scrapped their old open buses and replaced them with something newer. Three forward-entrance PD2/40s (51/53/54), new in 1965 and converted for one-man operation in 1968, replaced the 1947 buses in 1976-77 and these were lent to Liverpool regularly from 1978 for use on one hour City Tours.

Southport fought gallantly to retain their red and cream livery and the PTE eventually agreed to use it as an open-top livery. L677 was repainted in Southport livery on conversion. In 1982 the ex-Southport fleet was renumbered to satisfy a computer which could handle only four-digit numbers so the three PD2s became 0651, 0653 and 0654. By this time L677 was the only bus with a prefix letter so it became 0677. It was used as a treelopper in 1983 and withdrawn in 1984, the last of the Liverpool Corporation Atlanteans.

Four PTE Atlanteans were converted to open-top, 1449 (which had been vandalised) and 1551 in 1983, 1612 in 1984 and 1524 in 1985. 1494 was put aside for conversion but was eventually scrapped in 1986. Except for 1612, all the open-top conversions were done at Southport. Numbers 1551 and 1612 were painted in Merseyside County Council blue and yellow livery but both were repainted red and cream after the demise of that body and 1612 was based at Walton. The other bus, 1449, was specially painted and lettered 'City Heritage Shuttle' in 1989.

Leyland PD2 0654 was withdrawn in 1984 and placed on permanent loan to a Preservation Group; 0651 survived to be transferred to Merseybus and was still in service in 1990.

Inter-Divisional Transfers

By 1973, agreement had been reached over comprehensive one-man operation of double-deck buses in the Wirral Division and there was a need for a massive injection of suitable vehicles so that the changeover could be made as soon as possible. There were only 67 rear-engine front-entrance double-deckers in the Wirral fleet, the remainder comprising Leyland PD2 rear-entrance double-deckers from the Birkenhead fleet dating from 1957 to 1963. Practically all the ex-Wallasey half-cab buses, which dated from 1951-52, had been withdrawn from service and none was involved in the vehicle transfers. The only ex-Wallasey bus to cross the river was 399, a petrol-engined Bedford J2 19-seater which was used for staff transport at Edge Lane Works from December 1975 at least until 1977.

The absorption of the St. Helens and Southport undertakings in 1974 brought more Leyland PD2s and, in the case of St. Helens, AEC Regent V's into the PTE fleet, the most recent AEC being only seven years old. One-man operation in both towns had been accomplished using mainly single-deck buses, Leyland Panthers and Nationals in Southport and AEC Swifts in St. Helens. The Swifts had no equivalent in the ex-Liverpool fleet but all the other models were compatible.

By 1973 some of the ex-Liverpool PD2s and Regent Vs were older and in worse condition than the ex-Birkenhead vehicles. When new Atlanteans and Daimler Fleetlines were placed in service on Wirral routes converted to one-man operation, it was logical to send the displaced vehicles across the river for use on the two-man operated peak hour services, and withdraw older ex-Liverpool buses.

The first ex-Birkenhead buses went to Liverpool in April 1973. They were Nos. 86 and 80 of the 1963 batch of PD2/40s with Massey 65-seat bodies and OCM registrations. They were allocated to Green Lane depot

This ex-St. Helens AEC Regent V with Metro-Cammell body was new in October 1962 and was numbered L34 in the St. Helens fleet. Renumbered A455, it is finished in full Liverpool-style livery with the short lived square 'Merseyside' logo and is seen approaching Pier Head Bus Station in October 1974.

Several ex-Birkenhead Leyland PD2s were transferred to St. Helens and 63W (formerly 33 and 119) is seen in Prescot Road, Liverpool on service 317 in July 1975 in red and cream livery. Fourteen years later it was still in use as a training bus.

Seen in Prince Alfred Road depot in 1975, this Weymann Aurora-bodied 1956 Leyland PD2/20 carried fleet number 450 without the L prefix; it was new to Southport Corporation (32). The inclusion or omission of cream window surrounds on the transferred buses appears to have been a matter of chance.

Ex-Birkenhead 83 (L459), seen at Derby Square in Verona green livery in June 1975, had a Massey 65-seat body on a Leyland PD2/40 chassis. It has had an unusual front indicator treatment and, like most of the transferred buses, had no logo.

and renumbered L370-1. Further examples from this and the almost identical 1962 batch with MCM registrations were transferred during that summer together with three 1960 63-seaters (33, 35 and 36) and two 1961 vehicles with East Lancashire bodywork (49 and 54), which took the series up to L379.

In September 1973, 30 Leyland PD2/40s (Birkenhead Nos. 110-39) with Massey 66-seat bodywork were earmarked for transfer. These were 1965-66 models with BBG-C and DBG-D matching registrations. Nineteen were transferred to Liverpool immediately, a further five by the end of the year and two early in 1974. Fleet numbers L400-29 were allocated to the batch in the correct order but the numbers L403, L405, L409 and L421 were not used as Nos. 113 and 131 went to St. Helens on 1st April 1974, the day the undertaking was absorbed in the PTE, having already been painted red, and they were followed by 115 and 119 in May. They received the numbers 30, 32, 33 and 31 in the local series but in September 1974 they were renumbered 60W, 62W, 63W and 61W, the W presumably signifying 'Wirral'. In 1976, the survivors, 60 and 61, dropped the W and these two and 147 were destined to be the last open-back buses in St. Helens, two going into the training fleet and one becoming a towing vehicle. 60 (ex-Birkenhead 113) survived until 1982 and 61 and 147 passed to Merseybus being renumbered 8100 and 8087 in the service vehicle fleet in 1987.

Between July and September 1974, a further seven ex-Birkenhead PD2s of the 1963 batch were transferred to St. Helens and numbered 34-40 at first but changed to 64W-70W in September; an eighth vehicle (70) went to Southport in December 1974 when it became 170 being joined there by 321 (formerly 21) of the 1959 batch and 85 (now 70W) from St. Helens. When more AEC Swifts, ordered by St. Helens Corporation before the merger, were delivered in 1975, all these buses were transferred to Liverpool together with another 33 buses direct from Birkenhead. One-man operation at Southport was extended by transferring three ex-Birkenhead two-door Leyland Leopards (92-4) which had been rejected by Green Lane where their narrow doors and manual gear change were not liked. They had been earmarked for the 'Railride' service between Central and James Street Stations in company with some ex-St. Helens Swifts, but Panthers were soon substituted for both. They remained at Southport until withdrawal. They were joined by two rare single-deck Atlanteans (95-96) with 40-seat Northern Counties bodies, which had been ordered by Birkenhead but delivered to the PTE in 1970. They were eventually transferred to Liverpool in 1979 and finally withdrawn in 1981. Additional one-man requirements at Southport were met by moving Panthers from Liverpool to augment the 22 similar vehicles inherited from Southport Corporation.

The 33 vehicles transferred from Birkenhead included all the survivors of the 1959 batch, nine of which had been sent to Wallasey in 1970 to enable their 19-year old veterans to be scrapped. Buses 21-23, 25-30 had at first been renumbered by adding a B suffix to distinguish them from similarly numbered ex-Wallasey Atlanteans and then, in November 1971, by adding 300 to their numbers. Six Weymann bodied ex-Southport Leyland PD2/20s were moved to Liverpool, four in 1974 and two in 1975; another moved to St. Helens. Eight ex-St. Helens AEC Regent Vs dating from 1958-62 were also transferred to Speke depot and received fleet numbers A454-61. The Bedford coach mentioned earlier was transferred from St. Helens to Edge Lane.

All Leylands transferred to Liverpool in 1974 and up to August 1975 were given fleet numbers in a series between L450 and L474 but, unlike the earlier transfers, the numbers were allocated in a random fashion without regard to the previous identity of the vehicle. A number of vehicles carried the fleet number without the 'L' prefix. After August 1975, no ex-Birkenhead buses were renumbered as their existing numbers did not clash with anything else running in Liverpool; for the most part, this

These pictures taken at Stanley open air depot show the different treatment given to the ex-Birkenhead buses. In the left view taken in January 1975, both buses have been given full ex-Liverpool livery and prefixed fleet numbers though L406 still has a full set of Birkenhead blinds. In the picture on the right, taken in November 1973, four of the five buses are ex-Birkenhead. Number 407 is apparently still in Wirral blue livery. The rear indicators have been treated in different ways.

could have been done from the start. Some vehicles carried four different fleet numbers in the space of less than twelve months e.g. ex-Birkenhead 82-85 which became successively St. Helens 37-40 then 67W-70W then L470/459/464/461.

On arrival in Liverpool, buses in blue or red livery were usually repainted before entering service, in Liverpool green until October 1974 and thereafter in Verona green and jonquil. Similarly, those which went to St. Helens originally received the local red and cream livery with the exception of the odd one from Southport the livery of which was almost identical. By the time they left Birkenhead, most buses had had their generous Birkenhead style indicators with destination and intermediate blinds and two column route number blinds, front and rear and side route blinds, reduced by blanking out all but the front destination and front and rear number blinds. Some of the original route number blinds were replaced as the Birkenhead 'units' blind ran 0-9, 0A-9A and 0B-9B. Liverpool needed C, D and E suffixed numbers and St. Helens needed three digit numbers so that two figures had to be squeezed into the 'tens' aperture. Often, the former front intermediate aperture was used for the destination. Ex-Southport bus 39 (L472) was fitted with a Liverpool style three column route number display but retained its Southport-style single column aperture also.

Many of the transferees did not last long enough to don the Verona green livery. Some of them worked in Liverpool for very short periods before withdrawal and it seems

certain that the policy was to carry out no major repairs. If an expensive failure occurred, the bus was immediately taken out of service and eventually scrapped. For example, ex-Birkenhead 322 entered service in Liverpool in November 1975 and was withdrawn five months later.

The 41 buses which remained were all taken out of service on 10th January 1977, ending an interesting interlude in the story of the PTE fleet. Ex-Birkenhead PD2 67 has been preserved and restored to its original livery and 131 was still being used as a trainer bus by Merseybus in 1990.

Transfers from Liverpool

Bus movements across the Mersey were not all one way. Two of the ex-Liverpool Royal Tigers, SL175-6, which had had a fixed 'Private' destination display, were equipped for one-man operation, fitted with a single-track route number blind and reseated from 40 to 38 in April 1970. Renumbered 98 and 97, they were repainted in Wirral blue livery and, based at Laird Street, Birkenhead, were used mainly on routes 12, Seacombe-Charing Cross, 45, New Ferry-Brookhouse Estate and 97, Woodside-Oxton Village, until 1972. After withdrawal, 97 was scrapped but 98 became a Traveller Ticket sales bus, painted red, shedded at Prince Alfred Road and standing all day in Clayton Square. There were facilities for taking photographs and issuing identity cards and these duties lasted until June 1975 when the Williamson Square enquiry office took them over.

Four ex-Liverpool Atlanteans, L508, L515, L533 and L623 were among those selected for reinstatement in 1976 after withdrawal and were sent to Laird Street for overhaul to relieve pressure on Edge Lane. After completion, they entered service there, losing their L prefixes to avoid confusion with 1508 etc. which were also based there. They returned to Liverpool in 1980 and ran for a few more months. Several ex-Liverpool Panthers also saw temporary service in Wirral.

These Leyland Titans ex-Birkenhead (left) and Southport (right) are seen on driver training duties at Edge Lane in 1977; neither had seen passenger service in Liverpool. The Southport vehicle was one of four forward-entrance Titans (43-46) converted to one-man-operation in 1970. Three served as training buses.

Ex-Birkenhead 110, a Leyland PD2/40 of 1965, with 66-seat Massey body, was still in good condition when seen in Church Street, Liverpool on 15th September 1973 in all-green Liverpool-style livery and bearing fleet number L400.

The last cross-river movements involving pre-PTE buses took place in 1979-80 when Birkenhead's final batch of twin-door Atlanteans, 168-182, were sent to work out of Garston depot. These buses dated from 1969 and had Northern Counties bodies seating 44 on the upper deck and 27 in the lower saloon. They had been designed for one-man operation which had commenced at Birkenhead

with double-deckers just prior to the take-over by the PTE. The reason for these transfers is obscure and one report says that 167, which was the last of a previous batch of Atlanteans, also worked in Liverpool but this has not been confirmed. They were all withdrawn in 1981, the last being 180 in November of that year, thus becoming the last pre-PTE bus to be withdrawn from service.

54 DEPOTS AND WORKS

During the later municipal years and the PTE era many detailed improvements to depots aided efficiency, productivity and comfort in the workplace. The trade unions certainly exerted influence, but management also recognised that men work better in warm, clean and attractive conditions. From 1974, the Health and Safety at Work Act added statutory impetus. Heating costs were reduced by concentrating only on the maintenance bays which were enclosed with folding doors.

The old tram depots had generally had a face lift during conversion to bus garages in the fifties. Walton was the exception as it was so old that demolition of a substantial part of the structure and rebuilding was the only possible remedy. Garston suffered subsidence in 1971, extensive repairs being made to the administration block. Roof repairs to the 80-year old Smithdown Road shed and its much newer neighbour at Prince Alfred Road were necessary in the seventies.

Modernisation of bus washing and steam cleaning procedures brought new machinery to most depots and, by the early eighties, a second generation of fully-automatic bus washers was being installed.

Long, rear-engined buses caused many problems. Pits built for 26ft.-long front-engined vehicles now had to serve

(Above) All depots were equipped with automatic bus washers which were designed to clean the whole exterior but the rear profiles of some buses defied the ingenuity of the designers and some manual work was still necessary. This picture was taken at Gillmoss; the water was filtered and recycled.

Heat retention and general garage efficiency were prime considerations during the seventies and eighties. Edge Lane depot, built alongside the works, had been a long narrow tram depot and had to have one-way traffic. The rubber doors were very effective though they had a limited life. Buses were always refuelled immediately on entry.

Edge Lane works was equipped with a double steam cleaning bay near the rear entrance of the former tram depot. The weight of accumulated mud could affect the performance of a bus as well as encouraging corrosion and the chassis had to be steam cleaned before being presented for certification. This vehicle, A361, was one of 75 AEC Regent IIIs delivered in 1948-49 which retained the 7.7-litre engine and crash gearbox as used on earlier Liverpool Regent orders. It was renumbered A561 in January 1957 and withdrawn in 1962.

the needs of 36ft.-long rear-engined buses. In almost every case, the layout of premises precluded lengthening the pits and vehicles had to be driven in, reversed then backed in.

The transformation of Walton depot which was closed on 15th October 1962, the vehicles being transferred to Gillmoss. The building was then extensively reconstructed as a bus garage but retaining much of the outer walls and roof. The picture on the right shows part of the old 1901 tram shed prior to completion of the filling in of the tramway pits, the great depth of which was a reminder of the underground stables of the

The Head Office building at 24 Hatton Garden was also improved. The offices vacated by the Electricity Board, successor to the once closely related Corporation Electric Supply Department, provided space for the staff needed to handle the work previously performed by the various Town Clerks' and Treasurers' departments. The building was rewired and the old lifts replaced by modern equipment. A stand-by generator ensured the uninterrupted availability of power for the Traffic Control room, stairways and corridors.

Walton

Walton was the oldest depot in the city, the original structure having been built by the Liverpool Tramway Company in 1870. It had been altered and added to many times over the years and, because of the general layout and the many stanchions, proved very difficult to use as a motor bus garage

By 1959, Walton operated a higher mileage than any other garage and so many buses were based there that some had to be parked in side streets to the annoyance of residents and other road users.

Plans were drawn up for the demolition of the 1870 horse tram building, leaving only the outer walls, roof and roof supports of the 1901 electric tram shed intact. New workshops and a three-storey administrative block were proposed.

On 15th October 1962 all Walton's buses were transferred to the new Gillmoss garage and reconstruction work commenced soon after. An electricity sub-station,

previous century. Overleaf is the office block which replaced the Liverpool United Tramway and Omnibus Co building on the corner of Carisbrooke Road and Harlech Street, under construction in August 1963, whilst the picture below (left) shows the modern entrance doors for buses in the 1901 Harlech Street facade after the alterations were completed in January 1965. The depot was closed in 1989.

which had been built in to the structure years before, was relocated in the basement which had originally housed the horse tram stables. The rest of this huge void was filled in. On the Carisbrooke Road side, the building line was brought forward by 10ft, absorbing the former external tramway sidings, thus making it possible to erect the administrative block on the corner of Carisbrooke Road and Harlech Street with the maintenance block, equipped with nine inspection pits and two greasing pits adjoining it. Each pit was was fitted with shutter gates and the roof was insulated to retain heat.

The parking area was completely resurfaced, 120 buses being accommodated in nine rows, head to tail, facing north. Entering by the west door in Harlech Street, they proceeded through to a refuelling island where they passed through the familiar sequence of vacuum cleaning, radiator top-up, fuel and engine oil. Vacuum cleaning points were provided at upper and lower deck levels, enabling a shorter hose to be passed through an open upper deck window. The vacuum equipment stored refuse in bulk bins to await disposal so that no incinerator was needed. Dawson and Essex washing machines were installed. The new canteen and traffic offices were of the most modern design with a night safe system which automatically stored the money in a basement strongroom, avoiding the need for cashiers to work late at night. The three gables facing Harlech Street were stripped of all ornament and folding doors replaced the open, round-top arches but the basic shape of the facade remained.

The garage was reopened on 25th January 1965 on which date Dingle depot closed. Walton was allocated 112 buses to work routes 1, 2, 3, 20, 25 and 30. Routes 1, 3, 20 and 25 had been worked by Dingle while 2 and 30 had run out of Gillmoss. At the same time route 26 was transferred from Dingle to Edge Lane and the odd vehicles for 80E and 94 went to Prince Alfred Road.

Surprisingly, the PTE found it necessary to modernise and improve office accommodation in 1971 and the concrete floor soon began to break up, being renewed in 1978-79.

Walton depot was closed by Merseybus on 30th June 1989 following reduced demand, full size buses being transferred to Gillmoss and minibuses to Edge Lane. After almost 120 years at Walton, continuity is now provided only by the nearby Tramway Hotel.

BLOCK PLAN OF
WALTON GARAGE

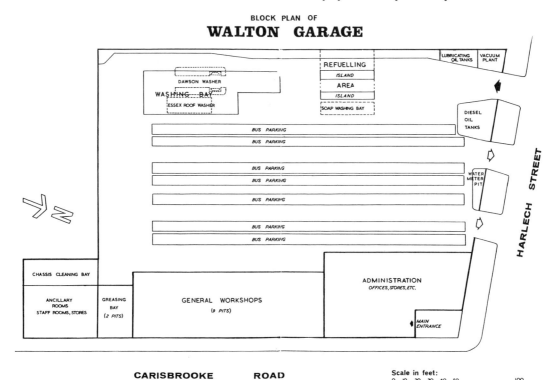

Gillmoss

Although first considered in 1948, Gillmoss depot, situated on the East Lancashire Road near the city boundary, did not open until 15th October 1962. On this day it took in the whole of the vehicle allocation from Walton, a courageous stroke which seems to have passed without too much difficulty.

Gillmoss was planned on the same lines as Speke and benefitted from the experience gained there but the seven acre site was double the size with 24 heated maintenance pits enclosed by separate folding doors. As at Speke, compressed air was laid on for small tools. In accordance with general policy, a new steam cleaning plant was installed in 1972 and the heating was improved in 1977. In 1984, a recycling plant for used oil was put in, waste oil from all the depots being processed. The output in the first few months supplied all the heating oil requirements for Edge Lane Works and later St. Helens and Birkenhead's needs were also met.

The 1985-88 Transport Plan included a scheme for roofing the site and it is of interest to note how the arguments put forward in the fifties in favour of open air parking were turned round to support the opposite view. However there were new factors to consider not the least of which was vandalism. Gillmoss was in a particularly vulnerable area and a number of rather vague and inconsistent statistics were invoked to prove the point. Over a two year period ending three years earlier, the PTE had lost 2,221 fire extinguishers of which 330 belonged to Gillmoss. In a more recent three month period 1,739 pieces of trim had been repaired at a cost of £8.33 per piece; 300 (17%) of these repairs were to Gillmoss vehicles.

Other factors were the greater expectations for comfort of both drivers and passengers and the resultant complaints about cold buses. Thirty years earlier, it was expected that buses would be cold first thing on a winter's morning and no Corporation bus was even equipped with a heater until 1958. The driver was eventually warmed by the engine and the passengers put up with cold conditions for the relatively short duration of the journey.

Further arguments included damage to vehicles in the parking area by intruders, despite the erection of new pallisade fences at all the open air depots in 1981 and installation of CCTV in 1983; lost mileage caused by failure to start and reduction in body and paint life through rapid weathering. Laudable as the scheme undoubtedly was, the estimated cost was £926,000 and the money was not available.

At deregulation, the Gillmoss-based fleet increased following the closure of Litherland depot and when Walton closed on 30th June 1989, it became the only Merseybus depot in the north of the city.

Gillmoss depot was the last completely new depot to be built by Liverpool Corporation, having been opened in October 1962. The tower blocks of Kirkby new town can be seen in the distance but the intervening area is now built up with the M57 motorway slicing through the wooded area.

Open air parking at new depots reduced capital expenditure but took its toll on cold winter mornings; later vandalism became a problem and the fence was strengthened and CCTV installed. This was Gillmoss on the opening day — 15th October 1962.

Carnegie Road, Stanley and Green Lane.

The trio of interdependent locations continued to function in the way planned in the fifties. Stanley and Green Lane were running depots and all maintenance was centralised at Carnegie Road. At the time of its opening in 1939, the latter had been hailed as a model of efficiency and modernity but 40 years later, progress had overtaken it in no uncertain manner. The need to ferry vehicles between the running depots and the workshop was expensive and the layout of the building was unsatisfactory. The 26ft.-long pits were arranged round three sides of the building, four having been added to the original seven in 1949. To do a full chassis inspection, they needed to be lengthened to 44ft. to avoid the need to shunt buses but to do so would have reduced the width of the circulating area to only 36ft. which was both impractical and dangerous.

The PTE did what they could. High mast lighting was erected at Carnegie Road in 1971 and Stanley in 1972; a new switch room with modern switchgear was installed at Carnegie in 1974 and modern fume extractors and roof ventilating equipment in 1975. New North Divisional offices were erected at Stanley in 1981-2.

By the early eighties the concrete parking area at Stanley had suffered water penetration over a period of years and the slabs were cracked and uneven. A scheme to lay a drainage system and relay the concrete was costed at £300,000. There was also a plan to roof the area on similar lines to Gillmoss at a cost of £900,000. Lengthening the pits on two sides of Carnegie Road would have cost £100,000.

Following the renewal of its heating boilers in 1981, Carnegie Road became the waste oil burning centre, a 12,000-gal. waste oil storage tank and five space heating units being installed. A 4,000-gal. road tanker was purchased for collecting waste oil from all the garages. However, in 1984, the PTE prepared a £3.6 million scheme to sell Carnegie Road and transfer maintenance to a rebuilt Stanley. Shortage of money prevented implementation and after deregulation the reverse happened, when Carnegie Road took over the entire engineering function for the North Division. Use of the old tram shed at Green Lane as a running shed was gradually reduced and ceased altogether by about 1964. Disused buses were stored in the yard for some time and on 12th February 1967, tram 869 was brought there for restoration by the Merseyside Tramway Preservation Society. The building had part of its roof renewed in 1977-78 and, after 869 left, a small shopping arcade was built inside the shed but there were several closures and reopenings. Weekend markets have been held in the depot with access from the open yard. The 1901 tram shed facade is virtually unchanged.

Garston & Speke

The old-established Garston depot had become a running shed with only basic servicing facilities though it had been extended by taking in some adjoining premises. In 1972 the compressed air system was renewed to enable modern impact tools to be used. It received a new automatic wrap-round bus washing machine in 1974, capable of washing sides, front and rear but this seems to have been

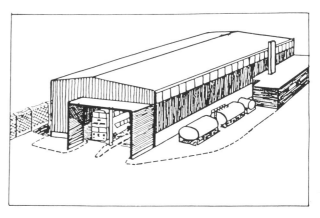

A drawing of the Stanley servicing bay planned in 1984 to replace the facilities at Carnegie Road. The scheme was dropped through lack of funds.

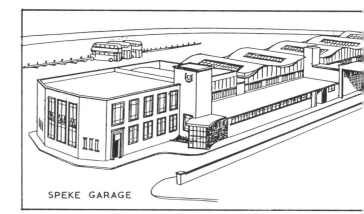

SPEKE GARAGE

This inside view of Speke workshop demonstrates an alternative method of achieving the essential pillarless interior, a concrete barrel-vaulted structure. There are nine 1957 AEC Regent V buses and one Leyland Royal Tiger parked over the inspection pits.

unsatisfactory as a new Britannia washing machine was installed in 1978 when the fuel bays were also renewed.

Speke, too, acquired an automatic bus washer in 1974 and a steam cleaning plant with roof protection for the operatives a year later. The maintenance bays, which also catered for the Garston fleet, were modernised and lengthened in 1975-76. In 1981 the centre islands were lowered to reduce skirt damage. As with the other open air parking depots, security fencing was strengthened in 1981 and there was an abortive scheme to roof it over in the mid-eighties.

Following the contraction of the fleet, Garston was closed on 30th June 1989, the vehicles being transferred to Speke except for the minibuses which went to Edge Lane.

Prince Alfred Road and Smithdown Road

A large new office block was built fronting on to Church Road in 1967. The PTE made many improvements to the depot itself in 1971, the offices and stores being modernised and the heating system in the covered garage renewed. The workshops were enclosed and the gates

motorised. High mast lighting was installed in 1972 to improve security for buses parked outside and part of the roof was replaced in 1977-78. In 1980-1, all maintenance work was transferred to a new workshop built in the 1902 Smithdown Road shed this being made possible by a new ramp which descended through the rear wall of the former tram shed. A new oil-fired warm air heating system was installed. New purpose-built South Divisional offices were built in 1981-2. The garage was closed on 25th October 1986 and the allocation transferred to Edge Lane.

Litherland

Litherland depot, in common with the others, had its heating upgraded, the boilers being replaced in 1979. More work was done in 1980-81, shutter doors and fume extractors being fitted; the canteen was also refurbished.

On 25th October 1986 the depot ceased to be operational, the vehicles being reallocated to Walton and Gillmoss. It was used as a vehicle store for a time and then offered for sale.

Edge Lane Depot and Works

It is probably true to say that Edge Lane Works was uneconomic at least from the early fifties. Increases in craft wages, shortages of skills, the growth of trade union militancy and intensification of restrictive practices conspired to increase the cost of all aspects of vehicle maintenance. Furthermore, the works, designed in the mid-twenties as a tramway works, was far from ideal in modern circumstances. The conversion to a bus overhaul and repair works was tolerably well done, a major job being the replacement of the tramway traverser by a concrete runway. But, by the sixties, costing of individual activities was more advanced and the financial liabilities of the works were better revealed. There was a tendency for more and more work to be done at the depots and Dingle became a centre for engine overhauls and unit exchanges until its closure in January 1965. The Department clung to

old-fashioned practices and bus bodies were still being removed from chassis for overhaul in 1966, long after other operators had abandoned the practice as unnecessary.

Conversion from a tramway to a bus works required considerable alterations to be made at Edge Lane. This concrete runway replaced the tramway traverser which enabled trams to be moved laterally and run on to the many tracks. It was illustrated on page 157 of Volume Three. This view shows many aspects of the work undertaken. The bonnet of one of the ex-London Bedford canteen prime movers is visible (lower left) while the rear of another canteen can be seen near the door. Three newly-delivered Atlantean chassis await their journey to the bodybuilders whilst a mechanic moves AEC Regent III A804 with the aid of a battery operated trolley. Outside the door is the stores van WR6, built in the works on the chassis of AEC Regent I A10 (BKA 610) of 1935, a vehicle which gave 17 years service as a bus and 12 as a van. The picture was taken on 26th April 1962.

At the time of the formation of the PTE, there were about 450 men and women employed at the works, about half the original number, and this decreased by about 100 in the first three years. No doubt the functions of the Birkenhead and Wallasey works could easily have been absorbed at Edge Lane and, whilst there was a degree of centralisation, there were often good reasons for leaving the work where it was. Indeed, some ex-Liverpool Atlanteans were overhauled at Birkenhead in 1976.

When MoT testing of private cars commenced, many municipal transport undertakings set aside a section of their works, seeing this as a useful source of additional revenue. Edge Lane was no exception but there was plenty of competition. A typical year's throughput was 2100 tests which in 1973 brought in only £3,600.

By 1971 the PTE had standardised maintenance procedures throughout the system with the emphasis on more frequent inspections and services. By rectifying faults which were still minor, the need for heavy formalised overhauls in the course of which much unnecessary work was done, was considerably reduced. The bodyshop assumed greater importance as, with the increase in road traffic, higher speeds and changing attitudes, the number of accidents increased dramatically. Vandalism, too, added to its toll and the works were kept busy repairing and replacing seats, removing graffiti and, as things got worse, repairing serious fire damage. In one year 25 buses were damaged by arsonists. It is a sobering thought that, in one year, passengers caused more damage than was caused by enemy action in six years of war.

Plastic laminates adopted in the late seventies brought new techniques and a modern fibreglass shop was commissioned in 1978 and completed in September 1981. One section which was always busy was the paint shop which had to cope with the livery changes of the early seventies and the repaints necessitated by inter-divisional transfers in the days before the standard livery. In 1981, a new paint spray booth was equipped with a 12-tonne capacity Zeeta double scissor hydraulic lift with a maximum drop of 16ft. This enabled a double deck bus to be painted without resort to working from scaffolding. The old paint booth was modified for chassis spraying.

One of the most successful sections in the works was the central stores which, with the aid of a very efficient computer system, coped well with the increased inventory resulting from the entry of new makes and types of vehicle into the fleet.

The purchase of hundreds of new vehicles under the stimulus of the bus grant scheme reduced bus maintenance requirements and it was accepted that the nearest thing to a major overhaul would be the preparation for renewal of the initial seven year Certificate of Fitness. In 1979, a feasibility study of VMS (Vehicle Maintenance System), a management information system developed by Chicago Transit Authority, commenced. All aspects of vehicle performance were monitored and the system was formally adopted in 1981. The PTE was well to the fore in developing computerised vehicle maintenance monitoring and, after further refinement, its system was later adopted as a model by the Department of Transport.

From 1st January 1982, a new national vehicle testing system was introduced. An annual inspection was done, initially at the MoT Testing Station at Simonswood, but eventually a Test Centre, manned by MoT personnel, was located at Edge Lane.

As deregulation approached, central works were virtually a thing of the past throughout the industry. The place for maintenance work was in the depot where the staff knew the idiosyncrasies of the fleet. In an address to the Bus and Coach Council's conference in 1989, one of the new generation of post-deregulation entrepreneurs described central works as 'a bastion of union militancy and a drain on resources'.

Whilst Merseyside's local politicians could not be expected to express such a view, in the run up to deregulation in 1986 it was recognised that no company could act commercially and, at the same time, support Edge Lane Works in its traditional role, curtailed as that may have been compared with an earlier era. The offices in which the modern trams of the thirties had taken shape and which had been added to in 1978-79, became the headquarters of the new operating company. The eastern section of the works was vacated and quantities of tram track excavated to the horror of local tramway preservationists who discovered too late what was afoot. The floor was relaid and a new running shed created which took in the allocation from Prince Alfred Road on the Appointed Day. This was run as part of the existing depot and, from July 1989, following closure of other garages, all the company's minibuses were based there. The specialist unit overhaul and fibreglass workshops and the paint shop remained but the general workshops served only the needs of the South Division.

COMPANY DEPOTS

Liverpool, Skelhorne Street (Ribble)

The combined bus and coach station and depot occupied a sloping site bounded by Skelhorne Street, Hilbre Street, Copperas Hill and Bolton Street and was brought into use for traffic purposes between April and June 1960. The upper level served as an express coach station and the lower one provided the usual Ribble style nose-on loading for stage carriage services. Although allowance had been made for 30ft.-long vehicles, the limitations of the site made for a cramped station and great care was needed, particularly when reversing from the platform on the lower level. When 36ft.-long vehicles came along the situation was made worse. Some cynics said that the station was more dangerous than the kerbside loading in Skelhorne Street which had been tolerated for 30 years without serious mishap. The building also housed the area offices of Ribble which had hitherto been at Aintree.

For the first few months, the 35 buses and coaches allocated to Liverpool depot continued to occupy the cramped depot at Collingwood Street, taken over in 1927 with Ribble's first acquisition on Merseyside but, at the end of 1960, a small maintenance area was opened on the

Aintree depot was opened by Ribble Motor Services Ltd in 1951 and until 1960 it housed the area as well as the depot offices. Situated on the main A59 road less than a mile outside the Liverpool city boundary, it was close to Aintree racecourse and provided coach parking for those vehicles without a place on the course for the Grand National and other race meetings. It is shown after transfer to North Western. After a period of closure it was re-occupied early in 1991.

Hilbre Street servicing area was originally part of Ribble's Liverpool depot but was completely separate from the bus and coach station lower down the hill which was used as a depot at night. North Western Leyland Olympian 612 with Eastern Coach Works body (formerly Ribble 2151) is seen outside the closed maintenance bay.

east side of Hilbre Street, across the road from the coach station. This provided for refuelling, inspection and simple rectification of faults, all major maintenance work being done at Bootle depot. The vehicles were parked overnight in the station and occasionally in the streets during the day.

In March 1980, Hilbre Street servicing area was handed over to National Travel (North West) and the Ribble stage carriage vehicles, now reduced to 12, were transferred to Bootle depot. However, after deregulation it was used by North Western who vacated the whole site on 11th September 1989.

Bootle, 503 Hawthorne Road (Ribble/North Western)

In October 1979, Ribble closed its depot in Hawthorne Road, opposite Staley Street which it had occupied since 1934, and moved to new premises costing £750,000 about 300 yds further north.

The two-acre site was almost 50% larger and, in conformity with the fashion of the time, consisted mainly of open parking with offices and covered maintenance facilities. Poor ground conditions required 26ft.-deep piled foundations.

The workshop occupied about one third of the site; it was of the 'swimming bath' type with ten pits provided with compressed air, low voltage power points and exhaust extraction pipes. All pits had waste oil disposal equipment. The stores and locker rooms, messroom and engineering offices were located above the workshop.

The drive-through fuelling and cleaning bay was in a separate building with 25,000-gallon fuel tanks above ground, shielded by a wall bearing the NBC logo. The garage was originally planned to maintain the 23 vehicles based at Liverpool and 26 at Southport in addition to its own allocation. It was taken over by North Western prior to deregulation and became the registered office of that company.

Love Lane (Lockfields)—Crosville and North Western

Love Lane depot had been built by Tate and Lyle Ltd. in the post-war era to house and maintain their immaculate fleet of lorries and tankers. When Tate and Lyle left Liverpool, the properties were bought by the Merseyside Development Corporation who used the former refinery site for housing. The transport depot was separate from the other buildings being bounded on the west side by the electric railway to Southport, Ormskirk etc., on the east by the Leeds and Liverpool Canal and on the north by the staircase of locks which connected the canal with the Stanley Dock.

The depot was leased by the Development Corporation to the National Bus Company and Crosville buses, having run out of Edge Lane on Saturday 3rd August 1985, ran into Love Lane that night. Edge Lane depot was sold, the buildings demolished and a DIY supermarket erected on the site.

Love Lane was well equipped with offices, canteen and workshops with adequate pits but vehicles were parked outside in the yard. The Crosville booking-on point and canteen at Mann Island was downgraded to an enquiry office and drivers' rest room.

The initial allocation was about 65 vehicles of which 50 were Bristol VRs, with a staff of about 150 drivers. Immediately prior to deregulation, Crosville secured contracts for several tendered services and over 100 more drivers and many additional vehicles were needed. On 5th January 1987 the drivers went on strike, refusing to drive some hired VRs which were not equipped with power steering. Following a measure of agreement, buses ran from the depot again on 13th and 14th January but the strike was resumed on the following day. The strikers were dismissed on 24th and staged a sit-in for several days but the depot was never again used operationally by Crosville.

After lying idle for two years, during February 1989 it was taken over by North Western Road Car Co Ltd who closed Aintree depot and transferred their registered office from 503 Hawthorne Road, Bootle. However, the Development Corporation intend to build on the site and the company must vacate the premises. The buses were moved to Aintree early in 1991.

Bentley Road, Princes Park (Lancashire United Transport)

These premises, originally known as Sefton Mews, were used as stables from the 1880s. The original owner was John Wilson, jobmaster, who sold out to White's Carriage Co about the turn of the century (see Volume Two, page 237). The buildings passed to the Liverpool Carriage Co who sold them, on 27th August 1919, to Lancashire United Tramways Ltd who were developing an excursion and private hire business with charabancs based in Liverpool.

The official capacity of the garage was 24 vehicles but half of it was sublet to G. A. A. Roberts for use by Avery and Roberts, motor dealers, who also had a showroom in Renshaw Street. Roberts also acted as manager of the LUT coach business and Avery and Roberts had other bus interests in North Wales. They went into liquidation in 1931 and LUT, by then the Lancashire United Transport and Power Co. Ltd, assumed direct control.

Buses for the Liverpool-Manchester express service were based there from 1929 and after the company joined the Tyne-Tees-Mersey limited stop pool in 1932, the garage housed not only LUT vehicles but those of any of the other pool partners which finished their journeys in Liverpool. The building was requisitioned by the military on 16th October 1940 and not returned to LUT until June 1948.

It was intended to close the garage from 25th October 1965 but, because of difficulties with a sub-tenant, it remained in use until 2nd October 1966. Thereafter one double deck bus and three coaches lodged at Liverpool Corporation's Edge Lane depot until 26th April 1974.

The interior of Love Lane depot workshop with Atlanteans and a National undergoing maintenance. Note the fume extractors and the absence of any obstructing pillars. This was successively a Crosville and a North Western depot.

55 MANAGERS AND MEN

Staff shortages had plagued the road passenger transport industry since the war years and, although Liverpool had often experienced a higher rate of unemployment than the national average, the coming of new industries and the increased mobility of labour had resulted in many experienced transport workers forsaking the buses for jobs with more pay and regular working hours. By 1960 the schedules required 4,250 drivers and conductors but the actual strength was 3,580, a deficiency of 16%. The shortages were not evenly distributed; for example Speke depot was 25% short of conductors and 10% short of drivers.

The dearth of platform staff had many diverse effects. Much work was covered by overtime but men became tired and selective in their choice of shifts. Some buses did not run at all but in other cases, there were no relief crews available and passengers would be turned off a bus during a journey because there was no driver to carry on. For example, at Broad Lane, Norris Green, where there was a cash office and canteen manned throughout the day by an inspector, 55 crew reliefs were scheduled on weekdays. When no men were available, the bus was parked to await

collection by engineering staff but on many occasions, to avoid congestion, the inspectors had to leave their duties to drive buses back to depot. There were cases of children and youths driving the buses around and, in one case, abandoning the vehicle broadside across the road.

Discipline suffered and the level of service to the public deteriorated as men were engaged who did not really measure up to the Department's standards. Men became more militant and openly defied their supervisors.

Staff shortages spread to the engineering department, wastage rates in 1965-66 being 32.6% for platform staff and 14.6% for maintenance workers. There were constant labour disputes with the craft unions, particularly at Edge Lane Works, where working methods were, in some instances, archaic. By 1966, Liverpool was the only municipality in the country where the general practice was

Both the Corporation and the PTE trained a steady flow of craft apprentices; this group, photographed at Edge Lane about 1957, probably gave the photographer a hard time. A local agreement with the unions allowed for about one apprentice for each ten craftsmen employed.

Seven mobile canteens passed from Liverpool Corporation to the PTE in 1969. AEC Regal A177, new in 1939 had already been scrapped in 1963, having been a canteen for ten years but its sister A178 survived to pass to the PTE as a static canteen being scrapped in April 1970.

to overhaul front-engined buses with the body removed and the AEU was demanding extra pay for overhauling buses with the body in situ. Demarcation disputes were common and buses sometimes stood for long periods in a dismantled state, awaiting the resolution of some argument as to what grade of worker should replace panels or insert rivets. The AEU showed contempt for the General Manager and, in 1966, wrote to the Town Clerk saying that they considered that no useful purpose would be served by negotiating with him further as he could make no decisions without reference to the Committee. They proposed to take up all matters direct with the Committee. This, of course, was true and, at times, the Committee would be more on the side of the workers, irrespective of the merits of the case. In September 1966, a closed shop policy was adopted for all full-time non-craft manual workers.

By 1965 the labour shortage on the buses of all operators had reached alarming proportions. Lengthy discussions were held with the unions to allow direct entry of drivers to the Corporation service, a practice which had always been adopted by the companies. The traditional municipal practice of all new entrants starting as conductors was a severe handicap in the existing conditions as many qualified public service vehicle drivers were deterred from joining. After many meetings and refusals, the point was finally conceded by the unions and, whilst the staff position was not markedly improved, there was a slowing down in the rate of deterioration. The men were disillusioned by what they saw as the remote and ponderous National negotiating machinery which could not be adjusted to meet local needs. To try to attract labour to the buses, the Corporation opted out and established its own rates of pay, a policy which was also followed by other cities including Manchester, Birmingham and Coventry. In return the unions agreed to co-operate in the introduction of one-man operation.

The 1968 Strike

A further settlement with the unions awarded an increase of 23/- per week which was approved by the City Council

on 20th December 1967. A national award of £1 was referred to the Prices and Incomes Board along with similar local settlements at Belfast and Glasgow; Liverpool deferred payment of the 23/- pending the outcome of these proceedings, as if they had not, the Government would undoubtedly have stepped in and frozen the award. There was considerable resentment amongst employees and trouble started suddenly during the morning of 11th March 1968 when Litherland depot staff stopped work. The strike spread from depot to depot and within six or seven hours every Corporation bus was off the road, the first complete transport stoppage in the city since the General Strike of 1926; before the day was out the initial protest about delay in paying the award had developed into a demand for a basic £17 for a five day week.

Despite an endless series of meetings and a warning from the General Manager that similar strikes elsewhere (including Birkenhead and Wallasey just across the river a few weeks earlier) had resulted in a permanent revenue loss of up to 15%, the strike dragged on for eleven weeks. Neither the Transport and General Workers nor the General and Municipal Workers Unions recognised the strike as official, though from early April both paid 'hardship money' of £4 per week, a similar amount to strike pay. Many of the men were quite unable to stand the financial hardship which the strike caused and left the Corporation's service for other employment, thus aggravating the already serious staff shortage. A new pay award was negotiated but the Prices and Incomes Board in their report, issued on 23rd May, rejected it on the grounds of manpower, productivity and comparability factors but suggested that under the Board's suggested tier system, Liverpool's crews' pay would probably rise by about the same amount. This was so much bureaucratic hot air and the award was paid; services were resumed on 27th May but the staff was so depleted that full services could not be restored and some of the suspended services were never resumed.

Inspectors

The road staff shortage during the sixties had repercussions on the inspection staff as the amount of overtime available made it possible for a driver to earn more than an inspector's salary. After the creation of the North and South divisions in 1962, the duties of the ticket inspectors and route supervision inspectors were merged to make the job more variable and satisfying. There was an establishment of 100 road inspectors and 42 timekeepers but, by 1966, the inspectorate was 36 below this level. If it were to be brought up to strength (assuming that sufficient suitable applicants were forthcoming), the already depleted driving staff would be reduced further.

Within each division there were groupings covering, in the North division, Prescot Road, Huyton, West Derby, Breck Road, Stanley Road and the Dock services and, in the South, Edge Lane, Wavertree, Smithdown Road, Park Road and the city centre. Inspectors worked early, middle and late shifts and, by mutual agreement, operated on one group for a week in the South division or for a month in the North.

Peak hour supervisory duties at factories and important traffic points resulted in very little ticket checking being done at those times when it was most needed. In December 1966 the trade unions agreed to the recruitment of 40 conductresses with a view to alleviating the road staff shortage and it was resolved to try to bring the inspectorate up to strength.

As operational conditions changed so did the role of the inspectors; their work became more demanding as indiscipline and lawlessness increased. The widespread adoption of one-man operation led to an increase in overriding. These trends were soon identified and at an OMO Liaison Committee in August 1968, inspectors were told to check one-man buses from the back as the overriders tended to sit at the rear, the centre exit door providing a means of escape.

As the seventies advanced, road inspectors were given radio-equipped patrol cars enabling them to move quickly from route to route and mount surprise checks. In 1977, the PTE sought Parliamentary powers to impose on-the-spot penalties for overriding which was estimated to cost several million pounds annually but the Bill, which was mainly concerned with ferries, was talked out. The powers were subsequently obtained and from 22nd October 1979 excess fares were fixed at 150% of the normal fare. However, from 23rd March 1980 they were were fixed on a sliding scale from 150% on a 10p fare to 106% on the maximum 82p fare. More ticket inspectors were appointed.

However, detecting offenders and demanding excess fares was one thing and securing payment was another. Attacks on drivers and inspectors were regular occurrences and part of the mobility strategy was to enable inspectors to work in pairs. In more recent times, 'enforcement teams' have become even stronger in numbers.

(Right) These notices as displayed in buses, make it seem that conductors were valued more highly than inspectors, at least by the magistrates. Assaults on staff became more frequent and more vicious as time went on and were a serious social problem.

Improving inspectors' mobility brought greater efficiency in dealing with problems on the road. Faced with an Atlantean breakdown, Inspector Postlethwaite reports the details to Control by radio while the driver looks disconsolately inside the rear engine compartment.

PROSECUTION

AT THE CITY MAGISTRATES' COURT RECENTLY,

A PASSENGER WAS

FINED £1

FOR ASSAULTING AN INSPECTOR.

PROSECUTION

AT THE BOOTLE MAGISTRATES' COURT RECENTLY,

A PASSENGER WAS

FINED £10

FOR ASSAULTING A BUS CONDUCTOR

The use of radio communication gradually changed from a novel refinement to an essential element in operational control and in 1980-81 the first major phase of the replacement of equipment was put in hand. Following comparison tests, new Motorola hardware had been ordered the previous year and separate channels were allocated to buses and supervisory inspectors. New transmitters were located on the Royal Liverpool Hospital building and at sites in Wirral, St. Helens and Southport. No fewer than 120 portable handsets were supplied for the use of inspectors and 100% coverage of the bus fleet was within sight. The control room was eventually relocated in the tower at Edge Lane Works.

Radio played an important part in combating the scourge of violence and vandalism as it enabled drivers and inspectors to summon aid. Many road staff suffered serious injury from attacks by passengers and from time to time drivers would refuse to work late journeys into the worst affected areas. There was constant liaison with the police and inspectors gave talks and demonstrations at schools which were said to be effective. The absence of a conductor encouraged bad behaviour and top deck fires, started by pyromaniacs who promptly left the bus to watch the results of their efforts from a safe distance, became an expensive problem. Fire resistant seats were tried but long term thinking has turned towards high capacity single deck buses where no one is totally out of sight.

Another by-product of one-man operation was poor timekeeping; drivers became oblivious of intermediate timing points and sometimes traffic conditions made it impossible for buses to 'wait for time'. In 1980 a number of mobile timekeepers were appointed, resulting in some improvement.

Senior Management

In contrast to the high turnover at the working level, senior management of the undertaking was very stable. The General Manager, W. M. Hall, had joined the Department as Deputy General Manager on 1st November 1946 and took over the senior job on the retirement of W. G. Marks on 12th July 1948. He was replaced as deputy by F. H. Clayton, a mechanical engineer by training, on 1st February 1949. The Traffic Superintendent, F. A. Moffatt was Liverpool-born and had served with the Department since 1933, apart from the years 1952-55 when he moved to Bradford as Assistant Traffic Superintendent, to broaden his experience.

W. M. Hall died in office on 14th July 1965. The Committee seemed to be in no hurry to choose a successor and it was February 1966 before they appointed Albert Burrows, the General Manager of Chesterfield Corporation Transport, who took up office in April. It was unusual for the manager of a relatively small undertaking to move directly into a plum job like Liverpool.

Burrows was born in Warrington on 3rd November 1919; there was transport in his blood as his father was a tram driver and after leaving grammar school, he joined Warrington Corporation Transport Dept. as a junior clerk.

He enlisted in the Territorial Army and was mobilised in August 1939, serving in both the Lancashire Fusiliers and the Royal Engineers. He completed his service with the Control Commission for Germany and, on demobilisation in 1946, returned to his job at Warrington.

In 1949 he moved to Nottingham as Commercial Assistant and, after further experience as Accountant at Portsmouth from 1953, obtained his first command as General Manager and Engineer, Lancaster City Transport in 1956. In 1958 he was awarded the Institute of Transport Commercial Users Road Transport Research Fellowship, allowing 14 weeks of study travel in Western Europe. He moved to Barrow-in-Furness as General Manager in 1961 but did not stay long, transferring to Chesterfield the following year.

When the first four PTEs were set up in 1969, Burrows was the only General Manager of a constituent undertaking to secure the Director General's job in the same Area which gave Merseyside great advantages in continuity and this was reflected in the absence of any radical change of policy in the early years.

The Passenger Transport Executive

The management structure of the PTE was quite different from that of a municipal transport undertaking. The Executive had a legal existence; the Act said there must be at least three directors and not more than eight. Its function was to interpret the policy of the Authority and put it into effect, having regard to the provisions of the 1968 Act. The Authority, a political body by its very nature, was not a management committee like the Transport Committees

Albert Burrows, General Manager, Liverpool City Transport 1966-69 and Director General, Merseyside PTE, 1969-72.

of the old municipalities, as much of the decision making was in the hands of the Executive. This was resented by some politicians who made the lives of the executive members very uncomfortable by constantly meddling and complaining. Burrows was often harrassed by councillors by telephone at his home late at night.

One of the other directors was appointed from within the combined undertaking; F. S. Brimelow, who became Director of Operations was General Manager of Birkenhead Municipal Transport. Born in 1915, he, too, had begun his career with Warrington Corporation in 1931, subsequently rising to Chief Assistant. In 1950 he moved to Middlesbrough Corporation as Deputy General Manager and, seven years later returned to the north west as General Manager of the Stalybridge, Hyde, Mossley and Dukinfield Joint Transport Board, later also becoming Clerk to the Board. In 1962 he moved to the neighbouring Stockport undertaking as General Manager before taking up his appointment at Birkenhead in 1964. During the transitional period, before the PTE was operational, he crossed the river to 24 Hatton Garden, his duties at Birkenhead being assumed temporarily by F. A. Moffatt, the Liverpool Traffic Superintendent.

The other directors were newcomers; P. I. Welding, Planning and Development from London Transport and J. Brooksbank, Borough Treasurer of Grimsby, Finance and Administration. Brooksbank resigned in 1974 and his successor was Leslie W. Latter whose previous experience had been entirely in the field of municipal finance in London and Kent.

The undertaking was divided into three Divisions—North, South and Wirral—each with a Divisional Manager. Moffatt took over South and Clayton went to Wirral until he retired in 1973. However, in August 1970 Moffatt was appointed Director of Operations for West Midlands PTE and was succeeded by K. R. G. Hannis, formerly Assistant Traffic Manager (East) of Crosville. North Division was managed by E. Haughton until 1975 when he was appointed Chief Engineer and succeeded by C. Millward.

On 23rd December 1972, Burrows died suddenly at the early age of 53.

A New Regime

The new Director General was F. A. (Arthur) Moffatt who returned from Birmingham to his native Liverpool. Having spent the greater part of his career on Merseyside, his knowledge of local conditions and transport needs was unsurpassed. No radical changes of policy followed his appointment which took effect from 4th June 1973.

As stated in chapter 48, the vacancies created by the resignation of Peter Welding in 1974 and the retirement of Frank Brimelow on 30th June 1976 were not immediately filled, causing a serious situation as the Executive had less than the statutory three members.

However, following Moffatt's retirement on 28th February 1977, Leslie Latter, Director of Finance was promoted to Director General and W. Gwyn Thomas,

L. W. Latter, Director of Finance, 1974-77 and Director General, Merseyside PTE 1977-86.

Uniforms were brought up to date from time to time. The style illustrated above was new in 1973. The bus is Bristol VR 2080, and the Bus Economy Ticket (BET) sign can be clearly seen.

Divisional Manager, Wirral since 1974 was appointed Director of Service Operations. The position of Director of Service Planning and Co-ordination was offered to one of the applicants for the Director General's job, Samir Rihani, Technical Director of the County Council's Joint Transportation Unit (JTU). A new Director of Finance (B. Foulds) was also appointed.

The new Labour-controlled County Council's Cheap Fares policy, introduced in October 1981, and extended two years later, placed further strain on relations between the Authority and the Executive. The former was quite deliberately defying a government directive that fares must not be reduced at ratepayers' expense. This was but one aspect of a wider confrontation policy between certain left wing local councils and the right wing government. As the statutory duties of the Authority and the Executive were intertwined, the Executive was forced into the invidious position of implementing purely politically motivated policies with which it could not agree on economic grounds. There was further anxiety in that the well-publicised defiant acts of the Militant Left-controlled Liverpool City Council, which came to power in 1983, threatened to bankrupt the city and thereby cut off a large part of the income from precept.

The Council ruled that the PTE's financial function should be exercised by the Director General in consultation with the County Treasurer and the once more vacant post of Director of Finance should be abolished. This was the first step in a process of blurring the separate existence of the PTA and PTE, as enacted in 1968, as executive functions were to be carried out by the County Treasurer who was also a member of the Authority.

Labour Relations

In tramway days, platform staff belonged to the Municipal and General Workers' Union and, as bus development progressed, all bus staff joined the Transport and General Workers' Union. With the conversion from tram to bus, staff retained their union affiliation so there was a mix of the two unions at most garages with obvious complications in labour relations. Management tried to encourage the unions to rationalise but membership was fairly evenly divided and, although senior union officials recognised the logic of this, no real progress was achieved at garage level. Only when a completely new garage, such as Speke, was built did one union at a garage become established.

There was similarly a wide variation of working arrangements. At some garages, rosters were sectionalised into routes whilst at others there was a common rota where crews worked all services run from that garage. The tempestuous labour relations of the first decade of the PTE must be viewed against the depressed economic circumstances on Merseyside which arose from the decline of the port and the modernisation of industry. The MALTS Survey had assumed population growth but, between 1966 and 1976, 100,000 people left Merseyside for areas with better prospects. Since 1961, the number of people travelling daily to work in Liverpool had fallen by 56,000 and Merseyside had lost 34% of its city centre jobs, more than any other major UK city.

At the time the PTE was created, the bus undertakings had not fully recovered from the strikes of 1968, especially Liverpool where the strike had lasted longer and a large part of the work force had been lost. A serious shortage of drivers which persisted throughout 1970 was aggravated by implementation of revised drivers' hours regulations in March 1970 and demands for a 40-hour five day week by the platform staff. Following a relaxation of the regulations in May 1971, conditions improved and natural wastage took care of staff reductions. During 1972-73 the staff position became more settled and there were no serious problems.

The Transport Act 1968 placed an obligation on the PTE to establish adequate negotiating procedures and the already elaborate machinery set up by the municipalities was integrated as far as possible and developed to the extent necessary to comply with the Act. Five joint committees were created in addition to three already working. As time went on, these committees proliferated and, by 1978, there were 18 of them, involving nine trade unions. The Industrial Relations Act, 1971 increased the PTE's obligations in the field of labour relations.

In the case of a merger such as the PTE, the unions naturally wanted to adopt the most advantageous conditions amongst the constituent undertakings, a potentially expensive procedure. Common wage rates were agreed in 1970 and common conditions of service in 1971. In 1971-72 there was a changeover from a six- to a five-day working week for operating staff, the last depot to change being Speke on 14th February 1972. It was found that all kinds of unofficial working practices had been adopted at different depots and agreed by the Depot Inspectors. These included minimum overtime payments of three or four hours for short periods of work.

The high turnover in platform staff, particularly conductors, averted any redundancy problems in the early stages of the conversion to one-man operation. All suitable conductors were given the opportunity to train as drivers but there were always the older men who could not adapt. In 1973, agreement was reached with the unions for such men to transfer to other grades and they were paid a lump sum, depending on length of service, provided they agreed to accept the rate of pay applicable to the new grade The Authority agreed to adopt a policy of no redundancy and a hard core of conductors who were untrainable as drivers and could not or would not accept regrading, remained. In 1981 there were still 88 conductors on the payroll; they were employed as attendants on school buses on Mondays to Fridays but as the schools were open for only 40 weeks a year, there were occasions when there was nothing for them to do. A slowly dwindling band, they were a drain on the PTE's resources until deregulation. The additional pay and added variety of driver-only operation certainly reduced the turnover rate for platform staff. From a high of 28.4% in 1970 it more than halved to 13.93% in 1971 and 9.95% in 1972. After a slight rise in the following two years, it fell to 8.89% in 1975-76.

During the late sixties and seventies, there was constant interference by the government in free bargaining, with the object of curbing inflation, and disputes occasionally flared up because of the employer's inability to implement what both parties were prepared to agree to. In general, the PTE's strike record was better than many others. In 1974-75, man-days lost amounted to less than 0.5% of man-days worked; in 1975-76, it was even lower at 0.366% and only in 1977-78, when there were six disputes, including a month long craft workers' strike, did it reach a high figure. Man-days lost totalled 41,515 or 2.99% of working days.

In July 1976 drivers in both Liverpool divisions embarked on a non-co-operation campaign, reporting every minor defect and adhering strictly to every regulation, in protest against further cuts in services. Half the scheduled buses were very soon off the road. A PTE spokesman summarised the situation in the following words:-

'An extremely difficult industrial relations situation lies ahead. There is a major confrontation with the operating staffs' trade unions and unyielding political support for the Executive is essential for the financial objective to be achieved'.

By 1979-80, the Executive believed that there were signs that the loss of passengers was being contained which was all the more surprising in view of the disruptions caused by industrial action in that year, resulting in 9,314 lost man-days. A further craftmen's dispute from February to April was followed by a series of damaging one day strikes by drivers which continued until the end of June. Ribble, too, was disrupted on four major occasions at Aintree and Bootle depots and Crosville suffered a vehicle shortage which compounded industrial and other troubles. The company experienced difficult industrial relations in Liverpool, there being five periods of disruption during 1980-81, resulting in a large proportion of its mileage being lost. On the PTE buses, one day strikes over wages were resumed.

In 1982 the Authority and the Executive worked out a new organisation structure to facilitate dealing with industrial relations matters more expeditiously. The Controller of Industrial Relations was given decision-making powers within policy guidelines without the need for reference back to full meetings of the Executive. The personnel section merged with the Industrial Relations department later in the year. The new system eliminated some of the frustration caused by delays and relative peace prevailed from 1982. A further settling influence was the removal of the threat of job losses when the practical results of the County Council's public transport policies became apparent. Another important factor was decentralisation of control whereby, from 1st September 1981, Divisional General Managers were given much greater autonomy in the fields of operations, routine engineering, administration and personnel. Potential trouble could, therefore, be swiftly nipped in the bud.

What annoyed the travelling public most was the complete disregard of the staff for their convenience. Whereas in days gone by, grievances would be aired at midnight meetings, there were several cases of drivers taking their buses to depots during the day just for the purpose of holding a union meeting, leaving the unfortunate public stranded and unaware of the reason for the sudden absence of buses. These incidents contributed substantially to loss of passengers and have continued into the deregulated era.

Reducing Staff

The PTE started operations with a staff of 6,165 which, by the end of 1973, had fallen to 5,275, a reduction of 14.4%. The inclusion of St. Helens and Southport increased the staff to 6,007 but by March 1979 it had again fallen to 5,266. However, these figures concealed persistent staff shortages and it was not until the recession of the eighties that these were overcome. In 1979-80, driving strength increased from 2,302 to 2,457 (6.7%) and the inspectorate was at last brought up to establishment by an increase from 263 to 299 (13.7%). Lack of alternative job opportunities created a more settled staff, turnover falling to around 5% in the mid-eighties. By March 1985, the numbers employed had risen to 5,600, perhaps reflecting an element of job creation in the political climate of the times.

The need to monitor the changing pattern of traffic continuously introduced a new grade of employee—the 18 SCRAM investigators appointed in October 1979 who travelled on the buses and trains, conducting continuous surveys. With their green blazers with PTE logos on the pocket, they soon became a familiar sight throughout Merseyside.

The staff achieved substantial benefits during the seventies. Holiday entitlements and bonuses were increased and, in some cases, consolidated. A 38-hour week for manual workers was conceded in 1982.

Welfare and Recreation

Welfare and recreational facilities had been well established in Liverpool Corporation passenger transport days and the club rooms and sports ground at Finch Lane, Dovecot were a model for other undertakings. Under the PTE regime, the club facilities were extended to the enlarged staff and, in 1972, the previous voluntary administration having shown difficulty in coping with modern demands, the PTE appointed a full time Administration Officer and opened its accounting and auditing facilities to the club free of charge.

The Club fought a losing battle against vandalism of the Finch Lane ground and matters became so serious that eventually they had to consider transferring the annual Retired Members' function to the Royal Iris as it was felt unsafe to hold it at Finch Lane. The Club was disbanded and the Finch Lane site sold after deregulation.

From 1st July 1971 the PTE extended its medical organisation, inherited from Liverpool Corporation, to replace the facility for medical examinations previously supplied by the Liverpool Health Department. In 1975 the

Edge Lane ambulance room was replaced by a modern medical centre and a new welfare office was built. Each year employees were trained to St. John's Ambulance first aid standards. Welfare assistants paid regular visits to the homes of sick employees and advised on social benefits.

A sine qua non for the average busman was the canteen. The depot canteens had long since graduated from tea and bun affairs to the provision of full meals and often figured in depot improvements (see chapter 54). The mobile canteens, too, were a familiar sight at various agreed locations throughout the operating area. The two wartime Bedford-Dyson articulated buses, GKA 287-8, served as canteens until March 1960 and were replaced by second-hand Bedford artics. bought from London Transport. There were eventually four of these one of which has been preserved in its London state. New in 1947-9, they were not much younger than those they replaced but they had very long lives, being withdrawn by the PTE in 1971-3. They were then replaced by new Bedford articulated combinations.

Two of the four 1940 AEC Regals became canteens, A177 from 1952 to 1963 and A178 from 1957 to 1970 by which time it was a static unit. The most remarkable of all was KJ 2578, a Leyland TD1 new to Redcar Services in 1931. After arduous war service in Liverpool, it became a driver training vehicle in October 1947, a stores van in July 1949, a canteen in October 1951 and served as such well into PTE days. It was eventually purchased for preservation in 1980.

On occasions, unconverted vehicles were pressed into service as canteens, as witness the arrangements at Hall Road described in chapter 50.

The Military Band

A happy reminder of more leisurely days was the PTE Military Band, successor to the Liverpool Tramways Band. Every year the band performed at 60-80 engagements, including Town Hall functions, Cenotaph services, old age pensioners' clubs, garden fetes, the Liverpool Show and Christmas concerts. There were also twice-weekly lunch time summer concerts at the Pier Head. In 1972, the Lord Mayor of Liverpool requested that the band be given a greater share of engagements at the Town Hall and, in that year, they attended 16 functions. Perhaps the pinnacle of their achievement was playing for the opening of the second Mersey Tunnel in 1971, in the presence of HM The Queen. The band became a victim of the drive for economies in the mid-eighties but was reformed as the Red Rose Band and played at the retirement function for Director General Ken Swallow in 1989.

Management Reorganised

Following the abolition of the County Council, the Passenger Transport Authority set up a support staff in Tithebarn House, Tithebarn Street with a Clerk, Treasurer and Transportation Adviser, a measure which had not been found necessary in the pre-County Council days between 1969 and 1974. After a period of ill-health, Leslie

Latter retired as Director General immediately after deregulation in November 1986. His successor was Kenneth Warwick Swallow who was born in Liverpool in 1935 and educated at Holt High School. He joined Liverpool Corporation Passenger Transport in 1951 and was one of the first young men to be accepted for the Municipal Passenger Transport Association executive training scheme when it was established in 1960. During the three year course, he served at Derby, Halifax, Manchester and Sheffield. Returning to Liverpool, he had experience in various sections but in the sixties became involved in public transport planning, a role which continued in the early years of the PTE. In 1974 he was appointed the first Public Transport Co-ordinating Officer for West Sussex County Council but later the same year he returned to Merseyside PTE as Planning Manager, assuming responsibility for bus and local rail service planning. He is a Justice of the Peace and a Fellow of the Chartered Institute of Transport.

The reconstituted PTE, with no direct responsibility for operations, other than the ferries, was a somewhat shrunken version of its predecessor. The former Director of Service Operations, W. Gwyn Thomas, had joined Liverpool Corporation Passenger Transport as a junior clerk in 1945 and, apart from a period as Traffic Superintendent of Wigan Corporation Transport in 1966-70, his whole career had been spent on Merseyside. He now became Managing Director and Chief Executive of Merseyside Transport Ltd (Merseybus) and successfully steered the company through its first three years. He retired on 31st December 1989 and was awarded the OBE in the Birthday Honours List, 1990. He was succeeded by Peter Coombes, formerly Director of Strategic Development for Babcock Thorn Ltd at Rosyth Royal Dockyard.

The Authority made it clear that they intended to reduce the Executive to the status of a local authority department and the other directorships of the PTE were filled by the Clerk, Treasurer and Transportation Adviser of the Authority thus destroying the separation of the two bodies as envisaged in the 1968 Act. By the time it moved into vacant offices at 24 Hatton Garden in the summer of 1988, the Authority's staff had swollen to 40. Determined to complete the emasculation of the Executive, the Authority proposed to turn it into an inter-disciplinary body with each director, including the Director General, having equal authority. This was clearly an unworkable arrangement and Ken Swallow, the Director General, took early retirement in October 1989. The weakness of the proposed chain of command was evidently recognised as the new Director General, appointed in February 1990, was also appointed Chief Executive.

1986-89 Director General Ken Swallow (right) during the course of 'showing the sights' to the 1988/89 President of the Chartered Institute of Transport, Alastair Pugh. One of the three former Birkenhead Corporation ferry boats, Mountwood, forms a backcloth in its pre-1990 refurbishment livery.

56 DEREGULATION AND AFTER

Although the authors set out in this volume to chronicle the events from 1957 to 1986, an account of subsequent happenings is desirable, if only to enable the observer to understand the enormous changes that the Transport Act, 1985 brought to public transport in Liverpool. Nevertheless, they hasten to explain that no attempt has been made to record events in the depth accorded to earlier developments. The truth is that, four years after deregulation, the public transport scene on Merseyside is so different from that of 1986 that, without explanation, the reader might be excused if he doubted the veracity of the earlier narrative. However, it is the authors' conviction that a definitive account of post-deregulation events should be delayed until the perspective of time can clarify the true import.

Public transport management had been both protected and frustrated by the licensing rules laid down by the Road Traffic Act, 1930 which had been little changed over the years and, for 55 years, had given operators security which they did not always deserve. Often used as a political football, their actions had perforce been defensive as the problems of social changes, declining revenue, labour shortages and inflation had been compounded by swingeing taxes and restrictive legislation. When subsidies came along to prop up the activities seen as necessary, a generation of bus managers grew up who regarded these conditions as normal and saw no merit in striving for new business or cutting costs. For the most part, their seniors had never known the cut-and-thrust of the pre-1930 days. Too much of the status quo was taken for granted and traditionalism reigned when innovation and enterprise were needed.

When long distance services were deregulated in 1980, the licensing rules for stage carriage operations were relaxed to the extent that the onus was shifted to the existing operator to prove that a new applicant's service was not necessary rather than the other way round but few took advantage of this concession. The legal expenses of obtaining the licence in the teeth of entrenched opposition were high and thereafter the operator was confined within the inflexible discipline of the Traffic Commissioners with no easy mechanism for altering times, fares and routes with the speed that competitive business demanded. The only serious challenge, in Cardiff, came to grief after costing the promoters dear.

After deregulation, it became illegal for a bus service to be subsidised unless competitive tenders had first been invited and a contract made. It also became possible for any number of newcomers, hitherto excluded by the protective clauses of the licensing structure, to take to the road on routes of their choice, at times and fares selected by them.

Many of the new municipal companies and, to a lesser extent the NBC companies, can be likened to soccer teams suddenly finding themselves playing rugby. Some players were unsure of the rules and picking up the ball and running with it were anathema. In the competitive struggle that was to follow, they were handicapped in that their staffs were thoroughly conditioned to the sheltered life and high cost structures of the old regime. While a few were soon bankrupt and went out of business, many adapted quickly, sometimes with the help of new men brought in from outside to exploit the commercial possibilities fully. Merseyside PTE had some advantages in that it had developed a marketing function with a distinctly commercial mien and this was passed on to the new operating company.

In all the PT Areas there was a lack of trust between some commercial operators and the PTE. The staffs of the old Executives were split up between the new PTEs and the PTA-owned operating companies so that people who had been close colleagues for many years found themselves in two very different camps. The other operators believed that, with the best will in the world, it was unlikely that old loyalties could be entirely cast aside and therefore some favouritism towards the PTA-owned companies was inevitable. Certainly the latter had benefited from the great store of statistical information amassed over the years and some believed that there were still hidden subsidies through services performed by Councils at less than economic prices. At the political level, the directors of the PTA-owned companies were members of the same bodies which made up the PTA and appointed the PTE. The law permits members of the PTA to be directors of the company but they may not receive remuneration; in the case of Merseybus, no PTA members, only ex-members, have been appointed to the Board.

Understandably, left wing politicians were reluctant participants in the whole deregulation and privatisation process. On Merseyside, the PTA's financial involvement was greater as the leasing debt was so enormous that it was commercially insupportable and the government had approved a partly paid-up share arrangement whereby the PTA continued to make payments for three years. Nevertheless, there is plenty of evidence of PTE officials bending over backwards to achieve impartiality. In this respect, the status of the Director General differs from that of the directors who are also chief officers of the Authority. The Director General, who had functional responsibility for bus service tendering, would frequently leave a meeting with members of the Authority when matters directly affecting Merseybus were discussed and this procedure was recognised by members. In reports to the Executive, tendering companies were identified by numbers, changed on every occasion, so that the dual role directors could not be accused of prior knowledge of which contracts were being awarded to the Authority's company.

Fares Policy

The PTA continued its Cheap Fares Policy in the only way open to it. On the subsidised routes it laid down a fare scale which was below the commercial scales generally adopted by the operators without there being any agreement between them. This led to a state of affairs which many members of the public found very confusing with different fares applying on the same route at different times of the day. Subsidised routes had different route numbers, usually made up of the commercial number plus 100 but there were many variations from this method, particularly when the commercial number was prefixed or suffixed by a letter. Bus stop signs were plastered with route numbers, many of which meant nothing to the majority of passengers. All subsidised buses were obliged, in terms of their contracts, to display a sign indicating that they were operating a 'Merseytravel' service, this being the marketing name of the new PTE.

Both the subsidised and commercial fare scales incorporated peak and off-peak differentials and off-peak maxima. Initially they were set at the following levels:-

Distance Miles	Peak		Off-Peak	
	Commercial	Subsidised	Commercial	Subsidised
	p	p	p	p
1	20	12	20	12
2	30	20	30	20
3	40	30	40	30
4	50	40 max	50	30 max
5	60		60	
7	70		60	
9	80		60	
12	1.00		60	
15	1.10		60	
18	1.20		60	
21	1.30		60	

As in the previous five years, the Cheap Fares policy was controversial as some 'Merseytravel' services ran all day and competed over common sections of route with commercial services. The practice was unsuccessfully contested in the courts by Crosville and North Western. There has been a gradual process of eliminating the differential between the two scales and one can speculate that, in time, it will disappear completely.

The Initial Period

An operator was obliged to give the Traffic Commissioner 42 days' notice of an intention to commence or discontinue running a service. This was then published in Notices and Proceedings, giving those concerned time to alter subsidised services or invite new tenders. It also gave the opposition, if any, an opportunity to plan retaliatory measures. However, during the official Initial Period from 26th October 1986 to 25th January 1987, no alterations were permissible.

Merseyside entered the new era with only the well-known established operators on the road, the main difference being that some of the buses were running on unfamiliar routes. Crosville secured contracts to run several ex-PTE routes including the all-day 192 (ex-part of 92) between Halewood and Walton, the 125 (ex-25) between Garston and Walton (which, surprisingly, Merseybus had not registered), the 111 (ex-part of 11) between Stockbridge Village and Pier Head and the 130 between Everton Valley and Pier Head, which was reminiscent of a long gone version of tram route 30. Several early morning, late evening and weekend contracts took the dark green buses to unfamiliar places such as Hall Road, Knowsley and Lyme Cross. Initially North Western stayed within the traditional Ribble area. The only newcomer to register a commercial route—between Maghull and the city centre—failed to start, having ceased trading before Deregulation day, and four taxi registrations came to nothing. Unlike many cities and towns, there was no large influx of minibuses, a type of vehicle which, in Liverpool, has tended to be mainly confined to routes on which the PTE has specified them on the grounds of sparse traffic or for access to roads of limited capacity.

Neither Merseybus nor Crosville was well-prepared for the new conditions. The former had let too many staff go and was seriously short of drivers; there were also no minibuses for use of tenders won. Crosville lacked both buses and staff to drive and maintain them and had the additional task of teaching drivers a host of new routes.

Deregulation brought Crosville buses through the tunnel from Birkenhead in addition to those on the company's traditional Liverpool routes now worked from Runcorn and Warrington depots. Leyland Olympian DOG162 on route C5 to Chester carries a 'Cheshirebus' sign in the front nearside saloon window, indicating that it is subsidised by Cheshire County Council while Bristol VR DVG453 is working the H25 service from Runcorn via Speke and Garston.

After deregulation, Merseybus hired minibuses from Crosville until the arrival of Dodge S56 vehicles, some with 22-seat Northern Counties bodies and others, like 7696 illustrated, with Alexander bodies. The two community services 100 and 101 were at first linked together but were soon worked separately once more.

Crosville hired 36 Daimler Fleetlines from the PTE, collecting them at the eleventh hour from Wallasey depot on Sunday 26th October, while Merseybus hired Crosville minibuses until its own were delivered. Some of the Fleetlines had previously been on long loan to Crosville, working from Heswall depot, and occasionally appearing in Liverpool on services 418-9. More than 100 drivers were recruited by Crosville but tendered services ran erratically and penalty clauses for failure to operate were invoked by the PTE more than once.

Exit Crosville

There were maintenance problems at Love Lane and the 1973 Fleetlines were elderly and unreliable. Nationals were drafted in from other Crosville depots and finally, ten Bristol VRs, ex-West Midlands PTE, were hired from dealers Martins of Middlewich. After preparation at Rock Ferry depot, Birkenhead, they were brought to Love Lane where they were due to enter service on 5th January 1987, still in WMPTE blue and cream but with Crosville fleetnames and numbers added

The company's Liverpool depot had experienced poor labour relations for a number of years and the drivers now refused to drive these buses because they were not fitted with power steering. There is no doubt that double-deck one-man operation in city conditions can be very hard work with manual steering and no manual one-man double-deckers had previously been used by Crosville for this type of work. There is evidence of some management obduracy as there was insistence on using these buses on all-day duties in the face of union requests for them to be allocated to split duties while the matter was discussed. Amazingly, one was allocated to the first duty out on 5th January and the drivers immediately went on strike. After a brief resumption on 14th, labour was again withdrawn the following day and on 24th the drivers were dismissed and the depot closed.

After intervention by the Traffic Commissioner early in February, the Runcorn and Warrington services were resumed from those depots; an attempt to persuade the Rock Ferry men to work H3, Liverpool-Rainhill Stoops, was unsuccessful. After a sit-in at the depot, a court eviction order and a period of picketing while appeal procedures were followed, half the ex-Crosville drivers were recruited by Merseybus who secured some of the temporary contracts which the PTE awarded to fill the void left by the withdrawal of Crosville. Many vehicles were removed from Love Lane depot at night by staff members. These included the PTE-owned 'Merseylink' buses for the disabled for which the company had won a minimum cost contract. Some men drove on the same routes for both operators. Other contracts were taken over by North Western. From February-March, new operators to the area, Shearings, an off-shoot of the Smith-Shearing touring group of Wigan, and Halton Transport took over some of the Huyton-Prescot routes.

The Villains of the Piece. Five of the hired Bristol VRs stand in the Crosville depot yard at Love Lane. They are still in West Midlands PTE blue and cream livery with the Crosville fleet name and leaping lynx logo superimposed. In the background is an ex-Merseyside PTE Daimler Fleetline. It was a dispute about driving the Bristols that finally closed down Crosville's Liverpool-based operations and this view dates from 22nd January 1987, a week after services ceased.

The First Year

Needless to say many miscalculations were made in the early days. One was the unnecessary change of familiar route numbers which added to public confusion. Thus route 46, successively a tram route and a bus route and virtually unchanged since 1927, was extended from Walton to Netherton and inexplicably renumbered 52. There are indications that more of this was planned as route 68 was shown in some publicity matter as 51, though this did not go ahead.

In 1986-87 bus passengers on Merseyside declined by approximately one third. This was partly due to the large fare increase on the commercial services and the confusion caused by the frequent route changes with which the passenger was confronted. There were also the unfamiliar buses, often without proper destination displays and the appearance of different buses on the same route but with strange route numbers at various times of the day or week. The validity of this argument is supported by the increase in rail traffic, reflecting the public perception of the permanence of the railway network. This was underlined by some press advertising by the PTE.

The nationwide upheaval which followed deregulation placed large numbers of second-hand buses on the market and the average age of the fleets tended to increase. These buses could be bought at bargain prices and North Western and the new operators who were to appear took advantage of the situation. The inflow of new buses to several fleets in 1989 was an indication of greater stability in the industry.

There is no doubt that the local taxpayer has benefited as revenue support from the buses declined from around £40 million to £8.6 million. History will judge whether the economy was worthwhile.

New Competition

The working of the new conditions during the initial period was studied with great interest, not only by the PTE and the existing operators but by a number of interested parties waiting in the wings and, from February 1987, new players came on to the stage. These can be divided into two kinds—the established coach operators who saw an opportunity to increase the utilisation of their assets by bidding for PTE tenders and newcomers who saw commercial opportunities. It soon became clear that there was no security for a business which sought to exist by tenders alone. Although contracts were initially awarded nominally for one year, they could be cancelled at relatively short notice if another operator registered a commercial service which fulfilled the same needs. For this reason, it was not unknown for an operator, having won a tender and found it to be wholly or partially a commercial proposition, to protect his interests by registering the service commercially and thus relinquishing the subsidy. Alternatively, on renewal, a 'nil tender' would be submitted. At a later stage Merseybus was criticised by other operators for registering commercially services for which their tender had been unsuccessful and thus unseating the successful bidder. More recently, contracts have been awarded for two or three years and the 1985 Act permits five years.

Fareway

The greatest impact on the status quo in Liverpool was made by three new operators all of whom obtained most of their revenue from commercial services. Fareway Passenger Services Ltd. was formed by four ex-PTE drivers towards the end of 1986. Using 13 Bristol VR East Lancs. bodied buses purchased from the PTE, a 20-minute service numbered F1 was started on 16th February 1987 between Kirkby Admin. Gate and Pier Head via Fazakerley and Walton, a route not exactly served by Merseybus. A half-hourly weekday evening service was given and by July an internal service in the Industrial Estate at peak hours and a half hourly Sunday service had been added together with a second route (F4) between Tower Hill and Pier Head via Southdene, Stonebridge Lane, Utting Avenue East and Breck Road.

Fareway's services were started with second-hand vehicles purchased from Greater Manchester and Merseyside PTEs, both of whom had surplus vehicles. This Bristol VR with East Lancs body, GKA 72N, was originally Merseyside 2120 dating from 1975 and carried a form of fleet name which was soon superseded by a script style.

Further services were started so that every main route between Kirkby and the city centre was covered including an ingenious service which took in a section of the 61 route between Old Swan and Black Bull. Fareway refused to adopt plain numbers for services other than tendered routes and there is a subtle relationship between some of the F numbers and the Merseybus numbers used in the same corridors. Thus F4, F8 and F9 cover much of the same ground as 14, 18 and 19. Later Merseybus reciprocated by starting routes 1, 2 and 3 over Fareway routes F1, F2 and F3. North Western also put minibuses on route F1.

In addition to the Bristols, of which two more were added via Lloyd of Maghull, the mainstay of the fleet were 40 Daimler Fleetlines from Greater Manchester PTE and a further 10 from London Transport via Hampshire Bus and Cumberland. However, five Northern Counties bodied Leyland Olympians were placed in service at the end of 1988 and another five six months later. With five Mercedes 19-24 seat midibuses, acquired for a tendered service serving Walton Hall Park and Croxteth Park, and three second-hand coaches, the fleet reached 75 by early 1990.

Fareway's operating base was established in premises in Hornhouse Lane, Kirkby and its success was derived from its identification with the local community who adopted the attractive blue and yellow buses as their own. The residents appreciated the moquette seats and the friendly drivers and Fareway was a serious threat to Merseybus.

Liverline

At the other end of the city, Liverline Travel Services Ltd, registered in March 1988 was also set up by people from the PTE and Merseybus. It started route 32 between Central Bus Station and Speke every 15 minutes on 11th April 1988. This route followed the Merseybus 82 service via Park Road and Aigburth Road but deviated via Garston Station, Springwood Avenue and Speke Hall Road instead of Speke Road. A half-hourly Sunday service was added on 29th May 1988 and there have been other minor changes since then.

Routes 35/35A between Central Bus Station and Halewood commenced on 15th August 1988 with a combined 15-minute frequency and two route variations at the Halewood end. The buses ran via Ullet Road, Menlove Avenue, Cromptons Lane, Woolton Road, Woolton village and Mackets Lane, there being no exact equivalent route by Merseybus or Crosville. The terminal variations proved to be confusing to passengers and all trips followed a slightly revised 35 route from April 1989. The third commercial service (36) took to the road on 22nd July 1989 between Central Bus Station and Garston via Smithdown Road and Brodie Avenue, every 20-minutes during the day and half-hourly evenings and Sundays. From 23rd October 1988, Liverline won the tender for the weekday evening and Sunday service 181 between Speke and Bootle from Merseybus and in 1990, commercial operations were extended to the Childwall Valley Road corridor.

Whilst Liverline's activities undoubtedly contributed to

Fareway was the first of the new independent operators to acquire new buses and this Leyland Olympian with Northern Counties body, No. 162, was one of ten placed in service in 1989

Ex-Greater Manchester Atlantean 7378 is seen leaving Roe Street *en route* to Kirkby on Fareway route F8 on 19th February 1988. The destination is 'Knowsley Industrial Estate' the new name for the Kirkby estate.

the closure of Garston depot, the company's impact in the south was not as strong as that of Fareway in the north, due perhaps to the rather run down appearance of the fleet in the early stages and the lack of identification with one cohesive community. Ten 1974-75 Alexander bodied Atlanteans, bought from Kentish Bus, had originated with Strathclyde PTE and another eleven slightly newer similar buses from the same source were soon added. In November 1988 maintenance problems necessitated hiring over a dozen vehicles from the contract fleet of Hyndburn Transport including some Atlanteans which had been with Plymouth Corporation, a Bristol RE, Leyland Nationals and two London Transport Routemasters

Ex-London Transport AEC Routemasters became a familiar sight in many parts of the country but their appearance in Liverpool was brief being due to a vehicle maintenance crisis for Liverline. Note the improvised destination indicator on RM811 which still advertised the London Transport Sightseeing Tour when seen in the Central Bus Station on 10th December 1988.

Service 32 was Liverline's first route being, in effect, a variant of Merseybus 82 between Pier Head and Speke. Scania No. 102 with Northern Counties body looks smart in the company's blue and white livery.

which, of course, needed conductors. At a time when Routemasters could be bought very cheaply and were appearing in towns all over the country, including Manchester (where route 143 was labelled 'the Piccadilly Line'), these were the only Routemasters to run in Liverpool. Some of the hired buses were later purchased and others were added in 1989. A single-deck Leyland Tiger with Plaxton bus body and three ex-Ribble Leopard coaches were also acquired. Seven new Scania double-deckers with Northern Counties bodies were acquired in 1989-90.

A depot was obtained in Naylor Street, off Vauxhall Road, to which the registered office was transferred.

Liverbus

One of the directors of Liverline left the company and, in due course, set up Liverbus Ltd, based at Huyton Industrial Estate. A fleet of 20 ex-Greater Manchester Atlanteans was used to start operations between Huyton and Liverpool by several routes, the first service (212), starting on 15th January 1990 though a free service was run on 13th to advertise the new facilities. The buses were owned by a separate company, Gemsam Ltd. Some contract operation was also obtained. The company used the generous-sized intermediate route indicator to display a detailed description of the routes.

These three commercial operators, running collectively over 100 double-deck buses, had a high profile in the city centre; there was scarcely a time during the day when one or other was not visible at Hood Street. There is no doubt that they represented a considerable threat to Merseybus.

Other New Operators

The three companies noted above have been picked out because of their high impact on the transport scene in Liverpool but there were many others and in September 1989 a total of 32 operators were contracted to the PTE;

Liverbus 33, an Atlantean with Northern Counties body, was formerly Greater Manchester PTE 7739 and good use is made of the typical Manchester destination indicator layout. The 212 route is so numbered because it is an extended version of Merseybus route 12. Also unloading in Roe Street is Fareway 150, a Northern Counties bodied Leyland Olympian.

nine others had had contracts and lost them. Few of these had any commercial bus operations and many were engaged solely on school or works contracts. The PTE adopted a series of 800+ numbers for industrial journeys; in most cases these numbers were determined by adding 800 to the original number, eg 877 and 883. Some of these could be worked by coaches and so attracted operators whose core activity was in a different field. Others found it worthwhile to purchase second-hand double-deckers for this work. Among these was Powneys Coaches Ltd,

(Right, upper) PMT 416 with Red Rider Mini-link fleet names is a Freight Rover Sherpa with the operator's own 20-seat bodywork. It is seen passing beneath one of the footbridges across Hood Street on the tendered 222 Albert Dock shuttle service, a route which has changed hands more than once since introduction in 1986. Note the continuous passenger shelter and the North Western Leyland National at the rear.

(Right) 'Red Rider' was adopted by PMT Ltd (the successor to the Potteries Motor Traction Co Ltd) of Stoke on Trent for some of its initiatives outside its normal North Staffordshire operating area. Route 116 was a tendered version of Merseybus route 6C from Huyton (Brookhouse Estate) to the Pier Head. The Red Rider Liverpool operations were not very extensive being worked from a yard in Moreton, Wirral. The livery is red and yellow but from 1990, PMT buses can also be seen in Liverpool in Crosville brunswick green livery.

Aintree which adopted the fleet name 'Acorn' and obtained several tendered routes.

Mention should also be made of PMT Ltd of Stoke-on-Trent, the descendant of a BET company which originated in the formative days of that great organisation in 1896. One of the first NBC companies to be sold, on 12th December 1986, it followed an expansionist policy, one of its ventures being the opening of an operating centre in a yard at Moreton. Running under the name of 'Red Rider', its operations were mainly in Wirral but it undertook tendered work in Liverpool and registered a 'Rapidride' service (475) between the city centre and Moreton so that its depot journeys could be run live. PMT was destined to play an even greater part in local transport on Merseyside as will be seen later.

Toppings Super Coaches Ltd of Wavertree, operating as Toppline, was an established coach operator which added Leyland Nationals and double-deckers to its fleet for tendered work. Another small operator which caused some heartache at Edge Lane was C&M Travel of Aintree which secured the Mobility Bus contracts, leaving Merseybus with some expensive conversions on their hands.

Halton Transport, the former Widnes Corporation, obtained many tendered services from south and east

Toppings Super Coaches Ltd were well established as coach operators and entered the tendered bus service field during weekday evenings and at weekends. This Bristol VR was second hand from the Brighton, Hove & District Omnibus Co. and still carried that operator's fleet number 562 when seen at Pier Head on a Sunday service to Huyton on 29th January 1989.

Merseybus Leyland Olympian 0031, in the maroon livery, is fitted with the new large electronic destination indicators. It is passing through Hood Street Gyratory *en route* from St. Helens to Pier Head. At the kerbside is Halton Transport Leyland Lynx No. 15 on the tortuous service 61 from Murdishaw.

Liverpool and also introduced a commercial service numbered 61 between Murdishaw, a suburb of Runcorn, and Liverpool (Hood Street). It had developed into a 20-minute service by January 1990, requiring 12 buses, almost a quarter of the fleet. The choice of number was unfortunate as it crossed the other 61 in Childwall; the origin of the number was the Crosville J61 between Runcorn and Whiston Hospital.

Privatisation of Crosville and North Western

Crosville and North Western were among the last companies to be sold off by the National Bus Company. On 16th March 1988, North Western, with a fleet of 320 vehicles and 870 staff, passed to Endless Holdings, part of the Drawlane Group, while on 25th of the same month, Crosville with 470 vehicles was sold to ATL (Western) Ltd of Rotherham.

Both these groups had already purchased other companies. However, in February 1989 ATL, whose investments in the bus business had not been very successful, resold Crosville to Drawlane. The Hon. Richard Stanley joined the Drawlane board and was elected chairman of Crosville; public statements were made predicting the return of the company to its former pre-eminent position. However, it continued to decline and in November 1989, in a general tidying-up exercise between Drawlane and the Stagecoach Group, (which by then owned Ribble and several other companies), North Western took over Warrington and Runcorn (and later

The fleet transferred from Ribble on formation of North Western in 1986 was augmented by several economical second-hand purchases. This 1972 PDR1/Atlantean with Alexander dual-door body was one of 10 bought from Lothian Transport of Edinburgh in 1988.

Northwich) depots of Crosville which was now confined to Birkenhead, Ellesmere Port and Chester. On 2nd February 1990, the services and part of the rump of a once great company was sold to PMT Ltd. The right to use the name Crosville for trading purposes was retained and, as such, the green buses could still be seen in Whitechapel, Liverpool on several through services to and from Wirral and Chester. The Crosville company, still possessed of a number of withdrawn buses, was renamed North British Bus Co Ltd on 30th March 1990.

In its dying months, Crosville's Merseyside routes were integrated with those of North Western with buses of both companies running across Liverpool from Southport to Warrington and from Ormskirk and Thornton to Runcorn. This followed the closure of Skelhorne Street bus station after the last bus on Sunday 10th September 1989; the coach station closed later in the month. Other services were extended to Dingle, Aigburth Vale or Penny Lane and, in one or two cases, to Pier Head or Central Bus Station. After the Drawlane rationalisation, the long through services became all North Western and operation benefited by once more having a central city operating base at Love Lane. The proposed sale of Skelhorne Street was an example of a strategy used by many of the new entrepreneurs, in this case not very successfully, as late in 1990 it was still on the market. In a business with small profit margins, any part of the infrastructure seen to be unnecessary, was disposed of. North Western had already displayed an aversion to paying terminal charges a year earlier when the PTE had imposed departure charges at its bus stations. It minimised its use of Pier Head and New Strand and took to the streets. The Pier Head terminal became Mann Island and in other cases, it linked services together, to avoid the need to visit bus stations. One of the results of this policy was to make what had originally been one of the shortest routes into one of the longest. Route 54, originally Seaforth-Netherton, had been extended to become New Strand-Fazakerley Hospital. It eventually became a complete circle, serving Page Moss-Huyton-City Centre-Bootle-Netherton-Fazakerley-Kirkby-Knowsley-Page Moss, operated with minibuses.

North Western acquired 26 Mercedes Benz L608D minibuses of which No. 4 (formerly 214) was one of six with Reebur 19-seat bodies with coach seats. It is seen on route 54 at Fazakerley Hospital in February 1987.

One of the most extraordinary developments was the closure of Pier Head Bus Station in March 1990 to enable the area to be turned into a stage for a Beatles commemorative concert! This location, once the hub of Liverpool's transport system, had become operationally irrelevant and was useful only as a parking place and canteen stop. The buses were moved to the site of Riverside Station, picking up the odd passenger at Princes Dock Gates in St. Nicholas Place North. Meanwhile, convoys of empty buses proceeded to run down to the waterfront where there was scarcely any traffic demand. A more efficient bus terminal has since been opened on the old site.

Meanwhile, Crosville Wales Ltd, which had been separated from the English company in 1987, had become a member of the National Express Holdings Group. In mid-1989, National Express bought Amberline of Speke and made it a subsidiary of Crosville Wales, though in June 1990, it became a direct subsidiary. The red dragon motif used on Crosville Wales' Little Dragon minibuses was cleverly transformed into a Liver Bird when a minibus service was put on between Speke and the city on 18th September 1989. This service eventually reached Warrington, with full size buses, a revival of the H1 service which had been abandoned by Crosville in 1986. As Crosville was still running H25 between Liverpool and Runcorn, it was in competition with Crosville Wales (disguised as Amberline) between Liverpool and Widnes.

Ticket Problems

The PTE continued to administer the concessionary schemes, Zone Tickets and Saveaways and the operators

Amberline achieved fame by taking over the National Express workings from Ribble but also entered the local service market, purchasing a number of PDR1A Atlanteans from Merseyside PTE. DD12 was originally 1264 in the PTE fleet and is seen on the 177 route between Hunts Cross and the Pier Head. Note the scruffy card destination indicator.

Buses of the six participants in the independent Rainbow anywhere ticket scheme lined up at Albert Dock for the inauguration of the initiative in May 1990. Left to right: Iveco minibus of Amberline (transferred from the parent Crosville Wales fleet); Leyland Lynx of Halton Transport; ex-Greater Manchester Transport Atlantean of Liverbus; new Olympian of Fareway Services; new Scania of Liverline and East Lancs-bodied Dennis Dominator of North Western.

accepted them. Payment was based on statistics compiled from the reports of the PTE's travelling investigators and, from time to time, doubts were expressed about the statistical accuracy of this information. In August 1988, North Western decided not to accept Saveaway tickets, an act which led to Merseybus putting on its own 321 service to Maghull and Lydiate so as to restore Saveaway coverage to that area. There were other points of dissatisfaction including children's fares

which were not uniform. It was finally agreed that these would be regarded as concessionary fares and subsidy paid and, from January 1989, North Western resumed accepting Saveaways. However, doubts about the accuracy of the payments continued and, on 19th May 1990, a rival unlimited travel facility, the Rainbow ticket, was launched by six companies led by North Western. The others were Amberline, Fareway, Halton Transport, Liverbus and Liverline.

The Future

In the first three years of deregulation, Merseybus lost ground and appeared to be a reactor rather than a proactor. In its first 18 months, its operating income was £71.2 million, producing an operating loss of £500,000. However, interest on investments of £200,000 and an extraordinary item of £600,000 resulted in a £300,000 surplus. October 1987 saw many tendered routes change hands and new operators take to the road. By early 1989, Merseybus was running only 63% of total mileage compared to 75% run by the PTE buses on 25th October 1986, and less than half the tendered services. Private operators accounted for 25% of tendered services but only 15% of commercial operations.

The government's privatisation policy had always envisaged the sale of the municipal and PTA companies and by the end of 1989, following an investigation by consultants into the best method of disposal, the PTA agreed in principle to the sale of the company to its workforce. The proposal was for the management team to take a 51% stake with the remaining shareholding distributed to the workforce through an ESOP (Employee Share Ownership Plan) similar to that already operating in the former Tyne and Wear and West Yorkshire PTA undertakings (Busways and Yorkshire Rider). To prepare itself, Merseybus implemented an economy package to eliminate projected losses as competition was by then present on every major corridor.

Merseybus Atlantean 1449 in Merseyside Development Corporation promotional livery overtakes Halton Transport Leyland Lynx 45 in Elliot Street by the St. John's Shopping Centre while working a very lightly loaded City Heritage Shutle in July 1989. The Lynx is on the commercial route 51 from Murdishaw via Runcorn, Widnes, Rainhill, Whiston and Huyton.

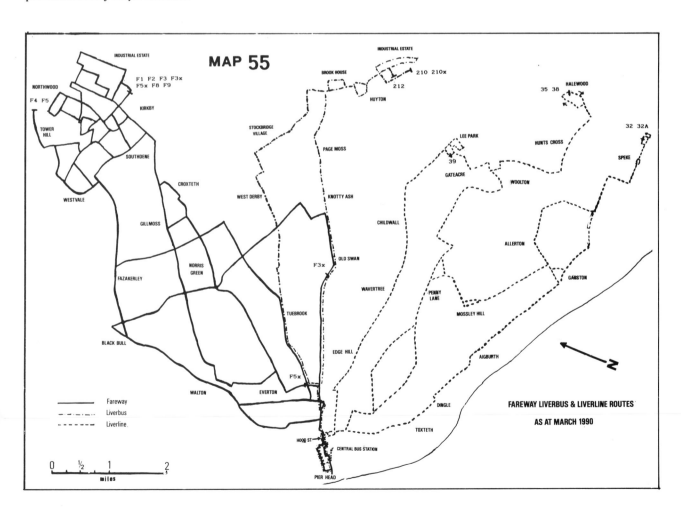

MAP 55

FAREWAY LIVERBUS & LIVERLINE ROUTES

AS AT MARCH 1990

APPENDICES
45 Conversions to One Man Operation

SD = Single deck   DD = Double deck

Date	Route	Description	Type
1.7.1968	68	Aigburth Vale-Seaforth	SD
3.9.1968	46	Penny Lane-Walton	SD
	99,99A	Penny Lane-Muirhead Ave.East-Gillmoss	SD
30.9.1968	4,5	Woolton-Castle Street	SD
	85,85A	Speke-Garston-Pier Head	SD
17.2.1969	17C	Fazakerley-Pier Head	SD
	17D	Utting Avenue-Pier Head	SD
	66	Garston-Naylorsfield	SD
16.6.1969	1,1A	Dingle-Seaforth	SD
3.11.1969	100	City Circle	SD
9.11.1969	500	Speke-Kirkby Limited Stop	DD
3.5.1970	3	Dingle-Walton	DD
17.5.1970	25	Aigburth Vale-Walton	DD
31.5.1970	20	Aigburth Vale-Fazakerley	DD
6.1970	88	Garston-Halewood	SD
14.6.1970	86,87	Garston-Pier Head	DD
30.8.1970	30	Aintree-Pier Head	DD
1.9.1970	33	Seaforth-Everton	DD
25.10.1970	80,82	Speke-Pier Head	DD
4.1.1971	9,10,510	Prescot Road Services	DD
	72	Hunts Cross-Pier Head	DD
	78	Halewood-Pier Head	DD
26.4.1971	86,87	Garston Circular journeys	DD
	97C	New service) Cantril Farm-Kirkby	DD
2.5.1971	81,81D	Speke-Bootle	DD
10.5.1971	11	(New service) Huyton Stn-South Castle St	SD
1.6.1971	61	Aigburth Vale-Seaforth	DD
27.9.1971	14,15	Kirkby-Croxteth-Pier Head	DD
	101	Tower Hill-Kirkby Trading Estate	SD
11.10.1971	60,60D	Dingle-Bootle	DD
6.12.1971	79,479	Netherley-Lee Park-Pier Head	DD
27.2.1972	12A	Page Moss-Pier Head	DD
	75	Huyton-City	DD
14.5.1972	19,44D,544	Kirkby-City	DD
16.7.1972	26,27	Sheil Road Circular	DD
3.9.1972	12,12C	Page Moss-Cantril Farm-City	DD
4.9.1972	412	Cantril Farm-City	DD
19.11.1972	18C,18D	East Lancs Rd-Muirhead Ave-Pier Head	DD
29.1.1973	73,73A	Woolton or Netherley-City	DD
	76	Broadgreen-Pier Head	DD
	79A	Belle Vale-Pier Head	DD
1.4.1973	28	Netherton-Old Haymarket	DD
16.4.1973	6C	Huyton (Brookhouse Estate)-Pier Head	DD
	40	Huyton Station-Pier Head	DD
6.5.1973	92	Bootle-Page Moss	DD
	92A,92B,93,493	Kirkby-City	DD
13.5.1973	16	Seaforth-Pier Head	DD
1.7.1973	42	Penny Lane-Edge Lane (postponed from 4th March)	DD
2.3.1975	56	Netherton-Old Haymarket	DD
28.9.1975	55,55A	Netherton-Old Haymarket or Pier Head	DD
3.11.1975	67	Old Swan-Seaforth	DD

46 List of Principal Services operated by Liverpool City Transport as at 30th November 1969

1	Seaforth-Dingle via Gt Howard Street, Pier Head and Sefton Street	O
1A	Seaforth-Dingle via Regent Road, Pier Head and Mill Street	OP
1E	Netherton-Dingle via Litherland, Regent Road and Sefton Street	P
*2/2E	Pier Head-Aintree via Scotland Road	
3	Walton-Dingle via Lime Street	
4	South Castle Street-Woolton (Hunts Cross Ave) via Wavertree and Menlove Avenue	O
*4B/5B	Pier Head-Wavertree-Smithdown Road Circular	
5	South Castle St-Woolton (Hunts Cross Ave) via Mount Pleasant and Smithdown Rd	O
*6A	Pier Head-Bowring Park (Sheppard Avenue) via Edge Lane	P
6C	Pier Head-Huyton (Brook House Estate) via Edge Lane	
6D	Pier Head-Bowring Park via Edge Lane	
*7C/7D	Pier Head-Stoneycroft via Kensington	
8C/8D	Pier Head-Pagemoss via Kensington	P
9	Pier Head-Lyme Cross via Prescot Road and Stockbridge Lane	
9A	Pier Head-Knowsley via Prescot Road and Stockbridge Lane	
9C/9D	Pier Head-Longview via Prescot Road and Woolfall Heath Avenue	
10	South Castle Street-Prescot	
10A	Green Lane-Prescot (Rye Hey Factory) via Manchester Road	P
10B	Pagemoss-Prescot via Woolfall Heath Avenue	P
10C/10D	Pier Head-Longview via Prescot Road and Liverpool Road	
*11	South Castle Street-Huyton Station via West Derby Road, Green Lane and Kingsway	
12	Pier Head-Pagemoss via West Derby Road and Melwood Drive	
12A	Sir Thomas St or Pier Head-Pagemoss via West Derby Road and Leyfield Road	
12C	Pier Head-Cantril Farm via West Derby Road and Melwood Drive	
14C	Pier Head-Croxteth via Everton Road and Breck Road	
14D	Pier Head-Croxteth via Shaw Street and Breck Road	
15	Pier Head-Kirkby Trading Estate via Breck Road and Hornhouse Lane	P
15B	Pier Head-Kirkby (Tower Hill Estate) via Breck Road and Southdene	
16	Pier Head-Seaforth via Vauxhall Road and Litherland	R
17C	Pier Head-Fazakerley via Heyworth Street, Utting Avenue and Lower Lane	O
17D	Pier Head-Utting Avenue via Everton Valley	O
18A	Pier Head-Kirkby Trading Estate via Muirhead Avenue and Croxteth	P
18C	Pier Head-Muirhead Avenue East via West Derby Road	
18D	Pier Head-East Lancashire Road (Lower Lane) via Muirhead Avenue	
19	Pier Head-Kirkby Trading Estate via Robson St, Walton Hall Ave and Hornhouse Lane	P
19A	Pier Head-Kirkby (Hornhouse Lane) via Robson St, Walton Hall Ave and Southdene	
20	Aigburth Vale-Fazakerley via Park Road and Scotland Road	
22	Pier Head-Fazakerley via Scotland Road	P
24	Old Haymarket-Seaforth via Stanley Road and Marsh Lane	
25	Aigburth Vale-Walton via Princes Park and Heyworth Street	
26/27	Sheil Road Circular	
28	Old Haymarket-Netherton via Stanley Road and Linacre Road	R
30	Pier Head-Aintree via Netherfield Road	
30E	Pier Head-Aintree (British Enka Works)	P
31	Pier Head-Walton via Heyworth Street	P
33	Everton Road (Grants Gardens)-Seaforth via Robson Street and Lambeth Road	P
34	Longview-Seaforth via West Derby and Sandhills Lane	P
35	Northwood-Seaforth via Fazakerley and Hale Road	P
36	Kirkby (5 Gate)-Seaforth via Walton Hall Avenue and Hale Road	P
37	Croxteth-Seaforth via Utting Avenue and Hale Road	P

38	Penny Lane-Seaforth via Netherfield Road and Sandhills Lane	P
40	Pier Head-Huyton Station via Edge Lane, Brookside Avenue and Woolfall Heath Avenue	
41	Eaton Road-Edge Lane (Southbank Road) via St. Oswalds Street	P
42	Penny Lane-Edge Lane (Southbank Road) via Mill Lane	P
44A	Pier Head-Kirkby Trading Estate via Everton Valley and Southdene	P
44D	Pier Head-Northwood via Everton Valley, Walton Hall Avenue and Southdene	
45	Longview-Edge Lane (Southbank Road) via Brookside Avenue	P
46	Penny Lane-Walton via Netherfield Road	O
47A	Croxteth-Edge Lane (Southbank Road) via Muirhead Avenue and Old Swan	P
48/49	Bootle Circular	R
50	Bootle Station-Ford (Fleetwoods Lane) via Orrell	PR
50A	Bankhall-Ford (Fleetwoods Lane) via Orrell	PR
51	Pier Head or Old Haymarket-Ford Cemetery via Hawthorne Road	R
52	Walton-Sefton Church via Hawthorne Road and Litherland	R
53	Black Bull-Netherton Village	R
53A	Black Bull-Netherton (Magdalene Square)	R
54	Seaforth-Netherton Village via Dunnings Bridge Road	R
55	Pier Head or Old Haymarket-Sefton (Almonds Turn) via Stanley Road	R
55A	Pier Head or Old Haymarket-Ford (Fleetwoods Lane) via Stanley Road	R
56	Old Haymarket-Netherton via Southport Road and Sterrix Lane	R
57	Pier Head or Old Haymarket-Orrell (Dunnings Bridge Road) via Worcester Road	PR
57A	Pier Head or Old Haymarket-Netherton via Worcester Road and Bridle Road	R
58	Pier Head or Old Haymarket-Litherland (Hatton Hill Rd) via Stanley Rd and Watts Lane	R
59	Pier Head or Old Haymarket-Old Roan via Stanley Road and Watts Lane	R
60	Dingle-Bootle (New Strand) via Ullet Road, Old Swan and Queens Drive	
60D	Smithdown Road (Ullet Road)-Regent Road (Millers Bridge)	P
61	Aigburth Vale-Seaforth via Childwall, Old Swan and Norris Green	
62	Speke (Western Avenue)-Kirkby via Belle Vale, Broadgreen and Knowsley	P
63	Speke (Ford Factory)-Kirkby via Belle Vale, Broadgreen and Knowsley	P
64	Edge Lane (Southbank Road)-Kirkby via Knowsley	P
65	Speke (Western Avenue)-Edge Lane (Southbank Road) via Belle Vale	P
66	Naylorsfield-Garston (Windfield Road) via Woolton	O
67A	Old Swan-Seaforth via Lower Breck Road and Sandhills Lane	P
68	Aigburth Vale-Seaforth via Wavertree, Old Swan, Walton and Hornby Road	O
*69	Aigburth Vale-Otterspool Promenade Smr	
70	Pagemoss-Huyton Industrial Estate via Huyton Hey Road	P
71	South Castle Street-Penny Lane via Park Lane	P
71D	South Castle Street-Penny Lane via Wapping and Parliament Street	P
72	Pier Head-Hunts Cross via Ullet Road and Hillfoot Road	
73	Pier Head-Woolton (Hunts Cross Avenue) via Ullet Road and Childwall	
73A	Pier Head-Naylorsfield via Ullet Road and Childwall	
*74	Pier Head or Sir Thomas Street-Dovecot via West Derby Road	
75	Pier Head-Huyton Station via West Derby Road and Pilch Lane	
76	Pier Head-Broadgreen via Wavertree	
77A	Pier Head-Speke via Crown Street and Springwood Avenue	P
78	Pier Head-Halewood via Wavertree and Hunts Cross	
78A	Castle Street-Hunts Cross via Wavertree and Woolton	P
79/79C	Pier Head-Netherley via Brownlow Hill, Wavertree and Childwall	
79A	Pier Head-Lee Park via Brownlow Hill, Wavertree and Gateacre Park	
79B/D	Pier Head-Lee Park via Pembroke Place, Wavertree and Childwall Valley Road	
79C	Pier Head-Lee Park via Brownlow Hill, Wavertree and Childwall Valley Road	
80	Pier Head-Speke (Western Avenue) via Ullet Road and Brodie Avenue	
81	Speke (Western Avenue)-Bootle (New Strand) via Woolton and Queens Drive	
81D	Speke (Eastern Avenue)-Bootle (New Strand) via Woolton and Queens Drive	
82C	Pier Head-Speke (Eastern Avenue) via Park Road and Aigburth Road	
83	Speke (Eastern Avenue)-Halewood via Woodend Avenue	P
85	Pier Head-Garston via Mill Street	O
85A	Pier Head-Speke via Mill Street	O
86	Pier Head-Garston Circular via Smithdown Road and Aigburth	
87	Pier Head-Garston Circular via Aigburth and Smithdown Road	

88/88A	Garston-Halewood-Netherley via Hunts Cross	O
90	St. Helens-Kirkby Station via Whiston, Prescot and Knowsley	H
91	Kirkby (Quarry Green)-Long Lane ROF via Fazakerley	P
91A	Kirkby (Quarry Green)-Gillmoss	P
92	Pier Head-Pagemoss via Walton, Fazakerley and Kirkby	
92A	Pier Head-Kirkby (Civic Centre) via Walton and Fazakerley	
92B	Pier Head-Northwood via Walton and Fazakerley	
93	Pier Head-Kirkby Trading Estate via Fazakerley and Southdene	
94	Dingle-Kirkby Trading Estate via Muirhead Avenue	P
95	Seaforth or Black Bull-Gillmoss via Lower Lane	P
95B	Netherton (Magdalene Square)-Gillmoss via Lower Lane	P
96	Black Bull-Kirkby Trading Estate via Fazakerley	P
97	Pagemoss-Kirkby Trading Estate via Knowsley	P
98	Huyton-Gillmoss via West Derby	P
99	Penny Lane-East Lancashire Road (Lower Lane) via Old Swan and Muirhead Avenue	O
99A	Penny Lane-Gillmoss via Old Swan and Muirhead Avenue	P
99B	Penny Lane-Kirkby Trading Estate via Wavertree, Old Swan and Muirhead Avenue	P
99C	Penny Lane-Kirkby Trading Estate via Childwall, Queens Drive and Muirhead Avenue	P
100	City Circle	
500	Speke-Kirkby via Lime Street and Fazakerley (Limited Stop)	D
*506	South John Street-Huyton (Brookhouse Estate) (Limited Stop)	P
*510	Central Station-Prescot (Limited Stop)	
544	South Castle Street-Northwood via Walton Hall Avenue (Limited Stop)	
*586	South John Street-Garston via Smithdown Road (Limited Stop)	P
592	Pier Head-Northwood via Walton and Fazakerley (Limited Stop)	
-	Liverpool (Tunnel Entrance)-Birkenhead (Tunnel Entrance) Night Service	B

CODE

C and D	suffixes on city routes denote via Church St. or via Dale St. respectively.
B	Jointly operated with Birkenhead Municipal Transport on behalf of Mersey Tunnel Joint Committee
D	Double deck one man operation
H	Jointly operated with St. Helens Corporation and Ribble
O	Single Deck one man operation
P	Operated at peak hours or factory times only
R	Jointly operated with Ribble Motor Services Ltd
*	Services licensed but suspended since strike of March-May 1968

AEC Regent III A287 with Metro-Cammell 62-seat body, was one of the last open-platform buses to be delivered to the Corporation, entering service in March 1958. Note the supplementary card indicator in the box in the end saloon window, later to be replaced by a roller blind over a reduced size route number. The body was a more substantial variant of the Orion design, the radiator grille and built-up nearside wing incorporating the parking light, being Liverpool design features. There were five rear facing seats along the front bulkhead. A287 was withdrawn in 1972.

47 Bus Services operated by Other Operators in Merseyside area as at 30th November 1969

1. RIBBLE MOTOR SERVICES LTD.

39	Liverpool (South John Street)-Manchester (Salford) via St. Helens and Leigh	L
101	Liverpool-Preston via Maghull, Ormskirk, Burscough and Tarleton	
201	Liverpool-Upholland via Aintree Lane, Melling and Skelmersdale	
203	Kirkby-Southport via Maghull, Shirdley Hill and Birkdale Cop Road	NSu
211	Liverpool-Upholland via Kirkby, Melling and Skelmersdale (Limited Stop)	NSu
300	Liverpool-Southport via Maghull, Halsall and Shirdley Hill	Irregular
301	Liverpool-Ormskirk via Melling and Aughton	
302	Liverpool-Southport via Maghull, Halsall and Kew	
303	Kirkby-Southport via Maghull, Shirdley Hill and Kew	
305	Liverpool-Rainford via Melling and Barrow Nook	TS
307	Liverpool-Melling (Rock Lane) via Altway	
310	Liverpool-Maghull (Moss Side Hospital, Park Lane Lodge) via Foxhouse Lane	
311	Liverpool-Blackburn via Ormskirk, Parbold and Chorley	
315	Ormskirk-Formby via Downholland	ThS
317	Liverpool (South John Street)-St. Helens via Prescot	H
320	Liverpool-Wigan via St. Helens, Haydock and Ashton	J
321	Liverpool-Lydiate via Maghull	
324	Ormskirk-Melling	Th
325	Ormskirk-Downholland via Halsall and Haskayne	ThS
328	Melling-Bickerstaffe	NSSu
331	Liverpool-Blackburn via Ormskirk, Parbold and Chorley	
337	Liverpool (Jubilee Drive)-St. Helens via Prescot	K
340	Liverpool-Maghull (Dodds Lane) via Northway	
341	Liverpool-Robbins Island via Maghull and Liverpool Road	
361	Liverpool-Robbins Island via Maghull and Northway	P & Sats.
381	Liverpool-Ormskirk via Crosby, Sefton and Maghull	
382	Liverpool-Ormskirk via Crosby, Sefton, Maghull and Town Green	
391	Crosby-Maghull via Seaforth, Orrell and Aintree	P
392	Bootle-Maghull via Orrell and Aintree	NSu
C 1	Thornton-Crosby via Blundellsands, Waterloo and Endbutt Lane (Flat fare)	NSu
C 2	Thornton-Crosby via Chesterfield Road, Waterloo and Blundellsands (Flat fare)	NSu
L 1	Liverpool-Crosby via Litherland, Church Road and College Road (Limited Stop)	
L 2	Liverpool-Crosby via Hawthorne Road, Litherland and Endbutt Lane	
L 3	Liverpool-Crosby via Litherland and Oxford Road	
L 5	Liverpool-Thornton (Nag's Head) via Seaforth Sands and Crosby	
L 6	Liverpool-Thornton (Long Lane) via Seaforth Sands and Crosby	
L 8	Liverpool-Crosby via Seaforth Sands and Endbutt Lane (Limited Stop)	
L 9	Seaforth Sands-Crosby direct	P
L11	Crosby-Little Crosby	
L15	Liverpool-Thornton (Runnells Lane) via Seaforth Sands and Crosby	
L25	Liverpool-Ford (Fleetwoods Lane) via Seaforth Sands and Crosby	
L30	Liverpool-Crosby via Seaforth Sands and Oxford Road	
L33	Liverpool-Freshfield via Seaforth Sands, Oxford Road and Crosby	Smr Su
L35	Liverpool-Thornton via Pier Head, Derby Road, Seaforth and Derby Road	
L47	Liverpool-Crosby (Hall Road) via Seaforth, The Northern Road and Bus Station	
L48	Liverpool-Crosby (Hall Road) via Litherland, The Northern Road and Oaklands Avenue	
L60	Seaforth Sands-Thornton (Nags Head)	P
L80	Liverpool-Crosby (Hillary Drive) via Seaforth Sands and Brownmoor Lane	P
L85	Liverpool-Thornton (Nags Head) via Seaforth Sands and Chesterfield Road	
L90	Bootle (Balliol Road)-Crosby via Seaforth Sands direct	P

L92	Bootle (New Strand)-Crosby via Hawthorne Road and Liverpool Road	NSu
S 1	Liverpool-Southport via Litherland, Crosby, Formby and Hillside	4 jnys
S 2	Liverpool-Southport via Litherland, Crosby, Formby and Birkdale	
S 3	Liverpool-Southport via Seaforth Sands, Crosby, Formby and Birkdale	P
W 3	Pier Head-Bold Colliery via Thatto Heath	HP
W 3	Burscough Bridge-Deysbrook Barracks via Skelmersdale and Kirkby	P
W 4	Bootle Depot-Bold Colliery	HP
W 6	Pier Head-Bold Colliery via Whiston	HP
W11	Seaforth Sands-Lydiate via Litherland and Maghull	P
W12	Crossens-Gillmoss	P
X27	Liverpool-Skipton via Crosby, Southport, Preston and Clitheroe (Limited Stop)	
X37	Liverpool-Southport via Crosby and Formby by-pass (Limited Stop)	

For services 16, 28, 48-59 and 90 see Liverpool City Transport list.
For service 89 see Crosville list.

The second generation of Ribble forward-entrance double-deckers was bodied by MCCW and entered service in 1961. The bodies were of very similar appearance to those of their Burlingham predecessors, the main difference being the positioning of the emergency door on the offside instead of centrally at the rear; they were also 2½in. wider. These buses were the workhorses of the Crosby and Ormskirk Road routes for many years and this picture of 1746, taken in June 1961, clearly shows the neat uncluttered lines of the full-fronted body. Note the illuminated offside advertisement panel, not yet in use.

2. CROSVILLE MOTOR SERVICES LTD.

H 1	Liverpool-Warrington via Speke and Widnes	
H 2	Liverpool-Warrington via Prescot and Rainhill	
H 3	Liverpool-Rainhill (Norlands Lane) via Old Swan and High Street, Prescot	
H 4	Liverpool-Rainhill (Norlands Lane) via Old Swan and Manchester Road, Prescot	
H 5	Liverpool-Warrington via Huyton, Cronton and Farnworth	
H 6	Liverpool-Runcorn (ICI Offices) via Huyton, Cronton and Widnes	P
H 8	Liverpool-Prescot via Huyton Quarry and Whiston Hospital	
H 9	Liverpool-Prescot via Wilson Road and Whiston Hospital	P
H10	Liverpool-Prescot via Wilson Road and Cross Lane	P
H11	Liverpool-Prescot via Huyton Quarry and Cross Lane	
H12	Liverpool-Prescot via Windy Arbour Road and Whiston Hospital	
H13	Liverpool-Prescot via Windy Arbour Road and Cross Lane	P and Sa
H14	Liverpool-Prescot via Huyton Village and Mosscroft Farm Estate	
H16	Liverpool-Huyton (Elizabeth Road) via Huyton Village and Seel Road	
H17	Huyton (Whiston Lane)-Longview School	Sch
H18	Mosscroft Farm Estate-Park View School	Sch
H19	Liverpool-Halewood (Derby Arms) via Woolton and Hunts Cross	
H20	Liverpool-Chester via Hunts Cross, Halewood and Widnes	
H21	Liverpool-Halebank (Carr Lane) via Woolton and Hunts Cross	P
H22	Liverpool-Frodsham or Helsby via Gateacre, Halewood and Widnes	
H23	Liverpool-Chester via Halewood, Halebank and Widnes	
H24	Liverpool-Frodsham via Gateacre, Tarbock Green and Widnes	
H25	Liverpool-Runcorn via Speke and Widnes	P
H26	Liverpool-Cronton Colliery via Huyton	P
79	Rainhill Stoops-St. Helens	H NSu
89	Speke-St. Helens via Woolton, Huyton and Prescot	H R
89F	Ford Factory-St. Helens via Woolton, Huyton and Prescot	H R P

3. ST.HELENS CORPORATION (Independent Services)

110	St. Helens-Kirkby (5 Gate) via Eccleston and East Lancashire Road	P
111	St. Helens-Walton Hall Avenue (Littlewoods) via East Lancashire Road	P
112	St. Helens-Walton Hall Avenue (Stopgate Lane) via East Lancashire Road	P
113	St. Helens-Gillmoss (Napier Factory)	P
114	St. Helens-Melling (BICC Factory) via East Lancashire Road and Kirkby	P
118	St. Helens-Fazakerley	Race Days

CODE

L	Operated by Lancashire United Transport Ltd. (jointly with St. Helens, Leigh and Salford Corporations).
P	Operated at peak hours or factory times only.
H	Operated jointly with St. Helens Corporation.
H R	Operated jointly with St. Helens Corporation and Ribble.
J	Operated jointly with St. Helens and Wigan Corporations and Lancashire United Transport Ltd.
K	Peak hour short workings on 317 operated by St. Helens Corporation.
	The number 337 was not officially recognised by Ribble.
T	Tuesdays only.
Th	Thursdays only.
S	Saturdays only.
Sch	School service.
Smr Su	Summer Sundays only.
NSu	Not on Sundays.
NSSu	Not on Saturdays or Sundays.

48 The Annals of Liverpool Transport (Traffics changes) 1957-1986

EXPLANATION OF NOTES

(a) Where exact dates are given every endeavour has been made to ensure their accuracy. If there is some doubt, a question mark (?) is added.

(b) When the event is a cessation, the date given is the last day of operation. If a change is involved, the date given is the day on which the new facility commenced.

(c) The letters in the column immediately following the date refer to the operator and/or the mode of transport viz:

B	Liverpool Corporation (1957-69) or Merseyside PTE (1969-86) buses.
C	Crosville buses.
M	Merseyrail.
P	Buses from outside the PTE Area (e.g. St. Helens Corporation up to 1974, LUT, Greater Manchester Transport).
Q	Private Operators.
R	Ribble buses.
Tr	Liverpool Corporation trams involving track changes.

31.3.1957	BPR	90 extended from Rockford Avenue to Leeside Avenue, Kirkby.
23.4.1957	B	1, 1A, 23, 33, 33A, 39 Diverted to Seaforth via Grove St. and Regent Road.
29.4.1957	B	1 Dingle-Seaforth increased to 6-minute service in peak hours.
	B	1A Dingle-Litherland reduced to 12 min frequency and period of operation cut.
	B	1B Park St.-Bankhall extended to Millers Bridge.
	B	1C Pier Head-Seaforth curtailed at Strand Road.
14.9.1957	Tr	OFFICIAL LAST TRAM 6A Bowring Park-Pier Head) Withdrawn and replaced by
	Tr	40 Pagemoss-Pier Head) buses during the afternoon.
	B	6A, 40 Buses took over from trams during the afternoon and operated to tram time-table. Services extensively revised from following day.
	B	74A Huyton Stn.-City via Kingsway and Eaton Road withdrawn.
15.9.1957	B	6C Brookhouse Estate-Pier Head via Edge Lane, Brownlow Hill.
	B	6D Bowring Park-Pier Head via Edge Lane, London Road, Dale St.
	B	40 Huyton Stn.-Pier Head via Woolfall Heath, Brookside Ave and Brownlow Hill.
	B	12 Pagemoss-South Castle St. via Melwood Drive, Town Row, London Rd., Church Street.
	B	12A/B Leyfield Rd-Sir Thomas St. or Pier Head.
	B	74 Huyton Stn.-Sir Thomas St. or Pier Head via Kingsway, Prescot Rd, Dale St.
	B	75 Huyton Stn.-Sir Thomas St.or Pier Head via Pilch Lane, Old Swan, Edge Lne.
	B	74D Finch Lane-Sir Thomas St. or Pier Head via Barnfield Dr., Eaton Rd., Dale Street.
	B	76 Broadgreen Stn.-Pier Head via Wavertree, Brownlow Hill.
	B	506 Brookhouse Estate-South Castle St.(in) South John St.(out) via Edge Lane.(LIMITED STOP).
30.9.1957	BR	28, 53A Extended to Netherton (Magdalene Square).
7.10.1957	B	92A All day service introduced. Kirkby (Admin)-Pier Head.
4.11.1957	B	47A Croxteth (Willow Way)-Southbank Road (peak hours) commenced.
9.12.1957	B	12A Revised as Pagemoss-Sir Thomas St. or Pier Head via Town Row, Islington, Church St. 12B Withdrawn.
	B	75 Reverted to original route via West Derby Road and Pier Head service operated IN via Dale St. OUT via Whitechapel.
	B	74D Pier Head journeys rerouted as for 75 above. No.74B allocated for journeys to Leyfield Rd.
25.1.1958	BR	50/50A operated at peak hours only.
	BR	57A Extended from Bridle Avenue to Hereford Drive.
	BR	57 Reduced to peak hours only and operated to and from Old Haymarket only.
10.2.1958	B	85/85A Alternate off peak buses diverted to Garston (Vulcan St) as 85B, 85E.
	B	66 Pay as you enter buses introduced. Termini altered to Windfield Rd. Garston and Lee Park Ave. Gateacre. Peak hour journeys to and from Vulcan St. as 66A.

	B	88 Pay as you enter buses introduced. Section of route via Chapel Rd, Island Rd & Horrocks Ave. withdrawn.
30.3.1958	C	143 Liverpool-Warrington via Cronton rerouted via Edge Lane & journey time reduced.
31.3.1958	B	85 rerouted to serve Exchange Stn, inward via Dale St. and Moorfields and outward via Tithebarn St. and Hatton Garden.
	B	544 Northwood-South Castle St. (in) South John St. (out) Limited stop commenced.
	B	44D Reduced in frequency.
	R	L80 Seaforth Sands-Hillary Drive (peak hours) commenced.
12.5.1958	B	79C/79D Extended to Lee Park (Lee Park Ave/Lee Vale Rd).
19.5.1958	B	17C Terminus altered to South Castle St.(in) South John St.(out).
	B	544 Terminus altered to South Castle St.(in and out).
	B	35 Seaforth-Fazakerley extended to Northwood.
31.5.1958	BR	57 Journeys to and from Pier Head reinstated.
18.8.1958	BR	56 Extended to Netherton (Magdalene Square).
28.9.1958	PR	W6 Pier Head-Bold Colliery via Whiston and Rainhill (Ribble and St. Helens Corporation).
18.10.1958	R	411, 412 Alternate buses on 411 diverted via Town Green and numbered 412.
20.10.1958	B	1 Diverted via Wellington Rd, Grafton St. and Wapping.
	B	Original route 1 via Park Lane renumbered 1A. 1A renumbered 1E.
3.11.1958	R	W1 Ormskirk-Kirkby Industrial Estate (peak hours Mon. to Fri.) commenced.
17.11.1958	BR	24, 28 Terminus moved from Lime Street to Old Haymarket.
6.12.1958	R	311 Through service licensed Liverpool, Ormskirk, Chorley and Blackburn.
8.12.1958	B	24 Terminus reverted to Lime Street.
29.12.1958	B	506 Reduced to peak hours and Saturday afternoons only.
	BR	56 Diverted via Bailey Drive in lieu of Watts Lane and Park Lane.
	B	85A/B Journeys via Cathedral withdrawn except on Sundays up to 7.00pm.
5.1.1959	B	586 Garston-Central Station via Mather Ave. (Limited Stop, peak hours & Saturday afternoons) commenced.
6.4.1959	B	35, 44D, 544 Extended via Old Rough Lane, Bigdale Dr. Brookhey Dr. to Roughwood Dr.
2.5.1959	R	305, 307 Rerouted via Old Roan and Altway in lieu of Melling Road. Journeys (307) introduced between Liverpool and Altway (Bullbridge Lane).
11.5.1959	B	34 Rerouted via Melwood Drive in lieu of Yew Tree Lane.
19.5.1959	B	88 Extended to Halewood (Derby Arms) on weekdays.
1.6.1959	B	586 Extended to South Castle St. (in) South John St. (out) & withdrawn Sats pm.
5.7.1959	C	All Crosville services renumbered.
7.1.1960	B	School services numbered from 601 up.
28.2.1960	BCPR	One way traffic scheme, Ranelagh St., Clayton Sq., Lime St. and Gt. Charlotte Street.
28.3.1960	B	15D Kirkby (Cherryfield Drive)-Pier Head via Westhead Ave, County Rd. Journeys to Admin as 15E not stopping between Lower Lane and Moorgate Rd. on outward journeys. 92B Northwood-Pier Head commenced.
1.5.1960	B	82E Speke-Pier Head via Hale Road withdrawn.
2.5.1960	B	82D Increased in frequency and renumbered 82C.
16.5.1960	B	66 Reverted to Vulcan St. terminus and Windfield Rd. journeys withdrawn.(PAYE ceased in March). 10D Outward journeys via Primrose Drive and Hillside Rd. rerouted via Liverpool Rd.
13.6.1960	R	All services entering the city via Aintree transferred to new Skelhorne St. Bus Station.
20.6.1960	R	411/2, L5/6/15, S1/2/3, X27/37 Transferred to new Skelhorne St. Bus Stn.
28.6.1960	R	L1/2/3/4/8/30 Transferred to new Skelhorne St. Bus Stn.
29.10.1960	PR	317 Wigan-Billinge-Liverpool Saturday service withdrawn.
31.10.1960	B	86, 87 Use of 86 for complete clockwise journey, 87 anti-clockwise.
27.11.1960	C	H28 Liverpool-Burtonwood USAF withdrawn.
23.1.1961	B	92B Diverted via Richard Hesketh Drive and James Holt Ave in lieu of Kirkby Row.
17.2.1961	R	W1 Ormskirk-Kirkby withdrawn.
20.2.1961	R	W3 Burscough Bridge-Deysbrook Barracks works service commenced.
27.2.1961	B	9A Knowsley (Sugar Lane)-Pier Head via Stockbridge Lane and Dale St. commenced.
	B	9 Reduced in frequency.
20.3.1961	B	17C Terminus altered from South Castle St./South John St. to Central Stn.
23.4.1961	BPR	90 Extended from Leeside Avenue to Kirkby Station.
30.4.1961	C	H15 Liverpool-Huyton Lane (Whiston Lane) short journeys on H14 replaced by half hourly through service to Prescot and all H14 journeys diverted through Mosscroft Farm Estate.
20.5.1961	B	85 Off peak service extended from Windfield Rd. to Airport. Vulcan St. journeys withdrawn.
26.6.1961	BR	57A Extended from Hereford Drive to Netherton (Magdalene Square).

21.7.1961	C	Opening of Runcorn-Widnes Bridge. New through services started at 5.30pm.
		H20 Liverpool-Hunts Cross-Halewood-Widnes-Runcorn-Chester.
		H21 Liverpool-Hunts Cross-Carr Lane (formerly H20).
		H23 Liverpool-Tarbock-Widnes-Runcorn-Rocksavage-Chester.
		H24 Liverpool-Halewood-Widnes-Runcorn-Frodsham.
		H25 Liverpool-Speke-Widnes-Runcorn (Workmen's).
24.7.1961	BR	95B Netherton (Magdalene Sq.)-Gillmoss (Napier Factory) commenced.
1.8.1961	B	79C Diverted outwards via Paddington in lieu of Elizabeth St. & West Derby Street.
25.9.1961	R	L47/48 Liverpool-Hall Road Station new services commenced replacing L4 and L7.
13.11.1961	B	79B Gateacre Park Estate-South Castle St. via Barnham Drive, Wavertree & Church Street.
18.11.1961	R	L80 Revised and some journeys extended from Seaforth Sands to Liverpool.
		L85 Liverpool-Thornton (Nags Head) via Chesterfield Road commenced.
4.2.1962	B	86/87 Circular journeys on Sundays between 10.30 and 17.30 diverted via Springwood Avenue and Woolton Road in order to pass Cemetery.
12.3.1962	B	71 One trip am & pm to run via Parliament St., Challoner St. Wapping & Canning Place as 71D.
4.1962	B	City terminus of Airport coach service moved from Lord Nelson St. to new station entrance in Skelhorne St.
7.5.1962	B	77 Peak hour journeys extended from Penny Lane to Speke (Western Avenue) via Mather Avenue, Springwood Avenue, Hillfoot Road & Speke Hall Road (Mons to Sats).
14.5.1962	B	62 Speke (Western Avenue)-Kirkby Civic Centre) New Services
	B	63 Hunts Cross (Old Hutte Lane)-Kirkby Civic Centre)) Mon to Fri. peak
	B	64 Edge Lane (Southbank Road)-Kirkby Civic Centre)) hours commenced.
	B	65 Edge Lane (Southbank Road)-Speke (Western Avenue))
1.10.1962	BCPR	63,81,82,89F,500 Journeys introduced to and from Ford Factory, Halewood.
	C	H6 Pier Head-Runcorn (ICI, Heath Road) via Bowring Park & Huyton commenced.
18.10.1962	B	80E Croxteth Rd.-Pier Head operated inward only in am peak and out only in pm peak.
29.10.1962	B	78 Hunts Cross (Mackets Lane)-Pier Head via Kings Drive, Woolton Road, Wavertree (New all day service). Former service 78 renumbered 78A.
1.6.1963	R	303 Southport-Shirdley Hill-Maghull-Kirkby commenced.
29.7.1963	B	19 Kirkby (Admin)-Pier Head via Hornhouse Lane curtailed off-peak at Lower Lane as 19C.
	B	19A Pier Head-Kirkby (Admin) via Moorgate Road extended off-peak to East Lancs Road (Hornhouse Lane) as 19E.
30.9.1963	R	340 Liverpool-Maghull (Dodds Lane/Moss Lane) via Hall Lane & Northway commenced.
	R	341 Liverpool-Robbins Island via Maghull & Liverpool Road commenced.
	R	361 Liverpool-Robbins Island via Northway commenced.
5.10.1963	B	22, 506, 586 W'drawn on Saturdays and many other services reduced in frequency.
28.10.1963	B	78A revised to run Hunts Cross (Old Hutte Lane)-Pier Head via Mackets Lane, Woolton Rd. & Wavertree (Peak hours).
29.10.1963	B	79B extended to Thurne Way and from South Castle Street to Pier Head.
13.1.1964	BR	51, 52, 55, 58 diverted in Litherland via Hawthorne Road in lieu of Sefton St. due to introduction of one way traffic scheme.
10.2.1964	B	592 Northwood-Pier Head Limited Stop introduced. Frequency of 92B reduced.
		92A Pier Head-Kirkby (Admin) via Quarry Green diverted via Civic Centre and Britonside Ave and extended to Pagemoss on Sats & Suns pm.
		44D augmented to Lower Lane (44E) Mon to Sat mornings and evenings.
		19E Pier Head-Hornhouse Lane renumbered 19A, 19C renumbered 19E.
		68 Diverted via Aigburth Vale, Queens Drive & Dovedale Rd. to serve Ministry of Pensions Hospital & Pier Head-Ministry of Pensions Hospital service withdrawn.
25. 5.1964	B	78 Extended to Leathers Lane via Higher Road.
		Airport coach service diverted via Ullet Road and Mather Avenue in lieu of Aigburth Road and picking up point introduced at Penny Lane.
27.6.1964	R	310 Rerouted in Maghull via Northway in lieu of Liverpool Road South and Hall Lane.
		340 Rerouted in Maghull via Liverpool Rd South & Hall Lane in lieu of part of Northway.
		305 Liverpool-Barrow Nook extended to Rainford.
20.7.1964	B	6D Extended to Sheppard Avenue as 6A.
5.9.1964	R	W11 Lydiate-Seaforth Sands peak hour service commenced.
26.10.1964	B	21 Dingle-Aintree withdrawn.
18.1.1965	B	20 Diverted northwards via Sir Thomas St. & Dale St.; southwards via Crosshall Street.
25.1.1965	B	15B Tower Hill Estate-Kirkby Civic Centre commenced.

29.1.1965	B	14A Gillmoss-Pier Head via Utting Avenue East withdrawn off peak.
30.1.1965	B	15B Tower Hill Estate-Pier Head (15D reduced in frequency).
22.2.1965	B	68 Diverted via Woolton Road in lieu of Taggart Avenue, Dunbabin Road & Queens Drive.
		73/73A Diverted in via Queens Drive, Woolton Road in lieu of part of Dunbabin Road and out via Queens Drive, Five Ways and Childwall Priory Road. (Due to construction of continuous island in Queens Drive).
11.4.1965	B	Pier Head Bus Station opened.
12.4.1965	B	12 Extended from South Castle Street to Pier Head.
		Cantril Farm-South Castle Street journeys numbered 12C.
25.4.1965	CP	79 Rainhill Stoops-St. Helens commenced.(Crosville & St. Helens Corporation).
1.5.1965	R	L25 Liverpool-Crosby-Thornton-Ford (Fleetwoods Lane) service commenced.
28.6.1965	R	211 Liverpool-Upholland via Kirkby Limited Stop industrial service commenced.
12.7.1965	B	9A Extended to Frederick Lunt Avenue, Knowsley.
2.8.1965	BCR	London Road and Islington became one way streets. Extensive rerouting of services.
31.8.1965	B	78 Extended from Leathers Lane/Higher Road to Halewood Village via Leathers Lane and Baileys Lane and increased from 20 to 15 minute frequency.
		83 Extended from Woodend Avenue via Higher Road and as 78 to Halewood.
5.9.1965	C	H19/20 Rerouted in Halewood via Leathers Lane in lieu of Baileys Lane.
4.12.1965	B	100 City Circle introduced.
1.1.1966	BR	Old Haymarket closed to ordinary traffic. Bus lane introduced in St. Johns Lane.
		51 to 59 Pier Head journeys rerouted outwards via Church Street, Clayton Square, Lime Street & St. Johns Lane.
		12A, 74, 74D and 75 outward journeys rerouted via Sir Thomas Street and Dale Street.
10.1.1966	B	33/33A/34 Diverted via Kirkdale Road, Smith Street in lieu of Whittle Street.
2.5.1966	B	586 Airport-South Castle Street/South John Street. All day limited stop service replacing Airport coach service.
	B	85/85A Airport journeys curtailed at Banks Road (Windfield Road).
8.5.1966	BCR	One way traffic scheme — Dale St., Tithebarn St., Whitechapel &c. General rerouting of services.
31.5.1966	B	88 Rerouted in Halewood via Leathers Lane in lieu of Baileys Lane. Sunday service extended from Hunts Cross to Halewood.
5.6.1966	BP	40, 74, 75, 89 Diverted southward in Huyton via Lathom Road instead of Derby Street.
25.6.1966	B	Outward Wavertree Road routes diverted via Mount Vernon and Towerlands Street.
1.8.1966	B	11 Extended to Huyton Station over route of 74 which was withdrawn.
7.8.1966	CP	79 Rainhill Stoops-St. Helens withdrawn evenings and Sundays.
30.8.1966	B	6C, 6D, 40 Rerouted inwards via Marmaduke Street in lieu of Towerlands Street.
5.9.1966	B	510 Diverted outwards via Erskine St., Low Hill in lieu of Moss St., Prescot Street.
12.9.1966	R	All services to Skelhorne St. Bus Stn diverted via Seymour St., Copperas Hill & Skelhorne St.
26.9.1966	BR	55 Rerouted to Sefton Estate (Buckley Hill Lane) via Almonds Turn.
	BR	55A Peak hour service on 55 to St. Nicholas Drive continued.
	R	201 Extended from Skelmersdale Arms to Tawd Bridge.
	R	101 operated in two parts. Liverpool-Ormskirk and Ormskirk-Preston.
	R	340 Rerouted via Eastway, Deyes Lane & Moss Lane.
31.10.1966	B	Erskine Street became one way out. All West Derby Road and Everton Road services rerouted inwards via Low Hill and Prescot Street.
7.11.1966	B	78, 83, 88 Terminal loop introduced at Halewood — via Leathers Lane, Wood Lane and Hollies Road, returning via Baileys Lane and Leathers Lane.
	B	(70) Diverted via Huyton Hey Road in lieu of Tarbock Road.
5.12.1966	B	586 Extended from South Castle Street to Exchange Station.
12.12.1966	B	900 Northwood-Aintree Station (Kirkby Rail Link) Mon-Fri peak hours commenced.
4.3.1967	B	84 Speke-Woolton-Penny Lane withdrawn.
11.3.1967	B	900 Withdrawn.
3.4.1967	B	74D Renumbered 74 and Finch Lane terminus redesignated 'DOVECOT'.
		81D Speke-Bootle — all journeys to Bootle numbered 81.
8.4.1967	BR	55A All day service introduced — St. Nicholas Drive-St. Johns Lane or Pier Head.
30.4.1967	B	23 Seaforth-Old Haymarket via Strand Road withdrawn.
1.5.1967	B	24 Seaforth-Old Haymarket rerouted via Marsh Lane instead of Knowsley Rd.
30.5.1967	B	586 Reverted to Mon-Fri peak operation to South Castle St. (in) & from South John St.(out).
12.6.1967	B	12C Cantril Farm (Haswell Drive)-Pier Head via Melwood Drive commenced.
7.8.1967	BR	1E, 16 Diverted on journeys from Seaforth to Litherland etc. via Crosby Rd. South and Church Road in lieu of Seaforth Road.

19.8.1967	R	221 Liverpool-Tawd Bridge Limited Stop (Sats and Suns) commenced.
	R	A.B.C. Formby Circulars commenced.
23.10.1967	B	London Rd./Church St. routes and 3 & 500 diverted inwards via Seymour St., Copperas Hill and Skelhorne Street.
11.3.1968	B	11 week municipal bus strike commenced.
19.4.1968	R	221 Withdrawn.
20.4.1968	R	201 Liverpool-Tawd Bridge extended to Hall Green.
5.5.1968	C	H8-13 terminus in Prescot moved from Hope Street to Grosvenor Road.
27.5.1968	B	Services resumed after strike.
		Services 2, 4B, 4C, 4D, 5B, 5C, 7C, 7D, 11, 13C, 17C, 24, 31, 74, 85, 100, 500, 506, 510, 586, 592 remained suspended.
		Services. 6D, 33, 39, 77 resumed only at Mon-Fri peak hours.
		Services 6C, 30, 40, 68, 71, 79B, 80, 81, 93 had restricted services only.
17.6.1968	B	12C Extended along Haswell Drive to underpass at Birtle Croft.
24.6.1968	B	86/87 Some journeys diverted via Mill St. instead of Princes Park as 85C in & 85E out.
29.7.1968	B	13C Reinstated with 30-minute frequency.
5.8.1968	B	60, 81, 81D Diverted to Bootle (New Strand) in lieu of Bootle (Oriel Road) Station.
9.9.1968	BR	48, 49 Bootle Circular commenced (joint with Ribble).
29.9.1968	R	L50 Bootle-Thornton withdrawn.
30.9.1968	B	5 Rerouted via Hunts Cross Avenue and Halewood Drive.
	B	85 reinstated as OMO and temporary 85C/E journeys withdrawn.
	R	General revision of services in Crosby.
		C1, C2 Crosby local services.
		L35 Liverpool-Thornton via Derby Road.
		L1/L8 made limited stop and converted to one man operation.
		391 Crosby-Seaforth-Maghull (peak hours).
		392 Bootle (New Strand)-Maghull (all day service).
		411, 412 Renumbered 381, 382.
14.10.1968	B	81 Diverted via Balliol Rd northbound in lieu of Merton Rd.
	B	24 Reinstated.
28.10.1968	B	12C Extended to Waterpark Drive-New Shopping Area and increased.
11.1968	BQ	Illegal service by H.F. Edwards (Reliance Coaches) between Cantril Farm and Edge Lane licensed to Corporation but operated by Edwards on hire.
4.11.1968	B	14A, 14C, 14D, 18A, 37, 47A Diverted via Storrington Ave in lieu of Carr Lane East.
9.11.1968	B	100 City Circle reinstated on Saturdays only.
2.12.1968	B	4, 5 Terminal arrangements at Woolton revised to Hunts Cross Ave (Halewood Drive) and 5 reverted to Manor Road route.
		99 Diverted southwards via St. Oswald's Street in lieu of Cunningham Road.
26.1.1969	B	85 Sunday diversion via Anglican Cathedral withdrawn.
17.2.1969	B	17C Reinstated and extended to run Pier Head-Fazakerley replacing 13C.
	B	66 Revised to operate between Garston (Windfield Road) and Naylorsfield.
	B	88A Temporary extension of 88 from Halewood to Netherley (Woodlands Estate) via Church Road and Gerrards Lane.
27.2.1969	R	314 Knowsley-Ormskirk (Th) withdrawn.
1.4.1969		MERSEYSIDE PASSENGER TRANSPORT AUTHORITY CONSTITUTED.
12.5.1969	B	73A Extended to Naylorsfield.
	B	73, 73A Peak period terminus removed from Castle St. to South Castle St. and inward peak hour journeys to be via Church Street not Dale Street (as 73C).
	B	79B Extended from Gateacre Park to Lee Park, off peak & renumbered 79A.
2.6.1969	B	500 Speke-Kirkby reinstated with 30 minute frequency.
	B	100 City Circle reinstated on Mondays to Fridays.
14.6.1969	B	33A Grants Gardens-Seaforth & 39 Pier Head-Seaforth withdrawn.
16.6.1969	B	1A, 1E Rerouted via Bath St., Waterloo Rd. and Regent Rd. and 1E extended from Litherland to Magdalene Square via Ford and Fleetwoods Lane.
	B	33 Extended from Breckfield Road to Grants Gardens via Breck Road & Everton Road.
	B	60 Rerouted in Bootle via Merton Road and Washington Parade in lieu of Stanley Road and Marsh Lane.
	B	81 Rerouted in Bootle via Balliol Road, Oriel Road and Washington Parade in lieu of Stanley Road and Marsh Lane.
23.6.1969	B	Various services between Gt. Crosshall St. and Islington diverted via northern tunnel relief

flyover (Churchill Way North). 72 and 85 excepted.

29.6.1969	R	L33 Liverpool Freshfield via Derby Road (Summer Sundays) commenced.
4.8.1969	B	1E Diverted via Sefton Street in lieu of Mill Street.
16.8.1969	C	H8/13 Supplementary journeys on Saturdays between Huyton Town Centre and Prescot.
8.9.1969	B	79 Netherley (Caldway Drive)-Pier Head via Brownlow Hill, Church St. commenced.
	B	79B/C/D Lee Park-Pier Head revised. 79D (Dale St./Tithebarn St.) service withdrawn on Mon-Fri evenings, all day Sats and Suns in favour of 79B via Pembroke Place, Lime Street and Church St. 79B Gateacre Park journeys renumbered 79A.
22.9.1969	B	85 rerouted via Churchill Way North in lieu of Byrom St. & William Brown St.
10.11.1969	B	93 Full service restored.
	B	592 Service reinstated.
	B	80 Diverted via Allerton Rd. and Queens Drive in lieu of Elm Hall Drive along which it had recently operated against the one way traffic flow.
1.12.1969	B	LIVERPOOL, BIRKENHEAD AND WALLASEY TRANSPORT UNDERTAKINGS ACQUIRED BY THE MERSEYSIDE PASSENGER TRANSPORT EXECUTIVE.
1.12.1969	B	15D Extended in Tower Hill Estate to Shevington's Lane (Highfield).
	B	85 Reverted to William Brown Street in lieu of Churchill Way North.
5.12.1969	B	510 Prescot-Central Station limited stop reinstated.
5.1.1970	B	Bus Economy Tickets introduced.
1.3.1970	BCR	Churchill Way South opened and all buses travelling inwards via St. Johns Lane, Whitechapel and Crosshall Street diverted.
27.4.1970	B	478 Halewood-Pier Head peak hour express commenced.
26.5.1970	B	79 Pier Head-Netherley extended to Woodlands (Winster Road).
	B	88A cut back from Woodlands to Halewood as 88.
13.6.1970	R	M1-5 Maghull Local Services commenced.
14.6.1970	B	86, 87 Circular working ceased except at peak hours and Sunday journeys via Springwood Ave and Allerton Cemetery withdrawn.
	B	480 Garston-Pier Head peak hour express commenced.
29.6.1970	B	London Rd./Church St. routes reverted inward to London Rd. (lower half) and Lime St. in lieu of Seymour St., Copperas Hill and Skelhorne St. 3, 500 remained on latter route.
	B	Ingoe Lane closed 92, 93, 500 diverted via Valley Road.
6.1970	BC	London Rd. inward routes diverted via Daulby Street and Pembroke Place in lieu of upper half of London Road.
10.8.1970	B	479 Netherley-Pier Head peak hour express commenced.
6.9.1970	C	H19-24, Some journeys converted to sd OMO.
7.9.1970	BC	9, 10, 510, H2-4 all outward buses diverted via Norton Street and upper part of London Road in lieu of Islington.
27.9.1970	R	L33 Liverpool-Freshfield via Derby Rd. (Sunday) withdrawn.
14.12.1970	B	20 Rerouted via Vauxhall Road and Boundary Street in lieu of Scotland Road.
25.1.1971	R	M1-3 Maghull Local Services withdrawn on Saturdays.
26.4.1971	B	412 Cantril Farm-Exchange Station peak hour express commenced.
	B	486 Garston-Pier Head peak hour express commenced.
	B	97C Cantril Farm-Kirkby works service commenced.
10.5.1971	B	11 Huyton Stn-South Castle St. new service replacing suspended routes 7, 11, 74.
15.5.1971	R	241 Liverpool-Upholland (SSu) via Tanhouse Limited stop commenced.
	R	301 Withdrawn on Saturdays and Sundays, 307 withdrawn on Sundays.
19.6.1971	R	C1 Extended in Thornton to Long Lane.
20. 6.1971	C	H12/13 One man dual purpose buses with Johnson Fare boxes introduced.
28.6.1971	B	Opening of Kingsway Tunnel — 31/32 Liverpool-Liscard-New Brighton commenced.
8.8.1971	B	Knowsley Safari Park tours commenced from Pier Head, Garston, Speke, Bootle, Netherton and Kirkby.
16.8.1971	B	65A Netherley-Edge Lane industrial service commenced.
6.9.1971	B	Bus Economy Ticket coverage completed on PTE buses.
25.9.1971	R	311 Through service to Blackburn broken up. Service operated between Liverpool and Ormskirk only.
27.9.1971	B	101 Kirkby Industrial Estate-Tower Hill commenced.
	B	92 Curtailed to operate Page Moss-Walton only.
	B	93 Curtailed to operate at weekday peak hours only.
	B	592 Withdrawn and replaced by 492 Northwood-Pier Head peak hour express non stop Civic Centre (Later James Hoult Ave) to Islington.
	B	30A Sefton Estate (Northern Perimeter Road)-Pier Head via Aintree commenced.

	BR	53, 53A Black Bull-Netherton reduced to a few peak hour trips.
	BR	55 Extended to new terminus at Northern Perimeter Road, Sefton Estate.
4.10.1971	B	405 Woolton-South Castle St 'Rapidride' service commenced.
31.10.1971	C	H19-24 Revised as follows and converted to OMO:-
	C	H19 Liverpool-Hunts Cross-Halewood.
	C	H21 Liverpool-Helsby or Chester-Liverpool via Halewood, Widnes and Runcorn Shopping City.
	C	H22 Liverpool-Chester or Helsby-Liverpool via Tarbock Green, Widnes & Runcorn Shopping City.
	C	H23 Liverpool-Chester or Helsby-Liverpool (Suns) via Tarbock Green, Widnes & Runcorn Cenotaph.
	C	H24 Liverpool-Frodsham via Gateacre, Halewood, Widnes and Runcorn Cenotaph.
8.11.1971	B	414 Croxteth-Pier Head 'Rapidride' service commenced.
30.11.1971	R	305 Liverpool-Rainford withdrawn.
26.12.1971	B	492 rerouted via Westvale.
3. 1.1972	B	New bus station at Kirkby Civic Centre opened.
8.1.1972	BCR	Weekly 'Traveller Ticket' introduced at £1.95.
30.1.1972	BC	New agreement between NBC and PTE. Minimum fares abolished on Crosville buses and limited stops introduced on certain sections within the city.
	C	H1, H25 diverted via Leece Street in lieu of Upper Duke St. and Canning St.
31.1.1972	B	66 Extended via Naylorsfield Dr. & Caldway Dr. to Netherley (Tothale Turn).
	B	73A Diverted at peak hours via Childwall Valley Rd. & Caldway Drive to Naylorsfield.
	B	100 Peak hour service between Exchange Station and Lime Street commenced.
26.2.1972	R	325 Downholland-Ormskirk (ThS) withdrawn.
27.3.1972	B	100 City Circle renamed 'Cityride'.
1.4.1972	B	'Soccerbus' services introduced from Gillmoss and Edge Lane.
10.4.1972	B	Two limited stop outward trips from Adelphi to Ford Factory numbered 582 but soon withdrawn due to lack of support.
17.4.1972	C	H8-13 Prescot terminus moved from Grosvenor Rd. to St. Helens Rd.(Grammar School).
6.5.1972	R	201 Rerouted in Skelmersdale via Gillibrands on Mon-Fri and renumbered 205. Unchanged on Sats and Suns.
	R	211 Rerouted in Skelmersdale and renumbered 265.
	R	266 Liverpool-Upholland via Kirkby and Digmoor (Limited Stop NSu) commenced.
8.5.1972	R	245 Liverpool-Upholland via Altway and Gillibrands (Mon to Fri) commenced.
	B	15D, 101 Extensions in Tower Hill-15D to Moorcroft, 101 to Highfield.
22.5.1972	B	78 Rerouted via Hunts Cross Avenue in lieu of Halewood Road.
21.8.1972	B	Eastbourne Street closed. 14D, 15, 15D, 19, 19A in via Low Hill, and Prescot Road, out via Brunswick Road and Everton Road.
29.8.1972	B	400 Speke, 438 Halewood & 439 Netherley-Seaforth 'Rapidride' services commenced.
4.9.1972	B	412 Cantril Farm-Exchange Station extended to Pier Head.
18.9.1972	R	M5 Maghull Local Service train connections established.
	C	H99 Mosscroft Farm-Huyton Station commenced.
21.9.1972	B	19 diverted via Breck Rd. & Everton Rd. inwards. (Queens Rd. & Aubrey St. closed)
28.10.1972	B	(Wirral Division) Soccerbus services from Bromborough introduced.
4.11.1972	C	H21, H22 New Runcorn Shopping City bus station opened.
20.11.1972	B	A1 Aintree-Netherton-Sefton rail feeder (returning via Giro) commenced.
10.12.1972	BPR	36, 90, 93, 101, 500 Rerouted via Britonside Avenue in lieu of County Road.
1.1.1973	B	34C Cantril Farm-Seaforth industrial service commenced.
	PR	39, 317, 320 Rerouted out via Brownlow Hill, Edge Lane & Holt Road, in via Towerlands St.
29.1.1973	B	73 Rerouted in Woolton out via Kings Drive, in via Manor Road.
	B	79A Rerouted via Grange Lane, Gateacre in lieu of Woolton Road & Gateacre Brow.
19.3.1973	B	36, 93, 101, 500 Rerouted via Park Brow Drive instead of part of Broad Lane.
	B	438 Rerouted in Woolton via Mackets Lane and additional stops introduced.
25.3.1973	B	72, 73, 85 diverted via Hood St. on closure of St. Johns Lane to inward traffic.
15.4.1973	C	New bus station opened at Church Street, Prescot — H8-14 diverted.
6.5.1973	B	92 Diverted to operate Page Moss-Bootle (New Strand) via Breeze Hill & Merton Road.
4.6.1973	B	43 Cantril Farm-Edge Lane (Southbank Rd) works service commenced.
9.7.1973	B	92 rerouted via Balliol Road in lieu of Merton Road.
8.1973	Q	Halewood-Old Swan minibus service operated under Sec.30 permit by J & M Coaches.
20.8.1973	B	42A Penny Lane-Edge Lane (Southbank Rd) via Wavertree Rd. & Durning Rd. works service.
	B	1, 1E rerouted via Beresford Road due to closure of Wellington Rd.
28.8.1973	B	44 Pier Head-Knowsley Industrial Estate (South) service commenced.
3.9.1973	R	W15 Crosby-Netherton and W16 Crosby-Litherland industrial services commenced.

21.10.1973	B	76 Broadgreen-Pier Head withdrawn.
	C	H16 Huyton (Elizabeth Road)-Pier Head & H19 Halewood-Pier Head withdrawn.
22.10.1973	B	11 Extended in Huyton to Pluckington Farm.
	B	40 Extended in Huyton to Elizabeth Road via Huyton Hey Road.
	C	H11 renumbered H7 to avoid confusion with 11.
	C	H12 Prescot-Pier Head via Windy Arbour Road diverted via Lickers Lane.
	C	H14 Prescot-Pier Head via Huyton Ln. diverted over 76 route and renumbered 76.
	C	H15 Prescot-Pier Head via Lickers Lane and Edge Lane (peak hours).
	C	H18 Prescot-Huyton Station via Lickers Lane (sd OMO).
	C	H20 Diverted via Gateacre & Hough Green and terminated at Runcorn Shopping City.
	B	66 Diverted via Belle Vale District Centre.
	B	79A Diverted to Belle Vale District Centre in lieu of Lee Park.
	B	79E Belle Vale District Centre-Pier Head (off peak) via Childwall Valley Road.
4.11.1973	C	H12 Reverted to original route via Windy Arbour Road.
10.12.1973	B	1, 1E diverted via Harlow St. in lieu of Beresford Road.
	C	418/9 Heswall-City Centre 'Rapidride' services commenced.
15.12.1973	BR	54 Revised as Bootle (New Strand)-Wango Lane(54) or Netherton (Village Green)(54A).
11.2.1974	B	100 Freeride experiment—Mons to Fris off peak and all day Saturday.
4.3.1974	B	79B/C/D Inward journey rerouted via Lee Park Avenue in lieu of Belle Vale Rd.
17.3.1974	BCPR	Church Street closed to vehicular traffic. Services diverted via Roe Street, Hood Street Gyratory and Whitechapel.
	BPR	11, 26/27, 39, 87/73 & 80 (peak), 317, 320, 544 diverted into new Central Bus Stn, Paradise St.
	B	510 City terminus moved from Central Station to South Castle Street.
24.3.1974	C	H6 Pier Head-Prescot via Lickers Lane commenced. H6, H15, H18 retimed.
1.4.1974	P	MERSEYSIDE PTE ABSORBED ST. HELENS AND SOUTHPORT MUNICIPAL TRANSPORT UNDERTAKINGS.
	B	80E Speke (Eastern Avenue)-Sefton General Hospital (service for visitors) commenced.
27.4.1974	BR	39, 317, 320 Ribble share passed to Lancashire United Transport.
5.5.1974	C	H1, H25 Rerouted via Central Avenue in lieu of Hale Road, Speke.
6.5.1974	B	Tunnel Night Service—some journeys extended to Lime Street Station.
9.9.1974	B	101 Tower Hill-Kirkby renumbered 13.
23.9.1974	B	18C Pier Head-Muirhead Avenue East extended to Fazakerley.
27.9.1974	Q	Edwards (Reliance) Cantril Farm-Edge Lane service withdrawn.
20.10.1974	R	Ormskirk depot closed. Skelmersdale depot opened.
25.11.1974	B	97C Extended to Barons Hey in Cantril Farm.
29.11.1974	B	92 Extended to operate Crosby (Hall Road)-Huyton (Civic Centre).
21.12.1974	B	30/30A All journeys operated through to Netherton.
31.12.1974	B	42A Penny Lane-Edge Lane via Durning Road withdrawn.
1.3.1975	R	201,241 Liverpool-Skelmersdale services withdrawn.
2.3.1975	R	101 Preston-Liverpool remaining through journeys split at Ormskirk.
	R	310 Withdrawn on Sundays. Converted to OMO.
	R	331 Ormskirk-Liverpool via Town Green and Maghull (NSu).
	R	340 Extended to Park Lane, converted to OMO and withdrawn on Sundays.
	R	341 Robbins Island-Liverpool diverted via Hornby Rd., Marsh Lane & Stanley Rd.
	R	350 Maghull (Park Lane)-Liverpool Sundays only replacing 310 and 340.
	R	381 withdrawn on Sundays when all journeys follow route 382 via Town Green.
	R	306 Liverpool-Ormskirk via Waddicar, Kirkby and Aughton replacing 301 journeys
	R	307 Liverpool-Melling Rock extended to Maghull (Green Park).
	R	355 Liverpool-Kirkby-Tanhouse-Up Holland commenced.
	R	205, 245 renumbered 305, 345.
	R	266 Revised in Skelmersdale, renumbered 336.
	R	265 Liverpool-Upholland-Pimbo, renumbered 335.
23.3.1975	R	Local passengers carried on Ribble buses between Rotunda and Black Bull.
18.7.1975	BM	Liverpool Central Low Level station closed for alterations and train service curtailed at James Street. Free bus service 'Railride' provided.
28.7.1975	Q	65B, 65C Halewood-Old Swan licensed to PTE but run by J & M Coaches minibuses on hire.
28.9.1975	BR	51, 57A, 58, 59 operated by Ribble only; 55, 55A to be operated by MPTE only.
	BR	57 Pier Head-Orrell reduced to one Mon-Fri journey.
5.12.1975	B	24, L30, L92 (and 392 on Saturdays) withdrawn.
6.12.1975	R	Minimum fares removed between Seaforth and Liverpool except on X27 and X37.

	R	L1, L8 Altered from limited stop to all stops & L8 rerouted via Marsh Lane.
	R	L5, L15 Reduced to occasional journeys & L25 to mainly peak hours & Sundays.
	R	L6 Most journeys extended from Long Lane to Freshfield as S3.
	R	L22, L23 Crosby-Fazakerley via Ford, Netherton and Aintree commenced.
	R	L85 Extended to Runnells Lane with alternate journeys via Edge Lane (L86).
18.12.1975	B	92 Diverted in Knowsley via East Lancs Road and School Lane.
16.1.1976	C	H6 curtailed as Prescot-Huyton Town Centre via Seel Road.
8.3.1976	B	1E Curtailed to operate Netherton-Pier Head only.
	R	29 Crosby-Fazakerley Hospital commenced replacing L22/23.
	B	30A Alternate trips diverted to Crosby via Thornton as 30C replacing L22/23.
19.6.1976	R	303 Kirkby-Southport curtailed to run between Kirkby and Lydiate Mons-Fris; withdrawn Sats.
12.12.1976	C	H2/3 Pier Head-Rainhill-Warrington converted to dd OMO. H4 (via Bridge Rd) withdrawn except for one peak hour journey.
10.1.1977	B	92 Huyton-Crosby (Hall Road) curtailed at Crosby Bus Station, rerouted via Knowsley Road in lieu of Linacre Road and diverted via Waterloo Interchange.
	R	211 New service Bootle (New Strand)-Kirkby via Sefton and Maghull commenced.
	R	351 New service Bootle-Ormskirk via Crosby and Maghull commenced replacing 382
	R	C3 New service (NSu) Crosby Bus Stn-Chesterfield Rd.-Waterloo-Crosby.
	R	C2, L1, L2, L5, L6, L8, L15, L25, L47, L48, L80, L90, S1, S3, 381, 382 withdrawn.
	R	L3 converted to OMO.
	R	L9 Diverted to operate Crosby (Bus Stn)-Waterloo Interchange (NSSu—peak hours).
	R	L21 New service Crosby (Hall Rd)-Bootle (New Strand) via College Road, Waterloo. Interchange, Sandy Road and Hawthorne Road commenced.
	R	L35 Curtailed to run Liverpool-Crosby Bus Stn and diverted via Oriel Rd. & Marsh Lane.
	R	L45 New service Liverpool-Thornton (Runnells Lane) via Knowsley Rd, Waterloo Interchange and The Northern Road.
	R	L85 Rerouted inwards via Edge Lane in lieu of Lydiate Lane.
	R	S2 Liverpool-Southport rerouted via Endbutt Lane and Waterloo Interchange.
	R	S4 New service Freshfield-Waterloo Interchange-(Liverpool peak) via Endbutt Lane.
	BR	50, 50A, 51, 52 Withdrawn.
	B	71, 87, 414, 492 Withdrawn.
5.3.1977	R	C3 Anti-clockwise journeys renumbered C4.
29.4.1977	M	Liverpool Exchange Station closed.
2.5.1977	M	'Link' railway line connecting Sandhills with Liverpool Central Low Level and Moorfields Station opened. Southport and Ormskirk trains extended and Kirkby electric railway service commenced.
9.5.1977	M	James Street-Liverpool Central Deep Level 'Loop' railway line opened.
	B	100 Peak hour Exchange Stn-Lime St. & Railride services withdrawn.
30.5.1977	B	69 New Hospital Service Netherley-Broadgreen Hospital commenced.
	B	71 New Industrial Service Speke-Huyton (Wilson Road) commenced.
	B	98D Journeys on 98 extended to Prescot (Oliver Lyme Rd.).
9.7.1977	R	211, 351, L21, L45 Journeys to New Strand via Marsh Lane in lieu of Merton Road.
11.7.1977	R	211, 351 Most peak journeys to terminate at Balliol Road instead of New Strand.
13.8.1977	R	59 Diverted via Hawthorne Road in lieu of Orrell Road, Watts Lane. Some peak journeys retained on old route as 59A.
3.9.1977	R	391, 392, L21 Converted to OMO.
2.10.1977	B	98D Withdrawn after operation.
30.10.1977	M	Lime Street low level station on 'Loop' line opened.
12.11.1977	R	305, 345, 355 converted to OMO.
11.12.1977	R	350 Some Sun. journeys rerouted via Eastway & Foxhouse Lane instead of Deyes Lane.
3.1.1978	M	Liverpool Central-Garston electric train service commenced.
16.1.1978	B	Tunnel Night Service extension to Lime Street Stn withdrawn.
28.1.1978	R	57A Converted to OMO.
1.4.1978	R	300, 302, 341 converted to OMO.
8.5.1978	M	Moorfields Wirral Line platform opened.
31.7.1978	M	Full Moorfields station concourse opened.
3.9.1978	C	H6 Prescot-Huyton extended to Pier Head by original route.
4.9.1978	C	H9 New service Prescot-Huyton via Whiston Hosp & Dragon Lane (NSu and evenings).
	C	H9, H10 Wilson Road journeys renumbered H8X and H7X respectively.
	C	H13 Diverted via Wilson Rd (double run between Cronton Rd. & Huntley & Palmers)
	B	3 and 85 merged as 85 Garston-Walton.

	B	9C Diverted to Lyme Cross via Primrose Drive and Knowsley Lane replacing 9 (withdrawn).
	B	11 Extended from Huyton to Cantril Farm via Longview Drive and Woolfall Heath Ave.
	B	12A Extended from Sir Thomas Street to Pier Head.
	B	16 Seaforth-Pier Head to be peak hour service only NSSu.
	B	20A New experimental service Field Lane-Aigburth, evenings and Sundays only.
	B	21 New experimental service Field Lane-Aigburth, evenings and Sundays only via Sir Thomas Street, Hood Street, Renshaw Street and Berry Street.
	B	25 Extended from Aigburth Vale to Garston, Banks Road.
	BR	48/49 Bootle Circular withdrawn.
	B	55A Ford-Old Haymarket/Pier Head withdrawn. 55 increased in frequency.
	B	66, 88 Linked as Circular. Garston-Netherley-Halewood-Garston.
	B	82C Pier Head-Speke (Eastern Ave) via Park Road renumbered 82.
	B	84 Speke (Eastern Ave)-Garston Station commenced.
	B	510 South Castle St.-Prescot limited stop service withdrawn.
30.9.1978	R	C1, C3, C4 w'drawn and replaced by reinstatement of C2 ext'd to Runnells Lane.
	R	L9, L45, L85, S2 withdrawn.
	R	303 Kirkby-Lydiate & 336/355 Liverpool-Skelmersdale withdrawn.
	B	30C Crosby-Pier Head withdrawn.
1.10.1978	R	C5 Crosby-Thornton (Long Lane) via Quarry Lane. 4 journeys NSSu.
	R	L22, L23 Crosby-Fazakerley reinstated and diverted via Waterloo Interchange replacing 29.
	R	L81 New service Thornton-Liverpool via Chesterfield Road, Waterloo, Knowsley Road, Balliol Road and Pier Head (L35 reduced to peak hours NSSu).
	R	S5 Freshfield Station-Liverpool replacing S2.
	R	S4 Freshfield Roundabout (Southport Rd)-Liverpool (off peak service only).
	R	211, 351 Rerouted via Green Park, Maghull.
	R	Formby Circulars revised and designated 1-4 instead of A,B,C,D,E.
	R	395-396 Skelmersdale-Kirkby commenced replacing 336, 355.
	B	92 Rerouted in Crosby via The Northern Road replacing L45.
29.10.1978		Zone Tickets introduced.
1.12.1978	R	X37 Liverpool-Southport limited stop withdrawn.
20.1.1979	R	315 Ormskirk-Formby extended from Cross Green to Town Centre.
27.1.1979	B	317 St. Helens-Liverpool withdrawn.
29.1.1979	B	89 Converted to OMO (PTE buses only).
12.5.1979	R	211, 351 extended from Bootle to Skelhorne St. to give Knowsley Rd. a city service.
4.6.1979	R	395/6 Skelmersdale-Kirkby extended from Bus Stn to Admin Gate Mons to Fris.
21.6.1979	C	OMO introduced on H6-8 Liverpool-Prescot, H9 Huyton-Prescot and 89 St. Helens-Speke. H12 converted from OMO sd to dd. (Delayed from 17.6.79 due to strike).
	C	H20-24 Limited Stop operation along Wavertree Road ceased.
1.7.1979	R	303 Southport-Kirkby summer Sunday service introduced.
15.12.1979	B	15C Tower Hill-Broadway diverted inwards via Lorenzo Drive and Broad Lane to Broadway.
28.1.1980	BR	57A Netherton-Old Haymarket renumbered 57. One remaining journey on 57 renumbered W57. 57B (or B57) Netherton-Bootle (New Strand) commenced.
13.4.1980	R	311 Ormskirk-Liverpool curtailed Suns to run between Robbins Island & Liverpool.
	BR	59 withdrawn & 54 Sunday service New Strand-Old Roan introduced.
6.5.1980	B	101 William Brown Street-Vauxhall 'Round-a-bout' introduced.
1.6.1980	B	13, 15D, 44D, 92A, 92B, 500, 544 withdrawn.
	R	311, 321, 331 converted to OMO.
2.6.1980	B	151 Kirkby Admin Gate-Tower Hill Circular — new service.
		152 Kirkby Civic Centre-Westvale-Northwood Circular — new service (part subsequently numbered 150).
		153 Kirkby Admin Gate-Kirkby Station — new service.
		154 Central Bus Station-Northwood via Walton Hall Ave — new service.
		155 Central Bus Station-Tower Hill via Townsend Ave — new service.
		156 Walton (Spellow Lane)-Tower Hill — new service.
		157 Pier Head-Northwood via Longmoor Lane — new service.
		158 Walton (Spellow Lane)-Southdene — new service.
		159 Broadway-Tower Hill (Saturdays) (15C renumbered).
		92 Extended from Huyton Station to Halewood (Derby Arms).
	BCR	89 Alternate journeys diverted from Speke to Halewood (Derby Arms) as 89A.
3.6.1980	P	39, 320 City Terminus removed from Central Bus Station to Old Haymarket.

29.8.1980	B	94 Dingle-Kirkby Withdrawn.
30.8.1980	B	100 Cityride service withdrawn.
1.9.1980	B	10, 11 Extended from South Castle Street to Pier Head.
		100 Central Station-Beresford Road (Toxteth Link-up) service commenced.
8.9.1980	P	39, 320 Rerouted outward via Whitechapel, Hood Street.
22.9.1980	R	705 Parbold-Skelmersdale-Liverpool (Skelhorne Street) limited stop — new service replacing journeys on 305, 345.
13.10.1980	B	144 Gillmoss-Pier Head peak hour trips commenced, replacing some 154 journeys.
19.10.1980	C	H22 Liverpool-Frodsham withdrawn and replaced by extra trips on H20 Liverpool-Runcorn (Shopping City). H21 rerouted in Runcorn.
		H24 Liverpool-Chester rerouted in Runcorn but most journeys curtailed to run Liverpool-Widnes only and withdrawn on evenings and Sundays.
		H25 Liverpool-Runcorn via Speke all day service introduced.
20.10.1980	B	101 Rerouted via Latimer Street to Silvester Street in lieu of Vauxhall Road.
6.12.1980	R	365 Liverpool-Skelmersdale via Aintree and Kirkby — replacing most journeys on 305 and all journeys on 395/6 (withdrawn).
	R	307 Liverpool-Maghull (Green Park) replaced by M6 Old Roan-Green Park.
8.12.1980	C	H7/H7X Rerouted via Huyton Hey Road, Victoria Road, and Seel Road instead of Hall Lane and all stops observed along Manchester Road, Prescot.
5.1.1981	B	17D Evening and Sunday service extended from Broadway to Fazakerley.
12.1.1981	B	16 Pier Head-Seaforth reduced to two journeys each way.
31.1.1981	R	211, L35, L81, S4, converted to OMO dd, S5 to OMO sd.
16.2.1981	B	100 Rerouted inward via Mount Vernon and Hall Lane.
17.2.1981	B	73 rerouted inward via Castle Street and James Street.
7.3.1981	R	705 Saturday service extended to operate Ashurst-Pier Head (Mann Island).
29.3.1981	C	76, H1 Converted to OMO. (Final Crosville conversion on Merseyside).
30.3.1981	R	M3 Extended to include Park Lane and School Lane.
24.4.1981	R	W52 Bootle-Sefton Industrial Estate withdrawn.
	B	111 St. Helens-Gillmoss (English Electric Works). Withdrawn.
	B	112 St. Helens-Walton Hall Avenue (Stopgate Lane). Withdrawn.
	B	114 St. Helens-Melling (BICC Works). Withdrawn.
27.4.1981	B	110 St. Helens-Kirkby reduced to 1 jny M-Th, 2 jny F from Kirkby only.
1.6.1981	B	Pier Head bus stands revised. 73, 73A, 79A moved from George's Dock Way to bus station. 73 rerouted inward via Water Street.
12.7.1981	B	72 outward journeys rerouted via Whitechapel and Hood St. in lieu of Wm. Brown Street.
18.7.1981	R	705 Timesaver extended from Ashurst to Blackpool via Chorley.
27.7.1981	R	M7 Melling (Prescot Rd)-Maghull (Green Park) 1 jny. M-F for shoppers.
26.9.1981	R	58, 351 Converted to OMO (Final Ribble conversion on Merseyside).
	R	L81 City terminus moved from Skelhorne Street to South John Street.
2.10.1981	R	M7 withdrawn.
3.10.1981	R	M6 Extended from Old Roan to Aintree Station.
11.10.1981	B	118 Green Lane (West Derby Road)-Croxteth Park Housing Estate commenced.
9.11.1981	B	1A Extended via Princess Way, Gorsey Lane and Fleetwoods Lane to Magdalene Square.
	B	1E Diverted to Northern Perimeter Rd. via Almonds Turn.
	B	55 Extended via Chapel Lane and Copy Lane returning via Northern Perimeter Road.
	B	Many industrial journeys withdrawn on 42 Edge Lane-Penny Lane; 62 Kirkby-Speke; 64 Kirkby-Edge Lane; 65 Edge Lane-Speke; 70 Page Moss-Huyton Ind.Est; 77 Speke-City.
	B	439 afternoon journey Seaforth-Netherley withdrawn-operated mornings only.
	B	60D Smithdown Road (Ullet Road)-Millers Bridge — last remaining journey withdrawn.
28.11.1981	R	L81 City terminus reverted to Skelhorne Street.
30.11.1981	B	61A/C Taggart Ave to Giro via 61 route to Northfield Road then via Southport Rd., Bailey Drive, Netherton Way, Bridle Rd. (Return journey to Aigburth Vale 61C).
2.1.1982	R	705 curtailed Sats Liverpool-Ashurst (4 jnys); M-F peak jnys to Parbold).
23.2.1982	B	15,18A,44A,97,97A,97C,99B Internal journeys in Kirkby Industrial Estate rerouted via Hammond Road, Woodward Rd. and Acornfield Rd. in lieu of Bradman Road temporarily.
15.3.1982	B	17C/17D officially converted to OMO dd having been mixed sd & dd for some time
29.3.1982	B	Temporary route in Kirkby Industrial Est. made permanent. (see 23.2.1982).
	B	161 new number for diversion of early journey on 151 via route of 153 for Kraft Factory.
5.4.1982	B	501 Ford Factory-Walton minimum fare restriction lifted.
2.5.1982	B	Lime St. Stn.-Langton Dock contract service to connect with resumed Liverpool-Belfast sailings

		by Irish Sea Ferries (0720 to 1040 daily — 50p flat fare).
9.5.1982	B	22 Pier Head-Fazakerley remaining journeys renumbered 93.
30.5.1982	B	Special traffic arrangements for Pope's visit. Early and extra buses.
		50 shuttle service Old Haymarket-Car Parks on North Docks, 25p fare.
1.6.1982	B	Revised peak hour schedules — economies — Speke Garage.
		Afternoon departures from Seaforth on 400 (Speke) and 438 (Halewood) withdrawn. Both now morning only as 439 (Netherley).
28-29.6.82	R	NUR National Rail Strike-Car Park space provided at Ribble's Aintree Garage and £1 park and ride ticket issued to Liverpool.
4-18.7.82	R	ASLEF Rail Strike — Similar arrangements.
5.7.1982	B	Revised peak hour schedules — economies — Green Lane and Gillmoss garages.
		36 Seaforth-Kirkby — some journeys extended to Tower Hill in lieu of 5 Gate via 155 route.
		62A Speke-Gillmoss withdrawn and many other journeys on other services withdrawn or retimed.
20.7.1982	B	TuF 66B/88B terminal arrangements at Belle Vale revised. 66B continues along Belle Vale Road to Childwall Valley Rd. in lieu of Besford Road to the Bus Station;
		88B return journeys start from Childwall Valley Road via Bus Station to Garston.
9.8.1982	B	Revised peak hour schedules — economies — Walton and Litherland garages.
		33 Grants Gdns-Seaforth reduced from 20-min. service to odd jnys. some extd to Containerbase.
		36 Remaining 5 Gate journeys extended to Tower Hill via 155 route.
16.8.1982	B	71 Speke-Huyton extended from Link Road via Wilson Road to new Lucas Aerospace Factory.
	B	70 Some journeys similarly extended and pm journey Wilson Road-Old Swan introduced.
10.9.1982	B	53 Last remaining journey Aintree (Park Lane)-Netherton withdrawn.
20.9.1982	B	8 Use of number for short journeys to Page Moss discontinued.
24.9.1982	R	C5 Crosby-Thornton (Long Lane) withdrawn. Bus saved used for 206.
27.9.1982	R	206 New experimental service, Crosby Bus Stn-Circular via Coronation Road, Warren Road, The Serpentine, Burbo Bank Road North, Hall Road, Merrilocks Road, Blundellsands Stn. & Coronation Road. Hail and ride in Blundellsands.
2.10.1982	R	Because of problems concerning passengers waiting for buses in Liverpool Road South, Maghull, outward buses after 1900 on 300, 302, 310, 311, 321, 331, 341, 350 rerouted via Northway & Hall Lane.
9.10.1982	R	705 Pier Head extension withdrawn and all journeys terminated at Skelhorne Street.
18.10.1982	B	94 Number allocated for Tunnel night service.
6.12.1982	B	Minimum fares removed from industrial services 14A, 18A, 34, 34C, 35, 36, 37, 41, 44A, 45, 47, 62, 63, 64, 65, 65B, 65C, 70, 70A, 91, 95, 95A, 95B, 97C, 98C, 99A, 99B. Minimum fares now apply only to 400+ services,12C, 43, 501/2 and Ribble services on Walton Road in evening peak.
11.12.1982	B	17 New Saturday shoppers' service Pier Head-Broad Lane via Gt. Homer St., Everton. Valley & Utting Avenue.
6.2.1983	B	55 Old Haymarket-Netherton extended from Dunnings Park to Old Roan Station via Northern Perimeter Road, Chapel Lane, Copy Lane.
11.2.1983	B	158 Southdene-Walton reduced to hospital visiting times.
21.2.1983	B	92 Crosby-Halewood rerouted to serve Belle Vale Centre via Childwall Valley Road, Hedgefield Road, The Centre Bus Stn and Besford Road.
11.3.1983	B	110 St. Helens-Kirkby via East Lancs. Road workers' service withdrawn.
14.3.1983	B	A1 Netherton-Aintree Station renumbered 29 am 29A pm. and extended back to Aintree as a circular.(Last day of A1 -11.3.83).
20.3.1983	B	30A extended in a loop from Northern Perimeter Rd. via Chapel Ln., Copy Ln. and Northern Perimeter Rd. (as previously followed by 55). All buses now show 30.
5.4.1983	BC	H26 Mann Island-Cronton Colliery via Wavertree, Roby and Huyton Quarry taken over by MPTE. Contract with NCB, 4 jnys M-F, 1 S.
11.4.1983	B	50 Kirkby Station-Rainford commenced-replacing evening railway service.
5.1983	B	Gillmoss Soccerbus service withdrawn.
19.6.1983	BC	89/89A Diverted at Belle Vale as route 92 (see 21.2.83) journeys to Dunlop Factory withdrawn.
5.7.1983	M	Garston train service extended to Hunts Cross.
1.8.1983	B	Experimental use of Autofare 3 equipment with fare boxes on 30 & am peak journeys on 16.
8.8.1983	B	102 New Service Walton (Spellow Lane)-Broadgreen Hospital via Croxteth Estate.
27.8.1983	B	Soccerbus services resumed from Woodside (900) and from Edge Lane Garage.
5.9.1983	B	94 diverted temporarily via Wallasey Tunnel.
12.9.1983	BC	London Rd lower section reverted to 2-way for buses. 9C, 10, 11, 12/A/C, 14C, 17C, 18C, 19/A/E, 30, 75, 79B, 155, H2/3 rerouted outward via London Rd instead of Islington.
17.9.1983	B	17 rerouted inward via Islington and Commutation Row and renumbered 117.

1.10.1983	R	M1-2-3 Maghull local services Saturday services introduced.
19.10.1983	B	B&I Dublin ferry moved north from Trafalgar Dock to Brocklebank Dock and contract service to and from Lime Street Station altered.
31.10.1983	R	206 extended to Hightown.
5.11.1983	R	X27 renumbered 727; rerouted via Princess Way and Crosby Road South in lieu of Cambridge Road and diverted to Colne via Accrington instead of Earby via Clitheroe.
12.11.1983	B	113 St. Helens-Walton Hall Avenue (Littlewoods) withdrawn.
14.11.1983	B	1,1A extended from Dingle to Aigburth Vale and w'drawn on Sats & Suns and M-F evenings except 3 trips for office cleaners between Pier Head and Dingle.
	B	1A, 1E combined as 1A with anti-clockwise loop through Netherton.
	B	55A New Strand-Northern Perimeter Road off peak supplementary service started.
	B	55B Balliol Road-Northern Perimeter Road peak hour supplementary service started.
	B	86C, 87C. The few remaining circular journeys withdrawn.
21.11.1983	B	71 Speke-Huyton rerouted in Halewood northbound via Baileys Lane.
16.1.1984	B	6D peak hour service rerouted via Hood St. Gyratory both ways. Use of No. 6A discontinued. Garston by-pass opened. 25, 82C, 85, H1, H25 rerouted inward via Dock Road and part of by-pass.
28.1.1984	B	50 Kirkby Station-Rainford Station withdrawn.
3.2.1984	B	1 extension beyond Seaforth to Containerbase withdrawn.
20.2.1984	B	80 extension beyond Western Avenue to Dunlop Factory withdrawn.
23.3.1984	B	109 St. Helens-Huyton Industrial Estate withdrawn.
2.5.1984	BCR	401 Pier Head-Garden Festival (Herculaneum Entrance) via Lime St. commenced.
		402 Aigburth Vale-Garden Festival (Fulwood Entrance) via Jericho Ln. commenced.
		403 Sefton Park (overflow car park)-Garden Festival (Herculaneum Ent.) never ran.
7.5.1984	B	94 operated permanently via Wallasey Tunnel.
12.5.1984	B	85B supplementary Sat journeys Dingle-Walton rerouted via Gt. Homer St. as 85C.
21.5.1984	B	Merseylink dial-a-ride service for the disabled commenced. Free service.
10.6.1984	R	S5 Liverpool-Freshfield Station withdrawn.
	R	S4 Liverpool-Freshfield Island increased and renumbered 284.
	R	W13 Crosby (Littlewoods)-Freshfield also operated under service Number 284.
	BC	Lime St.-Brocklebank Dock B&I Dublin contract transferred to Crosville.
1.6.1984	B	City Tours recommenced.
13.7.1984	R	54A Bootle-Netherton Village & 361 Liverpool-Robbins Island withdrawn.
14.7.1984	R	54 Bootle (New Strand)-Aintree (Wango Lane) extended to Fazakerley Hospital (Lower Lane) & rerouted via Irlam Road.
16.7.1984	R	W54 Bootle (New Strand)-Lydiate renumbered 254.
6.8.1984	B	102 experimental service made permanent, rerouted in Croxteth and via Westminster Road.
	B	118 extended from Oak Lane terminus to Stand Farm via Fir Tree Drive South.
18.8.1984	B	159 Tower Hill-Broadway (Sats) revised as Kirkby Civic Centre-Hood St.Gyratory, returning from Lord Street.
1.9.1984	B	610 Cronton Colliery contract withdrawn following final run down of colliery.
3.9.1984	B	161 early journey replaced by a trip on 151. (This was only journey to show 161).
28.9.1984	B	29/29A Aintree Station-Netherton circular withdrawn.
1.10.1984	B	103 Pier Head-Dingle via route 1, M-F evenings, Sats and Suns, introduced.
7.10.1984	B	Productivity deal at Green Lane depot. Services revised:-
	B	12 & 12C Pier Head-Pagemoss-Cantril Farm-Pier Head linked via Stockbridge Lane to form a circle — 12 anti-clockwise, 13 clockwise. Journeys via Leyfield Road as 12A/13A.
	B	17D Pier Head-Broadway and 18D Pier Head-Lower Lane linked via Townsend Avenue and East Lancs Road as a circle — 7D clockwise, 8D anti-clockwise. Sats 7/8 via Lord Street.
	B	18B journeys to Gillmoss withdrawn.
	B	117 Saturday shoppers service renumbered 17.
	B	12A, 75 extended to Pier Head and Sir Thomas St. ceased to be a terminus.
	B	41 Edge Lane(Southbank Road)-Knotty Ash withdrawn.
	B	43, 67, 70, 97, 97C reduced; 34, 34C, 47 retimed.
	B	Cantril Farm within Borough of Knowsley officially renamed Stockbridge Village but name not immediately used by MPTE.
14.10.1984	BCR	401-2 withdrawn as Garden Festival ends.
15.10.1984	B	100 rerouted officially via West Derby St. in lieu of Mount Vernon, Hall Lane, Prescot St. & Daulby St. (Actually happened 1.3.1984 due to industrial action).
	B	Journeys from Central Stn. rerouted via Lime St. & London Road in lieu of Skelhorne St., Copperas Hill and Monument Place.

23.11.1984	B	38 Penny Lane-Seaforth and most trips on 42 Penny Lane-Edge Lane withdrawn.
25.11.1984	B	Open days at all MPTE garages except Garston. Special services operated. Hunts Cross Hotel-Speke depot and Central Parade-Speke depot.
3.12.1984	C	H6X-H9X industrial journeys rerouted in Huyton Ind. Est. between Ellis Ashton St. & Wilson Rd. via Stretton Way in lieu of Link Road.
4.12.1984	R	Norton St. made two way again and services ex Skelhorne Street resumed old outward route via Norton St. in lieu of London Rd & Commutation Row.
7.1.1985	B	65B Halewood-Edge Lane withdrawn and replaced by extension of 65C from Netherley to Hunts Cross via Halewood as 65A.
25.1.1985	B	Huyton Link Road to M57 opened. Buses only link road from Stockbridge Lane to Waterpark Drive not ready and 11, 12/12A, 13/13A, 34C, 62-64, 92, 97 & 98C disrupted until 3.4.1985.
26.1.1985	B	67 Old Swan-Seaforth withdrawn also some M-F journeys on 34, 43, 47, 95, 96 & 97.
28.1.1985	B	118 Croxteth Park-Green Lane(West Derby Road) extended to Green Lane garage.
1.4.1985	BP	741 Liverpool(St.Johns Lane)-Heysham express service commenced twice daily.
15.4.1985	B	74 Pier Head-Wavertree Technology Park via Brownlow Hill, Edge Hill & Wavertree Road peak hour service commenced. 70 Old Swan-Huyton extended from Stretton Way via Ellis Ashton St. to Brickfields.
23.5-8.9.85	R	401 Skelhorne St.-Festival Gardens via Albert Dock service operated.
11.5.1985	B	Last day of operation of Soccerbus services.
2.6.1985	BCR	Crosville share of 89/89A/89F St. Helens-Speke/Halewood/Ford Factory transferred to Ribble.
3.6.1985	B	85 Walton-Garston (Windfield Road) extended to Airport Terminal Building.
8.7.1985	B	94 Most journeys continue to use Wallasey tunnel from Liverpool but return via Birkenhead tunnel. On Sat and Sun am, advertised frequency increased from 60 to 20 mins between 0215 and 0315. 3 trips use Birkenhead tunnel as 94A.
3.8.1985	C	Crosville Edge Lane garage closed and Love Lane garage opened.
4.10.1985	BP	741 Liverpool-Heysham reduced to 1 trip FrSaMo—operated by MPTE. Additional stops introduced at Washington Parade, Bootle and Aintree Station.
14.10.1985	B	34C Seaforth-Cantril Farm afternoon journey extended back to start from New Strand.
23.11.1985	B	85 extension to Airport withdrawn; terminus reverted to Windfield Road.
6.1.1986	B	741 Liverpool-Heysham service withdrawn.
15.1.1986	B	Asda free services to Huyton from Croxteth Park (906) and Rainhill Stoops (907) started.
17.2.1986	B	118 diverted from Green Lane Garage to Central Bus Stn. weekdays.
16.3.1986	B	Parker St. closed to through traffic. 100 to run to Canning Place to turn.
20.3.1986	BP	Old Haymarket ceased to be used as a terminus. 39, 320 rerouted to Whitechapel and 57 evenings and Suns. to Whitechapel, running out via Hood Street.
14.4.1986	B	Churchill Way South flyover from Islington to Dale St. closed for structural work. 4, 7D, 9D, 10D, 11, 14D, 18D, 75, 77, 79D, 412 to run inwards via Hood Street and Crosshall Street.
25.4.1986	B	906, 907 Asda store free services withdrawn.
28.4.1986	B	New Airport terminal opened. 80 extended via Hale Rd., Dunlop Rd. & Speke Hall Rd. officially on 19 May but some journeys ran before then.
27.6.1986	B	16 Pier Head-Seaforth, 33 Everton-Seaforth withdrawn.
	R	206 Crosby-Hall Rd.-Little Crosby-Hightown withdrawn.
	R	254 Lydiate-Bootle (New Strand) withdrawn.
	B	478, 479 Pier Head-Netherley/Halewood Rapidride services withdrawn.
28.6.1986	B	7, 7D, 8, 8D Pier Head-Lowerhouse Lane circulars withdrawn.
	B	55A, 55B Bootle-Netherton withdrawn.
	B	159 Tower Hill-Broad Lane withdrawn.
29.6.1986	B	Route 9C extended evgs and Su from Longview to Huyton Stn via Longview Drive as 9B.
	B	12A, 13A rerouted via Queens Dr., Alder Rd., Honeysgreen Lane in lieu of Town Row.
	B	17D Pier Head-Fazakerley via Everton Valley, Utting Ave. commenced.
	B	18 Pier Head-Croxteth Park commenced.
	B	155 Pier Head-Tower Hill rerouted via Kirkby Station.
2.7.1986	B	12A, 13A reverted to original route before 1800 Mons to Sats.
5.7.1986	B	12A, 13A withdrawn evenings and Suns and replaced by 22A/23A via Muirhead Ave, Queens Dr., Alder Rd., Honeysgreen Lane at these times.
7.7.1986	B	73B Pier Head-Childwall Park Ave withdrawn.
18.7.1986	B	412 Pier Head-Stockbridge Village Rapidride service withdrawn.
7.9.1986	R	North Western Road Car Co. took over Ribble Merseyside area routes.
24.10.1986	B	6D Bowring Park Avenue-Pier Head withdrawn.
	C	H99 Huyton-Mosscroft Farm withdrawn.

25.10.1986	B	1/1A Aigburth-Pier Head-Seaforth-Netherton withdrawn.
	B	11 Pier Head-Stockbridge Village withdrawn.
	B	18C Pier Head-Fazakerley withdrawn.
	B	22A/23A Pier Head-Stockbridge Village withdrawn.
	B	25 Garston-Princes Park-Moss St.-Walton withdrawn.
	B	28 Old Haymarket-Litherland-Netherton withdrawn.
	B	30 Old Haymarket-Walton-Netherton withdrawn.
	B	66/88 Garston-Halewood Circular withdrawn.
	B	84 Speke-Garston Station withdrawn.
	B	85 Garston-Mill St.-Lime St.-Walton withdrawn.
	B	150-158 Kirkby services withdrawn.
	C	H1 Liverpool-Warrington via Hale & Widnes withdrawn.

Deregulation marked the end of many sacred cows—including the Great Divide at Prescot with Liverpool services on one side and St. Helens services on the other. Atlantean 1763 in Merseybus maroon and cream livery leaves the Pier Head for St. Helens via Prescot and Eccleston Park.

49 Fleet List Summary

BUSES PLACED IN SERVICE BY LCPT & MPTE 1957-86

Fleet No.	Reg.No.	Chassis Make & Type	Body Manufacturer	Seats & Body Type	Year in Service	Year Withdrawn	Remarks
1. LIVERPOOL CORPORATION							
L245-79	VKB701-35	Leyland PD2/20	Crossley	H33/29R	1956-57	1968-76	
L280-309	VKB736-65	Leyland PD2/30	Cros./Met.Cam.	H35/29R	1957	1973-75	Stored until 1961
A168-202	VKB766-800	AEC Regent V(9.6)	Met.Cammell	H33/29R	1956-57	1973-75	
A203-32	VKB801-30	AEC Regent V(9.6)	Met.Cam./LCPT	H33/29R	1957-59	1972-76	
L310-44	VKB831-65	Leyland PD2/20	Crossley	H33/29R	1957-58	1968-75	
A233-67	VKB866-900	AEC Regent V(9.6)	Met.Cammell	H33/29R	1957	1970-75	
L345-69	WKF201-25	Leyland PD2/30	Crossley	H33/29R	1958	1971-73	
A268-92	WKF226-50	AEC Regent V(9.6)	Met.Cammell	H33/29R	1957-58	1972-76	
E1	371BKA	AEC Regent V(9.6)	Park Royal	FH40/32R	1959	1973	
E2	372BKA	Leyland PDR1/1	Met.Cammell	H44/34F	1959	1978	
E3	116TMD	AEC Bridgemaster	Park Royal	H45/31R	1958	1973	Ex-demonstrator
L500-699	500-699KD	Leyland PDR1/1	Met.Cammell	H43/33F	1962-64	1975-82	L677-1984
L700-59	CKF700-59C/D	Leyland PDR1/1	Met.Cammell	H43/35F	1965-66	1978-81	
L760-879	FKF760-879D/E	Leyland PDR1/1	Met.Cammell	H43/35F	1966-67	1978-82	
1001-70	FKF880-949F/G	Leyland PSUR1A/1	Met.Cammell	B47D	1968	1977-81	
1071-1110	RKA950-89G	Leyland PSUR1A/1	Met.Cammell	B47D	1968-69	1977-81	
2001-25	SKB671-95G	Bristol RELL6G	Park Royal	B45D	1969	1981-2	2017 - w/d 1970
							2022 - w/d 1977

The conversion of the tramway system to bus operation gave some older vehicles, such as this pre-war Regent, a new lease of life in the Training School.

Time to go home, all the shopping done, and the one-man era has yet to arrive.

Fleet No.	Reg.No.	Chassis Make & Type	Body Manufacturer	Seats & Body Type	Year in Service	Year Withdrawn	Remarks
2. ORDERED BY LIVERPOOL CORPORATION - DELIVERED TO MERSEYSIDE PTE							
1111-50	UKA562-601H	Leyland PDR2/1	Alexander AL	H47/32D	1969-70	1982	
2026-49	UKD520-43H/J	Bristol VRTLH6G	East Lancs	H49/31D	1970	1982-5	
1151-75	XKC773-802J	Leyland PDR2/1	Alexander AL	H47/32D	1971	1982-3	
1176-1235	XKC803-62K	Leyland PDR2/1	Alexander AL	H49/31D	1971	1982-4	1187 - w/d 1977
2051-85	YKF689-723K	Bristol VRTLH6G	East Lancs	H49/31D	1971	1982-3	
3. MERSEYSIDE PTE							
2086-95	YKB361-70J	Bristol RESL6L	ECW	B44F	1971	1982-84	Diverted from PMT
1236-95	BKC236-95K/L	Leyland PDR1A/1	Alexander AL	H43/32F	1972	1986-88	Diverted from BMMO 1271-95 Wirral Div.
4001-8	CKD401-8L	Scania BR111MH	MCW	B47F	1972	1982-86	Wirral Division
4009-20	CKD409-20L	Scania BR111MH	MCW	B44F	1972	1982-86	
1296-1395	DKC296-395L	Leyland AN68/1R	Alexander AL	H43/32F	1972-3	1985-	1356-70 Wirral Div.
3001-50	CKC301-50L	Daimler CRG6LXB	MCW	H43/32F	1973	1986-87	Wirral Division
1396-1445	EKD396-445L	Leyland AN68/1R	East Lancs	H43/32	1973	1986-	
1446-1545	GKA446-545L/M	Leyland AN68/1R	Alexander AL	H43/32F	1973-4	1986-	1446-93,1506-16/35-3 Wirral Division
4021	OKD579M	Scania BR111DH	MCW	H44/29R	1974	1984	
4022-31	PKD422-31M	Scania BR111DH	MCW	H44/29R	1974	1983-84	
4032-40	RKA432-40N	Scania BR111DH	MCW	H44/29R	1974	1983-84	
1546-53	OLV546-53M	Leyland AN68/1R	Alexander AL	H43/32F	1974	1988-	
1554-70	PKB554-70M	Leyland AN68/1R	Alexander AL	H43/32F	1974	1988-	
1571-85	RKA575-89N	Leyland AN68/1R	Alexander AL	H43/32F	1974		
1586-1612	GKA11-37N	Leyland AN68/1R	Alexander AL	H43/32F	1974	1988-	1586-1595 Wirral
2096-98	RKB96-98N	Bristol VRTSL6G	East Lancs	H43/32F	1974	1984-6	
2099-2145	GKA51-97N	Bristol VRTSL6G	East Lancs	H43/32F	1974-5	1986	
331-2	RKA423-4N	Leyland 550FG	Alex.(Belfast)	B22F	1974	1984	Wirral Division
1613-25	GKA38-50N	Leyland AN68/1R	Alexander AL	H43/32F	1975		
278-86	GEM598-606N	AEC Swift 505	Marshall	B42D	1975	1984-90	St.Helens
2146-55	GTJ382-91N	Bristol RESL6G	ECW	B47F	1975	1986	St.Helens
4041-4	HBG480-3N	Scania BR111DH	MCW	H44/29F	1975	1984-85	
4045-80	HWM45-80P	Scania BR111DH	MCW	H44/29F	1975	1983-85	

Mechanisation of garage activities was a feature of the 'sixties and 'seventies but the soap wash shown here was not a daily affair, being rostered at weekly or fortnightly intervals.

Fleet No.	Reg.No.	Chassis Make & Type	Body Manufacturer	Seats & Body Type	Year in Service	Year Withdrawn	Remarks
1626-85	HTJ626-85P	Leyland AN68/1R	Alexander AL	H43/32F	1975-76	1989-	1626-46 Wirral
1686-1725	JWM686-725P	Leyland AN68/1R	East Lancs	H43/32F	1976	1988-	
1726-55	LKF726-55R	Leyland AN68B/1R	East Lancs	H43/32F	1976	1986-	
1756-65	MTJ756-65S	Leyland AN68B/1R	East Lancs	H43/32F	1977		
1766-75	MTJ766-75S	Leyland National 1	11351A/1R	B49F	1977	1987-	Reno'd 6050-9 5/80
1000	OHF858S	Leyland National 1	11351A/1R	DP45F	1978		Reno'd 7000 1/79
1866-85	RKA866-85T	Leyland National 1	11351A/1R	B49F	1978		Reno'd 6060-79 5/80
1886-87	RKA886-87T	Leyland National 1	11351A/1R	DP45F	1978		Reno'd 7001-2
1776-1805	OEM776-805S	Leyland AN68A/1	MCW	H45/33F	1978		
1806-15	PKA720-9S	Leyland AN68A/1	MCW	H45/33F	1978		
1816-20	PHF557-61T	Leyland AN68A/1	MCW	H45/33F	1978		
1821	RBG821T	Leyland AN68A/1	East Lancs	H45/33F	1979		
1822-4	TWM209-11V	Leyland AN68A/1	East Lancs	H45/33F	1979-80		
1825-7	RBG825-7T	Leyland AN68A/1	East Lancs	H45/33F	1979		
1828-33	TWM212-7V	Leyland AN68A/1	East Lancs	H45/33F	1979-80		
1834	WWM917W	Leyland AN68A/1	East Lancs	H45/33F	1980		
1835-6	TWM219-20V	Leyland AN68A/1	East Lancs	H45/33F	1979		
1837-9	RBG837-9T	Leyland AN68A/1	East Lancs	H45/33F	1979		
1840	RBG840T	Leyland AN68A/1	East Lancs	H43/32F	1979		
1841-2	RBG841T/TWM221V	Leyland AN68A/1	East Lancs	H45/33F	1979		
6001-30	SKF1-30T	Leyland National 1	11351A/1R	B49F	1979	1987-	
6031-4	STJ31-34T	Leyland National 1	11351A/1R	B49F	1979		
6035-41	UEM35-41T	Leyland National 2	116L11/1R	B49F	1979-80	1988-	
6042-9	OFY1-8M	Leyland National 1	1151/2R	B46D	1974	1986-	S'pt 1-8 reno'd 5/80
6080-99	VBG80-99V	Leyland National 2	116L11/1R	B49F	1980	1988-	
6100	WWM905W	Leyland National 2	116L11/1R	B49F	1980		
6101-22	VBG101-22V	Leyland National 2	116L11/1R	B49F	1980		
6123-26	WWM906-9W	Leyland National 2	116L11/1R	B49F	1980		
6127-30	VBG127-30V	Leyland National 2	116L11/1R	B49F	1980		
6131-2	WWM910-1W	Leyland National 2	116L11/1R	B49F	1980		
6133	VBG133V	Leyland National 2	116L11/1R	B49F	1980		
6134-8	WWM912-6W	Leyland National 2	116L11/1R	B49F	1980		
6139-63	XLV139-63W	Leyland National 2	116L11/1R	B49F	1980		
1843-59	WWM920-36W	Leyland AN68B/1R	Willowbrook	H45/33F	1980-81	1989-	
1860-72	AFY180-92X	Leyland AN68B/1R	Willowbrook	H45/33F	1981-82	1986	
1873-1912	XEM873-912W	Leyland AN68B/1R	Alexander AL	H43/32F	1981		
1913-67	ACM913-67X	Leyland AN68B/1R	Alexander AL	H43/32F	1981-2		
2156-8	JUG352-4N	Bristol LHS6L	ECW	B27F	7/80	1984	Ex-WYPTE New 75
2159-60	MUA44-5P	Bristol LHS6L	ECW	B27F	7/80	1985	Ex-WYPTE New 76
6164-73	CKB161-70X	Leyland National 2	NL116A/L11/1R	B49F	1982		
1968-70	DKF683-5X	Leyland AN68D/1R	Alexander AL	H43/32F	1982		
1971-2	EKA171-2Y	Leyland AN68D/1R	Alexander AL	H43/32F	1982	1986-	
1973-91	DEM773-91Y	Leyland AN68D/1R	Alexander AL	H43/32F	1982		
1001-15	A321-35GLV	Leyland AN68D/1R	Alexander AL	H43/32F	1983		
1016-69	A96-149HLV	Leyland AN68D/1R	Alexander AL	H43/32F	1984		
1070	B926KWM	Leyland AN68D/1R	Alexander AL	H43/32F	1984		

A change from green to a predominantly cream livery with green roof, waistband and skirt, gave the Bristol REs a smart appearance despite the rather dated moulded waist of the Eastern Coach Works body. Number 2086 was parked at Carnegie Road on 4th March 1978.

Fleet No.	Reg.No.	Chassis Make & Type	Body Manufacturer	Seats & Body Type	Year in Service	Year Withdrawn	Remarks

EXPERIMENTAL VEHICLES

Fleet No.	Reg.No.	Chassis Make & Type	Body Manufacturer	Seats & Body Type	Year in Service	Year Withdrawn	Remarks
0001-8	Intended for vehicles eventually numbered 6001-8						
0009-13	Intended for Dennis Dominators/Willowbrook - order cancelled.						
0014-8	Intended for Leyland Titans/Willowbrook - order cancelled.						
0019-23	UKA19-23V	MCW Metrobus	MCW	H43/30F	1979-80		
0024-5	UBG24-25V	Dennis Dominator	Willowbrook	H45/33F	1980	1986	
0026	WWM918W	Dennis Dominator	Willowbrook	H45/33F	1980	1986	To Hong Kong
0027	WWM904W	Dennis Dominator	Willowbrook	H45/33F	1980	1986	
0028	WWM919W	Dennis Dominator	Willowbrook	H45/33F	1980	1986	
0029	BCK706R	Leyland Titan B15.05	Park Royal	H44/30F	On loan 5/80 to 3/82		
0030-4	ACM704-8X	Leyland Olympian ONTL11/1R	ECW	H46/31F	1982		
0035-6	ACM768-9X	Dennis Dominator	Alexander R	H45/33F	1982		
0037-41	ACM709-12/772X	Leyland ONTL11/1R	ECW	H46/31F	1982		
0042-3	ACM770-1X	MCW Metrobus DR104/9	Alexander R	H45/31F	1982		
0044-5	STV122-3X	Volvo Ailsa B55-10	Marshall	H44/35F	On loan from Derby 3/82 to 9/82		
0046-53	CHF346-53X	Dennis Dominator	Alexander R	H45/33F	1982		
0054-5	DEM821-2Y	Volvo Ailsa B55-10	Alexander R	H45/31F	1982		
0056-7	EKA156-7Y	MCW Metrobus DR102/29	Alexander R	H45/31F	1982		
0058-63	DEM758-67Y	MCW Metrobus DR102/29	Alexander R	H45/31F	1982		
0064-8	A316-20GLV	Leyland ONTL11/1R	Alexander R	H47/29F	1983		
0069-81	A151-63HLV	Volvo Ailsa B55 Mk.III	Alexander R	H44/37R	1984		
0082-6	B927-31 KWM	Quest 80B	Locomotors	B23FL	1984-85	1986	
0087	C8440BG	Quest 80B	Locomotors	B23FL	1985	1986	

COACH FLEET

Fleet No.	Reg.No.	Chassis Make & Type	Body Manufacturer	Seats & Body Type	Year in Service	Year Withdrawn	Remarks
201	KKU71F	Bedford VAM70	Duple	C45F	1974	1981	Ex-St.Helens
7000-2	See 1000 and 1886-7 above						
7003	WWM576W	Leyland PSU3F/4R	Duple Dominant	IC49F	1981	1988	
7004-7	XTJ4-7W	Leyland National 2	116AL11/1R	DP44F	1981		
7008	YKA8W	Leyland PSU3F/4R	Duple Dominant I	C49F	1981	1988	
7009-14	CKC623-8X+	Leyland TRCTL11/2R	Duple Dominant IV	C49F	1982		
7015-20	EKA215-20Y	Leyland TRCTL11/2R	Duple Dominant IV	C49F	1982		
7021-6	EKA221-26Y	Dennis Lancet	Duple	DP31F	1983		
7027	A996HKB	Dennis Lancet	Duple	DP31F	1983		
7028-30	EKA228-30Y	Dennis Lancet	Duple	DP31F	1983		
7031	BCK314Y	Leyland TRCTL11/3R	Duple Laser	C49F	1983		Ex-Duple New 10/82

+ Not consecutive.

The front-entrance London Transport AEC Routemaster RML1254 was the only one of its kind and worked briefly on the Sheil Road circular. It is seen outside Edge Lane works before entering service.

50 Inter-Divisional Vehicle Transfers

Orig. Fleet -No.	Reg. No.	Body Make	Seats	Date New	Date To St.H	Transferred To Sport	To Lpool	Date with drawn	Notes
1. FROM BIRKENHEAD.									
Leyland PD2/40									
16	HCM516	Massey	H33/28R	1959			9/75	3/76	
17	HCM517	"	"	"			12/75	7/76	
321	HCM521	"	"	"		12/74	7/75	10/76	Reno'd L462
322	HCM522	"	"	"			11/75	4/76	
323	HCM523	"	"	"			9/75	5/76	
325	HCM525	"	"	"			7/75	1/77	Reno'd L468
326	HCM526	"	"	"			9/75	8/76	Reno'd L474
327	HCM527	"	"	"			6/75	1/77	Reno'd L456
328	HCM528	"	"	"			9/75	1/77	
329	HCM529	"	"	"			11/75	3/76	
330	HCM530	"	"	"			11/75	3/76	
33	JBG533	"	H35/28R	1960			6/73	10/75	Reno'd L376
35	JBG535	"	"	"			6/73	1/77	Reno'd L377
36	JBG536	"	"	"			6/73	1/77	Reno'd L378
49	LCM449	E.Lancs	H37/28R	1961			7/73	8/76	Reno'd L379
51	LCM451	"	"	"			7/74	10/75	Reno'd L430
54	LCM454	"	"	"			5/73	5/75	Reno'd L372
61	MCM961	Massey	H35/30R	1962			11/75	1/77	
62	MCM962	"	"	"			7/75	1/77	Reno'd L465
63	MCM963	"	"	"			11/75	9/76	
64	MCM964	"	"	"			5/73	by7/75	Reno'd L373
65	MCM965	"	"	"			8/73	-/76	Reno'd L374
66	MCM966	"	"	"			9/75	4/76	
67	MCM967	"	"	"			1/76	1/77	Preserved
68	MCM968	"	"	"			1/76	1/77	
69	MCM969	"	"	"			8/75	1/77	Reno'd L471
70	MCM970	"	"	"		12/74	7/75	by9/75	Reno'd 170 at S'port & L463 in 7/75
71	MCM971	"	"	"			9/75	1/77	
73	MCM973	"	"	"			7/75	1/77	Reno'd L466
74	MCM974	"	"	"			11/75	9/76	
75	MCM975	"	"	1963			11/75	1/77	
76	OCM976	"	"	"			6/75	5/76	Reno'd L454 To Driving Sch.till 8/76
77	OCM977	"	"	"			8/73	8/76	Reno'd L375
78	OCM978	"	"	"			7/75	5/76	Reno'd L467
79	OCM979	"	"	"			6/75	3/76	Reno'd L455
80	OCM980	"	"	"			4/73	5/75	Reno'd L371
81	OCM981	"	"	"			6/75	10/75	Reno'd L457
82	OCM982	"	"	"	8/74		7/75	9/76	Reno'd 37 then 67W 9/74 & L470 7/75
83	OCM983	"	"	"	8/74		6/75	9/76	Reno'd 38 then 68W 9/74 & L459 6/75
84	OCM984	"	"	"	9/74		7/75	10/75	Reno'd 39 then 69W 9/74 & L464 7/75
85	OCM985	"	"	"	9/74	12/74	7/75	9/76	Reno'd 40 then 70W 9/74 & L461 7/75
86	OCM986	Massey	H35/30R	1963	9/74	12/74	4/73	1/77	Reno'd L370
87	OCM987	"	"	"	6/74			12/76	Reno'd 36 then 66W 9/74
88	OCM988	"	"	"	7/74		7/75	9/76	Reno'd 35 then 65W 9/74 & L460 7/75
89	OCM989	"	"	"	7/74		7/75	8/76	Reno'd 34 then 64W 9/74 & L469 7/75
90	OCM990	"	"	"			6/75	11/76	Reno'd L458
Leyland L1									
92	RCM492	"	B42D	1964		12/75		4/77	
93	RCM493	"	"	"		11/75		6/76	To Wirral Boro Counc.
94	RCM494	"	"	"		11/75		4/77	

Orig. Fleet -No.	Reg. No.	Body Make	Seats	Date New	Date Transferred To St.H	To Sport	To Lpool	Date with drawn	Notes
Leyland PDR2/1									
*95	OBG495J	NCME	B40D	1970		11/75	7/75	7/81	Back to Liverpool -/79
*96	OBG496J	"	"	"		11/75	7/75	2/81	Back to Liverpool -/79
Leyland PD2/40									
110	BBG110C	Massey	H36/30R	1965			9/73	?9/75	Reno'd L400
111	BBG111C	"	"	"			9/73	8/76	Reno'd L401
112	BBG112C	"	"	"			9/73	10/75	Reno'd L402
113	BBG113C	"	"	"	4/74			6/77	Reno'd 30 then 60W 9/74 60-/76 To Training School w/d /82
114	BBG114C	"	"	"			9/73	3/76	Reno'd L404
115	BBG115C	"	"	"	5/74			9/76	Reno'd 32 then 62W 9/74
116	BBG116C	"	"	"			9/73	1/77	Reno'd L406
117	BBG117C	"	"	"			9/73	1/77	Reno'd L407
118	BBG118C	"	"	"			9/73	-/76	Reno'd L408
119	BBG119C	"	"	"	5/74			12/76	Reno'd 33 then 63W 9/74
120	BBG120C	"	"	"			9/73	10/75	Reno'd L410
121	BBG121C	"	"	"			9/73	1/77	Reno'd L411
122	BBG122C	"	"	"			9/73	1/77	Reno'd L412
123	BBG123C	"	"	"			9/73	1/77	Reno'd L413
124	BBG124C	"	"	"			9/73	10/75	Reno'd L414
125	DBG125D	"	"	1966			9/73	1/77	Reno'd L415
126	DBG126D	"	"	"			9/73	1/77	Reno'd L416
127	DBG127D	"	"	"			9/73	10/75	Reno'd L417
128	DBG128D	"	"	"			9/73	1/77	Reno'd L418
129	DBG129D	"	"	"			9/73	1/77	Reno'd L419
130	DBG130D	"	"	"			9/73	8/76	Reno'd L420
131	DBG131D	"	"	"	4/74			-/78	Reno'd 31 then 61W 9/74 & 61-/76 To Training School
132	DBG132D	"	"	"			9/73	1/77	Reno'd L422
133	DBG133D	"	"	"			10/73	8/76	Reno'd L423
134	DBG134D	"	"	"			11/73	8/76	Reno'd L424
135	DBG135D	"	"	"			10/73	1/77	Reno'd L425
136	DBG136D	"	"	"			11/73	1/77	Reno'd L426
137	DBG137D	"	"	"			12/73	1/77	Reno'd L427
138	DBG138D	"	"	"			2/74	1/77	Reno'd L428
139	DBG139D	"	"	"			1/74	1/77	Reno'd L429
Leyland PD2/37									
140	GCM140E	Massey	H36/30R	1967			9/75	1/77	
141	GCM141E	"	"	"			9/75	1/77	
142	GCM142E	"	"	"			9/75	1/77	
143	GCM143E	"	"	"			9/75	1/77	
144	GCM144E	"	"	"			9/75	1/77	
145	GCM145E	"	"	"			9/75	4/76	
146	GCM146E	"	"	"			12/75	1/77	
147	GCM147E	"	"	"	12/75			6/77	Towing bus St.Helens
Leyland PDR1/2									
168	MBG368H	NCME	H44/27D	1969			-/79	-/81	
169	MBG369H	"	"	"			-/80	2/81	
170	MBG370H	"	"	"			-/79	-/81	
171	MBG371H	"	"	"			-/79	-/81	
172	MBG372H	"	"	"			-/79	3/81	
173	MBG373H	"	"	"			-?	5/81	
174	MBG374H	"	"	"			-?	5/81	
175	MBG375H	"	"	"			2/80	3/81	
176	MBG376H	"	"	"			-/79	9/81	
177	MBG377H	"	"	"			?	7/81	
178	MBG378H	"	"	"			-/79	6/81	

Orig. Fleet -No.	Reg. No.	Body Make	Seats	Date New	Date Transferred To St.H	To Sport	To Lpool	Date with drawn	Notes
179	MBG379H	"	"	"			?	3/81	
180	MBG380H	"	"	"			-/79	1/82	
181	MBG380H	"	"	"			2/80	11/81	
182	MBG382H	"	"	"			?	8/81	

2. FROM ST.HELENS.

AEC Regent V D3RV

Orig. Fleet	Reg. No.	Body Make	Seats	Date New	To St.H	Sport	Lpool	with drawn	Notes
1	ODJ941	MCCW	H36/28R	1961			7/75	1/77	Reno'd A458
2	ODJ942	"	"	"			7/75	5/76	Reno'd A459
4	ODJ944	"	"	"			6/75	10/75	Reno'd A457
33	SDJ353	"	"	1962			8/74	9/76	Reno'd A454 in 10/74
34	SDJ354	"	"	"			7/74	1/77	Reno'd A455 in 10/74
35	SDJ355	"	"	"			8/74	1/77	Reno'd A456 in 10/74
147	HDJ747	Weymann	H33/28R	1958			7/75	1/77	Reno'd A460
155	HDJ755	"	"	"			7/75	1/77	Reno'd A461

Bedford VAM70

Orig. Fleet	Reg. No.	Body Make	Seats	Date New	To St.H	Sport	Lpool	with drawn	Notes
201	KKU 71F	Duple	C45F	1968			10/74	8/81	Reno'd C201

3. FROM SOUTHPORT

Leyland PD2/20

Orig. Fleet	Reg. No.	Body Make	Seats	Date New	To St.H	Sport	Lpool	with drawn	Notes
32	LFY 32	Weymann	H32/28R	1956			6/74	-/76	Reno'd L450
35	LFY 35	"	"	"	4/74			5/75	Reno'd 135
36	LFY 36	"	"	"			6/74	5/76	Reno'd L451
38	MWM 38	"	H33/28R	1957			6/74	2/75	Reno'd L452
39	MWM 39	"	"	"			8/75	9/76	Reno'd L472
41	MWM 41	"	"	"			6/74	2/75	Reno'd L453
42	MWM 42	"	"	"			8/75	9/76	Reno'd L473

4. FROM LIVERPOOL TO WIRRAL

Leyland PSU1/13

Orig. Fleet	Reg. No.	Body Make	Seats	Date New			To Wirral	with drawn	Notes
SL175	SKB172	Crossley/LCPT	B40F	1956			4/70	4/72	Reno'd 98, Reseated to B38F 4/70
SL176	SKB173	"	"	"	"	"	4/70	4/72	Reno'd 97, Reseated to B38F 4/70

Leyland PDR1 Mk.II

Orig. Fleet	Reg. No.	Body Make	Seats	Date New			To Wirral	with drawn	Notes
L508	508 KD	MCCW	H43/34F	1963			/76	/81	Reno'd 508. Back to L'pool /80.
L515	515 KD	"	"	"			/76	/81	Reno'd 515. Back to L'pool /80
L533	533 KD	"	"	"			/76	/81	Reno'd 533. Back to L'pool /80
L623	623 KD	"	"	"			/76	/81	Reno'd 623. Back to L'pool /80

* Ordered by Birkenhead Corporation but delivered to Merseyside PTE.

51 Destination Indicators

A policy on destination indicators had been evolved by Liverpool Corporation in the early fifties following some pressure from the Passenger Transport Committee to augment the information currently being shown on buses, of a single destination at the front and three-track number indicators at the front, rear and nearside. Lettering was 6.25in. deep with an aperture of 10in. There were originally three blinds, one each for North, South and East Divisions and from 1951-52 an intermediate indicator with three names was fitted alongside the destination on all new buses.

The Committee had wanted a four-line intermediate blind but the manager fought against this on the grounds of excessive length with its attendant mechanical problems. The difficulties were somewhat exaggerated in a report which gave as an example 12 different 'shows' for route 82 and its short workings. But the three-line blind was troublesome and in 1958 a gradual change was made to a one-line intermediate blind with 6.25in letters similar to the destination. On city routes, this usually showed 'Dale St' or 'Church St' but other displays in common use were 'Limited Stop', 'Short Journey' and 'School'.

To supplement the frontal display, a box was fitted along the back of the nearside inward facing seat just inside the lower saloon and loose cards were used to display similar information or 'Minimum Fare'. This system was unsatisfactory as the cards tended to get torn or lost and from early 1962, the size of the side route number blinds was reduced and a small blind mounted above them with the same information which had been shown on the cards.

With reduced size apertures, Atlantean L734 displays the typical route indicators of the 'sixties with Gill-Sans capitals for the destination and lower case two-line intermediate blind.

230

Meanwhile, from March 1960, the depth of the front destination and intermediate indicator apertures was reduced by masking to 8in. (the same depth as the route numbers) and the spaces between the names on the blinds were reduced accordingly. At the same time the sparse intermediate displays were improved by the provision of a two-line blind. When the Atlanteans came into service, they adopted this layout, the only change being the use of lower case lettering for the intermediate blind only. This style of lettering was not applied to ultimate destinations in Liverpool until 1980-81. There were now two destination blinds, North and South, and to keep the number of 'shows' to a minimum, one general destination was used for several different points in the same district. Thus 'Woolton' could indicate Manor Road, Mackets Lane, the old tram terminus or Derby Arms. Eventually 'Speke (Ford Factory)' and 'Kirkby (Industrial Estate)' were added to avoid confusion.

When Atlanteans were converted to one-man operation, the front number and destination screens were repositioned at a lower level and the intermediate screen removed from the front though the little side screens remained. Rear route numbers lasted much longer than might have been expected but eventually disappeared in the eighties. During the changeover period, the remaining intermediate blinds on the older buses tended to fall into disuse.

The migration of buses from the neighbouring towns necessitated special non-standard blinds of odd sizes being made. Intermediate screens and rear destinations were invariably masked or painted over or even repanelled.

When the Leyland Nationals came into the fleet, they retained the standard National layout with deeper route numbers and a narrower destination. Most had rear route numbers.

From 1979, many new double-deck buses came equipped with four-track route numbers in readiness for the adoption of three digit route numbers as was done in 1980 for the Kirkby rationalisation scheme. However, Alexander-bodied buses delivered subsequent to this had three-track numbers.

In the early 1980s, a selection of new buses received electronic destination indicators, most of which were of the Transign dot matrix type. The first type had the route number and destination in line and, following criticism of the small-size number, 0048 and 0063 were fitted with 10in. number displays above a larger destination. In 1984, the design was approved and 31 vehicles were modified. National 6098 had ripple type destination equipment fitted. At a later stage, dot matrix indicators were fitted from new to Leyland Olympians.

Olympian 0032 with Eastern Coach Works body is seen passing the Empire Theatre en route to Prescot. The route number on the electronic destination display was adjudged to be too small and was replaced by much larger centrally placed figures.

Crosville

In conjunction with the revised route number system introduced on 5th July 1959, Crosville adopted a standard indicator layout comprising a destination and a three-track number display at the front. Route numbers were shown to the rear for a time but were gradually eliminated.

The older Bristol K and L buses with the post-war Tilling layout of a long destination indicator surmounting a combined 'via' and number screen had the whole unit sheeted over, leaving a small gap at the centre of the top aperture which now housed the route number, and a standard destination indicator below. Those with separate numbers had the top line blanked out and used the intermediate box as the destination.

Apart from the Nationals which had the normal equipment of that model, this standard layout continued for over 30 years, the only modification being placing the number to the offside to facilitate its operation from the cab.

Ribble

Ribble retained its standard arrangement of a three-track route number and a 5in. deep. destination blind. Rear numbers were gradually phased out from about 1964. In the seventies there was a change to lower case lettering and blinds of a depth of only 3.5in., the same in-line display being used on both single and double-deck buses. However, some double-deckers retained the 5in. numbers. North Western inherited the Ribble layout but later installed deeper destination blinds with bolder upper case lettering.

Ribble PD3 1978 was originally owned by Scout Motor Services of Preston, acquired by Ribble in 1961, and had a half-cab front end. The indicators had been altered to the Ribble standard layout. The Crosville Bristol VR exemplifies the indicator layout which evolved gradually from the ambitious Tilling layout of the late 'forties.

52 Liveries

The green livery with cream bands at cantrail and upper deck waist level and black mudguards, which had been adopted as standard for Liverpool Corporation buses in 1950, prevailed exclusively until 1960. In the mid-fifties a few buses and trams were repainted without the upper band but this was not favoured and there was soon a reversion to the normal livery.

Subsequent livery changes were made to enable hot-spray painting to be introduced. In 1960 the upper cream band was eliminated and the centre band soon succumbed also. The new scheme substituted cream surrounds to the windows on both decks and the staircase panelling on the lower deck, everything else being sprayed green. This included the mudguards except on a few of the first repaints e.g. L100 and L162 which retained their black mudguards. The labour required for masking was reduced very considerably. When the new livery was applied, gold fleet numbers were replaced by cream decals. The unpainted buses were given green window surrounds and cantrail bands when their turns came to pass briefly through the paint-shop while the single deckers (SL171-6) conformed to the double deck scheme except that their cream window surrounds extended round the front of the vehicle. From July 1960 attention was also given to the interiors, 20 buses being painted in a blue and brown scheme; the public's comments were invited and green and cream was eventually adopted as standard.

When the first production Atlanteans entered service in 1962 there was a further change as the cream was not taken round the front or rear of the vehicle. A similar style was adopted when repainting older vehicles and many changed directly from the two-band livery to the new layout. In due course, the cream on the upper deck was restricted to the window surrounds between the bulkheads, the first and last windows on each side being included in the green area.

The coat-of-arms was moved from the conventional place, centrally on the lower deck sides, to the front of the between-decks panels and the words 'City of Liverpool' were progressively added in gold from July 1965. The first to be so adorned were L90 and L524. Some two-band buses, including the experimental Atlantean E2, could still be seen until 1966. Mention should be made of L430 which alone had no cream relief at all.

A267, an AEC Regent V with 65-seat Orion style body, entered service in September 1957, the month the last trams were withdrawn. The Orion body had been introduced as a lightweight design with austere standards of interior finish but the version favoured by Liverpool was less spartan and nearer average in weight. The four-bay layout had become optional and was chosen, in line with Liverpool's standard of the period. The crew are about to take the bus out of Speke garage. These like many Liverpool buses had a rearward facing seat for five passengers across the front bulkhead.

The so-called City circle was operated by these specially appointed Leyland PD2/20s from December 1965 to September 1969 when Panthers took over. The Pier Head was not on the route but each of the four buses took time off for crew breaks at the staff canteen. In the right hand picture the same bus, L164, is shown entering Garston depot.

Reversed Livery

The five Leyland PD2s adapted for the City Circle in December 1965 were the first to carry a virtually all-cream livery, relieved only by green window surrounds. It was undoubtedly an attractive colour scheme, reminiscent of tram 293 in 1957, and probably influenced the choice of a somewhat similar arrangement for the experimental Atlantean one-man conversion, L749, and the Leyland Panthers which first took to the streets in July 1968. The Panther had a stepped waist rail and, to enable the green to be applied in a straight band, there was much more of it. Thus there was a broad green band above the forward bays and below the rear bays; the green was also continued round the front and back. The Bristol REs with their straight waist rail had much less green. The Atlantean also had the coat-of-arms and 'City of Liverpool' on the front panels above the relocated route indicators and whilst this was not adopted as standard, several other vehicles converted to the two-door layout also had this feature. On the single deckers, the crest and title were applied ahead of the centre exit door and in a corresponding position on the offside.

Towards the end of the Liverpool Corporation era, the only buses not finished in one or other of these styles were the four former airport coaches XL171-4 which carried a two-tone blue livery and the legend 'Liverpool City Airporter'. When the special airport service ceased in 1966, they were transferred to the Railway Stations-Princes'

Landing Stage services, 'Airporter' being replaced by 'Transport'. This livery prevailed until March 1972 when standard green and cream livery was substituted.

PTE Colour Schemes

After the formation of the PTE, the Liverpool divisions retained the Corporation's green livery but in March 1970 the Wirral division adopted a separate blue and cream colour scheme, embodying some features of the former Birkenhead and Wallasey liveries. This was done to appease the ratepayers of the Cheshire county boroughs who objected to being 'taken over' by Liverpool. The livery was not regularly seen in Liverpool until June 1971 when blue buses started running through the Wallasey tunnel into the city centre. There was a later version of this livery using a darker blue and lemon yellow. A logotype, sometimes described as a catherine wheel, was devised and applied on the sides in the position formerly occupied by the Liverpool coat-of-arms. The four hatched arms symbolised the Authority's pro-rail policy and the foundation year 69. It was applied in different colours depending on the background; thus it was cream on green or green on cream and, in Wirral, blue on cream. The first bus to carry the new symbol was L545 which was still the only example in May 1970 though its use spread rapidly later that year.

The early PTE livery in Liverpool evolved from that of Liverpool Corporation and these contrasting pictures show the metamorphosis from 'City of Liverpool' fleetname and coat-of-arms to the PTE's 1969

'Catherine Wheel'. The right hand picture shows a bus at Birkenhead North station on a rail replacement service during the reconstruction of the Mersey railway.

The only change in 1971 was the decision to repaint the cream single deckers in standard livery and 1006, 1082-3 were the first to have their colours reversed in April. However, by 1978 Bristols were being repainted cream with green roofs, waistband and skirt panels though eventually the waistband was eliminated. In mid-1972 units of the Training fleet appeared with cream panels between decks and 'Training Vehicle' in large red lettering on the cream area. Liverpool green was retained above and below but the styling, which had already been adopted in Wirral, seems to have influenced subsequent events.

When it was known that the Southport and St.Helens fleets were to be absorbed from 1st April 1974, the Executive decided that a standardised livery had to be chosen. Both towns' fleets were attractively painted in not dissimilar red and cream schemes and there was strong local feeling, (especially in Southport whose residents wanted nothing to do with anything Liverpudlian) that the status quo should be preserved.

However, early in 1974, the PTE announced that the whole fleet, including Southport and St. Helens when absorbed, would be painted in Liverpool green with cream between decks, as already used for the Training fleet. There was to be a new logo consisting of a square with 'Merseyside' in lower case lettering and different background colours for the various divisions and districts;

in Liverpool this was a cream square outline on a green background. The design was uninspiring to say the least and was short-lived, its demise being hastened by the threat of legal action by a coach operator who was already using the 'Merseyside' fleet name. Some sources say that its application in Liverpool ceased as early as April 1974 though some new buses were delivered with it in place later than that. The question of livery now came up for reconsideration and, in the meantime, Southport and St. Helens retained their liveries and buses transferred from Birkenhead to Liverpool or St. Helens were usually repainted in green or red and cream as appropriate. Several had no cream relief to the Liverpool livery.

In September 1974, Panther 1087 was repainted in existing style using a light green paint whilst Atlantean 1436 appeared in the same colour but with cream panels between decks. L862 followed soon afterwards together with a coach version (cream with green trim) on the ex-St. Helens coach 201. None carried any emblem.

The public was told in October 1974 that the new livery for double-deckers would be Verona green below the lower saloon waist line and above the upper deck waist line with jonquil cream between and, for single-deckers, Verona green with jonquil cream window surrounds. The colours closely resembled those used by West Yorkshire PTE, Verona green being slightly darker than the green used in the experiments.

Atlantean 1585 and Bristol 2103 were the last buses delivered in Liverpool green; the former entered service thus but the Bristol, several Atlanteans and two Leyland midibuses, delivered in blue and cream, were immediately repainted.

Early in 1975, use of the catherine wheel logo was resumed, the fleet title 'Merseyside Transport' in lower case letters being added alongside it. The first bus to carry it was new Bristol VR 2117. Great progress was made in 1975 in repainting the fleet and applying the new logo but the Liverpool green was slow to die altogether as the need for economies tended to put an end to costly premature repainting. Bristol 2102 and Metropolitan 4025 were still in the old colours in August 1981 and Green Lane's towing bus, 1956 Leyland PD2 L252, retained it until 1984 when it was repainted all over Verona green. The last bus in St. Helens red, PD2 No.44, was withdrawn in October 1977 but a few red ones lingered on in Southport and in 1977, red and cream was officially adopted as the livery for the open top buses used there on holiday services. The Leyland Nationals were finished mainly in jonquil cream with Verona green roofs and skirts and the earlier single-deckers adopted a similar style when repainted.

Detail Changes

A prominent feature of the ex-Liverpool Atlanteans was the stainless steel trim right round the bottom of the bodywork and those vehicles overhauled during 1976 had steel sheeting painted green substituted, altering the appearance considerably. The 1111 batch and some Bristols were similarly treated when they went through the works. No.1177 was overhauled in 1977 and painted a darker green which it wore until 1981. No more were done, however.

In 1977, in a somewhat half-hearted endeavour to promote local identities, different coloured logos were devised for the divisions and districts. The first indication of this was when 1265 emerged from Edge Lane with the fleet name in orange on the offside and purple on the nearside. No.1303 similarly had red on the offside and blue on the nearside. The colours adopted were brown for Liverpool North, purple for Liverpool South, blue for Wirral, red for Southport and orange for St. Helens. However, some green logos were applied in 1978, perhaps to use up stocks.

Atlantean 1560 was repainted in 1978 with the lower deck window surrounds in Verona green; 1655 then came out of the paint shop with dark brown window surrounds and bottom panels. Initially, it also had front and rear fleet number plates mounted on oval frames with a purple background (for Liverpool South division) and the words 'Merseyside' above and 'Transport' below. Normal rectangular plates were retained on the sides and the oval frames were removed by the end of the year. Bus 1840 was delivered in this style, being shown to the official photographer on 25th January 1979. The dark brown features were adopted permanently and, on subsequent new vehicles, the window surrounds were fabricated in dark brown Warerite plastic laminate. Inside the lower deck, the cove panels received long decorative streamers depicting a formalised Merseyside skyline in silhouette.

Crosby bus station was the scene with MCW Metrobus 0057 on service 92 and a Ribble Atlantean on the once-controversial L23 to Fazakerley. The latter displays the logos of both the NBC and the PTE.

There was some tinkering with the livery in 1986 when Atlanteans 1288-9 and a Daimler Fleetline had the brown trim reduced in area and cream applied around the front and rear windows while bus 1873 retained all the brown and had jonquil cream round the windscreen; there were other variations on the same theme. In November 1987 about 20 double-deckers and two single-deckers were painted in an experimental two-tone green scheme but this was not favoured and Merseyside Transport Ltd decided on a livery consisting mainly of maroon with cream relief around the windows of both decks, extending right round the vehicle. On some buses, the lower half of the dash panel was also cream. Some vehicles were done before deregulation when a new Merseybus logo which was adopted with Mersey in one colour and bus in another. The theme has been varied on single deck vehicles, the minibus version incorporating diagonal separation of the colours while the coaches carry the fleet name Merseycoach.

Special Liveries

Many individual buses have received non-standard liveries to mark special occasions and, from time to time, the PTE accepted contracts for all-over advertising. Atlantean 1237 (Yellow Pages), 1239 (Skelmersdale New Town), 1321 (Cohen's Furniture Store) and 1331 (Liverpool Central Hotel) were so treated from being new in 1972 but all were back in green livery by 1974. Numbers 1351, 1426, 1435 and 1494-5 were painted for various advertisers from new in 1973 and others were done from time to time. No.1495 (Vernons' Industries) became the last all-over advertisement bus for the time being in 1977 but there were to be many others in the eighties.

In May 1977, Atlantean 1745 entered service from Speke in a silver livery, sponsored by Barratts Homes, to mark the Queen's Silver Jubilee and, two years later, the same vehicle was one of six selected to receive traditional liveries of the PTE's constituent undertakings to celebrate an Open Day in 1979. The six were:

1615	'Scotch purple' and cream (Birkenhead)
1745 &	
4050	Crimson lake and cream (Liverpool)
1789	Primrose green and cream (Wallasey)
1766	Red and cream (St. Helens)
90	(ex Southport) Red and cream (Southport).

There was some debate about the validity of the crimson lake which seemed to be too dark.

It was 1982 before 1745 resumed fleet livery and 1789, which was often seen in Liverpool on the Cross-River Express, retained the old Wallasey colours until 1984.

After conversion to open-top, Atlantean 551 worked mainly from Southport where it is seen on a Circular Tour run for holidaymakers.

The next occasion justifying a special livery was the International Garden Festival in 1984 when Atlanteans 1915-6 were painted mainly red with yellow fronts, with Higson's Brewery advertisements, for use on the special Festival service 401. Two Ribble and two Crosville buses were also given yellow fronts and Festival lettering. The same year five Atlanteans were painted in a blue, white and yellow livery to support the campaign against the abolition of Merseyside County Council. These were 1950, 1971, 1980 and two open-toppers, 1551 and 1612.

In post-deregulation days, Atlantean 1893 was painted in the final green tramway livery in September 1987 to mark the thirtieth anniversary of the last tram to run in Liverpool. Open-top bus 1449 was painted in a 'City Heritage Shuttle' livery of turquoise blue, white and yellow for city tour duties in 1989. In the same year, Merseybus became the first company to launch a special vehicle to support the 'green' environment campaign, bus 1955 being painted with rural scenes and embellished with suitable slogans.

Merseyside County Council was not to work much longer. One of the five blue, white and yellow-liveried Atlanteans is seen against a background of a participant in the Tall Ships Race in 1984.

Company Liveries

Crosville and Ribble followed the national trend of simplifying liveries to facilitate more economical repainting and, by the early sixties, the double-deck standard was for the basic colour to be relieved only by a single cream band above the lower deck windows. Single-deck buses tended to become completely unrelieved though Crosville favoured retention of the cream waistband and this feature reappeared on Ribble buses when the first Bristol REs came in 1968.

Ribble retained its square-letter underlined fleet name but Crosville opted for a plain title in unimbellished capital letters in place of the gold serif-lettered underlined fleet name and this was in general use by 1968.

Following the formation of the NBC, both companies changed to a larger fleet name in the same style of white lower case characters, suggesting that this was a North West group decision; it was carried in the traditional position on the lower deck panels of all vehicles but a smaller version also appeared on the front of Ribble single-deck and fully-fronted double-deck buses.

In 1972, the NBC devised its 'corporate identity' livery which imposed common liveries on all companies, a choice of basic colours—poppy red or leaf green—being permissible in the same way as ex-Tilling companies had been able to choose between green and red. Many observers felt that the new colours, particularly the red adopted by Ribble, were a poor substitute for what had gone before. Relief was provided by a white band but NBC policy was to eliminate this when repainting 'to save a few pounds'. Crosville seems to have objected to this edict and their vehicles—and later those of Ribble, too—looked all the better for the addition of a white band at waist level.

Fleet names were in white capital letters accompanied by the NBC logo, a red 'N' over a blue reflected 'N' on a white ground. On single-deck buses, this was carried towards the front of the vehicle at cantrail level, ostensibly to leave the lower panels free for commercial advertising. Ribble fleet numbers became smaller and grey but Crosville retained their stick-on plates. A number of Ribble Nationals were delivered in cherry red and repainted before entering service.

The overall effect was very bland and the same colour schemes, with different fleet names, were repeated all over England and Wales.

A typical Crosville VR with Eastern Coach Works body displays the PTE and NBC logos when working on service H2 from Warrington via Prescot. This was the nationwide standard double-decker of the nationalised companies in the early 'eighties.

In the run-up to deregulation, there was a complete reversal of policy, eye-catching, often garish, liveries being considered a strong marketing tool. Crosville adopted Brunswick green as the basic colour with cream relief around and above the windows on both decks. The roofs of some double-deckers were painted orange but this feature was dropped in favour of cream, at an early stage. A similar style was also applied to single-deckers.

A new fleet title in capitals, with a large initial letter, was accompanied by a leaping lynx, a device which had already been in use for some time to market certain interurban products.

Ribble made no changes but, when its southern territory was hived off to North Western, the latter introduced a dramatic new livery to emphasise the change that had taken place. This comprised red and blue areas, separated diagonally by white and grey stripes, with the fleet name in large white lower case lettering. The initial reaction of the staff when they saw it was 'Great! Liverpool and Everton!'

A Ribble Bristol VR in Festival Bus livery in 1984 contrasts with post-deregulation North Western Atlantean and Dennis buses in the multi-coloured livery of 1987 and later.

53 Liverpool Corporation—Allocation of Routes to Depots November 1963

1	D G	26	D	55	L R	84	Sp
2	GM	27	E	56	L	85	G
3	D	28	L	57,57A	L R	86,87	G
4,5	G	30	GM	58,59	L R	88	G(Sp Su)
4B,5B,5C	PA	31	GM	60	PA	90	*S StH
6C 6D	E	33,33A	L	61	PA	91	E
7CD,8CD	GL *S	34	E S	62-65	E	92	GM *S
9,9ACD,10D	GL *S	35,36	GM L	66	G	93	GM *S
10	GL	37	L	67	E S	94	D
11	S	38	PA	68	E	95-98	E S
12,12A	S	39	L	71	PA	99	PA
13C	S	40	E	72	Sp	500	G M Sp
14CD	GM S	41	S	73	PA	506	E
15D	GM	42	E PA	74/D,75	S	510	GL
16	L	44D	GM	76	PA	544	GM
17C	GM	45	E GL	77/A	PA Sp	586	G
17D	S	46	PA	78	Sp	Airport	G
18CD	S	47	E	79	PA	Stations	PA S
19	GM *S	50	L R	80	Sp	Tunnel	BMT L
20,21	D	51	L R	80E	D		
22	GM *S	52	L R	81	Sp *PA		
23,24	L	53,53A	L	82C	Sp		
25	D	54	R	83	Sp		

KEY

BMT	Birkenhead Municipal Transport	PA	Prince Alfred Road
D	Dingle	R	Ribble (Bootle)
E	Edge Lane	S	Stanley
G	Garston	Sp	Speke
GL	Green Lane	St.H.	St.Helens Corporation
GM	Gillmoss		
L	Litherland	*	Peak hour augmentation

These models of Liverpool tramcars are in the custody of Merseyside Museums. The older red and cream car had no prototype.

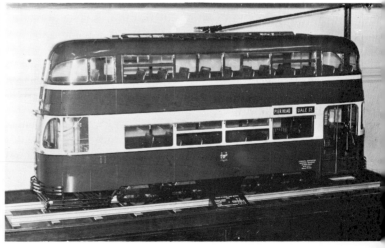

54 Preservation

Considerable interest has been shown in the last 30 years in the preservation of transport relics and literally hundreds of tramcars, buses, and railway locomotives and rolling stock have been rescued from all kinds of locations and lovingly restored to original condition. The establishment of the National Tramway Museum at Crich in 1959 added a fillip to the preservation movement.

Horse car 254 was discovered built into a bungalow at Leasowe in 1984. Permission was eventually obtained to recover it but it broke up and only the parts remain as a very long term replication project. It was similar to the car illustrated on page 92 of Volume One. Attempts by North Wales preservationists to acquire a Milnes car of the 21-32 series and a Brush car (464-8) were unsuccessful.

Local enthusiasts tried to persuade Liverpool Corporation to preserve Bellamy-roof car 544 which outlasted all others of its type and was finally withdrawn in 1949. Others secured similar car 558 and 1898 Hamburg trailer 429, which had languished in Garston depot and they were stored at Kirkby from 1951-54. However, apparently discouraged at their inability to find a secure home for these interesting old timers, their custodians abandoned them and they were destroyed. Another victim of arsonists was an American car, the body of which was taken from Newsham Park to Green Lane in February 1979 and then stored in Otterspool Park.

The successful preservation movement owes its origins to the efforts of a group of Liverpool University students led by Martin Jenkins, now a BBC radio drama producer. Overcoming apparently insuperable difficulties, they purchased streamliner 869 for £50 from Glasgow Corporation to whom Liverpool had sold it in 1954. They transported it first to Leeds and then to Crich where it lay for several years in a queue of trams awaiting restoration. Frustrated by the lack of progress, members of the Merseyside Tramway Preservation Society which had been formed in 1960, raised funds and brought it back to Liverpool where the Corporation, and later the PTE, found it a home in Green Lane depot in 1967. These enthusiasts gradually restored it to its 1954 condition, working mainly at weekends and, in October 1979, it was returned to Crich where it was hoped to operate it on the museum tramway. Alas, it was found to be unsafe due to a cracked bogie frame and it languished in the restoration queue until repairs were started in 1990.

Streamliner 869, newly restored by members of the Merseyside Tramway Preservation Society, was displayed at the Big Bus Show at Edge Lane in 1979. Behind is a preserved AEC RT of St. Helens Corporation.

Two four-wheel Baby Grands were preserved. Number 245 was acquired by the Liverpool Museums but kept hidden away in Edge Lane Works until 1978 when it was sent on loan to Steamport Museum at Southport. It had many defects when it went to Southport and the leaking roof there did not improve its condition; after considerable agitation by local preservationists, it was brought back to Liverpool in 1988 to be housed at the Large Objects Store at Princes Dock and there is a possibility that it will be refurbished to go into service at Blackpool. Number 297, the official Last Tram in a special reversed livery, crossed the Atlantic to the Seashore Trolley Museum, Kennebunkport, Maine where, by all accounts, it is now somewhat the worse for wear.

In 1972, the body of horse car 43 was found doing duty as a summer house and shed in a garden in Cressington, and was purchased by MTPS members for £25. As recorded on page 152 of Volume One, the car had been sold in August 1902 to T.W. Wilson of Lark Lane. With the aid of a giant crane, it was safely extricated and taken to Green Lane. Some specialised work on the wooden underframe was done by a firm of Mossley Hill coachbuilders but, thereafter, restoration was done by Society members. Work was completed in 1983 since when the car, complete with period advertisements, which help to fund restoration, has taken part in several local events.

The Survivors. Baby Grand 293 on the tracks of the Seashore Trolley Museum in Maine, USA (top left) and No. 245 while in store at Edge Lane Works. In the lower picture, 245 passes Wavertree Clock Tower on an outing to Liverpool Show.

In 1977, the lower saloon of 1931 English Electric bogie car 762 was rescued, in a semi-vandalised state, from Newsham Park where it had been used as a bowling club pavilion for 22 years. It was taken to Green Lane and work started in 1979. In July 1981, the Society had to leave Green Lane and 762 was stored in the open air at Netherley for 18 months. New accommodation was found at Speke where work continued in 1982 and bogies were purchased from Blackpool Corporation the same year. Very substantial progress has been made, including the building of new platforms, vestibules and an upper deck.

In 1985, the Museums Department established the Large Objects Store at Princes Dock and the trams were duly accommodated there as part of the Merseyside Transport Collection. Apart from providing secure storage and a place where work could proceed in relative comfort, the Society gained considerable publicity when the public was admitted. They have also restored a 1946 Guy Vixen tower wagon and are working on Birkenhead and Wallasey trams.

In 1990 the Large Objects Store was closed in preparation for the redevelopment of Princes Dock and the trams were found temporary accommodation in Birkenhead, pending the building of a tramway and museum in part of the redundant docks near Woodside.

The Restoration Scene. Top left is a row of trams undergoing restoration at the Large Objects Store, River Dock with Wallasey 78, Liverpool 762, Birkenhead 20 and Liverpool 245 in evidence. Top right shows fully restored horse car 43 with a Guy Vixen tower wagon. Lower left is a close up of Birkenhead 20 while, lower right, lightweight 43 goes on one of many outings.

Buses

No fewer than 25 ex-Liverpool Corporation and early PTE buses have been preserved. Their condition varies widely but a great number, having been acquired soon after withdrawal, are in a good state of repair. This is due to the efforts of the Mersey and Calder Bus Preservation Group founded in 1971 which has tackled its projects in a well-organised and professional manner. The Group has had the use of premises at a disused airfield at Burscough to house some of the vehicles. Two of the buses in the care of this Group are, in fact, the property of Merseyside Transport Ltd and are on permanent loan.

However, the most interesting relics are undoubtedly a 1928 Karrier WL6 (KD3185) and a 1931 Thornycroft FC (KF1040). Both have clerestory-roof bodies built at Edge Lane works. The former is in a remarkably good state of preservation after half a century's use as a holiday home in the Severn Valley. Its owner, Mr G. Lumb, also has a somewhat similar vehicle from Ashton-under-Lyne Corporation. By contrast, the Thornycroft, which was one of those converted into an ambulance in 1939, was in an advanced state of dilapidation when recovered from a field near Reading in October 1969 by Mr T. Hollis of Queensferry. a noted collector of old buses at that time. However, circumstances prevented any real progress being made and the vehicle was purchased by Merseyside County Museums in 1981 and eventually placed in the Large Objects Store. In 1989 the chassis was completely restored to immaculate condition by Ribble Engineering and it is hoped that replication of the body can soon be tackled.

Two survivors of a bygone age are valuable restoration projects. The chassis of Thornycroft KF 1040 has already been fully restored by Ribble Engineering but a new body will need to be replicated. In the lower picture Karrier KD 3185 is being winched down a slope during recovery from a Severn Valley site.

These three AECs and one Leyland PD2 are now in safe hands thanks to the efforts of diligent and enthusiastic preservationists. They are, from top to bottom, AEC Bridgemaster E3; the first unpainted Regent III, A40; 7ft. 6in.-wide Regent III A544 and PD2 L227 in final Corporation livery.

Two of the ex-London buses, acquired by Liverpool Corporation in 1940, have survived and are stored at St. Helens Transport Museum in the former tram and bus depot in that town. One of them, ex-canteen KJ2578, is in a shortened, cut-down state but the other, KR1728, is recognisable for what it was but considerable effort will be needed to restore it. Also at St.Helens was ex-London Bedford articulated canteen JXC 6 but it was stolen some years ago and never recovered, while a similar vehicle, JXC 2, has been saved by the London Bus Preservation Group.

The other buses in the custody of the Mersey and Calder Group are broadly typical of the post-war Liverpool fleet. They range from a 1946 AEC Regent II (A233) to four Atlanteans and a Bristol single decker. Two airport buses (B1 and XL171), the first unpainted bus (A40) and two of the three experimental buses (E1 and E3) are also included. The youngest bus is Atlantean 1236 of 1971. L728 is preserved in the Isle of Man, after serving as Isle of Man National Transport No. 86.

Daimler CVA6 D553 was discovered in use as a children's playbus on a large farm at Altcar where it had sunk to its axles in soft ground. The aid of the Territorial Army was enlisted to recover it as a weekend exercise but the front brakes were found to be rusted on solidly and oxy-acetylene cutting gear was needed to free them. The bus was still reluctant to leave its rural home after 18 years and it took two days of effort by the TA and preservationists before it was extricated.

Experimental forward-entrance AEC Regent V with Park Royal body is now preserved. Top left it is seen at the Pier Head soon after entering service, while its present condition is shown at the Mersey & Calder Bus Preservation site at Burscough. The means of gaining access to the engine compartment is shown in the lower picture.

In 1980 Ribble showed commendable enterprise by restoring a 1927 Leyland Lion PLSC1 bus, CK3825 (originally Ribble No.295). It had been sold in 1938 and, after periods as a showman's van and a static caravan, it was purchased in 1973 by a Mr Hatfield of Northwich for preservation. Eventually Ribble took it over and restored it to near-original condition. There is a link with Merseyside in that it incorporates several parts from Wallasey Corporation No. 8, a similar bus which had survived the war as an illuminated bus and had become a site office in 1954. Several other Ribble buses have been preserved including a forward-entrance Leyland PD3s Nos.1523, 1775 and

1847, the latter having spent the whole of its service at Bootle. There are also PD2s 1399 and 1467 and 1939 TD5 2057 with a 1949 Alexander body, which ran in Liverpool at one time.

Throughout the history of the preservation movement, with a few exceptions, officialdom has been strangely reluctant to give anything more than grudging assistance and it is extraordinary that priceless relics of bygone municipal enterprise should be restored solely by the efforts of enthusiastic amateurs who have periodically had to face and overcome accommodation crises. Their dedication deserves the highest praise and recognition.

For several years preserved trams and buses were housed in a shed at Princes Dock. This picture shows Liverpool tram 762 being rebuilt after use as a park shelter with Birkenhead tram 20 just visible above it; Ribble Leyland PD3 1775, Atlantean L835 and AEC Regent III A40, the first unpainted bus.

Two of the six buses painted in the old-fashioned liveries of the constituent undertakings are shown at a rally at Chester Castle on 10th June 1979. Metropolitan 4050 wore a crimson lake and cream livery which many criticised as not being quite the same shade as that used by Liverpool prior to 1933. Alexander-bodied Atlantean 1615, a Wirral Division bus, was finished in the dark chocolate (officially 'Scotch purple') Birkenhead bus livery, also superseded in 1933.

Atlantean L728 was registered CKF 728C when new in 1965 but had to be re-registered C57 MAN when sold to Isle of Man National Transport in 1979. It was withdrawn from service in 1984 and sold for preservation. It is seen outside Douglas railway station after restoration alongside an ex-Bournemouth Leyland Titan.

PHOTOCREDITS

We are grateful to all the photographers whose pictures we have used—especially so to Reg Wilson who has provided over 140 illustrations. Others have been provided as shown below:

Atkins, G. H. F.   68
BCVM, Courtesy of   46, 157(l)
Cadwallader, J.   232(left)
Chatburn, V.   244(u.both)
Crosby Herald   120
Forbes, N. N.   22(u & c), 23(all), 35(u), 47, 74, 83, 85(l), 104, 105(both), 121(u & c), 142(u), 234(r)
Horne J. B.   248
Horne J. B. Collection   11, 13, 16(l), 24(all), 243(u.l)
Gilberry, G. K.   138(u), 225, 232(r)
Jenkins, M.   28
Liverpool City Engineer   17, 31, 134, 137(u), 173(both), 223, 252
Mack, R. F.   95, 108, 247(u.l)
Martin P. B.   25(l)
Maund T. B. Collection   14(both), 15(both), 16(u), 18(all), 19(all), 20(both), 21(both), 22(l), 72(u), 145(both)

MPTE   9, 26(u), 39, 42(l), 45(l), 51, 53, 59, 60, 61, 62, 63, 66(all), 96(u), 97, 101, 103, 107(l), 109, 110, 117, 118, 122, 124, 135, 137(l), 138(l), 139(u), 148(l), 150, 151, 152, 170(both), 171(all), 172(both), 174(all), 175, 179, 181(all), 182, 183, 187, 222, 226, 233, 247(l)
North Western Road Car Co Ltd   177, 178, 196, 198(l)
Nye, J. G. E.   129
O'Brien, G.   70, 96(l), 247(u.r)
Phillips, A. R.   90(u), 99(l)
Quinn, L.   144
Ribble Motor Services Ltd   69
Scottish Tramway Museum Society   27
Senior, J. A.   149(l)
Swallow, K. W.   11, 12, 25(u), 26(l), 30, 32, 33, 35(l), 41, 42(u), 43(both), 44(both), 64, 126(c), 127(u,c,l.r), 128(u), 131, 132(u.l), 133(both), 139(l), 144(l), 146, 180, 186, 245(l)
Taylor, B.   243(l)
TPC Collection   84

ACKNOWLEDGEMENTS

The authors acknowledge with thanks the valuable assistance given by the following:-
J. Balderston, MBE, formerly Ribble Area Manager (South West); J. N. Barlow; W. Barlow; Jonathan Cadwallader of the Mersey & Calder Bus Preservation Group; C. P. Davies; R. W. Gregory, Managing Director of North Western Road Car Co Ltd; K. R. G. Hannis; C. W. Heaps; R. S. Jones of the Merseyside Tramway Preservation Society; F. A. Moffatt and K. W. Swallow, JP, both former Directors-General of Merseyside PTE; P. F. Rusk; C. D. Skelton; Alan Townsin, for indispensable help with technical details; Simon Watts of the Ribble Enthusiasts

Club; R. L. Wilson; Staff of the Merseyside Modern Record Office and Merseyside PTE; members of the Omnibus Society and the PSV Circle.

Documents consulted include the Annual Reports and Accounts of Liverpool Corporation Passenger Transport and Merseyside PTA/PTE, MALTS Interim and Final Reports, Fleet Histories PC12, PC13, PC15, 2PC17 and 2PC19 issued jointly by the PSV Circle and the Omnibus Society, the files of Buses and Motor Transport.

J. B. Horne
T. B. Maund

The cover painting was specially prepared by Deryk Bailey

Leyland National 6024 shows its new colours of maroon and cream in June 1988, heralding a new era in Merseyside transport.

INDEX

Just what this Crossley hit has been lost in the mists of time but the localised damage is noteworthy.

Mersey Ferries Volume 1
TB MAUND FCIT

The first volume of the long-awaited definitive history of the Mersey Ferries will be published in the Autumn of 1991. It covers the seven ferries from Woodside to Eastham - Woodside, Monks, Birkenhead, Tranmere, Rock, New and Eastham - all of which are described in meticulous detail. While recording the mediaeval origins of certain ferries the story concentrates on the period from the introduction of steam in the post-Napoleonic War era to the present day. The interdependence of the ferries with the railways in the mid-nineteenth century and the part played by cross river facilities in the development of Merseyside as one socio-economic unit are ably described.

In addition to a detailed account of the passenger ferries, the vehicular ferries - the famous 'luggage boats' - receive special attention, with a unique insight into the cattle trade of bygone days and the events leading up to the eclipse of vehicular ferries by the first road tunnel.

Mersey Ferries Volume One is profusely illustrated and includes comprehensive statistics and the most detailed Ferry Fleet List ever published. A history of Liverpool's landing stage adds an additional dimension to this fascinating story.

The author, a native of Merseyside and a life-long researcher of the local transport scene, is well known as co-author of the much acclaimed five-volume history of Liverpool's road passenger transport systems, *Liverpool Transport,* published by TPC, and also of *The Tramways of Birkenhead and Wallasey.*

Mersey Ferries Volume 1 is scheduled for publication this autumn in case bound format with colour cover. The price will be in the region £17-£20.

For further details please send SAE to TPC Ltd 128 Pikes Lane Glossop SK13 8EH

MAP 56 MERSEYSIDE PTE BUS ROUTES AS AT 1.1.86

For Rapidride Routes see Inset on Map 53

SPOILED

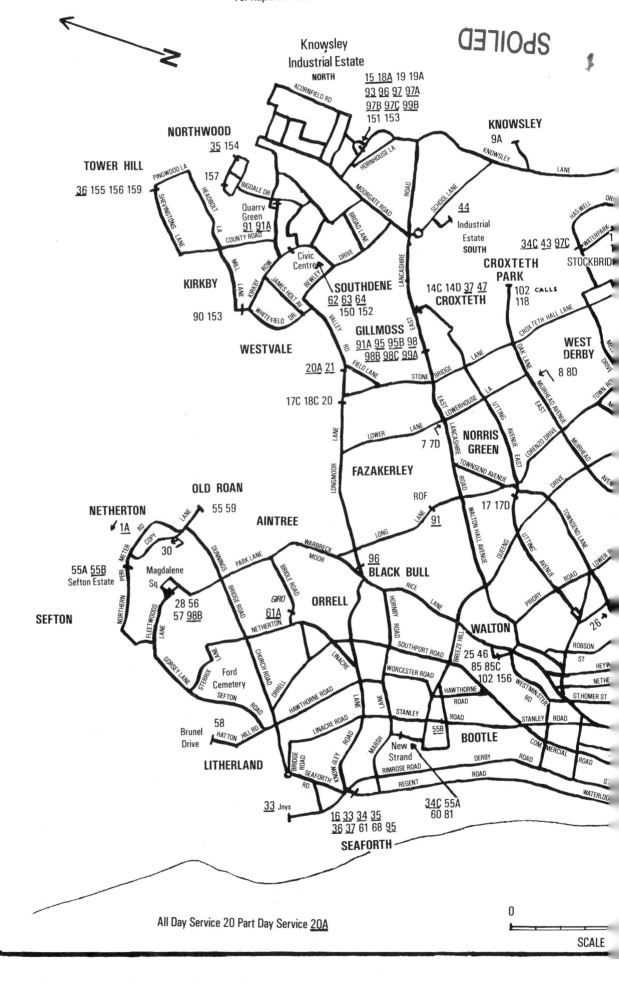

N

Knowsley
Industrial Estate

NORTH

15 18A 19 19A
93 96 97 97A
97B 97C 99B
151 153

KNOWSLEY
9A

ACORNFIELD RD

KNOWSLEY LANE

NORTHWOOD
35 154

157

PINGWOOD LA

TOWER HILL
36 155 156 159

SHEVINGTONS LANE

HEADBOLT LA

BIGDALE DR

Quarry
Green
91 91A

COUNTY ROAD

BROAD LANE

MOORGATE ROAD

SCHOOL LANE

LANCASHIRE ROAD

44
Industrial
Estate
SOUTH

HASWELL DR

WATERPARK

34C 43 97C

STOCKBRID

**CROXTETH
PARK**

102 CALLS
118

Civic
Centre

KIRKBY

90 153

MILL LANE

KIRKBY ROW

JAMES HOLT AV

WHITEFIELD DR

BEWLEY

DRIVE

VALLEY RD

SOUTHDENE
62 63 64
150 152

CROXTETH

14C 14D 37 47

EAST LANE

OAK LANE

MUIRHEAD AVENUE EAST

**WEST
DERBY**
8 8D

CROXTETH HALL LANE

MILL

DRIVE

TOWN RD

WESTVALE

GILLMOSS
91A 95 95B 98
98B 98C 99A

20A 21

FIELD LANE

STONE BRIDGE

LANE

EAST LANE

LOWERHOUSE LA

LANCASHIRE ROAD

UTTING AVENUE EAST

LORENZO DRIVE

MUIRHEAD

AVEN

17C 18C 20

LONGMOOR LANE

LOWER LANE

7 7D

**NORRIS
GREEN**

TOWNSEND AVENUE

DRIVE

TOWNSEND LANE

OLD ROAN
55 59

ROF

17 17D

NETHERTON
1A

AINTREE

LANE

91

UTTING AVENUE

QUEENS DRIVE

PRIORY ROAD

LOWER

30

LANE

COPY RD

PERIMETER RD

DUNNINGS LANE

PARK LANE

WARBRECK
MOOR

LONG

BLACK BULL
96

WALTON HALL AVENUE

26

55A 55B
Sefton Estate

NORTHERN PERI

FLEETWOODS LANE

Magdalene
Sq

28 56
57 98B

BRIDGE ROAD

GIRO

61A
NETHERTON

BRIDLE ROAD

ORRELL

HORNBY ROAD

RICE LANE

SOUTHPORT ROAD

WALTON
25 46
85 85C
102 156

ROBSON ST

HEYW

NETHE

GT. HOMER ST

WESTMINSTER RD

SEFTON

GORSEY LANE

STERRIX LANE

Ford
Cemetery

SEFTON

CHURCH ROAD

ORRELL

HAWTHORNE ROAD

LINACRE

LANE

WORCESTER ROAD

HAWTHORNE ROAD

STANLEY ROAD

STANLEY ROAD

COMMERCIAL ROAD

58

Brunel
Drive

HATTON HILL RD

LINACRE ROAD

KNOWSLEY ROAD

MARSH LANE

55B

New
Strand
RIMROSE ROAD

REGENT

BOOTLE

DERBY ROAD

ROAD

WATERLOO

LITHERLAND

33 Jnys

BRIDGE ROAD

SEAFORTH RD

16 33 34 35
36 37 61 68 95

34C 55A
60 81

SEAFORTH

All Day Service 20 Part Day Service 20A

0

SCALE